Give and Take

HARVARD EAST ASIAN MONOGRAPHS 413

Give and Take

Poverty and the Status Order in Early Modern Japan

Maren A. Ehlers

Published by the Harvard University Asia Center
Distributed by Harvard University Press
Cambridge (Massachusetts) and London 2021

The Harvard University Asia Center publishes a monograph series and, in coordination with the Fairbank Center for Chinese Studies, the Korea Institute, the Reischauer Institute of Japanese Studies, and other facilities and institutes, administers research projects designed to further scholarly understanding of China, Japan, Vietnam, Korea, and other Asian countries. The Center also sponsors projects addressing multidisciplinary and regional issues in Asia.

Library of Congress Cataloging-in-Publication Data
Names: Ehlers, Maren Annika, 1975- author.
Title: Give and take : poverty and the status order in early modern Japan / Maren A. Ehlers.
Other titles: Harvard East Asian monographs ; 413.
Description: Cambridge, Massachusetts : Published by the Harvard University
    Asia Center, 2018. | Series: Harvard East Asian monographs ; 413 | Includes
    bibliographical references and index.
Identifiers: LCCN 2017029386 | ISBN 9780674983878 (hardcover : alk. paper)
    ISBN 978-0674-25127-4 (pbk : alk. paper)
Subjects: LCSH: Social classes—Japan—History. | Japan—Social conditions—1600–1868. |
    Poverty—Japan—History. | Japan—History—Tokugawa period, 1600–1868.
Classification: LCC HN723 .E35 2018 | DDC 305.5/10952—dc23
LC record available at https://lccn.loc.gov/2017029386

Index by Robert Swanson
First paperback edition 2021

♾ Printed on acid-free paper

Last figure below indicates year of this printing
30 29 28 27 26 25 24 23 22 21

Für meine Eltern, Gerda und Herfried Ehlers,
in Liebe und Dankbarkeit

Contents

Contents

Maps, Tables, and Figures

Acknowledgments

It is now my turn to give thanks to the many people who have guided and supported me in my research. First I want to express my sincere thanks to David Howell, the adviser of my dissertation, which serves as the foundation of this book. My project would not have gotten off the ground without his patient guidance and owes much to his teaching and stance as a historian. The other members of my dissertation committee—Shel Garon, Martin Collcutt, and Daniel Botsman—also had a great influence on my understanding of Japanese history. Dani persuaded me to make the leap to the U.S. East Coast and has been a wonderful mentor ever since. Susan Naquin taught me how to write. I also thank Anthony Grafton, Theodore Rabb, Benjamin Elman, Joy Kim, Janet Chen, and Keiko Ono for making my time at Princeton so enjoyable and inspiring.

My long journey as a student of Japan began as an undergraduate at the University of Hamburg under the guidance of Roland Schneider, Manfred Pohl, Judit Árokay, Klaus Vollmer, Herbert Worm, Yamamori Takeshi, Miyazaki Noboru, and Klaus Saul, who sparked my interest in social history. I am grateful for their training and for the many bridges they built to universities and scholars in Japan.

Tsukada Takashi of Osaka City University introduced me to the interpretive layers of Tokugawa period documents and the society behind them. Thanks to his persistence, I mustered the courage to tackle such an empirically difficult project. Through Tsukada-sensei, I became connected to a wide network of researchers in Japan and beyond who have profoundly influenced my thinking through their criticisms and comments. The list of names has grown long over the years, and I want to give special thanks to Yoshida Nobuyuki, Morishita Tōru, Saga Ashita, Yagi Shigeru, Machida Tetsu, Kumagai Mitsuko, Yokoyama Yuriko, Mita Satoko, Saitō Hiroko, Yamashita Sōichi, Yamazaki Tatsuhiro, John Porter, Tim Amos, Matt Mitchell, Fujimoto Seijirō, and Sakaguchi Hiroyuki. Hirokawa Waka read parts of my English-language manuscript and offered important suggestions.

The publication of this book finally gives me the opportunity to recognize Katō Morio and Saitō Noriko from the Office for the Compilation of Ōno City History for their outstanding work. This book would not have been written without their tireless commitment to exploring, photographing, and protecting local historical sources and making them available for research. Their integrity and friendship has been an ongoing inspiration for me. I am also grateful to the mayor of Ōno, Okada Takao, for his unwavering support despite the often gloomy subject matter of my research. Araki Kyōko, Matsuyama Yōko, Yamamura Kazumi, Sasaki Shinji, and Sasaki Masasuke shared materials and ideas. I am grateful to all former and current employees of the Office for the Compilation of Ōno City History, the Ōno City Library, and the Ōno City History Museum who assisted me during my research. Finally, I thank all document owners who gave me permission to use, cite, and reproduce materials from their collections.

I am grateful to Matsuura Yoshinori, formerly of Fukui University, for the many hours he spent teaching me to read *kuzushiji* and sharing his vast historical knowledge. Matsuura-sensei introduced me to Ōno's documents, and because of him and Hayata Yoshihiko's farsighted work as editor of the Yōdome volume of Ōno City History, I became aware of the town elders' journals' potential for researching the history of marginalized people.

In Fukui, I benefited again and again from the sharp insight and deep bibliographical expertise of Sawa Hirokatsu, Yanagisawa Fumiko, Nagano Eishun, Hirano Toshiyuki, Kado Akihiro, and other members of the informal research group at the Fukui Prefectural Archive. I also thank Motokawa Mikio for many eye-opening conversations about the history of Echizen and Japan in general. Outside of Fukui, Kiyoyoshi

Eitoku, independent scholar in Niihama (Shikoku), expanded my idea of what a historical source looks like and how it can be approached.

As I turned my research into a dissertation and finally into a book, many advisers, colleagues, and friends shaped this manuscript through their feedback. I hope I have done justice to all the good advice I received, and all shortcomings remain my own. Kate Nakai helped me reorganize chapter 5 for publication as an article in *Monumenta Nipponica*. During my time as a postdoctoral fellow at the Reischauer Institute at Harvard University, I had the opportunity to organize an author's conference with Daniel Botsman, Andrew Gordon, David Howell, Federico Marcon, and Amy Stanley, who graciously agreed to read substantial portions of my draft. Their suggestions helped me square the circle of how to integrate the extensive Japanese historiography on urban society and status marginality into my narrative. My two (no longer) anonymous readers for the press, Amy Stanley and Fabian Drixler, provided many incisive comments, and so did Peter Kornicki, who offered to read the manuscript in its entirety. I am grateful to Brian Platt for his comments on chapter 6. In addition, many scholars have enriched this work through their comments, questions, and advice. Special thanks are due to Robert Hellyer, Shigehisa Kuriyama, Phil Brown, Steve Wills, Colin Jaundrill, Niels van Steenpaal, Doreen Mueller, Laura Nenzi, Beth Berry, Morgan Pitelka, David Spafford, David Ambaras, Patricia Sippel, Bettina Gramlich-Oka, Galen Amstutz, Helen Hardacre, Takii Kazuhiro, and Katsumata Motoi. I received valuable comments on chapters 5 and 6 from the participants of two workshops on charities in the non-Western world, particularly Thomas Dubois and Angela Leung.

My fellow graduate students and postdocs at Hamburg, Princeton, and Harvard Universities have been an immense source of friendship and inspiration. Of the many names that come to mind, I want to mention a few who frequently helped me think through research-related matters: Paul Eason, Brigid Vance, Fabian Drixler, Yulia Frumer, Daniel Trambaiolo, Daniel Koss, Danny Orbach, Nobu Kiyonaga, Nicole Fujimoto, and Ryoma Sakaeda.

My colleagues at the History Department of the University of North Carolina at Charlotte have provided an ideal environment to pursue my work on this book. Special thanks go to Christine Haynes, Mark Wilson, Ritika Prasad, Steve Sabol, Shep McKinley, Cheryl Hicks, Dan

Dupre, Gregory Mixon, Erika Edwards, Chris Cameron, Jim Hogue, Peter Thorsheim, and John David Smith for reading and commenting on parts of my manuscript.

Yasuko Makino, Kris Troost, and Kuniko McVey helped me gain access to much of the literature needed for this project. I thank Stacie Matsumoto from the Reischauer Institute for her assistance, and Patrick Jones at UNC Charlotte for producing the maps for this book. An earlier version of chapter 5 appeared in *Monumenta Nipponica* (vol. 69, no. 1) under the title "Benevolence, Charity, and Duty: Urban Relief and Domain Society during the Tenmei Famine." A precursor of chapter 6 was included in the volume *Charities in the Non-Western World* (ed. Rajeswary Ampalavanar Brown and Justin Pierce, Routledge, 2013) under the title "Charity Reconstructed: The Transformation of Social Welfare in Rural Japan in the Nineteenth Century." I thank both publishers for permitting me to use these two articles as the basis for chapters in this book.

I am grateful to Robert Graham, my editor at the Harvard University Asia Center, for his thoughtful and professional work in preparing my manuscript for publication, and to Laura Poole for her effective copyediting.

I began this project many years ago as a visiting doctoral fellow at the University of Fukui, where I was studying on a Japanese Ministry of Education (Monbukagakusho) Research Scholarship. The Japan Foundation funded another year of archival research in Ōno and at Osaka City University, and the Mrs. Giles Whiting Foundation supported the completion of my dissertation during my final year as a graduate student at Princeton University. I was able to take additional time off for writing thanks to a postdoctoral fellowship at the Reischauer Institute at Harvard University and a Junior Faculty Research Grant from the University of North Carolina at Charlotte. Additional summer travel to Japan was made possible by two faculty research grants from UNC Charlotte and a Frances Lumsden Gwynn Endowment Award.

I dedicate this book to my parents, Gerda and Herfried Ehlers, who have always encouraged me to learn and whose love and support have kept me going in difficult times. I wish my father had lived to see the publication of this book and hope the result would make him proud. I also thank Justin for his patience and competent support in the final stages of completing this book.

Note to the Reader

All Japanese names are given with surnames first. To facilitate tracking references, months and dates are kept in the lunisolar calendar format in which they appear in the primary sources (month/day or year.month. day, with intercalary months preceded by the letter *i*). Years, on the other hand, are converted into the Western calendar for better readability. Because the lunisolar and solar calendar years do not precisely overlap, this method occasionally fails to place a date within the correct Gregorian calendar year. Readers interested in determining the exact date will need to complete the conversion based on the month and day given. Macrons are used to indicate long vowels, with the exception of certain terms and geographic names familiar in English.

MAP 1 Location of Ōno town.

INTRODUCTION

Every few days, the town elder of the castle town of Ōno took up his journal, brush, and ink stone and recorded whatever he considered relevant to the administration of this small town of about 6,000 people, clustered on a fertile high plateau in the mountains of central Japan in Echizen Province (see map 1). Most of his entries concerned mundane matters like road repairs, festivals, processions, snow shoveling, blocked sewers, trade regulations, night patrols, adoptions, divorces, and petty crime. Only rarely did a fire or other dramatic event disrupt the peaceful rhythm of town life. Today we have the records for forty-nine years from the period between 1740 and 1870—volumes of sturdy mulberry paper, thick like telephone books, filled with thousands of entries in black ink and more or less graceful calligraphy, some preserved in their entirety and others in fragments of several months.

These journals provide more than just a colorful glimpse of small-town life in early modern Japan (1603–1868). They allow us to zero in on myriad interactions and negotiations between rulers and subjects that together helped the Tokugawa state maintain its stability over a period of 270 years. These interactions were shaped by the Tokugawa status order, a system of reciprocal relationships between rulers and subjects that developed toward the end of the civil wars of the 1500s. When the early Tokugawa shoguns established their new state in the seventeenth century, they asserted control by recognizing many of the self-governing groups that already existed among their subjects. Historian Takagi Shōsaku

has used the term "garrison state" for this new polity because it was designed to facilitate the mobilization of subjects for auxiliary tasks in a
military emergency.[1] All subjects were required to join occupation-based
groups that discharged specific duties vis-à-vis the authorities at times of
peace and war. In return, rulers invested the status groups with extensive
powers of self-government and various other privileges, which could
range from occupational monopolies and tax exemptions to the right to
wear certain clothes and other status markers. Initially, the Tokugawa
shogunate and its coalition of subordinate warlords (daimyo) established
this system to pacify the war-ravaged country and consolidate their
power against ambitious lower retainers. Over time, the status order
grew into a flexible mechanism of governance that accommodated social
change and inspired people's energies and aspirations.

This book is a study of government in the context of the Tokugawa
status order. Instead of focusing on samurai officials, it highlights ordinary
subjects who participated in the administration of society through their
occupational groups and the duties performed for the authorities. These
subjects included not only wealthy merchants and village headmen but
also small house and landowners, tenants, and even those on the margins
of society, such as entertainers, laborers, outcastes, and itinerant clerics. Under
the status order, any subject was able to play an active administrative role if
he (and in rare cases, she) was a full member of an occupation-based group
that enjoyed official recognition. Even a town of Ōno's size was home to
a great variety of self-governing groups, from wholesale merchants and
carpenters to cormorant fishermen and blind performers. The ties that
developed among these groups, as well as between them and the government, were interdependent and locally specific and are therefore best
examined in a small, well-documented locality.

I use responses to poverty as a lens on governmental practice because
few areas of statecraft were as central to the stability of the Tokugawa
regime as the management of poverty. Poverty control and relief constituted one of the most active areas of ruler–subject interaction because East
Asian monarchs legitimized their power with their ability to practice
Confucian-style "benevolent rule"; in other words, they used poor relief
to maintain social order and win the trust of subjects. Confucian ideas

---

1. Takagi, *Nihon kinsei kokkashi no kenkyū*, 1–32, 107–64.

about good governance provided subjects in distress with some leverage because they could take their rulers at their word and remind them of their benevolent obligations. The status order constituted the framework through which Tokugawa lords put benevolent rule into practice. By managing status groups and their various mutual relationships, the authorities tried to address one of the main concerns of benevolent rule, namely, the relief of the poor and their integration and placement within the polity. The issue of poverty is well suited to shed light on one of the status order's least acknowledged aspects—its adaptability to change. Because poverty was a source of instability for the individual and society at large, it required a flexible response.

This book approaches the status order from two different angles. Two of the chapters zoom in on specific status groups—one on Ōno's beggar guild (the so-called Koshirō), and the other on the town's guilds of blind performers. Although these groups were made up of marginalized people, they had much in common with the mainstream status groups in terms of their external relationships and internal structure. As groups with begging privileges, they played an important role in the management of poverty because the recognition of mendicant groups constituted one of the main strategies rulers used to control and govern destitute people in Tokugawa Japan. The remaining chapters investigate the interplay and cooperation between various status groups and the domain government as they tried to control poverty and implement various forms of welfare, such as beggar relief, famine relief, and health care. The book can be read in three different ways: as a history of government under the status order, as a local history of Ōno town, and as a history of poverty control and relief in Tokugawa Japan. On the following pages, I briefly sketch out these three fields and identify their interconnections.

The Tokugawa Status Order

For most of the twentieth century, historians understood the Tokugawa status order as a hierarchy of four estates—samurai, peasants, artisans, and merchants—and regarded status (*mibun*) as the preserve of the "honorable people" (*ryōmin*), excluding outcastes and entertainers. This interpretation closely followed the ideological proclamations of government officials and intellectuals from the period. But the Confucian concept of the four estates (*shimin*), which originated in ancient China, did not reflect the social reality in Japan, not even in the Tokugawa iteration, which substituted the samurai for the Chinese gentleman-scholar.[2] When educated people in Tokugawa Japan wrote of the "four estates," they often used them as a metaphor for society as a whole, which they imagined as a harmonious, hierarchical body of people contributing to the common good on the basis of their occupation. Government officials invoked this concept for the purpose of moral indoctrination. In Ōno, for example, the domain leadership issued a proclamation in 1851 that started off with a detailed exposition of the four estates and their respective roles in society and went on to condemn "idlers" (*yūmin*), described as people who shunned hard work and gave up agriculture for a supposedly easier life in the city.[3] The intent of this proclamation was to enforce a work ethic that served the interests of the ruling class.

In reality, the people of Tokugawa Japan were organized not into four estates but into a countless number of small, occupation-based groups of mostly local range. These groups did not necessarily relate to each other in a hierarchical way. To be sure, the samurai unquestionably occupied the top position as a hereditary ruling elite, and the outcastes were confined from birth to a stigmatized existence at the bottom of society. But in between there was the broad and complex field of "commoners" (*heimin, heijin*), which included merchants, artisans, peasants, and many others and generally permitted social mobility between occupational communities. In addition, many people of marginal occupations other than outcastes—such as nuns, priests, and entertainers—were integrated with the commoner class through bloodlines, residence, or marriage. If we took the metaphor of the four estates literally, we would run the risk of misrepresenting this large and dynamic core of Tokugawa society. My

2.   Asao, "Kinsei no mibun to sono hen'yō," 7–40. A number of studies in English on the structure of the status order have provided incisive critiques of the concept of the four estates; see Hall, "Rule by Status in Tokugawa Japan," 39–49; Howell, *Geographies of Identity*, 24–27; Ooms, *Tokugawa Village Practice*, 298–99.

3.   On-ryōbun muramura kyōyusho, Yasukawa Yozaemon-ke monjo; On-jōka chōchō kyōyusho, Urata Takeshi-ke monjo. For details on these and other manuscript sources, see the bibliography.

approach to the status order rests on two premises. First, I regard the status groups not as local manifestations of a uniform standard that applied countrywide but as products of a specific local environment. Second, I emphasize not only groups but also relationships, both between status groups and the authorities and between one group and another. I propose to imagine the Tokugawa status order as a web—a tangled fabric of reciprocal relationships that radiated from every status group into many different directions. The status order had three basic elements: (a) the groups themselves, each anchored in a particular place (*ba*) and occupation (*shokubun*), (b) the customary relationships between status groups, and (c) the ties of privilege (*gomen*, etc.) and duty (*yaku*, *goyō*) that connected status groups to the authorities. This description draws on the analytical framework of the Status Marginality Research Group (Mibunteki Shūen Kenkyūkai) in Japan, which in 1990 began to reinvestigate the Tokugawa status order by taking groups (*shūdan*), relationships (*kankei*), and places (*ba*) as its points of departure.[4]

One can identify two major categories among the status groups: those that were based on land and those that were not.[5] The warrior authorities particularly valued communities that engaged in the agricultural or commercial exploitation of land, that is, the villages (*mura*) and the block associations (*chō*), which represented communities of urban house owners and typically comprised the two rows of houses on either side of a block-long street section. Villages and block associations were subdivided into so-called five-people's groups (*goningumi*) of about five households each. The shogun and the lords (daimyo) regarded the villages and block associations as the mainstays of the Tokugawa order, imposing land tax on them and requiring them to keep population registers, supervise their

4. Tsukada et al. (eds.), *Mibunteki shūen*; *Shiriizu Kinsei no mibunteki shūen*, 6 vols.; *Mibunteki shūen to kinsei shakai*, 9 vols. For survey articles of this research project, see Ono, "Mibunsei shakairon to iu shikaku"; Morishita, "Mibunteki shūen no keifu to hōhō"; Yokoyama, "Zen-kindai mibunsei kenkyū no dōkō." On the genealogy of the status marginality research project, see also Botsman, "Recovering Japan's Urban Past" and Carré, "Les marges statutaires dans le Japon prémoderne." In English, David Howell and Daniel Botsman have built on the work of the project to develop new perspectives on Japanese modernity and national identity; see Howell, *Geographies of Identity*; Botsman, *Punishment and Power*.

5. In making this distinction, I follow Yoshida Nobuyuki, *Seijuku suru Edo*, 32–38, and Tsukada, "Mibunteki shūen to rekishi shakai no kōzō," 82–88.

members, and issue identification documents. Most subjects were part of
a household in a village or a block association. The only alternatives were
to affiliate oneself with a retainer band (typically as a temporary samurai
valet), an outcaste association, or a monastic community or live without
a registration altogether. These were the status groups in the narrow sense.
At the same time, the authorities recognized many other occupational
groups, such as trade and craft guilds and confraternities, which were able
to exist on top of the primary status groups because they did not lay claim
to productive land. Before the formation of the Status Marginality Research Project, scholars did not perceive the common ground that existed
between guilds and confraternities and the land-based groups because the
latter played distinct roles for the state in the areas of registration and
taxation. However, subsequent research has revealed fundamental structural similarities between these groups, and I therefore refer to guilds and
confraternities as status groups in the broader sense.

When comparing status groups, one needs to keep in mind that the
villages and block associations constituted not only spatial units of administration but also communities of homeowners who managed their
own occupational affairs—land use, trading practices, irrigation, and
more—in the manner of a trade or craft guild.[6] Villages and block associations had come into being during the civil wars of the sixteenth
century and shared a common ancestor in the fortified villages (*sōson*) of
the Kinai region, whose residents had carved out a measure of autonomy
from warlords, imperial aristocrats, temples, and other medieval authorities.[7] Both kinds of units were responsible for delivering taxes on land,
though in the case of the block associations, members usually organized
around a shared craft or trade rather than agriculture and were often exempt from the land tax (at least in larger towns). Both were self-governing
and issued rules to regulate the social life and land use within their respective communities. However, because only members who owned a
plot of land with a homestead had a voice in communal affairs, tenants
and all other persons who did not head a household—which included

6. The most sophisticated English-language study of Tokugawa village government
is Herman Ooms's *Tokugawa Village Practice*. Machida Tetsu's more recent *Kinsei Izumi
no chiiki shakai kōzō* builds on the findings of the Status Marginality Research Project
and analyzes village society as a conglomeration of overlapping interrelated groups.

7. Asao, "Sōson kara chō e," 323–62; Yoshida Nobuyuki, "Chōnin to chō," 151–88.

most women—were automatically confined to a subordinate position within their village or *chō* (block association; this book alternates between the English and Japanese terms).

All occupational groups, whether they organized around productive land or not, had a core body of stakeholding members with a shared occupation who jointly regulated the group's affairs. These groups drew on similar notions of collective property.[8] In the case of the villages and the *chō*, full group membership was linked to land ownership and (in rural areas) access rights to the commons. Villages and block associations exercised a strong collective claim over the land; some villages went so far as to regularly reshuffle fields among cultivators.[9] Land owners within a *chō* usually had to ask the other owners for permission if they wanted to sell a plot to an outsider. In the case of trade and craft guilds, members shared a usually finite number of so-called stocks (*kabu*)—business licenses with responsibilities vis-à-vis the authorities and the group—that were recognized by the government and could often be traded and pawned among members, sometimes to outsiders. The concept of group property was so deeply entrenched that it even shaped the structure of marginal associations, such as mendicant confraternities and guilds of itinerant entertainers. These kinds of groups typically treated access to a particular cluster of *chō* or villages as their collective property—a turf, so to speak—and often divided it up into shares that could be inherited and in some cases traded and pawned without the local residents having any say in the matter.

All occupational groups interacted with the authorities through exchanges of privileges and duties. As well as paying the land tax, villages and block associations were responsible for performing various duties (*goyō*) for the authorities that either involved the delivery of goods or the provision of services, for example in form of corvée (unpaid labor). Some of these goods and services were designed to help the lord run his residence, mobilize his military, and discharge his feudal obligations toward the shogunate. Others were of a more public nature; they included firefighting, patrols, road maintenance, and other activities benefiting society

8. "Shinpojiumu tōron: Mibun o toinaosu," 184–93; Yoshida Nobuyuki, "Kojiki/kanjin to geinōsha no shoyū ni tsuite."
9. Brown, *Cultivating Commons*.

as a whole. In towns, the house-owning members of a block association often hired others to perform these duties in their stead. The villages and *chō* were expected to exercise mutual supervision and suppress or report any criminal activity of people in their midst. In return, villagers and townspeople enjoyed collective privileges, which usually included self-government and various tax exemptions, occupational monopolies, and permission to display markers of rank in public. But these conditions also applied to groups that were not anchored in ownership of productive land. Guilds and confraternities served as vehicles for the authorities to control subjects and mobilize them at peacetime and during military campaigns, for fortress construction, commodity price regulation, provision of tools, or jail guard work, to name a few of many possible duties.

Because the trade and craft guilds and confraternities lacked a connection to productive land, they were more flexible than the villages and *chō*; for this reason, shoguns and lords increasingly relied on them to recognize and regulate new forms of economic activity and allowed them to coexist with the land-based communities. The authorities' willingness to work with occupational groups other than the land-based communities increased over the course of the early modern period.[10] In the middle of the seventeenth century, the Tokugawa shogunate was still eager to break the power of the medieval guilds and did not recognize professional associations that transcended villages and block associations except in a few key occupations such as wholesalers of lumber, rice, sake, and oil; brokers of silk thread, rice, fish, and some other sensitive commodities; and artisans and entertainers who performed important services for the authorities. Nonetheless, many of the late medieval trade and craft associations survived the transition to the new regime and continued to operate without official recognition. During the seventeenth century, the country experienced a period of economic and demographic expansion that led to the emergence of many new guilds, and by the end of the century, the Tokugawa authorities began to change their strategy and proceeded to acknowledge many of these groups. In Edo, for example, merchants had developed associations of long-distance wholesale traders as mutual

10.   On the Tokugawa regime's shifting policies toward occupation-based groups, see Yoshida Nobuyuki, *Seijuku suru Edo*, 36–38; Yoshida Nobuyuki, "Dentō toshi no shūen," 33–64.

insurance against the loss of goods in transit. The shogunate co-opted and expanded this system and in 1721 completed the edifice of guild control in Edo by pushing ninety-six types of merchants and artisans to form groups and submit records on membership. From that point onward, associations of powerful wholesalers began to dominate the economic and political life of most Japanese towns. They oversaw the import and export of goods and supervised the guilds of many of the less lucrative local trades and crafts.

The formation and recognition of new status groups was a process that continued until the beginning of the Meiji period. The greatest expansion of trade and craft guilds occurred in the 1770s and 1780s, when shogunate elder Tanuma Okitsugu used the recognition of dues-paying guilds as a strategy to cultivate new sources of revenue for the shogunate. By the 1830s, the distribution of duties and privileges had become so complicated and the discrepancies between residential registration and various status group memberships so confusing that the shogunate began to see a need for a simplified system of registration and considered—for the first time in its history—creating a few group-transcending categories of registration such as "samurai," "peasant," and "townsperson." The Meiji government in fact briefly introduced such categories in 1868 before abolishing the status order altogether.[11] In 1841, shogunate elder Mizuno Tadakuni dissolved all trade and crafts guilds (*kabu nakama*) because he suspected them of driving up commodity prices; ten years later his successors permitted them once again in a looser form, acknowledging the guilds' ordering influence in economic life. The opening of ports for foreign trade in 1858 undermined the wholesaler's hegemony for good.[12]

Occupation was essential to the construction of public identity in Tokugawa Japan because membership in an occupational community was the only way for subjects to become taxable and governable in the eyes of the authorities. As David Howell has shown, occupation created a link between everyday economic activity and the political order and imbued people's livelihoods with political significance—a nexus he calls

11.   Yokoyama, *Meiji ishin to kinsei mibunsei no kaitai*, 325–27; Yokoyama, "Meiji ishin to kinsei mibunsei no kaitai," 27–61, 204–36.

12.   Yoshida Nobuyuki, "Dentō toshi no shūen," 51–63. On the processes and reforms that led to the dismantling of the status order before and after the Meiji Restoration, see Yokoyama, *Meiji ishin to kinsei mibunsei no kaitai*.

the "politics of the quotidian."[13] But because many commoners belonged to trade and craft guilds or confraternities on top of their affiliation with a village or a *chō*, they could end up with more than one occupational identity and switch identities as the situation demanded.[14] A house owner who resided in a *chō* dominated by innkeepers, for example, could also be part of a sake brewer guild or an association of physicians, whereas a village peasant might have doubled as a shrine priest or rapeseed broker and belonged to self-governing groups in these capacities. These two examples refer to commoner elites, but among the lower classes, membership in guilds and confraternities was arguably even more important because people without land were denied a voice in the affairs of their village or *chō*. By forming associations of peddlers, petty craftsmen, porters, entertainers, backstreet clerics, and so on, they could forge alternative bases of power and establish direct links to government officials. Many leaders of such marginal status groups were crafty negotiators who used strategic petitioning to engage the authorities. Whenever possible, they framed their requests in an idiom of occupation, privilege, and duty because this was the language most likely to resonate with the government. At the same time, warrior officials actively sought out the expertise and cooperation of self-governing groups and took advantage of their resilience and cohesion. By disagreeing with the government over specific occupations, privileges, and duties, the people of early modern Japan actually reinforced these principles as the bedrock of the Tokugawa order.

Throughout the Tokugawa period, new status groups took shape in every area of Japanese society and overlaid the infrastructure of the primary status groups like an invisible web. The main propeller behind this development was the gradual evolution of the economy. New commodities entered the market; new transportation routes circulated them to new regions and carried migrants to wherever they were needed to provide new kinds of labor. Sooner or later, these economic changes led to the formation of new occupation-based groups that sought protection against competitors. The impetus for their recognition could come from either above (the government) or below (the group). When the government encountered

---

13.   Howell, *Geographies of Identity*, 45–78.
14.   On the situational nature of status, see ibid., 39–40.

an unprecedented problem—fraudulent traders, for example, disruptive street performers, or an outbreak of rabies—officials could simply order one of the existing status groups to take care of it. If that group refused to take action, the administration might entice it with new privileges, or—if the problem was caused by a new type of professional—ask some powerful representatives of that profession to form an entirely new group that would discipline the transgressors in their midst. The transaction could also be initiated from the subjects' side. For example, some of the traders or street performers in question could offer to form a new group that would control disorderly colleagues on the authorities' behalf before the authorities even realized that these professionals posed a problem. An existing group could complain about intruders into their territory and petition for permission to suppress them.[15] In these scenarios, the government sanctioned and channeled social processes that were already in place. When a group was recognized for the first time, it usually had to submit a written pledge that spelled out its privileges and duties and hand in a roster of its members. To enhance their chances of recognition, some groups produced founding legends or other documents to prove historical ties to a powerful warrior house or courtier family, temple, or shrine. Although officials were in no position to verify the truthfulness of most of these claims, they rarely questioned their authenticity, probably because these fictions allowed them to govern society in a flexible way while appearing to adhere to tradition.[16]

15. These processes could play out in a great variety of ways, some of which are described in later chapters, but two examples suffice to illustrate the point. In the late eighteenth and early nineteenth century, groups of peasants who doubled as street vendors of candy competed over sales territory in Echigo Province, and they justified their attempts to discipline competing groups with some sort of recognition they had obtained from the shogunate or a family of court aristocrats in Kyoto; see Kanda, "Ameuri shōnin." In Osaka, various associations of wholesalers of fresh and salted fish and fish fertilizer coevolved over the eighteenth century, differentiated from each other by supply and sales routes and the perishability of the commodities in which they traded. They occasionally clashed over the delineation of market space and tradable goods and repeatedly separated and (re)merged, often as a result of petitions to the shogunate city authorities; see Hara, "Akinai ga musubu hitobito."

16. Kurushima and Yoshida, *Kinsei no shakai shūdan—Yuisho to gensetsu*; "Shinpojiumu tōron: Mibun o toinaosu," 154–64.

The status order gradually evolved over time. New groups took shape and others declined; some groups had to subordinate themselves to others, and some suddenly became useful to the authorities in ways they had not anticipated. For certain groups, the occupation that had once constituted their raison d'être ceased to matter, and they needed to come up with new ways to make a living and develop new duties to render themselves valuable to the authorities. In that sense, the society of Tokugawa Japan resembled a giant ecosystem where self-governing groups gradually developed new traits to adapt to their changing environment, stumbling toward an ever elusive equilibrium. The recognized occupational groups always coexisted with large fringes of unlicensed associations and unrecognized social relationships. These fringes were not necessarily a sign that the status order itself was becoming obsolete. Rather, the shogunate and domain governments generally tolerated such fringes, which were often structured similarly to the recognized status groups and indirectly supervised by them.[17] In some cases, officials found it expedient to leave an occupation unregulated. Dealers of discarded paper in Edo, for example, repeatedly submitted requests for guild recognition but were turned down each time because the shogunate wanted to give the poor townspeople who collected paper for these dealers the chance to engage in this activity without burdensome fees and controls. Officials remained unpersuaded by the petitioners' argument that a formal guild would help the urban underclass because it would lower the price of the end product—recycled paper.[18]

Although the shogunate and lords always insisted on having the last word in matters of government and could exercise coercion if needed, they preferred to work through the recognition, regulation, mobilization, consultation, persuasion, and mediation of and between occupation-based groups.[19] Under the status order, subject autonomy and state control were not at odds with each other but expanded hand in hand. John Whitney Hall has captured this paradox in his metaphor of the "container society," whose "containers" (self-governing groups) both constrained

17. Tsukada, "Mibunsei no kōzō," 136–47; Tsukada, "Mibunteki shūen to rekishi shakai no kōzō," 82–86.

18. Yoshida Nobuyuki, *21-seiki no "Edo,"* 84–90.

19. On this point, see also McClain, "Edobashi: Power, Space, and Popular Culture in Edo," 127–31.

the freedom of subjects and protected them from willful intrusion from above.[20] To be sure, groups also had internal hierarchies that could be quite complex, and some were headed by hereditary bosses, but at their core was a communal body of full members. Even the social units of samurai—the retainer bands, which were more strictly hierarchical than other collectives because they subordinated members to an individual lord as part of his extended household (*o-ie*)—had a council of high-ranking vassals at the top and groups (*kumi*) that bundled the hereditary households of lower-ranking samurai.[21] Occupation-based self-government and collective decision making were thus manifested in every corner of the social order despite an often strong emphasis on vertical hierarchy. Occupation-based groups allowed even poor people and outcastes to play a public role and use it to their advantage. Although the manipulation of relationships of privilege and duty did not amount to a head-on confrontation with the powerful, it was not a subversive "weapon of the weak"[22] but a legitimate, publicly sanctioned exercise of political agency.

Local History and the Status Order

The proliferation of occupation-based groups complicated the political geography of early modern Japan because many groups had territories that did not neatly overlap with the units of warrior lordship. This was true for some of the older, land-based groups, as the lands of one village community could be divided between one or more tax-collecting overlords. But the phenomenon was much more widespread among guilds and confraternities that were not defined by land ownership. Although these groups maintained reciprocal relationships with the lords on whose territories they operated, their sphere of influence could be larger or smaller than one domain, and they could acquire additional privileges from the shogunate, a temple, a shrine, or a family of imperial aristocrats

20. Hall, "Rule by Status in Tokugawa Japan."
21. Morishita, *Bushi to iu mibun*, 10–30.
22. Scott, *Weapons of the Weak*.

in Kyoto.[23] The domain governments needed to take these overlapping geographies of status[24] into consideration and navigate an always-changing landscape of narrowly defined duties and privileges of varying geographical reach. Warrior officials and their subjects tried to keep track of the allocation of duties and privileges within local society because they would have been unable to interact politically without such knowledge. For this reason, historians who seek to understand Tokugawa government also need to familiarize themselves with occupations, duties, and privileges precisely as they were distributed in a specific time and place. The easiest way to achieve this is with a local history.

A small-sized castle town such as Ōno is particularly well suited for an inquiry into the governmental process because its administrative structure was comparatively simple. In bigger cities, individual town officials would have dealt with only a small part of the urban area or have been too far removed from the lives of ordinary townspeople in the *chō* to deal with their everyday affairs. In Ōno, however, the town elders were directly involved with many specific cases, coordinating townspeople's self-government while overseeing the affairs of the entire town on behalf of the domain. They also kept track of certain rural matters because Ōno town was home to many farmers and was economically intertwined with the surrounding villages, also across domain borders. I emphasize Ōno town rather than the domain because I want to highlight the autonomy of status groups that were based in the castle town but maintained turfs that did not coincide with the territory of the domain. To be sure, even the study of a small town constitutes a major challenge because it requires piecing together many fragments of evidence scattered across administrative journals and other kinds of sources. Administrative records and communications in early modern Japan were handwritten in the epistolary style (*sōrōbun*), a formal style of written Japanese that drew almost exclusively on Chinese characters and required the reader to reorder and supplement the graphs according to the Japanese syntax, following the same conventions used in Japan for reading classical Chinese texts. The vast majority of these records remain untranscribed, and insofar as printed

23. On the importance of the imperial court as a source of privileges, see Wakabayashi, "In Name Only."
24. This term is borrowed from Howell, *Geographies of Identity*, 37.

editions exist, they usually constitute just the tip of the iceberg of un-published documents. Still, a small town makes the task of analyzing these records more manageable because officials like Ōno's town elders had deep and broad jurisdiction over a relatively limited body of people and reflected the perspectives of many different social groups in their jour-nals. The journal format has proven especially valuable for examining politics under the status order because it recorded not only final outcomes but also informal precedents and the process of confidential negotiations.

Ōno was the castle town of a relatively small domain of the same name that was assessed at a productive capacity of 40,000 *koku* and gov-erned by the Echizen branch of the House of Doi. The domain's territory consisted of four more or less distinct clusters of land scattered across Echizen Province. In terms of shape and size, Ōno thus differed quite dramatically from the large and politically prominent domains such as Tosa, Kaga, and Chōshū that most non-Japanese historians have favored in their studies on domain rule.[25] But these large territories coexisted with a much greater number of small and middling domains. In 1730, for example, 82 percent of all domains were assessed at 90,000 *koku* or smaller, and about 60 percent fell into the bracket between 30,000 and 10,000 *koku*, which was the smallest fief size a lord of daimyo rank could hold.[26] Although Tokugawa specialists are aware that domains came in many forms, the bias toward larger, contiguous domains has created a default image of a territorially coherent, comprehensive social entity that was mutually exclusive vis-à-vis other units of its kind. By concentrating on a castle town in a region of scattered lordship, I hope to shift the focus toward the status groups and make them stand out more clearly as independent variables that neither coincided with the political geogra-phy of samurai rule nor were entirely legislated from the top down. This is not to say that studies of domain rule have ignored the political agency

25. One factor that contributed to the image of the domain as a contiguous unit was the series of case studies on domain rule included in Hall and Jansen, *Studies in the Institutional History of Early Modern Japan.* Monographs on domain rule in English have also focused almost exclusively on large, contiguous domains; see, for example, Craig, *Chōshū in the Meiji Restoration*; Brown, *Central Authority and Local Autonomy*; Ravina, *Land and Lordship in Early Modern Japan*; Roberts, *Mercantilism in a Japanese Domain.*

26. Nojiri, *Kinsei Nihon no shihai kōzō to han chiiki,* 20.

of commoners. Luke Roberts, for example, has drawn attention to the system of the petition box, and Philip Brown has emphasized villagers' involvement in matters of land tenure and village administration.[27] But because these works are ultimately interested in the institution of the domain, they do not map out self-governing groups and their social ties, except to explain the character of the domain's top-down policies.[28] Even Herman Ooms's study of village rule, which offers otherwise detailed descriptions of village self-government and its relation to warrior rule, does not delve deeply into the issue of relationships between coexisting occupational groups.[29]

Despite some particularities, small domains can provide insights that apply to domains of any size because even lords of large territories had to govern through relationships of give and take with self-governing groups.[30] To illuminate these relationships and draw attention to the overlapping geographies of status, I envision the domain not as a bounded territory but as a node in the social fabric. The lord served as a privilege-granting center, around which the self-governing groups on his lands clustered while also spinning threads into other directions. The fundamental unit of Tokugawa society was the status group, and each group could cultivate a whole bundle of relationships—with the local lord, with other local status groups, with groups in other domains, with lords of other domains, with far-away peer groups, with the shogunate, with distant temples or shrines, and with houses of imperial court aristocrats. These relationships were not all of the same quality. Some of them involved

27. Roberts, *Mercantilism in a Japanese Domain*, 103–33; Brown, *Central Authority and Local Autonomy*.

28. This is true also for Luke Roberts's latest work, but its description of Tokugawa politics as a negotiation between dominant and subordinate autonomous spaces is generally compatible with and helpful for my understanding of the status order; see Roberts's *Performing the Great Peace* and the conclusion of this book.

29. Ooms, *Tokugawa Village Practice*.

30. Another concept used in recent scholarship is that of "domain worlds" (*han sekai*) or "domain regions" (*han chiiki*), which has informed a number of collaborative research projects on the multidimensionality of domain society; see, for example, Okayama-han Kenkyūkai, *Han sekai no ishiki to kankei*; Watanabe, "Han chiikiron to chiiki shakairon"; Watanabe, *Han chiiki no kōzō to hen'yō*; Kishino, *Owari-han shakai no sōgō kenkyū*.

exchanging duties and privileges and served the purpose of obtaining recognition from a privilege-granting entity. Others were ties of patronage—for example, between a powerful merchant house and a block association in a town or between a mendicant confraternity and a village. It is impossible to analyze these two types of relationships in isolation because ties of patronage, even though they did not support the state directly, often had a semi-public character and could affect the ability of an occupational group to perform its official duties. The ties between status groups and samurai authorities were not homogeneous, either. For example, one group could interact separately with multiple bureaus of the same domain administration. Generally, the more relationships a group maintained, the greater its leverage, and the greater the duties it needed to perform.[31]

Horizontal ties mattered as much as vertical ones.[32] The block associations of Ōno, for example, were linked together in the so-called *machikata* (town) under the leadership of the town elders. Villages often formed leagues on the regional level that regulated issues such as irrigation and shrine maintenance and could include villages from more than one warrior jurisdiction.[33] Among entertainers, artisans, and clerics, it was common for equivalent groups in different parts of the country to affiliate themselves with the same temple, shrine, or family of court aristocrats and use that institution as an anchor for countrywide networks with regional subunits. To be sure, there were many occupational groups that lacked such region- or nationwide associations, but even they were usually able to identify peer groups in other places that were similar in terms of occupation, duties, privileges, and cultural traditions. Networks played an important role in the Tokugawa status order because they connected

31. For an exemplary study that considers a group's whole bundle of relationships, see Tsukada, "Hinin–Kinsei Osaka no hinin to sono yuisho."

32. Tsukada Takashi has emphasized the need to study both "layers and combinations" (*jūsō to fukugō*), that is, the hierarchical layers forming within and between equivalent status groups, and the relationships forming between heterogeneous groups; see Tsukada, *Kinsei Nihon mibunsei no kenkyū*, 353–57; Botsman, "Recovering Japan's Urban Past," 12.

33. See, for example, Walthall, "Village Networks: Sōdai and the Sale of Edo Nightsoil."

local groups to the rest of the realm and facilitated the exchange of people and ideas. In recent years, historians of Tokugawa Japan have devoted particular attention to the cultural networks among educated elites, which took the form of overlapping artistic and intellectual circles and facilitated the formation of a politically informed bourgeoisie.[34] Such networks between intellectuals must be distinguished from the transregional ties between status groups because they did not usually concern themselves with the defense of occupational privileges. It is worth keeping in mind, however, that these cultural networks occurred in a context in which networking in general was relatively common and not limited to the educated classes.

Like any place in Tokugawa Japan, Ōno had many distinctive local features. If its case is representative, then it is so only in the sense that it illuminates the operation of occupation, privilege, and duty in local society—principles of political interaction that pervaded the whole realm. In Ōno, we can observe how they played out in the context of one castle town community. As such, Ōno adds a new dimension to the urban historiography of Tokugawa Japan, which has been strongly biased toward larger castle towns, such as Kanazawa, and the grand shogunal metropolises of Edo, Kyoto, and Osaka.[35] No matter what size, each town was situated in a distinctive cultural and geographic environment that influenced the size and character of its occupational groups and produced a coherent, interdependent body of block associations, guilds, and confraternities, all internally layered and interconnected with crisscrossing ties. Some of this variety can be grasped through the conventional typology of Tokugawa towns, which distinguishes between castle towns, post stations, port towns, rural market towns, and so on. At the same time, a more finely grained analysis is needed to investigate how power was

34. Ikegami, *Bonds of Civility*; Gramlich-Oka, *Thinking Like a Man*; Beerens, *Friends, Acquaintances, Pupils, and Patrons*.

35. The number of English-language monographs on Japanese urban history is relatively small and includes McClain, *Kanazawa*; McClain et al., *Edo and Paris*; McClain and Wakita, *Osaka*; Leupp, *Servants, Shophands, and Laborers*; Hur, *Prayer and Play*. In Japan, urban history has been a very active field of research since the 1980s; see Botsman, "Recovering Japan's Urban Past;" Tsukada, "Toshi ni okeru shakai=bunka kōzōshi no tame ni."

distributed and negotiated among various kinds of self-governing groups in town society.[36]

Poverty and the Status Order

In the Japanese capital of Edo, a city of approximately one million people, there were about 300,000 residents in the nineteenth century who were classified as "earning just for the day" (*sono hi kasegi*; that is, people without any reserves) and thus eligible for aid from urban relief institutions at times of high prices.[37] In smaller towns like Ōno, the absolute number was less overwhelming, but all urban communities in the early modern period had high concentrations of poor or at least economically vulnerable people who kept the authorities on their toes. Towns and cities therefore offer rich fields for investigating governmental responses to poverty. Although small urban centers in rural areas lacked some of the structural complexity of the big cities, they provide direct insight into the relationship between urban and rural poverty because these were places where town and village poor mingled and moved between various types of urban and agricultural labor.

The underclass in Tokugawa towns and cities was an amorphous category and included many kinds of people who were "earning just for the day." Nevertheless, one can identify three large and interconnected populations: back-alley tenants (*uradanagari*); day laborers (*hiyō*), who comprised servants, valets, construction workers, porters, and so on, working for either merchant or samurai employers; and mendicants (*kanjinsha*), who included such diverse types as beggar monks and nuns, street performers, outcaste beggar bosses (*hinin*), and casual beggars.[38] The economic

---

36.   Yoshida Nobuyuki has proposed to study castle town society through what he calls "segmental structures" (*bunsetsu kōzō*), that is, the social and physical spaces around large temple complexes, merchant houses, palace compounds, marketplaces, and other social nodes that structured interactions between various kinds of town dwellers; see *Dentō toshi/Edo*, 37–70.

37.   Yoshida Nobuyuki, *Kinsei kyodai toshi no shakai kōzō*, 15–21.

38.   Yoshida Nobuyuki, "Nihon kinsei toshi kasō shakai no sonritsu kōzō"; Yoshida Nobuyuki, "Nihon kinsei ni okeru puroretariateki yōso ni tsuite."

context in which this underclass subsisted slowly changed over time. In the seventeenth century, many villagers sought their luck as workers, traders, and entertainers in the emerging castle towns and contributed to the formation of an urban underclass of unprecedented size.[39] As the population grew and transportation improved, trade between castle and post towns and the surrounding countryside intensified, and by the late eighteenth century, long-distance trade had engulfed and transformed even the remotest parts of the archipelago. Availability of consumer goods increased, and dependent village households became better able to supplement their income with seasonal wage labor and tenant farming and gradually distanced themselves from the protection of their paternalist landlords. But the growing freedom to work and consume also made poor villagers and townspeople more vulnerable to economic risk and widened the gap between rich and poor. By the late eighteenth century, the Japanese economy had become so interconnected that most regions were participating in the national market through cash crop and craft production or proto-industrial manufacturing. Rural and urban entrepreneurs could draw on sophisticated financial markets complete with a gold standard, futures trading, and interbank lending to finance their endeavors. On the downside, villages and regions that failed to adjust to the vagaries of the market suffered from population decline and decay. Cash crop cultivation also contributed to food insecurity because grain exports to other regions became more common, and authorities often stepped in at times of scarcity by placing strict bans on food exports that could have saved lives in other regions. In the 1780s and 1830s, Japan experienced especially long and harrowing famines that claimed the lives of several hundred thousand of people.

The term "poverty" requires careful definition. In a social order that was hierarchical by design, relative poverty was normal and not a source of political concern. There were three big hereditary categories in Tokugawa society—samurai, commoners, and outcastes—and even

---

39. This overview draws on the following works of Tokugawa economic history in English: Thomas C. Smith, *The Agrarian Origins of Modern Japan*; Hauser, *Economic Institutional Change in Tokugawa Japan*; Howell, *Capitalism from Within*; Howell, "Hard Times in the Kantō"; Metzler, "Policy Space, Polarities, and Regimes"; Toby, "Both a Borrower and a Lender Be." On forms of poverty, see Yoshida Kyūichi, *Nihon hinkonshi*, 41–106. On mountainous areas, see Gotō and Yoshida, *Yamazato no shakaishi*.

though people were able to move within these categories, they usually formed households that maintained a specific rank. While some affluent commoners entered the ruling class through marriage, adoption, or the purchase of rank, few wealthy households were willing to take on the occupational responsibilities and limitations that came with a transition to full warrior status. For outcastes, who suffered from hereditary stigma, a rise to commoner status was generally impossible unless they obscured their origins. The three categories were composed of many different status groups whose internal rank distinctions loosely corresponded to differences in wealth and whose membership could range from comfortably affluent to desperately poor. As Dean R. Kinzley has noted, the Japanese did not imagine "the poor" as a distinct social category until the late nineteenth century, when journalists and other modern elites spearheaded a "discovery of poverty."[40]

The Japanese standard of living rose considerably over the course of the early modern period, allowing even small townspeople and villagers to enjoy improvements in the quality and availability of housing, clothing, and food.[41] But as already mentioned, lower-class people faced a growing risk of falling into absolute poverty. Economist Amartya Sen defines absolute poverty as the lack of material means for a healthy and respected existence and cites as indicators starvation, a lowered life expectancy, and social isolation.[42] Technically, this definition does not qualify as "absolute." In a debate with Sen, Peter Townsend pointed out that poverty cannot be measured in absolute terms because even physiological definitions of deprivation are influenced by social norms and circumstances. Nutritional requirements, for example, hinge on work roles that are socially constructed, and an absence of "avoidable disease" depends on what medical technology is available and how a society defines disease.[43] Yet the relativity of poverty as a concept does not make

40. Kinzley, "Japan's Discovery of Poverty."

41. Hanley, *Everyday Things in Premodern Japan*; Hanley and Yamamura, *Economic and Demographic Change in Preindustrial Japan*. Howell emphasizes the growing vulnerability that went hand in hand with this increased standard of living; see his "Hard Times in the Kantō."

42. Sen, *Poverty and Famines*.

43. Townsend, "A Sociological Approach to the Measurement of Poverty—A Rejoinder to Professor Amartya Sen"; Sen, "A Sociological Approach to the Measurement

poverty a matter of mere perspective because the effects of poverty on the individual can be irreversible and absolute.

Assistance for the poor always contributes to the construction of notions of poverty because it requires identifying and labeling the poor and making assumptions about the material and moral causes of destitution. Even relief measures that actually succeed at alleviating poverty can have a stigmatizing effect, for example, when they exclude certain individuals as undeserving or establish relationships of dependency and control.[44] Whereas Tokugawa shoguns and lords never attempted to define poverty in general terms, they were very concerned about two of its side effects— starvation and the dissolution of tax-paying households. Government officials often used these two issues as thresholds to determine eligibility for relief.[45] The Tokugawa authorities undertook many poverty surveys in the eighteenth and nineteenth centuries, and in them they rarely made a terminological distinction between disaster victims, the chronically poor, and the unemployed, although in practice they often devised different types of relief for these various forms of deprivation. They also continued to cite Mencius's classic Confucian definition of the deserving poor—"the widowed, the lonely, and the invalid" (*kanka kodoku haishitsu*)—even as they gradually began to acknowledge unemployment as a legitimate cause of poverty and provided unemployed people with aid.[46]

The most stigmatized people in Tokugawa society were the outcastes, who were not always materially deprived but were still associated with

---

of Poverty: A Reply to Professor Peter Townsend." Sen's opposition to a relative definition of poverty stems from his concern that a preoccupation with social context could result in relativizing and dismissing the wealth gap between rich and poor nations. Michel Foucault sees poverty as relative and attributes the concepts of absolute and relative poverty to two different approaches to public assistance: the redistributive, socialist model, which employs a relative definition because it aspires to the elimination of wealth differentials; and the neoliberal model, which favors an absolute poverty standard because it sees public assistance primarily as a means to preserve a healthy labor force; see his *Birth of Biopolitics*, 204–7.

44. Foucault, for example, understands the modern welfare state as a disciplining entity; *The Birth of Biopolitics*. For a summary of critical approaches to the history of modern social welfare, see O'Brien and Penna, *Theorising Welfare*.

45. Fukuda Chizuru, *Bakuhanseiteki chitsujo to oie sōdō*, 128–42.

46. Yoshida Kyūichi, *Nihon hinkonshi*, 46–51.

poverty because destitution was a major factor in pushing people out of their land-based occupational communities and into disrespected and unprofitable livelihoods. Tokugawa outcastes were hereditary pariahs who often took on tasks despised by the rest of society, which allowed commoners to dissociate themselves from necessary but disreputable labor. One of two major types of outcastes, besides leatherworkers, were the beggar bosses (*hinin*), who held begging privileges and formed guild-like associations. Ōno's beggar guild was known as the Koshirō and played an important role in the supervision and relief of street beggars. Most literature on Tokugawa outcastes has singled them out as exceptional because of their stigma, but in chapter 2, I use the case of Ōno's Koshirō to argue that structurally speaking, outcastes were integrated into the social order in the same way as the more respected members of society. They were organized into local occupation-based groups, maintained ties of privilege and duty with the authorities, and negotiated reciprocal relationships with other status groups around them. Their stigma could increase or decrease as their roles in society shifted over time and their position changed in relation to other local groups. The outcomes of negotiations over occupation, privileges, and duties depended largely on the mechanics of each group's specific bundle of reciprocal relationships. This situation explains why outcaste hierarchies in Tokugawa Japan differed so greatly from place to place and why it is so difficult to generalize about outcastes' roles and social stigma.

Beggar guilds played an especially important role in the regulation of begging, but the management of poverty also depended on the contributions of many other occupational groups. I argue that the status order constituted the framework that shaped responses to poverty in Tokugawa Japan. Because the status order had developed in the process of pacifying the country, it was designed to ensure the preservation of order and the extraction of resources from the population.[47] These goals also characterized the authorities' approach to poverty throughout the Tokugawa period. Governments were especially bothered by the inability of destitute subjects to pay taxes and their potential to disturb the public peace, and they used status groups to support and contain such people. At the

47. As Ooms has noted, the Tokugawa order resembled a colonial regime in that respect; see Ooms, *Tokugawa Village Practice*, 89–97.

same time, status groups also afforded the population, even the poorest people, considerable freedom to govern themselves and defend their own interests. The mendicant status groups, for example, were the product of two conflicting tendencies in Tokugawa society: the capacity of poor people to engage in aggressive solicitation, and a strong desire on the part of governments and well-to-do commoners to minimize direct confrontations with the poor. Chapters 2, 3, and 4 take up the mendicant status groups that resided in Ōno town—the Koshirō and the two gender-specific guilds of blind performers—to investigate how these groups were situated within local society, and what roles they played in the management of mendicancy as an important means of controlling and relieving the poor.

In Tokugawa Japan, the status order coexisted with the idea of benevolent rule (*jinsei*), which was shared by East Asian monarchies contemporaneous to the Tokugawa regime.[48] The two meshed well because both operated on a notion of reciprocity. Mencius (fourth century BC), one of the first Confucian thinkers to elaborate on the idea of benevolent rule, argued that nourishing the people was necessary for producing virtuous and peaceful subjects: "A sage governs the kingdom so as to cause pulse and grain to be as abundant as water and fire. When pulse and grain are as abundant as water and fire, how shall the people be other than virtuous?"[49] The warlords at the beginning of the Tokugawa period emphasized the idea of benevolent rule to reinvent themselves as models of Confucian virtue and legitimize their hegemony over the pacified realm. Over time, the concept grew deep roots within the popular consciousness and allowed the common people some leverage over their rulers because according to the Confucian canon, failure to govern with benevolence could provoke the loss of Heaven's mandate, and popular unrest could be a manifestation of heavenly discontent.[50] In uprisings and petitions, subjects tried to shame their self-proclaimed "benevolent" lords into taking their Confucian obligations more seriously. The idea of benevolent rule became the foundation of a Tokugawa moral economy, not

48.   Will and Wong, *Nourish the People*, 507–25; Woodside, *Lost Modernities*, 56–76.
49.   Mencius, *The Works of Mencius* 7.23, 463.
50.   Matsumoto Sannosuke, "The Idea of Heaven"; Scheiner, "Benevolent Lords and Honorable Peasants."

unlike the one described by E. P. Thompson for eighteenth-century England—a cultural censoring of exploitive rule and self-interested profit seeking that could serve as a script for popular protests.[51] Many Tokugawa uprisings constituted organized attempts to claim the benevolence due to "honorable" tax-paying subjects.

The idea of benevolence undergirded not only the ruler's aid for subjects in distress but also the charity practiced by wealthy commoners. Seigneurial benevolence had much in common with charity because it was anchored in personal virtue, not legal entitlements, and was considered an expression of the ruler's compassionate feelings. At the same time, Confucian governance imbued the charity of subjects with public significance.[52] Neo-Confucian scholars believed that not only the ruler but all members of society had the capacity to cultivate their inner moral nature and align the social order with the principle of Heaven by practicing virtues such as righteousness (*gi*), loyalty (*chū*), and benevolence/humaneness (*jin*), especially within the core human relationships between ruler and subject, parents and children, husband and wife, among friends and siblings, and toward living beings in general. Scholars of the Confucian school of Ancient Learning, which rejected the neo-Confucian premise of a cosmic principle knowable to man, tended to be more skeptical regarding the ability of ordinary subjects to publicly act as people of virtue. Ogyū Sorai (1666–1728), a leading proponent of that school, wrote: "People endeavor only to live. Their goals are limited to providing for themselves, they do not aspire to provide welfare for all. Since their aspirations are limited they are mere men [*shōjin*]." But he still assigned to them an auxiliary role: "All people are to act as officials, assisting the sovereign in establishing benevolent rule."[53] No matter who

51. Sippel, "Popular Protest in Early Modern Japan"; Walthall, *Social Protest and Popular Culture*; Scheiner, "Benevolent Lords and Honorable Peasants"; Makihara, *Kyakubun to kokumin no aida*; Fukaya, *Hyakushō naritachi*; Yasumaru, *Nihon no kindaika to minshū shisō*, 234–452; Asakawa, "Notes on Village Government in Japan After 1600," part 1. On the "moral economy" as a term and concept, see Thompson, "The Moral Economy of the English Crowd."

52. Yoshida Kyūichi, *Nihon shakai fukushi shisōshi*, 186.

53. Matsumoto Sannosuke, "The Idea of Heaven," 195–96. The Sorai quotes follow Koschmann's translation of Matsumoto's essay, which cites from Ogyū Sorai, "Benmei," *Nihon shisō taikei*, vol. 36, 182; and "Sorai Sensei tōmonsho (jō)," in *Nihon rinri i-hen*, vol. 6, 151.

practiced it, benevolence was not a private matter but carried implications for the stability of the whole society. If rulers' and subjects' benevolence were imagined to be so closely intertwined, we need to ask how rulers and subjects collaborated in practice to provide poor people with relief. Chapter 5 uses the example of the Tenmei famine in the 1780s to examine how Ōno's domain authorities interacted with various self-governing groups in town society to provide relief to the starving. I argue that the status order served as the framework for mobilizing charity and coordinating different forms of aid.

In this book, I use the phrase "poor relief" rather than "social welfare" to refer to assistance for the poor because social welfare is strongly associated with the modern welfare state, which has been much more ambitious and comprehensive than the Tokugawa state in addressing the lives of the poor. The concept of benevolent rule only partially overlapped with that of social welfare. Although its commitment to public health and education was relatively weak, it strongly emphasized criminal justice and economic policy and included potentially any economic intervention that helped raise subjects' prosperity.[54] Benevolent governance also called for policies that did not target poverty per se but fostered and rewarded altruistic behavior, such as Shogun Tsunayoshi's Laws of Compassion of the 1680s, which banned the slaying of dogs and other creatures for the sake of promoting respect for life and went hand in hand with "actual" welfare policies such as foundling care and support for sick travelers.[55] A blending of welfare and moral suasion also took place in the official rewards for filial children, which promoted the Confucian virtue of filial piety while simultaneously alleviating the economic plight of recipients.[56] As I argue in chapter 6, only in the final years of the Tokugawa regime did authorities begin to significantly expand their involvement in

54. For the early Tokugawa period, Fujita Teiichirō has identified "seigneurial relief" (*osukui*) as a broadly conceived program of economic policy that combined loans, tax breaks, relief granaries, riparian works, transportation, and other measures to ensure the viability of the small peasant economy. According to Fujita, this approach was replaced by mercantilism (*kokueki* thought) in the eighteenth century, and the meaning of *osukui* narrowed to refer only to famine relief; see *Kinsei keizai shisō no kenkyū*, 15–60.

55. Tsukamoto Manabu, *Shōrui o meguru seiji*; Nesaki, *Shōrui awaremi no sekai*.

56. Van Steenpaal, "Kankoku kōgiroku—Bakufu jinsei no pafōmansu."

public health and education and thus moved the parameters of benevolent rule closer to the modern concept of social welfare.

In the twentieth century, historians of social welfare in Japan began to take an academic interest in Tokugawa benevolent rule and charity, but the conceptual lens of "social welfare" has prevented them from fully acknowledging the social context of governmental welfare measures. In their groundbreaking work on the history of social welfare in Japan, historians Yoshida Kyūichi and Ikeda Yoshimasa examined Japan's past for the seeds of a democratic welfare tradition. They ascribed particular significance to mutual relief practiced within Tokugawa village and town communities and identified the paternalist concept of benevolent rule as a major obstacle to the development of independent communal welfare institutions.[57] But although Tokugawa society failed to pave the way for democratic institutions of modern welfare, it does not yield much ammunition to conservative opponents of state welfare either, who in both the pre– and post–World War II era tried to promote premodern Japanese practices of community mutual aid as alternatives to costlier Western models.[58] After all, Tokugawa rulers in the nineteenth century tended to spend far greater amounts on poor relief than the Meiji state that followed.[59] What historians of social welfare have not yet taken into account is the structure of the Tokugawa status order, specifically the reciprocal relationships between governments and occupation-based groups that shaped practices of aid and were to a large degree locally contingent.

While the status order and the concept of benevolent rule both stressed the give and take between high and low, there was also an element of tension between these types of reciprocity because the relationship between lord and subject in Tokugawa Japan was impersonal and bureaucratic, notwithstanding the emotional appeals to quasi-parental bonds that pervaded the discourse of benevolent rule. At the end of the Warring States period, the shogun and most lords stopped governing their territories through vassals who resided directly in their fiefs and

57. Ikeda and Ikemoto, *Nihon fukushishi kōgi*, 26–33; Yoshida Kyūichi, *Nihon shakai fukushi shisōshi*; Yoshida Kyūichi, *Shin-Nihon shakai jigyō no rekishi*, 7–11, 99–120.

58. For example, Inoue Tomoichi, *Kyūsai seido yōgi*. On the genealogy of this interpretation, see Goodman, "The 'Japanese-style Welfare State.'"

59. See, for example, Garon, *Molding Japanese Minds*, 34–36.

established bureaucracies in their castle towns that managed self-governing status groups largely from afar. This structure made it impossible to maintain a paternalistic relationship between warriors and peasants except in the most abstract sense.[60] Still, the idea of benevolent rule created the fiction of a perpetual dialogue between high and low that involved the exchange of not only rituals and rhetorical gestures but also concrete privileges and duties. It left its mark on poor relief because it portrayed seigneurial relief as an extraordinary favor and thus discouraged subjects from feeling entitled to it.

Besides Confucianism, Buddhism supplied important rationales for charity in Tokugawa Japan. The various Buddhist schools all emphasized the importance of compassion (*jihi*) in their teachings, and many clerics promoted good works as a way of accumulating merit (*kudoku, riyaku*) for the afterlife, for example, by publishing stories of cold-hearted misers who suffered karmic retribution.[61] The language of charity in Tokugawa Japan was overwhelmingly Buddhist. In institutional terms, however, Buddhist temples in Tokugawa Japan did not play a leading role in the relief of the poor. When I embarked on the research for this book, I initially assumed temples to have been heavily involved in charity because during the so-called medieval era that preceded the Tokugawa period, Buddhist monasteries frequently provided aid for beggars on a grand scale, to assert their own influence and to serve the warrior authorities and the imperial court.[62] But the power and charitable role of Buddhist institutions declined considerably when warlords unified the country in the late sixteenth century and subdued monastic organizations as well as the communities of the powerful True Pure Land sect. To be sure, even after that point some temples actively engaged in charity for religious reasons, and many occasionally served as sanctuaries for widows, orphans, and

---

60. On this point, see Hall, "Rule by Status," 44–45. Abercrombie and Hill define paternalism as an economic institution with an ideological dimension. Unlike patronage, which is personal, paternalism does not require face-to-face contact between people and can become a "strategic institution" of the social order as a whole; see "Paternalism and Patronage," 413–16.

61. Kouamé, *Pèlerinage et Société*, 148–52; Kondō, *Shikoku henro*, 110–21.

62. Matsuo, *Chūsei no toshi to hinin*; Amino, *Chūsei no hinin to yūjo*; Takahashi Bonsen, *Nihon jizen kyūsaishi*.

other abandoned people.[63] It was also extremely common for temples to offer healing rituals and prayers for attaining material wealth. But the vast majority of temples behaved similarly to the secular elites in their local communities: they helped their tenants, neighbors, and affiliate status groups in distress; they set up rice gruel kitchens for starving locals; and they made their grounds available for the activities of other benefactors. Rarely, however, did temples become charitable institutions in their own right. It is significant that even on the island of Shikoku, which was teeming with Buddhist pilgrims and experienced a boom of Buddhist charity in the second half of the Tokugawa period, most giving took place without active temple involvement.[64] There were certain places (such as Kyoto) where temples did take on a bigger role, but overall, Buddhist institutions did little to structure the flow of alms from the rich to the poor. At the same time, Buddhist faith remained a powerful motivator for all forms of individual and collective almsgiving on all levels of Japanese society.

The chapters in this book are arranged both thematically and in loose chronological order, each addressing one aspect of Japan's responses to poverty in the Tokugawa period. Some highlight a particular status group and its web of relationships, whereas others are more concerned with the interplay between groups. The first chapter presents an overview of the society and geography of Ōno town and domain as background for the subsequent discussion. In chapter 2, I focus on one of Ōno's two outcaste associations: the Koshirō, a group of beggar bosses (*hinin*) that performed various duties for the domain, including managing the town's beggar hospice and patrolling and policing the castle town and villages. The Koshirō maintained reciprocal relationships with townspeople and villagers within and in some cases outside of the domain. Beggar guilds such as the Koshirō were a widespread phenomenon in Tokugawa towns and cities. Throughout the seventeenth century, authorities across the country tried to address the problem of vagrancy by granting begging privileges to associations of homeless begging paupers; over time, these

63. Ikeda, *Nihon shakai fukushishi*, 107–14; Taniyama and Yamazaki, *Bukkyō shakai jigyōshi* (jō), 60–75; Taniyama, *Nihon shakai jigyōshi*, 419–22; Asano, *Nihon bukkyō shakai jigyōshi*.

64. Kouamé, *Pèlerinage et Société*, 141–86.

groups developed into self-governing institutions dominated by collectives of hereditary households. Each group, however, was embedded somewhat differently into the social fabric. The chapter outlines one of many possible configurations in which a *hinin* group could interact with local society.

Chapter 3 shifts the focus from the structure of the beggar guild to the most prominent part of the Koshirō's portfolio of duties: the management of mendicancy. The chapter engages primarily with the eighteenth and nineteenth centuries because documentation from the Ōno area is concentrated in that period. In Tokugawa Japan, it was not uncommon for impoverished villagers and townspeople to beg for alms for survival because the stability of villages and block associations and their constituent households often depended on the ability to withdraw support from unproductive members, either permanently or for limited periods of time. The management of these and other kinds of itinerants required various interlocking arrangements between local status groups and the warrior authorities. Ōno's domain government maintained a beggar hospice and seasonal rice gruel kitchens in the castle town to support seasonal beggars and showcase the lord's benevolence. It also relied on the self-governing capacities of the Koshirō, the villages, and the *chō* to manage and control the beggars' presence. But in the nineteenth century this model of beggar management became difficult to maintain because the increasing presence of criminal drifters in the area began to blur the distinction between harmless beggars and deviant vagrants. The abolition of the status order in the 1870s eventually allowed local governments to do away with managed mendicancy completely and suppress existing begging customs.

Chapter 4 takes up Ōno's two guilds of the blind—the male *zatō* and the female *goze*. The guilds of the blind illustrate in exemplary form how lower-class people in Tokugawa towns defended their interests through self-governing, occupation-based groups. Because the blind were physically impaired, the Tokugawa authorities considered them especially deserving of assistance. Yet they extended official protections only to a small occupational subset among them: itinerant performers. The male performers in particular asserted their interests through a powerful national guild with a steep internal hierarchy that enjoyed shogunal patronage and a monopoly on occupations customarily practiced by the blind: the performance of certain stringed instruments, massage, and acupuncture. The guild also asserted begging privileges for its members. It maintained headquarters in the imperial city of Kyoto and was one of several occupational groups that leveraged its ties with the shogunate and the imperial court to challenge the territorial hegemony of lords. Ōno's gendered blind associations were examples of many local groups that existed under the umbrella of the national guild of the blind. The chapter shows how the two groups in Ōno used collective action and appeals to privilege and seigneurial compassion to assert their interests vis-à-vis their domain government and other groups in domain society. One of the guilds' greatest concerns was to avoid stigmatization as outcastes because their begging privileges resembled those of the Koshirō. They managed to evade that fate largely thanks to their connection to an influential countrywide association.

Chapter 5 discusses poor and famine relief in Ōno's castle town and uses these topics as a starting point to investigate social groups among the townspeople and their relationships to the domain government. The chapter focuses on the years around the Tenmei famine in the late eighteenth century, a time when Ōno and many other governments across Japan sought to improve relief for impoverished townspeople. It introduces three mutually complementary schemes of aid: seasonal rice gruel kitchens for beggars, domain-funded grain loans for starving townspeople, and pooled rice donations from wealthy townspeople for their poor neighbors. The people of Ōno town were involved in these schemes through groups such as the sake brewer guild, the purveyor guild, the beggar guild, and the block associations. The example of hunger relief shows that even in the late Tokugawa period, rule by status still constituted a flexible and potentially innovative mechanism of governance. Authorities and subjects continued to rely on the principles of occupation, privilege, and duty to respond to new challenges in town government. Because wealthy commoners and domain officials had a shared interest in preventing unrest among lower-class townspeople, they benefited from coordinating commoner charity and seigneurial relief.

Chapter 6 explores the changes that occurred to the management of poverty in Ōno under the influence of nineteenth-century mercantilism. After the Tenpō famine in the 1830s, Ōno's domain government launched a mercantilist reform program to overcome its chronic budget deficit and in the course of these reforms began to promote poor relief and public health as important means to cultivate a productive labor force and generate economic growth. Drawing on the theme of reciprocity between high and low, it demanded donations from wealthy commoners and sought to elicit gratitude from recipients of poor relief and medical care so they would repay the seigneurial "favor" with obedience and hard work. After the Meiji Restoration, commoner elites were finally free to engage in charity on their own terms, but the domain's mercantilist vision of welfare lived on, for example, in the domain's former trading enterprise, which remained in the hands of former domain vassals and developed into the region's leading charitable donor. Other former vassals and commoner elites in the Ōno region also went on to practice philanthropy in a nominally private but de facto public fashion, working for local prosperity while supporting Meiji state-building from below.

The theme of rule by status runs through all the chapters. I chose not to organize chapters around particular features of the status order because none of these features operated in isolation. Many of them surface again and again throughout the book: the overlapping geographies of status, the autonomy of groups, the efforts of lower-class groups to better themselves by leveraging and triangulating relationships, the habit of warrior authorities to mobilize self-governing groups through exchanges of duty and privilege, and the interplay between the status order and the idea of benevolent rule. The responses to poverty in Ōno domain highlight the importance of these structural characteristics, although they were ultimately only one of many areas of public life in Tokugawa Japan that were shaped by self-governing status groups and their relationships.

CHAPTER I

The Castle Town and Domain of Ōno

The best view of Ōno is from Kameyama hill, the site of the domain's small castle keep. From there, one overlooks the entire Ōno plain: the town on the hill's eastern foot; the fields and groves dotted by tall, sturdy farmhouses; the mountain streams cutting through the land; and the ring of mountains surrounding the plain, with the triangular peak of Mt. Arashima retaining some snow until early summer (fig. 1). The high plateau has been settled since prehistoric times. In the Tokugawa period, most visitors took the highway from the lowlands of Fukui near the Sea of Japan, hiking for about thirty kilometers up the Asuwa River and then through the narrow Haniu Valley before entering the plain (see map 2).[1] Travelers from Mino Province in the east took the more arduous route along the Mino Highway through the remote Anama Valley, following the Kuzuryū River downstream. The mountain ranges around the Ōno plain culminate in Mt. Hakusan, a peak of 2,702 meters with a long history as a holy site that brought many pilgrims to the area. But Mt. Hakusan is not visible from Ōno town, not even from Kameyama hill.

Because of its proximity to the Sea of Japan, Echizen Province is exposed to heavy snowfall during the winter, and people living on the Pacific side of Honshū Island have always associated this area with deep snow. Although the Ōno plain offered favorable conditions for growing rice, agricultural development here lagged behind the more densely

1. In this region, Haniu (rather than Hanyū) is the preferred pronunciation.

FIGURE I View of Ōno town from Kameyama hill, with Mt. Arashima visible toward the right. Photo by the author.

settled plains on Honshū's Pacific side, particularly in the mountains, where villagers cultivated their dry fields with primitive slash-and-burn methods during the Tokugawa period. The cultivation and national marketing of cash crops took a big leap forward only in the nineteenth century. But despite their remote location and harsh climate, the people of Ōno were not isolated from the rest of the country, and they interacted with it in many different ways.

With an assessed productivity of 40,000 *koku*,[2] Ōno domain occupied no more than a tiny corner on Japan's early modern map. Even within Echizen Province the domain was not the most prominent fief. In the Tokugawa period, the sixty-six provinces of Japan's ancient imperial state served as units of nationwide surveys and for mobilizing troops

2.   In Tokugawa Japan, large amounts of rice were usually measured either in bales (*hyō*) or in *koku*, with 1 *koku*=180.39 liters=47.55 gallons, and 1 bale (in Ōno) equaling 4.56 *to*, that is, 82.26 liters=21.73 gallons.

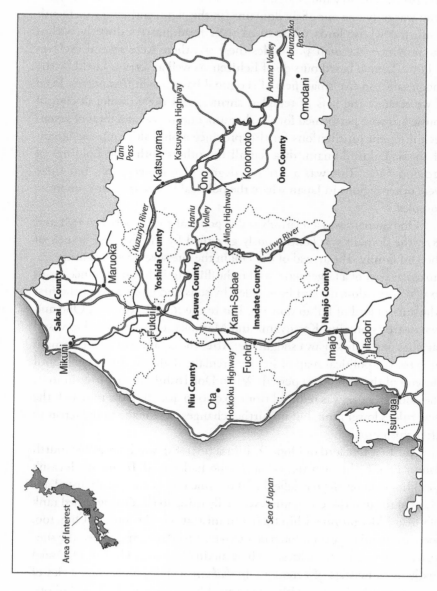

MAP 2 Major roads and rivers in Echizen Province in the Tokugawa period. Adapted from Fukui-ken, *Zusetsu Fukui kenshi.*

and corvée, but their political importance had faded because warlords had divided the country into shogun and daimyo domains. Within Echizen, Ōno was only one out of six domains (in the eighteenth and nineteenth centuries) whose lords maintained their headquarters directly within the province (see map 3). Besides these six, there were several exclaves held by daimyo based outside of Echizen, as well as territory held by the shogunate and five small fiefs of shogunal bannermen (*hatamoto*). Even if we exclude the fiefs of temples, shrines, and the Kōwaka (a clan of musicians who performed for the shogun), one arrives at a total of seventeen different jurisdictions for this province alone, although the largest of them, Fukui domain, dwarfed all the others with land holdings of 320,000 *koku*. This was a striking degree of fragmentation, but there were other regions in Japan where the political landscape was even more complex.

Ōno domain was a relatively stable political entity. Between 1682 and 1871, the domain was continuously governed by the Echizen branch of the Doi family. The arrival of the Doi in the late seventeenth century occurred as part of a larger territorial reshuffling in Echizen Province, prior to which the domain had been ruled by sons and grandsons of the first Matsudaira lord of Fukui domain. But in the 1670s and 1680s, Ōno and two nearby domains, Katsuyama and Maruoka, were entrusted to vassal families of the Tokugawa shogunate. After the creation of Sabae domain in 1720, the political map of Echizen remained almost unchanged until the end of the Tokugawa period. When Doi Toshifusa took over in 1682, the domain's size was reduced from 50,000 to 40,000 *koku* to match the new ruler's lower rank, but no further changes were made to the territory after this point.

The first Doi lord of Ōno, Toshifusa (1631–83), was born as the fourth son of Doi Toshikatsu (1573–1644), who had served Tokugawa Ieyasu's son Hidetada on the battlefield and became one of the most trusted advisers of the first three shoguns, eventually rising to the distinguished rank of Great Elder (*tairō*) within their administration. The lords of Ōno, too, spent every other year on tours of alternate attendance and served the shogunate in various capacities, such as auxiliary guards (*kaban*) of Osaka castle or as masters of ceremony (*sōshaban*) in Edo. They forged ties of marriage and adoption with other vassal lords such as the Ii of Hikone

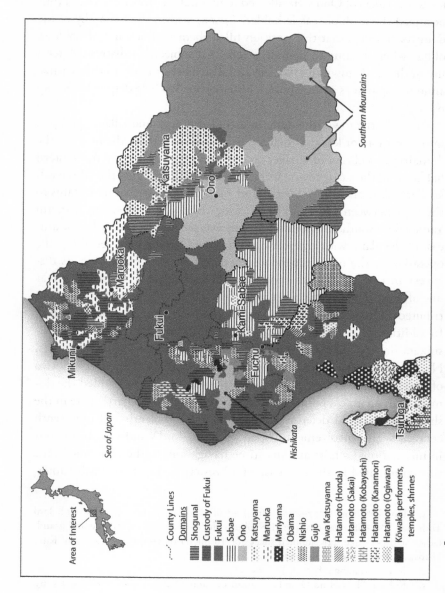

Area of Interest

Sea of Japan

Mikuni

Maruoka

Fukui

Kami-Sabae

Eichū

Nishikata

Tsuruga

Katsuyama

Ōno

Southern Mountains

County Lines
Domains
Shogunal
Custody of Fukui
Fukui
Sabae
Ōno
Katsuyama
Maruoka
Mariyama
Obama
Nishio
Gujō
Awa Katsuyama
Hatamoto (Honda)
Hatamoto (Sakai)
Hatamoto (Kobayashi)
Hatamoto (Kanamori)
Hatamoto (Ogiwara)
Kōwaka performers,
temples, shrines

MAP 3 Ōno's domain territory in 1770. Adapted from Fukui-ken, *Zusetsu Fukui kenshi*.

domain and the Kuze of Sekiyado domain.[3] Unlike many other smaller lords, the rulers of Ōno were allowed to maintain a proper castle and thus occupied the rank of "castle holder" (*jōshu*) within the hierarchy of the daimyo. It seems that this position filled them with a sense of noblesse oblige when it came to providing relief for subjects in distress. After a fire in the castle town in 1789, the lord distributed money to the victims, announcing that as a castle holder, he felt obliged to help despite his empty purse.[4]

Besides the town, the domain included ninety-one villages grouped into four more or less well-defined parts (see map 3). At the heart of the domain was a cluster of villages on the Ōno plain, mostly on the western half around the castle town. Second, the domain included the "three valleys" (*mitani*) of Ashimi, Haniu, and Ajimi in the adjacent mountains to the west between Ōno and Fukui. The third part was called Minami Yamanaka (Southern Mountains) and was located in the valleys southeast of the plain, with an exclave around the Omodani copper mine. The operation of the mine experienced several ups and downs after its discovery in the seventeenth century until its closure in 1922, but it was one of Tokugawa Japan's most productive copper mines and greatly contributed to the recovery of domain finances in the nineteenth century.[5] In addition to these three clusters, the Doi also held the so-called Nishikata fief (Nishikata-ryō) or Ota fief, an exclave of twelve villages in Niu County about thirty kilometers west of the castle town.[6] Only two of these villages bordered directly on the sea, but they provided the domain with an access point to the ocean and forced it to participate in the shogunate's coastal defense plans in the late eighteenth and nineteenth centuries. This involvement helped spark the lord's and vassals' interest in international affairs and maritime navigation; in the 1850s and 1860s this culminated in the purchase of a Western-style schooner, the initia-

3.   Doi Toshinori (1777–1818), fifth lord of Ōno and father of the seventh lord Toshitada (1811–68), was a son of Ii Naohide, the twelfth lord of Hikone and grandfather of Ii Naosuke. His adopted successor Toshikata (1783–1818) was a son of Kuze Hiroakira, fourth lord of Sekiyado.

4.   MT goyōdome 1789.7.21, YH 360, 262.

5.   Kobata, "Kinsei no Omodani dōzan ni tsuite"; *Izumi sonshi*, 378–413, 453–63, 499–504; *Fukui kenshi*, Tsūshi-hen 4, 110–11, 337–44.

6.   In Echizen, Niu (rather than Nyū) is the preferred pronunciation.

tion of regular trade with Ezochi (Hokkaido), and the establishment of a colony on Kita-Ezochi (Sakhalin).[7]

As this description suggests, Ōno's domain territory was not only small but also fairly incoherent. It did not even cover the entirety of the Ōno plain, of which the eastern half was a mosaic of jurisdictions under several domains, including Gujō (Mino Province), Katsuyama, Fukui, Sabae, and the shogunate. Echizen's interior (which roughly overlaps with Ōno County and is known as Oku-Echizen in Japanese) thus constituted a region of scattered lordship. In that sense it was comparable to the Kantō and Kansai regions, but unlike those regions it did not include a city under the shogun's control whose administrators would have exercised oversight over surrounding fiefdoms.[8] Among the people in this area, those within Ōno domain were likely to have been relatively conscious of their identity as domain subjects because their lord's castle was visible from almost every corner of the plain, but they also cultivated identities that connected them to peers in other jurisdictions. Whether they married, traded, or looked for entertainment or employment, the people of inner Echizen behaved more as residents of a geographical region than as subjects of a particular domain.[9] Some of the local poor took advantage of territorial fragmentation. Indigent peasants and townspeople, for example, often moved into the households of relatives during times of distress, including those who lived in a different domain. Once there, they could apply for relief from the government as regular household members. During the Tenpō famine (1833–38), this phenomenon took on such proportions that the domain, on the suggestion of Ōno's town elders, temporarily suspended admissions of subjects of other domains who wanted to move into the town (relief was easier to obtain there than in the villages).[10]

---

7. Azuma, "Ōno-han no Ushoro basho keiei"; *Fukui kenshi*, Tsūshi-hen 4, 825–61.

8. Fukai, *Kinsei no chihō toshi to chōnin*, 25; Yasuoka, *Nihon hōken keizai seisaku shiron*, 112–45. However, only one Ōno village—Koyato—was a shared-revenue (*aikyū*) village, that is, it had more than one feudal overlord. Shared-revenue villages were a relatively common feature in other regions with scattered lordship.

9. See, for example, the analysis of moves and marriages in and out of Ōno town in *Fukui kenshi*, Tsūshi-hen 4, 309–15.

10. MT goyōdome 1837.2.11, SSM. For details on all manuscript sources, see the bibliography.

The complicated political geography forced the government to tread carefully in its relationships with its neighbors. Ōno's domain officials kept regular contact with their peers in the nearby castle town of Katsuyama and with Gujō domain's administrative outpost in Wakaino. Although the officials in Katsuyama and Wakaino were close enough to keep an eye on their territories on the Ōno plain, the same could not be said about the shogunate's outpost Honbo in distant Niu County, which governed some villages on the plain on behalf of the county intendant's (*gundai*) office in even farther-away Takayama. Ōno's domain government appears to have regarded the shogunate's villages as a source of disorder. According to an undated petition drafted in the nineteenth century, Ōno's lord planned to ask the shogunate to entrust him with the administration of its eleven villages—not because of the tax revenue, which he intended to forward to the shogun as before, but because he wanted to keep them under tighter reins to keep out criminals and stop residents from picking fights with his own villagers over irrigation and other matters. He also hoped to coerce these villages into selling rice to his Omodani copper mine at a lower price. Although it is unclear whether the lord ever submitted this petition, the document illustrates some of the challenges of governing in an area of scattered jurisdictions.[11]

With a total population smaller than that of modern Ōno City (15,876 in 1682,[12] 24,254 in 1726,[13] 31,115 in 1870,[14] compared with 35,024 for Ōno City in 2015), domain rule in Ōno had more in common with the government of a township plus hinterland than a territorial state. Even the highest decision-making organ of the government, the Council of Vassals (*retsuza*) that advised the lord, often bothered itself with seemingly marginal details, especially when it came to the administration of the town. At the same time, the townspeople and other status groups enjoyed a high degree of independence, and the principle of self-government by status was taken very seriously, even in the castle town, where enough warrior officials would have been available to exercise tighter control. The relative number of vassal households in the domain was small in com-

11. Untitled source in TKM.
12. *Fukui kenshi*, Tsūshi-hen 3, 180.
13. Ōno go-ryōbun yonmangoku-chū chōzai ninzū-yose, 1726, SSM.
14. Kōshi bibō, 1870, Ōno Kōtō Gakkō Ōkuma-ke monjo.

parison with the nearby Fukui domain: 631 in 1682, about 500 in the 1770s, and 540 in 1871, when the new Meiji government sorted all warriors into two categories and identified 292 *shizoku* (higher-ranking warriors) and 248 *sotsu* (foot soldiers, etc.) among Ōno's vassal band. Some were stationed at the domain's mansion in the shogunal capital of Edo.[15] The vassals also hired townspeople and peasants of small means to serve them as valets, porters, and firefighters (*chūgen*) and changed the registration of these servants so they became warriors for the duration of their employment.[16]

The castle town was administered more carefully than the rest of the domain. Its population was 5,081 in 1756, but grew noticeably during the subsequent 120 years (6,166 in 1856; 6,547 in 1861).[17] The domain officials directly in charge of the town included the town governor (*machi bugyō*) and the governor of temples and shrines (*jisha bugyō*, often held in personal union with the town governor). The governor of temples and shrines oversaw not only clerics but also townspeople who resided in houses on temple land. The town governor directed the two town elders (*machidoshi-yori*) of commoner status. He was assisted in these duties by the town corps (*machigumi*), a division of lower-ranking vassals.[18] The villages of the domain, on the other hand, were under the rule of the county governor (*kōri bugyō*), who lived in the town and supervised three rural intendants (*daikan*), whose point persons in the peasantry were the so-called village group headmen (*ōjōya*), drafted from the ranks of powerful landowners. The village group headmen represented the peasants vis-à-vis the domain, but because they had their office in the castle town, they had to divide their time between the town and their home villages. To improve control, for much of the Tokugawa period, the domain's two exclaves—the

15. Funazawa, "Ōno-han kashindan no shokusei to kyūroku," 54; Kōshi bibō, 1870, Ōno Kōtō Gakkō Ōkuma-ke monjo; Araki, "'Monogashira-yaku tsutomekata tehikae'"; Matsuyama, "Uchiyama Kaisuke no jinbutsuzō."

16. Ōjōya goyōdome 1860.5.19, YH 1154, 825–28; MT goyōdome 1785.1.26, SSM.

17. "Ōno hanryō muramura hondaka iekazu ninzū oboechō," 1756, in *Fukui ken-shi*, Shiryō-hen 7, 228–29; MT goyōdome 1856.6.14, YH 1086, 789; MT goyōdome 1861, YH 1254, 887.

18. The post of town governor was typically held by vassals with a stipend of 120–240 *koku* who oversaw their own small band of retainers (*kumi*). Upon appointment to the position of town or county governor, these vassals turned their retainers into the town or county corps and used them for various auxiliary tasks, such as town patrols; see Araki, "'Monogashira-yaku tsutomekata tehikae.'"

Southern Mountains and Nishikata—each had their own village group headman, who resided directly in those areas.[19]

Nishikata was situated near the Sea of Japan and was important to the domain for economic and military reasons. Socially it belonged to an entirely different regional microcosm. The residents of Ōno's core area in inner Echizen did not customarily interact with the people in Nishikata and hardly ever mentioned them in their documents. The mountain villagers, by contrast, were heavily dependent on their exchanges with the castle town and had many reasons to travel to the Ōno plain.

Castle Town Society

Ōno was the textbook example of a Tokugawa castle town. The early modern town settlement was established in 1576 by Kanamori Nagachika, a vassal of prominent warlord Oda Nobunaga. Instead of occupying one of the medieval fortresses on the Ōno plain, Nagachika built an entirely new castle on top of Kameyama hill and constructed a town at its foot. The new town was laid out according to a plan (see fig. 2). At the eastern foot of Kameyama hill, Nagachika placed the lord's palace and residences of higher-ranking retainers, separated from townspeople's residences by a moat. Along the eastern edge of the town, Nagachika and his successors lined up about seventeen temples of various Buddhist affiliations as a line of defense toward the open plain. The townspeople's quarters filled up the space between the temples and the moat like a grid. The residences of low-ranking retainers were situated around the northern and southern exits of the town and along the western foot of Kameyama Hill, where conditions were moist and undesirable. If there was anything unorthodox about the structure of this town, it might have been its openness toward the surrounding countryside, a relatively unusual feature among castle towns in this part of the country that perhaps reflected Nagachika's interest in trade.[20]

Ōno town served as an important urban center for the residents of Ōno County. It shared this role with Katsuyama, a somewhat smaller

19.   YH, "Kaisetsu," 18–22.
20.   Fukai, *Kinsei no chihō toshi to chōnin*, 30–33.

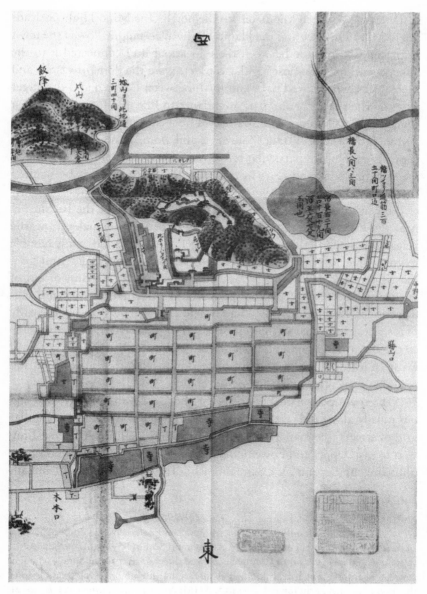

FIGURE 2 The castle town of Ōno, circa early 1680s. *Source*: *Shokoku tōjō no zu* in the Asano Bunko collection. Courtesy of Hiroshima Shiritsu Chūō Toshokan.

castle town about ten kilometers to the north. The Mino Highway leading to Mino Province and the Haniu Highway to Fukui allowed the town
to participate in trade between these locations and connected it to the
outside world.[21] The most regular travelers were the domain vassals and
their valets, who moved back and forth between Echizen and the larger
cities on their tours of alternate attendance to Edo and for guard duty at
Osaka Castle. Commoners also traveled frequently, although they needed
permission for long-distance journeys, and women and commoner officials were subject to particular scrutiny. Town doctors, for example, im-
mersed their sons and heirs in the latest intellectual trends by sending
them to study in Edo or Kyoto.[22] Wealthy merchants and peasants traveled for business and pleasure, visiting holy sites such as the Ise Shrines
near the Pacific Ocean or the hot spring resort of Yamanaka in nearby
Kaga Province.[23] In the second half of the Tokugawa period, many humble
townspeople and peasants also visited Fukui, Kyoto, Osaka, and Edo,
mostly to work or to learn a trade but sometimes as pilgrims or out of
curiosity. The flow of people, goods, and information was not one-
directional. In 1815, Ōno town had nineteen innkeepers, and in the early
1840s, these inns hosted an average of 771 to 916 travelers each month.[24]
In the Bakumatsu period (1853–68), the small town thrived as a center of
Western learning and attracted educated men from the entire Hokuriku
region and even from Osaka and beyond.[25]

The townspeople area consisted of about a dozen *chō* that were laid
out mostly along the vertical north–south axis of the town's rectangular
grid of streets (see map 4). These *chō* were conveniently numbered from
west to east: Upper and Lower Ichibanmachi (First *chō*), Upper and Lower
Nibanmachi (Second *chō*), Sanbanmachi (Third *chō*, and so on), Shiban-

21. Fukui-ken Kyōiku Iinkai (ed.), *Mino kaidō/Katsuyama kaidō*.
22. The Sasajima family of town doctors, for example, received its training in Edo.
In the 1790s, one member of this family, Amenomori Sōshin (Gyūnan), introduced the
eclectic school (*setchūgaku*) of Confucianism and thus replaced Ogyū Sorai's school of
Ancient Learning, which had dominated intellectual life among Ōno's vassals until
that point; Tenmei hachi tomeki, 1783.10.2, AHM; *Nihon jinmei daijiten*, vol. 1, 120–21;
Fukui kenshi, Tsūshi-hen 3, 711–12.
23. See, for example, Goyōdome, 1790.7.10, 1795.3.26, Hanakura-ke monjo.
24. *Fukui kenshi*, Tsūshi-hen 4, 300–301.
25. Ibid., 635–36, 718–26.

machi, and Gobanmachi. In Ōno, where the water flows from south to north, "upper" (*kami*) referred to the southern and "lower" (*shimo*) to the northern section of the town. Among the horizontal streets, only Shichikenmachi and Yokomachi constituted self-governing block associations. Shichikenmachi was home to the town's market, which attracted many peasants from the surrounding countryside.[26] In total, the town area had twelve (sometimes thirteen) *chō*, including two block associations made up of artisans: Kajimachi (blacksmiths) and Daikumachi (carpenters). The other *chō* were not as exclusive in their occupational orientation and included house owners of many different trades, although most of them had some form of occupational concentration. Lower Ichibanmachi, for example, included many innkeepers, whereas Bikunimachi specialized in cheap hostels for poorer travelers. There was a community of sawyers within the territory of Yokomachi and coopers in Lower Nibanmachi. Occupational matters played an important role in the self-government of these block associations.

In addition to the *chō*, the town included five branch villages (*edamura*), Noguchi, Kanazuka, Shinokura, Seiryū, and Saihōji, which were located along the southern limits of the town. Some of these villages had a distinct occupational character. Kanazuka was a community of fowlers and cormorant fishermen with a hunting privilege from the lord. Together with Noguchi, it constituted one of the town's most impoverished neighborhoods and often had to request relief loans from the domain. The "villages" of Seiryū and Saihōji had hardly any residents, but Shinokura was a community of more than 100 people, dominated by a few shrine priests who served at the ancient Shinokura Shrine. The southernmost section of the town area was covered by fields and an undeveloped wilderness called Shindenno, which served the townspeople as a commons for fodder, fertilizer, and firewood.

It was not unusual for Ōno townspeople to work in agriculture. The owners of agricultural land in the town were known as "town peasants" (*machibyakushō*) or "land owners" (*takamochi*), and they had an organization with officers (*sōdai*) to represent their interests.[27] In their role as

---

26. Tsutomekata oboegaki Tamura-hikae, 1810, TKM; MT goyōdome 1852.10.28, SSM; Takahashi, "Shichiken no asaichi."

27. MT goyōdome 1792.3.6, YH 398, 283–84; 1860. 9.1, YH 1194, 853–54.

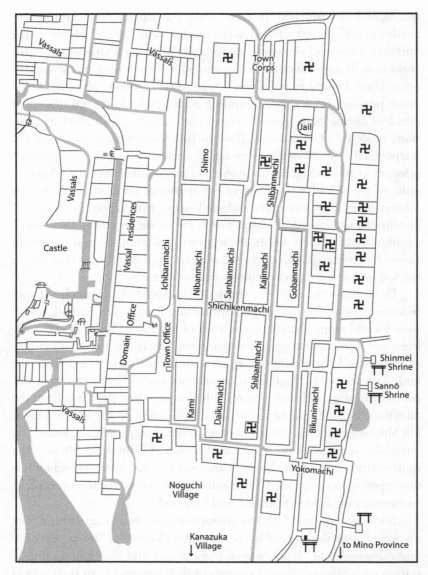

MAP 4 Ōno town, based on a map copy from 1820. Adapted from Ōno-shi Rekishi
Minzoku Shiryōkan, *Ezu ga kataru Ōno*.

peasants, they paid their rice tax not to the town governor but to one of the rural intendants in the same manner as the villagers of the domain. But even the nonfarming townspeople of Ōno were not exempt from paying taxes on their land—not even on their residential plots (*yashikidaka*).[28] This distinguished them from the residents of many larger castle towns, who often enjoyed an exemption from the land tax. Almost every piece of settled land in the town was assessed a "yield" that reflected the profitability of its business location, and the townspeople paid the tax in monetary form.[29] In the 1830s, the castle town was assessed at a yield of over 5,206 *koku* of rice, a figure that included residential land and cultivated fields.[30]

Even those who did not own land often engaged in farming, either as tenants or as seasonal laborers. In 1777, more than 230 townspeople submitted a petition for relief loans in their capacity as tenant farmers and day laborers, and as it turned out, there were between seventeen and forty such applicants in almost every *chō*, including Noguchi village.[31] These people asked for aid because they had lost their belongings in a large fire two years earlier, leaving them with no one willing to refinance their loans and no items to pawn. To make matters worse, some of the applicants were still living in temporary shacks and had no firewood in the depth of winter. This petition illustrates not only the hardships faced by fire victims but also the importance of moneylenders for small townspeople hoping to survive tough times.

Ōno town was vulnerable to fire, especially in the spring, when warm and dry foehn winds spilled over to the plain from the south. In the second half of the Tokugawa period, the town experienced at least eight large fires that each destroyed between 10 and 2,000 buildings.[32] To minimize the danger of fire, in 1822 the domain government forced the whole village of Noguchi and some residents of Upper Ichibanmachi, Upper Nibanmachi, and other *chō* to move to new quarters on the outskirts of the town, which partly developed into slums because of their bad

28. The same was true for many other castle towns in the Hokuriku region; see Fukai, *Kinsei no chihō toshi to chōnin*, 34–35.

29. Ōno-machi danmen ezu, 1743, copy of 1775, TKM.

30. *Ōno shishi*, Chiku-hen, 13.

31. MT goyōdome 1777, second month, YH 123, 100–101.

32. Sakata, "Jōkamachi no seiritsu to yonhyakunen no keika," 47; *Fukui kenshi*, Tsūshi-hen 4, 105; *Ōno no ayumi*, 110.

location.[33] The government regarded fire prevention as a top priority and ordered additional fire patrols in times of dry weather. Throughout the eighteenth and nineteenth century, administrators tried to force the townspeople to thatch their roofs with wooden planks instead of reed or straw, but progress on this matter was slow because the latter material happened to be much cheaper. The frequent fires inflicted a major burden on the domain budget and the livelihoods of the townspeople.

Ōno's block associations were home to a wide variety of trades and crafts: merchants and peddlers of rice, salt, vegetables, fish, tofu, miso, soy sauce, tea, sweets, lamp oil, medicine, textiles, paper, tobacco, copper, medicine, tools, horses, and more; artisans including sake brewers, blacksmiths, carpenters, sawyers, dyers, coopers, and spinners; and other lines of trade such as inns, bathhouses, hairdressers, entertainers, doctors, and pawnbrokers. Most of these livelihoods were organized into one or more than one professional guild, which usually selected an annual and a monthly representative (*nenban* and *tsukiban*) each to communicate with the town elders and the domain.[34] From the 1830s onward, a few new guilds emerged as the domain government began to promote the domestic production of woven textiles, thread, lacquer, paper, tobacco, and other commodities.[35]

The hierarchy of rank within the townspeople's community was loosely correlated to wealth. Like most Japanese towns in the eighteenth and nineteenth centuries, Ōno's town society was dominated by a group of wealthy wholesale merchants.[36] Many of these enjoyed so-called tax-exempt (*gomenchi*) status, which freed them from paying taxes on part of their land. Although this category did not constitute an actual institution of town government, its members were treated as a class apart in many official situations.[37] Overlapping with the tax-exempt were the purveyors (*goyōtashi*), privileged townspeople who regularly served the domain lord as financiers and in other capacities. The purveyor merchants were organized in the so-called purveyor guild (*goyōtashi nakama*), which included

33. *Fukui kenshi*, Tsūshi-hen 4, 293.

34. Ibid., 297–302.

35. Ibid., 814–17.

36. The "wholesalers' hegemony," in Yoshida Nobuyuki's terminology; see "Dentō toshi no shūen," 33–64.

37. For example, the town elders did not include them in the circulars they sent out to the townspeople but informed them in a separate letter.

the tax-exempt and played an important role in regulating the town economy. The domain government usually appointed the two town elders from among the purveyor merchants for a period of several years.[38] From 1789 or earlier, there was also an intermediate rank called *nakadōri*, probably for merchants who were on the way of qualifying for promotion to purveyor.[39] The majority of townspeople, however, were simple house owners (*honke*), land tenants (*jinago*, who rented land but owned their homes), and house tenants (*kashiya*). Among these, only the house owners counted as full members of the block associations and shouldered the townspeople's status privileges and duties. The town doctors (*machi isha*) and the blind professionals (*zatō* and *goze*) had occupational groups of their own and were treated differently from the other townspeople in some settings, but if they owned land in the town, they maintained a separate identity as full members of a block association. They all resided within the *chō* and were recorded in the same population registers as the other townspeople.

Clerics and outcastes, by contrast, were excluded from the townspeople collective in terms of status, registration, and residential space. In 1856, the town had 104 Buddhist priests (including at least 8 mountain ascetics (*yamabushi*)), 1 full-time shrine priest (*kannushi*), and 2 nuns (*bikuni*) of the Ji sect.[40] The outcastes comprised two groups: the beggar bosses (*hinin*, also known as Koshirō) and the leatherworkers (*eta*, also known as *kawaya*). Although the outcaste groups were independent from each other, the beggar bosses were a larger group and more influential. The leatherworkers lived in a row of three or four households on the edge of Yokomachi and collected the carcasses of farm beasts and other animals to manufacture drums and other leather items. Sometimes they were derogatorily referred to as *eta* (literally: "very polluted") by the authorities and even by the Koshirō, but it is unknown whether they were discriminated against more severely than the beggar bosses were.[41] Documentation on the leatherworkers is scarce. The beggar bosses, however, frequently

---

38. For the duration of their term in office, the elders were excluded from the purveyor guild.

39. MT goyōdome 1789.7.21, YH 360, 262.

40. MT goyōdome 1856.6.14, YH 1086, 789–90.

41. On the leatherworkers, see, for example, MT goyōdome 1741.6.26, SSM; MT goyōdome 1769.9.5, YH 61, 56; 1815.6.20, YH 599, 422–23; MT goyōdome 1852.6.21, 1852.8.6, 8.8, SSM.

communicated with the domain government through the town elders and left many traces in the town elders' journals. Their settlement was located on the southeastern periphery of the town, and their total population hovered around thirty throughout the second half of the Tokugawa period.[42]

The structure of town society slowly changed over time. Although the overall number of households was growing, the growth was limited to the highest and lowest rungs of the townspeople's social ladder. In 1741, the town had only twenty-three purveyor merchants (plus nine tax-exempt), as well as 709 house owners, 68 land tenants, and 453 house tenants.[43] In 1864, by contrast, there were fifty-two purveyors (plus sixteen tax-exempt), 672 house owners, and 856 tenants (land tenants and house tenants combined).[44] As these figures show, the ratio of tenants to house owners was on the rise; by 1806, it had already slightly increased to 47 percent from 44 percent in 1741.[45] To be sure, this proportion was never as high as in the central districts of Edo, Osaka, or Kyoto, where absentee landlords were common and back alleys were often filled with row houses (*nagaya*) populated with many tenants.[46] Cadastral records show that many of the house owners in Ōno possessed no more than the plot they lived on, and much of the rented space was located in ordinary town houses.[47] But as far as tenancy was concerned, Ōno was on the higher end among the castle towns of the Hokuriku region. In the late eighteenth and first half of the nineteenth century, many towns in Echizen experienced population increases and growing tenant ratios, not so much as a result of economic growth but because of an influx of landless villagers.[48] Maps

42.   Ōno machi ezu, 1730, SSM. See also Sakata, *Ōno machi ezu*.

43.   MT goyōdome 1741.12.8, YH 25, 23–24

44.   MT goyōdome 1864.9.26, YH 1293, 916. This number does not include the six privileged townspeople who were directly ruled by the town governor (*jiki-shihai*).

45.   MT goyōdome 1741.12.8, YH 25, 23–24; Horikane goyōdome, 1806, YH 564, 384–86. Townspeople on temple land are counted as tenants.

46.   Yoshida Nobuyuki, *Kinsei kyodai toshi no shakai kōzō*, 196–204, 220–24; Yoshida Nobuyuki, *Kyodai jōkamachi Edo no bunsetsu kōzō*, 90–104. In Osaka during the Genroku era (1690s), tenants made up 61 percent of the total population (excluding servants); "Settsu-shō," 1688, in *Osaka hennenshi*, vol. 6, 278–79.

47.   Aside from house sale records, a few cadastral registers (*mizuchō*) have survived for certain *chō* from the years 1763, 1829, and 1864; see SSM.

48.   Fukai, *Kinsei no chihō toshi to chōnin*, 42–43, 58–62. Also see *Katsuyama shishi*, vol. 2, 447–49, 480–83.

show only twelve row-house tenements for townspeople for 1730, but by 1844 this number had risen to sixty-nine. Most of them were owned by wealthy merchants and temples.[49]

Although not all tenants in Tokugawa towns were poor, poor people were likely to be tenants. In Ōno, it seems that even many house owners were economically quite vulnerable. For example, house owners constituted the majority of applicants in a petition for starvation aid in 1777.[50] In this particular case, the high rate of house-owning applicants was probably related to the fire of 1775 that affected everyone regardless of wealth, but house owners also featured prominently in many other instances of poor and starvation relief. In 1783, for example, the house owners of the branch village of Noguchi submitted a petition in which they described themselves as tenant farmers and laborers who had sunk into a state of "extreme poverty" (*goku-konkyū*) and depended mostly on day labor for survival.[51] Poor individuals like these seem to have been reluctant to sell their homes even when their economic situation had become difficult, probably because they took pride in their status as house owners and hoped to convey it to their descendants.

The gradual expansion of Ōno's tenant class seems to have gone hand in hand with a concentration of wealth at the top of local society. The most important elements in the business portfolios of the purveyor merchants were moneylending and sake brewing. Of the twenty-five purveyor merchants in 1784, fourteen belonged to the brewer guild and thirteen were members of the pawnbroker guild.[52] Almost all purveyor merchants belonged to at least one of these two associations. Many pawnbrokers in Ōno were far more than just petty moneylenders.[53] The most common

---

49. Yoshida Jun'ichi, "Hanseiki ni okeru Ōno jōka/Katsuyama jōka no machiya," 150–62; Sakata, *Ōno machi ezu.* After a great fire in 1775, for example, the tax-exempt merchants obtained permission from the domain to build new tenements and take in new land tenants to support their financial recovery; Tenmei hachi tomeki, 1783, sixth month, AHM.

50. MT goyōdome 1777.2.1, YH 122, 98–99.

51. Tenmei hachi tomeki, 1783, second month, AHM.

52. MT goyōdome 1785.2.27, YH 247, 178–79; 1786.10.26, YH 290, 215–17.

53. In Osaka, for example, there were "big" and "small" pawnbrokers (*ōjichiya* and *kojichiya*), with big pawnbrokers specializing in real estate and small pawnbrokers in mobile items. *Ōjichiya* and *kojichiya* also appear in Ōno's town elders' journals (MT goyōdome 1741, fourth month, SSM). On pawnbrokers in urban society and their

pawns in Ōno were agricultural land and rice, the latter of which was often pawned in form of bills (*tegata*).[54] For this reason, the pawnbrokers in Ōno town not only held remarkable reserves of rice but also accumulated land each time their debtors forfeited collateral. By the 1780s, the peasants of Noguchi had lost almost all their farmland to a small group of six townspeople, five of whom can be identified as pawnbrokers and four as purveyor merchants.[55] Three of these purveyors, Hiiragiya, Nabeya, and Kameya, also belonged to the exclusive circle of the tax-exempt. The family of the fourth, Kamiya Mataemon, supplied several town elders in the course of Ōno's history.

The eighteenth century saw the ascendancy of powerful new merchants in the town. The most conspicuous of them were Nabeya Seizaemon and Kameya Moemon, who built a fortune through money-lending, sake brewing, and trade[56] and by the 1780s had become so rich that they funded more than half of the starvation relief distributed to the town poor during the Tenmei famine. As the domain government began to tap the wealth of these two men, it invested them with ever higher privileges.[57] In 1785 and 1788, respectively, Nabeya and Kameya were lifted above the other purveyors and tax-exempt and placed under the direct rule of the town governor.[58] Perhaps this strategy was designed to reward these men without openly demoting other, traditionally privileged merchants, some of whom were now on the decline.[59] A similar change of guard among purveyor merchants took place in Edo during the very same decades.[60]

---

connection to sake brewing, see also Gay, *The Moneylenders of Late Medieval Kyoto*, 46–55, 206–9.

54. *Ōno chōshi*, vol. 3, 434.

55. Tenmei hachi tomeki, 1733, second month, AHM.

56. *Ōno chōshi*, vol. 2, 903–9, 1177–83; vol. 4, 538–40; MT goyōdome 1786.10.26, 11.6, YH 290 and 292, 215–19 (Kameya); Sakata, "Jōkamachi Ōno no dōro."

57. *Fukui kenshi*, Tsūshi-hen 4, 108–10.

58. *Ōno chōshi*, vol. 4, 538–40; MT goyōdome 1785.11.14, 12.2, SSM; MT goyōdome 1785.11.16–21, YH 260, 190–91.

59. Katō Kyūzaemon, for example, the highest-ranking tax-exempt, had attained this rank by the early 1700s, but in 1813 was forced to sell his tax-exempt house to Kameya. The household managed to reverse its fortunes; see *Ōno chōshi*, vol. 2, 1319–22.

60. Takeuchi, "Kansei kaikaku to 'kanjōsho goyōtashi' no seiritsu."

Many (perhaps most) members of the town elite were not only merchants but also large holders of agricultural and forest land.[61] In 1741, for example, two flood-prone villages on the Ōno plain lost an extensive amount of land, which they had collectively offered up to Nabeya as collateral to borrow money for tax payments.[62] The habit of pawning forest and other land to moneylenders in Ōno town had spread among mountain villages in the valleys of Anama, Uchinami, and Nishitani, many of which were not part of Ōno domain. The archive of purveyor merchant Mugiya contains countless IOUs collected from a number of mountain villages in Uchinami and Anama over a span of more than 100 years, as well as from a few villages on the western rim of the Ōno plain.[63] Most villages in the mountains had become the long-term clients of particular town merchants. The wholesalers supplied them with rice, salt, and loans for food and taxes in bad years and purchased the goods they produced: lumber, charcoal, medicinal herbs, turned woodcrafts, and more. The miners' settlement near the Omodani copper mine essentially operated on a similar exchange model. Most mountain villagers grew millet for their own consumption, but they imported rice, salt, and other commodities from the plain.[64] The provision of the hinterland was a typical business pattern for the wholesale merchants who had come to dominate most small Japanese castle towns by the end of the seventeenth century.[65]

The symbiotic relationship between merchants and mountain villagers became a problem whenever rice was scarce and the grain price in Ōno town rose slower than in Fukui and the interior part of Mino Province directly adjacent to Echizen. The resulting price difference was an invitation for profiteers, and the townspeople of Ōno were extremely vigilant about merchants who exported rice in such situations. In bad years, they often demanded price interventions and export controls. The town elders and domain officials were almost always able to prevent such unrest

---

61. On the same phenomenon in another part of the country (Shōnai), see Kelly, *Deference and Defiance*, 44–49.

62. *Ōno chōshi*, vol. 2, 1178–83.

63. *Ōno chōshi*, vol. 3, 640–46; Mugiya monjo.

64. MT goyōdome 1783.12.1, 1783.12.21, 1784.3.2, SSM; Kobata, "Kinsei no Omodani dōzan ni tsuite," 20–21; *Ōno shishi*, Minzoku-hen, 58–69, 141–51; Yoshida Mori, *Nishitani sonshi*, vol. 1, 338–40.

65. Fukai, "Kinsei toshi no hattatsu," 159.

from escalating, but in the Bakumatsu era, townspeople increasingly resorted to arson and anonymous denunciations to intimidate wealthy merchants.[66]

The poor of Ōno town belonged to a variety of status groups. They even included some members of the ruling class—low-ranking retainers who had to subsist on shrinking stipends and were banned from many profitable by-employments. Many samurai families were heavily in debt, and the only aid they were allowed to accept was from the lord or their relatives, who sometimes included well-to-do commoners connected through marriage or adoption. Among the townspeople, each block association and branch village included a mix of richer and poorer people, and even the Koshirō—the beggar bosses, who lived on alms—were not all equally deprived. Poverty-related petitions suggest that applicants often engaged in one of the following livelihoods: tenant farmer, farm laborer, construction worker, porter, lumberjack, servant, samurai valet, maker of small craft items such as straw sandals or lamp wicks, tobacco cutter, craftsman's assistant, cormorant fisherman, itinerant cleric, peddler, entertainer, beggar boss, and watchman. Some of these livelihoods could be practiced by both men and women and by members of any status group, but they were often structured or overseen by some form of occupational organization. In other words, status and class intersected in multiple ways. Although many occupational groups were tilted toward one end of the socioeconomic scale, each comprised people of different material means.

Village Society

The structure of village government mirrored that of the town. Each village had a headman (*shōya*), an assistant headman (*osabyakushō*), and a peasant representative (*sōdai*). Like the block associations, villages were internally divided into groups of five or more households for mutual supervision and support. The equivalents of the town elders in the countryside were the village group headmen, whose journals were less detailed than those of the town elders and preoccupied with agricultural matters.

---

66. *Fukui kenshi*, Tsūshi-hen 4, 106–8; MT goyōdome 1860.5.21, 5.26, YH 1155, 828.

Thirty-three such journals have survived from the period 1739 to 1869, and for some villages in the domain, they can be supplemented with the house journals of wealthy peasants and journals of village headmen.

The ninety-one villages of Ōno domain were very diverse, and each had its own character as a self-governing community. The biggest contrast was between villages in the mountains and those on the plain, although the line between them is not always easily drawn. In the villages on the plain, rice was by far the most important crop. The peasants there irrigated their fields with water from the Kuzuryū, Mana, and Akane Rivers, but these mountain streams were difficult to tame and residents had to be on guard against flooding (see map 5).[67] The domain occasionally drafted townspeople and peasants as laborers for riparian works. All agricultural communities in the domain and the townspeople participated in associations for the maintenance of irrigation systems and river ferries. These associations usually spanned several domains, reflecting the flow of water and transportation rather than the borders of individual fiefdoms.[68]

Even on the plain, the long and snowy winters made double-cropping almost impossible. From late December until late March, the land was covered in a thick layer of moist and heavy snow and yielded only a very small rye harvest in the spring.[69] The people of Ōno invested much time and energy into clearing their streets and roofs from the crushing snow masses; some of them were drafted for snow removal at the lord's castle.[70] The snow was a burden for anyone in the domain and caused particular hardships for the poor, who could not expect to find employment in construction or agriculture during the winter. Digging up roots and herbs was not an option when they ran out of reserves, and they needed a long-lasting supply of firewood to survive the winter on their own. For the poor

67. Especially the villages Sabiraki and Gojōhō; MT goyōdome 1740.7.29 and later, SSM.

68. Saitō et al. (eds.), *Okuetsu bunka*, vol. 7; *Katsuyama shishi*, vol. 2, 426–30; Yōroku, 1852, SSM.

69. *Izumi sonshi*, 15–22. In this region, precipitation during the winter is about as much as it is during the Japanese monsoon season in June/July.

70. Tsutomekata oboegaki Tamura-hikae, 1810, TKM. On the mobilization of snow labor in Katsuyama, see *Katsuyama shishi*, vol. 1, 1023–24.

MAP 5 Aerial photograph of Ōno town and surroundings. Bold letters refer to villages of Ōno domain, light letters to villages of other jurisdictions. Adapted from *Ōno shi-shi*, Chiku-hen.

of Ōno, self-help during the winter was far more difficult to achieve than for poor people in warmer regions.

Some of the village communities on the Ōno plain were dominated by large landowners whose lineages went back to the early Tokugawa or even the late Muromachi period (1336–1573). Ōno's wealthiest peasants, Hanaguro (Matsuda) Yosōzaemon in Nakano and Nojiri Gen'emon in Yokomakura, fell into this category. They enjoyed extensive tax and rank privileges and served the lord as financiers and occasionally village group headmen. Their landholdings were located both in- and outside the domain. To cultivate them, they relied partly on their own servants and partly on tenants, whom they tried to keep in a paternalistic relationship. When hiring agricultural laborers became too costly in the late Tokugawa period, the proportion of tenant-held land gradually increased.[71] Hanaguro's home village, Nakano, was directly adjacent to the town, and its large population (641 in 1756) was heavily skewed toward landless households (114 landless versus 28 landowning households), indicating a large presence of tenant farmers.[72] Some domain villages also had high concentrations of part-time laborers. In Hakariishi, Ōmiya, and Ōkubo, for example, many peasants supplemented their income by working as porters on the Haniu Highway.[73]

The peasant economy in most mountain villages differed radically from that of the plain. The mountain ranges and valleys in the Ōno area were part of a wide zone of slash-and-burn agriculture unfolding on the foothills of Mt. Hakusan. Here the typical crops were foxtail and barnyard millet (*awa* and *hie*), soybeans, *azuki* beans, and buckwheat. Peasants also harvested vegetables, goldthread (*ōren*, a medicinal herb), chestnuts, wasabi, and other mountain plants.[74] In addition, many of

71. *Fukui kenshi*, Tsūshi-hen 3, 766–71; Tsūshi-hen 4, 190–99.

72. "Ōno hanryō muramura hondaka iekazu ninzū oboechō," 1756, in *Fukui kenshi*, Shiryō-hen 7, 243.

73. "Haniudani muramura jōmen/natsunari men gin osame negai," 1728, in *Fukui kenshi*, Shiryō-hen 7, 887; "Ōrai jinba chinsen ni tsuki Ōmiya/Ōkubo-mura gansho narabi ni saikyo," 1768, in *Fukui kenshi*, Shiryō-hen 7, 891–94.

74. *Ōno shishi*, Minzoku-hen, 141–59; Ogura, *Uchinamigawa ryūiki no dezukuri seido*; Tachibana Reikichi, "Hakusanroku no yakihata kenkyūshi"; Yamaguchi Takaharu, *Hakusanroku/dezukuri no kenkyū*; Yoshida Mori, *Nishitani sonshi*, vol. 1, 331–45; Sugimoto, *Nōsanson keizai no kisoteki kenkyū*, 438–69.

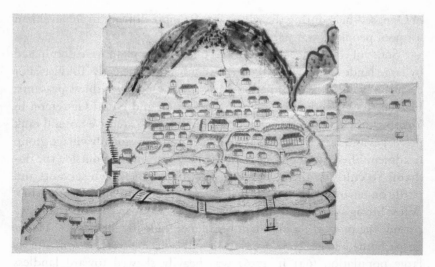

FIGURE 3 The village of Omodani at the Omodani copper mine. *Source*: Omodani yashiki narabi ni mura no zu, 1843, Yokota-ke monjo.

them cut lumber and manufactured charcoal, silk, and paper. Some of the charcoal and lumber they produced supported operations at the Omodani copper mine (fig. 3) and at other smaller mines in the vicinity.[75] Other products were bought up by merchants in Ōno town and exported to more distant markets. In the valley of Nishitani, for example, semi-itinerant groups of wood turners (*kijiya*) produced tool handles, bowls, and other wooden crafts and sold them to town merchants. The copper from the Omodani mine was transported through middlemen in Ōno town to Osaka via ship and horseback.[76] In that sense, the mountain villages were no less integrated into the national economy than were the villages on the plain.

Because arable land was scarce in the mountains, many peasants engaged in a practice called *dezukuri*. They moved into narrow valleys and up the slopes of the mountains where they cultivated swidden (so-called *mutsushi*) as either landowners or tenants. Some stayed there year

75. *Izumi sonshi*, 397–400.
76. MT goyōdome 1784.9.12–14, YH 226, 168; *Izumi sonshi*, 331–60; Yoshida Mori, *Nishitani sonshi*, vol. 1, 338–40.

round; others lived in shacks that were too flimsy to withstand the snow in the winter. In the mountain valleys, the snow not only stayed on longer but regularly piled up to a height of several meters.[77] According to population registers from these areas, households in the valleys tended to be unusually large and sometimes counted more than ten members.[78] It is likely that younger siblings were prevented from establishing branch households by the narrow space and lack of economic opportunity in the valleys, not to speak of the trouble it took to heat and maintain a homestead during the winter.

The mountain villagers depended on Ōno town as a market and supply base, and the domain government was willing to facilitate this exchange. No matter what domain they lived in, the mountain dwellers (*yamaga no mono*) were allowed to spend the night in Ōno town without applying for official permission to do so.[79] For many of them, Ōno town was also the location of their family temple. Because the countryside of inner Echizen was populated almost exclusively by adherents of the True Pure Land sect of Buddhism, most villages did not have proper temples but community prayer halls (*dōjō*), which were run by so-called *dōjōnushi*—unordained farming members of the village community. Each prayer hall was affiliated with a head temple (*uwadera*) in Katsuyama, Ōno, or other towns, which had to confirm their parishioners' identity for the official population register.[80] During the winter and in times of famine, poorer mountain villagers often descended to the plains of Echizen to collect alms, and many of these came into Ōno town.

Every village was required to submit taxes (*mononari*) on its rice and dry fields and more levies (*komononari*) on other miscellaneous forms of produce. For the town, the tax on farmland was based on a fixed rate (*jōmen*), which brought gains in good years but made the authorities reluctant to lower taxes after a crop failure. The villages were subjected

---

77. On the tribulations of life in "snow country," see Suzuki Bokushi's bestseller *Hokuetsu seppu* of 1837.

78. Saku, *Echizen no kuni shūmon ninbetsu on-aratamechō*, vol. 2, 945–1037, vol. 3, 191–398. Folklorist Yanagita Kunio also made this observation when he visited the area in 1911; Yanagita, "Mino Echizen ōfuku," 103.

79. MT goyōdome 1741.7.19, SSM.

80. *Katsuyama shishi*, vol. 2, 534–42; Tsubouchi, *Hakusan sanroku no Shinshū hatten to dōjō no kenkyū*.

to the more flexible but less predictable system of annual inspections (*kemi*).[81] The tax burden on domain subjects is difficult to evaluate because many factors played into the equation, such as corvée substitutions, taxes on nonrice commodities, and conversion rates. The *History of Fukui Prefecture* contends that the overall tax burden in Ōno domain was not unusually high, with about three quarters of villages paying less than 40 percent of the inspected harvest as rice tax (*mononari*) in 1756.[82] Between 1764 and 1870, the domain's net income from the land tax (including *komononari*) ranged between 11,300 and 11,900 *koku* (ten-year averages) and was thus far lower than what one would expect from a fief with an assessed yield of 40,000 *koku*, possibly because the land survey in the late sixteenth century had assigned a very high yield to the land in this area. To support its chronically deficient budget, the House of Doi relied heavily on additional levies (so-called duty money=*goyōkin*) and loans from wealthy merchants and peasants in and outside the domain. It also "borrowed" from its vassals, in essence reducing their stipends to a point where unrest among retainers became a serious possibility.[83]

Although the countryside of Ōno domain experienced its fair share of conflict and discontent, there were relatively few incidents of open rebellion, especially when compared with neighboring Katsuyama domain. Only the protests of 1699 and 1809 reached a significant scale. In 1699, peasants directly petitioned the shogunate in Edo to demand tax relief after a bad harvest and ask for the elimination of tax increases the House of Doi had imposed after taking charge of the domain.[84] In 1809, Ōno's subjects rebelled against the early retirement of Ōno's fifth lord Toshinori, who had a reputation for benevolent rule, but the underlying motives of the protests remain obscure because most records of this incident were intentionally destroyed, for example, by tearing out relevant pages from official journals.[85] In addition, a few years after the Meiji Restoration the region experienced a large and violent rebellion directed

81.   MT goyōdome 1800.3.7, YH 512, 347; 1860.9.1, YH 1194, 853–54; *Fukui kenshi*, Tsūshi-hen 3, 335–38.

82.   *Fukui kenshi*, Tsūshi-hen 4, 100–101.

83.   Ibid., 100–111.

84.   Motokawa, "Jūhasseiki Echizen ni okeru hōkensei no tenkan," 61–63.

85.   Comment on Kasamatsu Sōemon-ke monjo in *Fukui kenshi*, Shiryō-hen 7, nos. 5 and 6, 894–95, 897; Sakata, "Miryoku aru hanshu Toshiyoshi [*sic*] ni tsuite."

against local elites and the new government's modernizing policies (discussed in chapter 6).

Religious Practices and Beliefs

Echizen Province was one of the heartlands of the True Pure Land school of Buddhism. This had implications for the way people understood and practiced charity in this region. Whereas most faithful Buddhists in Tokugawa Japan sought to accumulate merit through almsgiving and other good deeds, the True Pure Land school did not follow this pattern because Shinran, who founded this sect in the thirteenth century, taught that the invocation of the Amida Buddha's name was sufficient for achieving rebirth in paradise and did not recommend almsgiving and good works to improve prospects of salvation.

However, as elsewhere, motivations for charity in Echizen Province were complex and cannot be reduced to a single dogma or set of beliefs. First, the True Pure Land school was not categorically opposed to the giving of alms. Rather than rejecting charity outright, Shinran sought to democratize it by teaching that anyone, even ordinary believers, had the capacity to practice gratitude and compassion. Though the sect prioritized sharing resources among parishioners within the same community, it also valued charity toward strangers.[86] In Fukui, for example, major temples of the True Pure Land school handed out rice gruel to beggars during the Tenpō famine in the 1830s, and village officials did the same on the 600th anniversary of Shinran's death.[87] Some of the beggars from Echizen's mountain villages explicitly asked their donors for rice to offer to the Buddha inside their house altars,[88] an appeal that was likely to fall on sympathetic ears because for believers of the True Pure Land school, the house altar was not a place of ancestor worship but a shrine for the

86.　Ikeda and Ikemoto, *Nihon fukushishi kōgi*, 51–52; Yoshida and Hasegawa, *Nihon bukkyō fukushi shisōshi*, 45–57.

87.　Sawa, "Kinsei no chiiki chitsujo keisei to shūkyō," 47–49.

88.　Chiba and Saigusa, "Chūbu Nihon Hakusanroku jūmin," 271–76, 284, 291. On begging and almsgiving in areas of True Pure Land Buddhism, see also Rotermund, *Pèlerinage au neuf sommets*, 231, 258–59.

Amida Buddha and a site of praying for salvation. In other words, the True Pure Land school was capable of producing doctrinal justifications for almsgiving, not to accumulate merit but as a way of honoring the saints and Amida Buddha and reciprocating their grace (*hōon*).[89] The idea of the four favors (*shion*), which emphasized the interconnectedness of all living beings, was widely held among Buddhists of all persuasions and worked as a strong motivator of almsgiving and charity in general.[90] Second, claims of the sect's many critics notwithstanding, the spiritual lives of True Pure Land believers in the Tokugawa period were not marked by narrow-minded fanaticism but were subject to many competing influences. Although the people of Ōno and surroundings took their sectarian affiliation very seriously, they were not hostile to other popular religious trends of their time. They maintained village shrines, held festivals for Shinto gods, asked mountain ascetics to pray for rain, worshiped at the ancient Kannon temple in Kurodani, and made long-distance pilgrimages to the Ise shrines, Zenkōji temple, and the temple circuits of Shikoku and the Western Provinces.[91] Nor do the people of inner Echizen seem to have remained insulated from the idea that good deeds would help accumulate merit, which enjoyed extreme popularity elsewhere in Tokugawa Japan.[92]

Although most temples in Ōno's countryside belonged to the True Pure Land school, seventeen out of the thirty temples in the castle town had other affiliations, such as Nichiren, Pure Land, Shingon, Sōtō Zen, Rinzai Zen, and Ji. In the archives of all thirty temples, references to charity are almost completely absent. On the contrary, temple priests often expressed dismay over their inability to extract sufficient contributions

89.   On the ethics of gratitude in True Pure Land Buddhism, see Mikami, "Nihon kindaika to Shinshū chitai," 5–8.

90.   According to one definition, the "four favors" comprised favors from the parents, from other living beings, from the ruler of the country, and from the three Buddhist treasures (Buddha, his teachings, and the Buddhist clergy); see Fukaya, *Hyakushō naritachi*, 54.

91.   *Fukui kenshi*, Tsūshi-hen 3, 653–54, 662, 766–76. On the coexistence of religious groups and beliefs in early modern Japan, see Sawa, "Nihon ni okeru shūkyōteki tairitsu to kyōzon."

92.   In their research on begging customs in this area, folklorists Chiba and Saigusa encountered interviewees who expressed ideas of merit; "Chūbu Nihon Hakusanroku jūmin," 290.

from their parishioners to cover their temples' financial needs. Some priests engaged in moneylending, operated loan societies, or leased land and tenements for profit. Others practiced mendicancy themselves: Ōno's mountain ascetics (*shugenja, yamabushi*), of whom there were about six in the temples and shrines of Ōno town, seem to have collected alms from the local population in and around the domain.[93] This is not to say that temple priests in Ōno never engaged in charity or failed to preach it, but they can hardly have been a major factor in institutional terms. With the exception of the Shinokura Shrine, which had resident Shinto clerics, the Shinto shrines of the town were all taken care of by Buddhist priests or mountain ascetics.

A Note on the Town Elders and Their Journals

The best sources on town and village government in Ōno domain are the journals of domain, town, and village officials. Among these, the journals of Ōno's two town elders stand out in their number of surviving copies and the depth of their coverage (fig. 4). The elders occupied a pivotal position in the administration of the town because they were the highest officials of commoner status. Both of them were high-ranking wealthy merchants who served on a monthly rotation and commanded the help of one or two assistants (*gachigyōji*) and a runner.[94] The town elders represented the townspeople vis-à-vis the domain administration. They transmitted petitions, reported problems, suggested solutions, advised the domain on draft proposals, and objected to them if necessary. At the same time, the town elders served as an executive arm of the domain government in terms of the town. They transmitted the domain's orders to the towns-people and the outcastes and vouched for their implementation. They shielded the warrior officials from inopportune requests by prescreen-ing petitions and forcing conflict parties to solve their disagreements

93. Tokuganji, a Sōtō Zen temple, seems to have been especially involved in mon-eylending and land sales. The archives of the Kasuga Shrine, Shinmei Shrine, and Chōkyōji temple mention begging mountain ascetics and Zen monks; see *Ōno shishi*, Shaji monjo-hen, 32–67, 236–80, 461–81, 514–33.

94. YH, "Kaisetsu," 25–26.

FIGURE 4 Town elders' journal for six months in 1860. *Source:* NGM.

through mediation. They maintained a spy in the town at the domain's expense to collect sensitive information.[95] Ōno's town elders thus belonged to a stratum of officials Asao Naohiro and others have labeled the "intermediate layer" (*chūkansō*): commoner elites who mediated between samurai governments and subjects without exclusively representing either side.[96]

Town elders' journals have survived in Ōno for forty-nine of the years between 1740 and 1870.[97] Of these, twenty-two years are covered fully, and the remaining twenty-seven are in fragments of every other month,

95. MT goyōdome 1837.10.16, SSM.

96. Asao, "Jūhasseiki no shakai hendō to mibunteki chūkansō."

97. In addition to the volumes listed in YH, "Kaisetsu," 13–15, this count includes the journals of 1794 and 1798, as well as part of 1783. Photographs of all existing volumes can be accessed in the Office for the Compilation of Ōno City History. For a printed selection of 1,406 entries from the journals of town elders, village group headmen, town and county governors, and wealthy commoner households, see YH.

because each town elder usually kept his own journal and took notes only during the alternate months when he was on duty. There are two longer gaps in the record: one from 1742 to 1764—probably caused by a large fire in 1775—and one from 1816 to 1828. The shortest of the journals had just a few dozen pages, and the longer ones had more than 200 pages each. The longest surviving journal—for 1838—counts 384 pages. Each journal was filled with dozens or hundreds of entries, some just a few words, some several pages long, which were noted in chronological order. In some years, such as in 1740 and 1860, the town elders seem to have edited their notes at the end of the year and copied them into a fresh book. Embedded in these entries we find copies of domain edicts and announcements, petitions, testimonies, receipts, letters, certificates, passports, lists, compacts, and other sources. In some years, petitions were collected in a separate volume, a so-called petition book (*ganshodome*). The journal entries also recounted the town elders' own observations and their interactions with various officials, especially with their immediate superior, the town governor of the domain. Most of the journals were titled *goyōdome* or *goyōki*, literally, "record of official business," meaning that they dealt with governmental business rather than with matters pertaining to the elders' own households.

Certain items in the record repeated themselves with annual or even monthly regularity: the New Year audiences at the castle; various types of patrols; the updating of population registers; prices of rice, tofu, and other staple commodities; festivals; and the rice gruel handouts for beggars during the winter. Other events appeared as they happened: domain orders, arrivals of prominent visitors, debt and family conflicts, crimes, fires, fights, repairs, and many more. Although the town elders tried to take on a detached and bureaucratic persona in their journals, their temperament and convictions shone through on occasion. They produced many different styles of entries, from lengthy arguments and gripping narratives to bare-bones lists of facts. The journals often included records on certain procedures and conversations that were marked as "internal" (*nainai*). These "off-the-record" entries did not refer to strictly guarded secrets but to unofficial compromises and exceptions that facilitated the day-to-day conduct of government while keeping the letter of the law intact.[98]

98. On this issue, see Roberts, *Performing the Great Peace.*

The town elders needed to be meticulous about marking exceptions as unofficial because everything else in the journals could be cited as precedent in the future. The conservation of precedent was one of the journals' most important functions. Commoner and domain officials could ask to consult old journals at any time to look up past events and procedures.[99] It is therefore somewhat surprising that for a long time, the elders stored their journals not in an official location but in their own homes, even after their withdrawal from public office. In 1785, the domain government eventually became more interested in the town's record-keeping practices and ordered the elders to store the journals in the town office (*machigura*).[100] Even after that point, some journals ended up in the house archives of individual elders, but the domain's order clearly represented a step toward a more bureaucratic and accountable approach to the government of the town.[101]

Of course, the town elders were not the only officials who mattered in the self-government of Ōno's townspeople. The land-based status groups of the townspeople—the *chō*—were each administered by a headman (*shōya*) and two group leaders (*kumigashira*). Within the *chō*, all residents were organized into smaller subunits of several households— so-called five people's groups (*goningumi*)—for mutual support and control. The town elders regularly consulted with the headmen of the block associations but did not participate in the *chō*'s internal decision making. Unfortunately, the *chō* headmen do not seem to have kept administrative journals until very late in the Tokugawa period—at least none that have survived. The only preserved exceptions are the "Chōnai yōdomeki" of Lower Ichibanmachi, which covers the period between 1831 and 1948, and an untitled record from Yokomachi and its successor

99.   See, for example, MT goyōdome 1797.8.16–19, YH 459, 321–23; Tenmei hachi tomeki, 1783, sixth month, AHM.

100.   MT goyōdome 1785.2.16, 2.26, 4.21, 8.6, 10.20, SSM. On a similar transition in the castle town of Sunpu, see Aoki, "Kinsei toshi ni okeru monjo kanri ni tsuite."

101.   Today, the bulk of the journals are included in the family archive of Saitō Shūsuke, compiler of Ōno's first town history (Saitō Suzuko-ke monjo), but some are part of Adachi Hiromichi-ke monjo and Nunokawa Genbei-ke monjo, archives of former town elder families. Saitō seems to have obtained his part of the journals from Ōno's town hall. A few volumes were damaged or lost after Saitō's death, but some of the lost material can be retrieved from *Ōno chōshi* and an earlier compilation project in the 1920s.

communities for the time between 1860 and 1977.[102] The townspeople of Yokomachi prefaced their journal by stating that they had not had such a record in the past and had decided to create one because they wanted to keep better track of the precedents of their community. Unlike the town elders, neither of these block associations made entries on a regular basis.

Ideally, the town elders' journals would have to be read in conjunction with the journals of domain officials, but in Ōno, the most relevant domain records have not survived. There are only two journals each left from the town and county governors, who among higher-ranking domain officials interacted most frequently with the town elders and therefore gave the most detailed accounts of town government from the domain's point of view.[103] Precedent manuals for town governors also constitute an important source.[104] Although the domain archives are large and contain many other journals by domain officials such as members of the Council of Vassals, these types of records tend to be spotty and superficial regarding matters of town government. Even though there are few sources that can complement the town elders' journals from the top down, the journals themselves have plenty to say about the give and take between high and low, and their perspective offers an important corrective to histories of Tokugawa government written entirely from the warriors' side.

102. Chōnai yōdomeki, 1831–1948, Honmachi-shimo kuyū monjo; Chōnai yōdome, 1860–1977, Hiyoshi kuyū monjo.

103. Town governors' journals have been preserved for 1781 (Jisha machi goyōdome, NGM) and 1865 (Ōno-han jisha machikata goyōki, Echizen shiryō), and county governor's journals for 1865 and 1866 (Goyōdome, SSM). Goyōki (1764–81, Miyazawa Yoshizaemon-ke monjo) might also be a town governor's journal.

104. Tsutomekata oboegaki Tamura-hikae, 1810, TKM. Another important precedent manual is that of the town elders' assistants (*gachigyōji*); Yōroku, 1852, SSM.

CHAPTER 2

Beggars by Birth

An Outcaste Group in Domain Society

There was a quarter in Ōno town most people did not go to. It was located near the Sannō Shrine, behind the long line of temples that sealed the town off toward the eastern part of the plain. Maps of Ōno town did not always include this area because the people who lived there did not belong to the community of ordinary townspeople. A map of 1730 that was otherwise quite detailed labeled the space with a single term: "beggar dwellings" (see fig. 5).[1] The "beggars" in these dwellings were obviously not homeless, and although the map did not indicate this, Ōno's townspeople usually referred to this settlement as the Eastern Village (Higashi-mura). The Eastern Village was comparable to the other five branch villages of the town that were clustered along its southern edge, each with a distinct occupational orientation; Kanazuka, for example, was a community of fowlers and cormorant fishermen. But unlike the people of the other branch villages, Eastern Village denizens did not pay taxes on their residential land[2] and they were not usually welcome to mingle with the townspeople. They even occupied a separate section on the graveyard.[3] In 1852, a widow in the nearby neighborhood of Yokomachi complained to the town elders that the Koshirō, as the beggars were commonly called, kept visiting the public bathhouse she was running, no

---

1. *Kojiki yashiki*; see Ōno machi ezu, 1730, SSM.
2. Ōno on-ryōbun yonmangoku-chū chōzai ninzū-yose, 1726, SSM.
3. Yōroku, 1852, SSM.

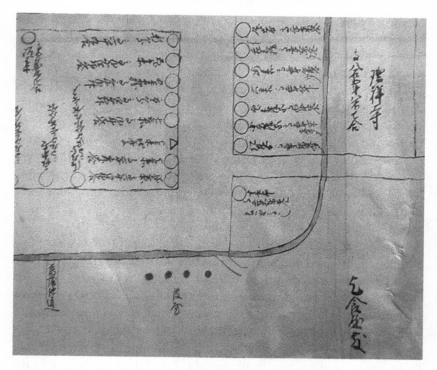

FIGURE 5 "Beggar dwellings" (*kojiki yashiki*), bottom right, and four houses of leather-workers (*kawaya*). *Source:* Ōno machi ezu, 1730, SSM.

matter how many times she told them to stay away.[4] The town elder on duty responded by sending his assistant to the Koshirō to put an end to this behavior. To him, the widow's complaint was entirely reasonable.

Who were the Koshirō, and why were they ostracized in everyday life? Historians of Tokugawa Japan writing in English have settled on the term *outcaste* to refer to those who were excluded from the communities of ordinary peasants and townspeople. This term is useful because it hints at the hereditary nature of their stigma and their organization into occupational groups.[5] But outcastes in Tokugawa Japan have remained

4. MT goyōdome 1852.10.26, SSM.

5. Amos and Groemer reserve the term "outcaste" for the members of stigmatized groups in the Tokugawa period and refer to their medieval equivalents as "outcasts" because in the latter case exclusion was less permanent and less hereditary; see Amos,

an elusive subject because there was no obvious common denominator between the many groups that fell into this category. Although occupation was often a factor, it was not always the decisive one. Moreover, there were major local differences in the organization of outcastes and the discrimination they experienced, even within the same region. Tokugawa Japan did not have a uniform outcaste hierarchy. Instead, it was populated by many marginal groups that suffered from varying degrees of stigma and were distributed unevenly over the Japanese islands, reflecting different local circumstances and historical trajectories. They were embedded in the status order the same way as other status groups, namely, by organizing around an occupation and cultivating long-term reciprocal relationships with the authorities and other groups in local society. Ōno's Koshirō can serve as an example.

Although outcaste status did not hinge on occupation alone, a few occupations do stand out as typical among outcastes. In its relevant edicts, the shogunate therefore usually referred to outcastes by listing the most common kinds of groups—for example as "*eta, hinin*, et cetera"—rather than using a single term such as the ancient Chinese *senmin* (base people), which appears in some writings of the time in reference to outcastes. *Eta* can be translated as "very polluted" and was a derogatory name primarily for leatherworkers, that is, people who flayed dead animals and processed their skins into leather. Another, somewhat less insulting term for leatherworkers was *kawata*. Because the Japanese in the Tokugawa period did not consume beef, these groups did not obtain hides by slaughtering live animals but by staking out turfs in the countryside and monopolizing the collection of carcasses of cattle and horses abandoned by the farming communities within them. The number and size of leatherworker communities was far greater in western Japan than in the east, but even in the Tōhoku and Kantō regions of eastern Japan, the

---

Embodying Difference, 8–9; Groemer, "The Creation of the Edo Outcaste Order," 264. To facilitate comparison, most scholars writing in English have framed discussions of Tokugawa outcastes in terms of caste and race while recognizing the limitations of these concepts in the Japanese context; see Cornell, "'Caste' in Japanese Social Stratification"; de Vos and Wagatsuma, *Japan's Invisible Race*; Brooks, "Outcaste Society in Early Modern Japan"; Ooms, *Tokugawa Village Practice*, 243–311. In English, see also Amos, "Portrait of a Tokugawa Outcaste Community"; Hermansen, "The Hinin Associations in Osaka."

shogunate and lords granted privileges to groups of artisans that supplied them with riding gear, drums, and other leather products.[6]

The second common type of outcaste group were the *hinin*—literally: "nonhumans"—though the term was often used in the sense of "beggar." When the shogunate used this designation in its edicts, it was referring to mendicant associations in various parts of Japan that went by different local names and organized around begging as an occupation, which could involve performing simple dances and rituals at benefactors' doors. Ōno's Koshirō belonged in this category of mendicant groups. Like the leatherworkers, the mendicant associations depended on the monopolization of certain areas, which provided them with access to households of almsgivers. The distinction between cadaver-collecting and alms-collecting groups is helpful in categorizing outcastes in a general way, but it was not always clear-cut. In the Kantō region, for example, a powerful leatherworker organization monopolized both carcasses and alms within its territory and entrusted its begging rights to local groups of beggar bosses, who were subordinate to the leatherworkers and provided services to them in return. In Osaka and Kyoto, by contrast, carcass collection and begging rights were divided more clearly between independent groups of outcastes.[7]

Begging and leatherwork were the most common occupations among outcastes because beggar bosses and purveyors of leather had proven especially useful to warrior rulers during the formative phase of the Tokugawa regime in the seventeenth century. Each group, however, developed along a locally specific trajectory, maintaining additional livelihoods or branching out into new ones over time. Besides, there were many miscellaneous outcaste groups that qualified as neither leatherworkers nor beggars even though some of these were also labeled *eta* or *hinin* on occasion: bamboo tea whisk makers (*chasen*), itinerant entertainers (*sasara*, etc.), monkey trainers (*sarukai*), certain groups of farmers (*shuku*), and others. Legal historian Ishii Ryōsuke has attempted to rank these groups by their distance from commoner status, placing the *kawata/eta* at the bottom, the monkey trainers and *hinin* above them, and other miscellaneous

---

6. Chapters "Tōhoku" and "Kantō," in Buraku Mondai Kenkyūjo, *Buraku no rekishi*, Higashi Nihon-hen, 189–366; McCormack, *Japan's Outcaste Abolition*, 38–40.

7. Tsukada, *Kinsei Osaka no hinin to mibunteki shūen*, 12–15.

groups somewhere in between *hinin* and commoners.[8] In his scheme, the leatherworkers were the most despised, although they also wielded the most power among outcastes. In reality, outcaste group hierarchies and levels of stigma differed significantly from place to place. Although the leatherworkers of Edo indeed constituted the most powerful out-caste group in the Kantō region, Edo's structure of outcaste rule was by no means representative of the country as a whole.

Tokugawa outcastes had one main feature in common: they were ex-cluded from membership and registration in the land-based status com-munities of peasants and townspeople, no matter what their designated occupation was or what livelihoods or other activities they actually en-gaged in. Groups of leatherworkers and beggar bosses were typically subjected to this form of exclusion. Other "base" people were often also excluded in this way, even though their communities were occupation-ally distinct from leatherworkers and beggar bosses, and in some cases they avoided intermarrying with them.[9] Beggar bosses did not necessarily fare better than leatherworkers when it came to attaining commoner status. Those who moved up were usually former commoners who had been integrated into the fringes of a mendicant outcaste group after fall-ing onto hard times and went back to a village or block association after finding work or support. The biggest factor driving discrimination against outcastes were the decisions of village and *chō* communities to accept or reject certain people as members.[10] These decisions were reinforced by discriminatory legislation on the part of local and shogunate authorities, which had their own motives for marginalizing outcastes—a concern for public order, for example, and a need for social groups that would take on unsavory but necessary jobs. But the discriminatory choices of villages, block associations, and other self-governing bodies weighed heavily, and domain laws and edicts on outcastes often merely confirmed and justi-fied what was already common practice among subjects.

8. Ishii, *Edo no senmin*, 13–49, 135–36; de Vos and Wagatsuma, *Japan's Invisible Race*, 25–28.

9. See, for example, the cases of *sekkyō* and *haruta-uchi* performers in the Shimo-Ina region; Yoshida Yuriko, "Manzai to haruta-uchi," 63; Yoshida Yuriko, "Chiiki shakai to mibunteki shūen," 24–25.

10. Asao, "Kinsei no mibunsei to senmin," 38–45.

If the decisions of status groups influenced the treatment of outcastes, each outcaste group must be carefully situated within the status order. This chapter puts the spotlight on Ōno's Koshirō. I examine the group's size, composition, and internal structure, and its relationships with the authorities, the villages and block associations, other outcastes, and physical space. The Koshirō are at the center of this discussion because they not only were the strongest outcaste group in Ōno domain but also played a central role in the management of poverty, like many other mendicant associations in Tokugawa Japan.[11] The recognition of beggar groups and their mobilization for beggar control and relief and related tasks constituted one of the Tokugawa authorities' most important strategies of poverty management. Although few new groups of beggars were recognized after the end of the seventeenth century, the existing ones remained active until the end of the Tokugawa period and increasingly gravitated toward police-related work.

The chapter consists of three parts. The first identifies the Koshirō's occupation and discusses popular attitudes toward mendicancy that contributed to the marginalization of this and other similar outcaste groups. The second part reconstructs the Koshirō's relationships of privilege and duty with the domain and their ties with local communities, including changes that occurred to these relationships over time. The third part examines the character of households among the Koshirō and raises the question of the beggar bosses' social mobility by introducing the case of a wealthy Koshirō household that tried to make inroads into commoner society. Throughout the chapter, I compare the Koshirō to groups of beggar bosses in other places to illustrate how the make-up and inner dynamics of local society led to differences in the status of otherwise similar groups.

11. Aside from a paragraph in Fukui's prefectural history, the only previous publication on the Koshirō is Tanaka Yoshio's "Kenkyū nōto: Ōno jōkamachi, hiningashira 'Koshirō-domo' to shūen no hitobito (1)." In this article, Tanaka, a specialist on outcastes in Kaga domain, paraphrased various sources in preparation of a more substantial study, but he passed away in 2009 before he could complete this project. For a preliminary study of the Koshirō, see also Ehlers, "Ōno-han no Koshirō."

Occupation

The origins of the name "Koshirō" (古四郎; sometimes Koshiro 古城) are
unknown,[12] but the fact that it was often used in the plural (Koshirō-
domo) leaves no doubt that it was not the name of an individual beggar
boss but a status designation for all residents of the Eastern Village, including family members. Next to the Koshirō village, on land belonging
to the *chō* of Yokomachi, was a small cluster of houses of another outcaste group: the leatherworking *kawaya* (a local name for *kawata*; see
fig. 6). The leatherworkers were associated with the shogunate's *eta* category, but Ōno's domain and town officials seldom applied the shogunate's outcaste nomenclature. In 1844, they noted that the "*eta* and *hinin*
are fighting over hegemony," and ruled that neither the *kawaya* nor the
Koshirō should have the upper hand over the other.[13] Normally they referred to these groups by their local names: Koshirō and *kawaya*. Both
groups submitted their population registers to the town elders and the
domain, though none of these registers have survived.[14]

The Koshirō's occupation can be identified quite easily. They were
professional beggars, though the modern English term "begging" is hardly
sufficient to convey the full range of meanings inherent in the Koshirō's
style of collecting alms. Nor do I mean to suggest that begging constituted their main daily activity or the professional identity under which
they themselves preferred to be known. Rather, begging constituted their
shokubun—the occupation by which they were situated in the status
order.[15] The group had a begging territory that covered most of the domain and some villages outside of it (especially on the plain). The Koshirō
went around in regular intervals to collect alms from villagers, townspeople, and samurai, and whenever they got a chance, they solicited additional money in ways that bordered on extortion. In a number of sources,
the Koshirō are referred to as *kojiki* (also *kotsujiki*) or *kojikigashira* ("*kojiki*

12.   Some local scholars in Ōno believe that the term, which literally meant "old
fortress" in its second transliteration, was originally a toponym. The Sannō Shrine next
to the Eastern Village might have been the site of the medieval Iyama fortress.

13.   MT goyōdome 1844.10.1, YH 885, 652.

14.   Tsutomekata oboegaki Tamura-hikae, 1810, TKM.

15.   Howell, *Geographies of Identity*, 46–47.

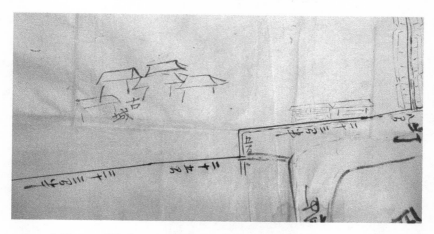

FIGURE 6 Houses of Koshirō and leatherworkers (*kawaya*). *Source:* Aza fukisho shimo, Sannō ushiro, Shinmei shimo kyōkai sokuryōzu, year unknown, SSM.

bosses"; see fig. 7). *Kojiki* was originally a Buddhist term for religious men-dicants, but the Koshirō had little in common with Buddhist clerics.[16] In Ōno, the terms *hinin* and *kojiki* were both used almost interchangeably for impoverished people who begged for alms. The Koshirō's occupational identity was expressed in their official status symbol: the begging bowl (*mentsū*). Even though the Koshirō had little use for such bowls in every-day life (they did not collect their alms in form of cooked food), they were required by domain law to carry them.[17] With several members of

16.   Ōno machi ezu, 1730, SSM; Zatō, goze, kojikigashira e shūgi fuse no oboe, 1791, Mugiya monjo; Chōnai yōdomeki (Honmachi kuyū) 1837, first month, YH 723, 520. The Portuguese-Japanese dictionary of 1603 defined the term "cojiki" as "poor person, mendicant." For a discussion of the terminology regarding beggars, entertain-ers, and outcastes as recorded in Portuguese missionary texts for language instruction, see Kuroda, *Nihon chūsei no kokka to shūkyō*, 399–410. Some begging outcaste groups, such as the lepers (*monoyoshi*) of Kyoto, took on the persona of Buddhist monks, but such cases became rare after the end of the medieval period; see Yokota Noriko, "'Monoyoshi'-kō."

17.   MT goyōdome 1796, seventh month, YH 939, 691. On the Tokugawa practice of displaying tools as status symbols, see Asao, "Kinsei no mibun to sono hen'yō," 27–29. The begging bowl is discussed in Hosaka, "Jūnanaseiki ni okeru komusō no seisei," 186. Another stereotypical marker of beggar status was the straw mat; see Kikuchi, *Kikin kara yomu kinsei shakai*, 70–93.

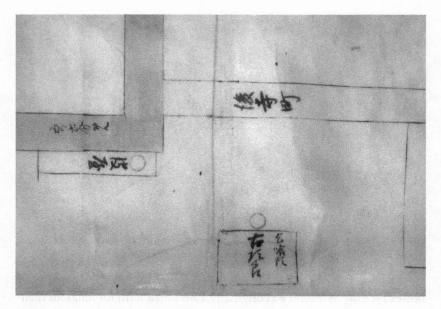

FIGURE 7 "Beggar bosses (*kojikigashira*) Kojirō" on a town map of 1743.
Source: Ōno-machi danmen ezu, TKM.

equivalent rank, the structure of the group mimicked the structure of villages, block associations, and trade and craft guilds, and both outsiders and the Koshirō themselves used the term *nakama* (guild) to refer to the group.[18] Unlike the larger and more complex beggar guilds of Kyoto and Osaka, the Koshirō here did not have a supraordinate council of leaders who represented the guild collective vis-à-vis the authorities. All full members were capable of speaking on the group's behalf. The Koshirō do not seem to have performed any itinerant entertainment, although they might have delivered blessings when making their rounds after New Year's.[19] They engaged in some agriculture on the side, probably as tenant farmers.[20]

18. MT goyōdome 1834.4.20, SSM, 1837.8.12, SSM, 1860.3.12, NGM.
19. On itinerant performers in the Ōno area, see Nagami, "Echizen Ōno no kado-zuke geinō"; MT goyōdome 1855.3.9, 3.10, YH 1066, 782; and chapter 4 of this book.
20. MT goyōdome 1786.4.28, YH 273, 200–201.

Although the Koshirō were beggars by occupation, I refer to them as beggar bosses because by the time under discussion they were heavily involved in the control and relief of beggars. Their duties included managing the domain's beggar hospice, running town patrols, working as jail guards, and a host of other tasks related to supervising vagrants and removing pollution. The reciprocal structure of the status order required a clear distinction between occupation and duty. Even though town patrols, policing, and so on could be very time-consuming and would certainly conform to our modern understanding of work, they constituted the Koshirō's duties, not their occupation. This was true even in the late Tokugawa period, when many beggar groups tried to reinvent themselves by obscuring their mendicant roots and portraying their duty work—especially policing and beggar boss responsibilities—as their original calling.[21]

There is hardly any evidence on the Koshirō's origins, but the group was already in existence before lord Doi Toshifusa moved to Ōno in 1682. The death register of Hondenji, the Koshirō's family temple, indicates that the mother of a Koshirō Kahei died in Ōno in 1668.[22] This suggests that the beggars had already established families by the second half of the seventeenth century and were affiliated with a temple of the True Pure Land school that also counted townspeople among its parishioners. A more detailed picture begins to emerge in 1740, the time of the first preserved town elders' journals. Although the dearth of early sources makes it impossible to establish exactly when and why the Koshirō obtained

---

21. Historians have disagreed over the characterization of *hinin* duty in medieval Japan. Kuroda Toshio framed *hinin* status as a phenomenon of economic and social exclusion, whereas Amino Yoshihiko, Ōyama Kyōhei, and others emphasized the outcastes' constructive ritual roles as removers of pollution. Subsequent scholarship has resolved this debate by combining the two viewpoints and characterizing the removal of pollution as a duty, which was performed by people forced into such tasks by economic deprivation and exclusion; see Kuroda, *Nihon chūsei no kokka to shūkyō*; Amino, *Chūsei no hinin to yūjo*; Ōyama, *Nihon chūsei nōsonshi no kenkyū*; Mieda, "Chūsei inu jinin no sonzai keitai."

22. Death register (*kakochō*) of Hondenji, 1667–1734. Further Koshirō and their relatives are recorded for 1674, 1685, 1692, and 1693. They seem to have belonged to at least three different households. One of them, San'emon, was identified by a head priest in 1850 as the ancestor of a Koshirō house still in existence. No death registers have survived for the time between 1775 and 1868.

their begging privileges, we can make some inferences by examining groups with similar occupations in other places.

From the end of the sixteenth century onward, during the big age of castle town construction, samurai authorities across the country began to recognize associations of beggars in their castle and market towns to manage a rootless population of paupers and masterless samurai. Often, lords seem to have picked bosses from among the local vagrants and used them to guard their jails and control unattached people. In some places, these new groups merged or clustered with existing outcaste communities of older origin, such as lepers and itinerant performers.[23] Sometimes the beggar bosses took leatherworkers under their wing, though in some localities like Edo and Wakayama the order was reversed, and leatherworkers ended up exercising control over groups with a mendicant character.[24] Throughout the seventeenth century, new groups formed as towns experienced periodical surges of vagrancy. The second big wave of beggar group formation occurred in the second half of the seventeenth century, when administrators across the country established beggar hospices in years of famine to intern beggars temporarily and later placed the survivors under the rule of existing beggar bosses as subordinate groups (see chapter 3). The emerging hierarchies also reflected power struggles among the beggars. The *Hinin Taiheiki*, an illustrated book printed in 1688 (see fig. 8), narrated the encounter between old and new beggars in Osaka during the famines of the Enpō era (1670s) as a battle tale in the mode of the Taiheiki, a fourteenth-century warrior epos that was wildly popular in seventeenth-century Japan.[25]

The guilds were thus a product of the beggars' desire to engage in collective action and the authorities' desire to control mendicancy. It seems possible that the Koshirō in Ōno emerged during the earlier wave of vagrant control, within the first few decades after the castle town's founding

23. For example, in Kyoto and Iida; see Sugahara, "Kinsei zenki Kyoto no hinin," 179–83; Yokota Noriko, "'Monoyoshi'-kō," 4–14; Yoshida Yuriko, "Shinshū Shimo-Ina chiiki ni okeru mibunteki shūen."

24. Tanaka Yoshio, "Kaga-han ni okeru hisabetsu buraku"; Tanaka Yoshio, "Kaga-han 'tōnai' no kenkyū"; Kishū-han Rōbangashira-ke Monjo Hensankai, *Jōkamachi keisatsu nikki*, 829–33.

25. *Hinin Taiheiki*; Wada, "Taiheiki o matou kanazōshi"; Okamoto, *Ran/ikki/hinin*, 3–17; Selden and Young, "Hinin Taiheiki."

FIGURE 8 Beggar bosses expelling homeless beggars. *Source: Hinin Taiheiki*, 1688.

in 1576. At a later point, the group must have been put in charge of Ōno's beggar hospice, which was established in an unknown year before 1730 and was populated by sick and abandoned paupers. This pattern would conform to what is known for other castle towns. The four beggar confraternities of Osaka, for example, which resembled the Koshirō in their independence from the leatherworkers, were granted residential land in 1594, 1609, 1622, and 1626, not long after the founding of Osaka's early modern town settlement. Tsukada Takashi has investigated the lineages of some of their oldest and most influential members and found that many of them were descendants of homeless migrants from the countryside or other towns.[26] In 1655 in the castle town of Tottori in western

26. Tsukada, *Kinsei Osaka no hinin to mibunteki shūen*, 15; Tsukada, *Toshi Osaka to hinin*, 5–36; Tsukada, *Osaka no hinin—Kojiki/Shitennōji/Korobi-kirishitan*, 24–74.

Japan, the authorities relocated a small beggar group with older roots and made them integrate homeless beggars who had arrived more recently.[27] In the 1620s in the castle town of Hirosaki on the northeastern end of Honshū, the new domain lord placed vagrant control in the hands of beggar boss Chōsuke; in 1695, a year of famine, the lord built the first of several beggar shelters and eventually placed their few surviving occupants under Chōsuke's control.[28]

If begging was de facto treated as an occupation, the question arises what "occupation" meant to the Tokugawa authorities and how contemporaries understood and distinguished between work and mendicancy. As Eiji Takemura has noted, the Japanese language of the early modern period knew two groups of terms that loosely corresponded to the modern concept of work. On one hand, it included expressions such as *nariwai*, *sugiwai*, *kasegi*, and *tosei* that described work as a livelihood for the purpose of gaining sustenance. The other word cluster—*shokubun*, *tenshoku*, *kagyō*—referred to "occupation," an assigned social role (*bun*) within the status order that defined the identity of a household and its members.[29] Neither set of terms made a statement on whether the performed activity was actually productive and could therefore apply to begging as well. Ōno's town elders, for example, were not being ironic when they described the begging of poor mountain villagers in the area as *fuyu-kasegi* (earning a winter living). By recognizing beggar bands as occupation-based groups, the Tokugawa authorities turned the beggars' livelihood (*kasegi*) into a *shokubun* or *kagyō*, a publicly recognized social role with concomitant duties.

This is not to say that governments in seventeenth-century Japan did not try to turn beggars into productive subjects. They used some of them for the reclamation of land or coerced them to work in other settings. Between the 1670s and early 1700s, for example, the shogunate went against the spirit of its own antislavery policy and tolerated the operation of labor agents in Osaka and Kyoto, who gathered homeless people from the streets and shipped them off on long-term labor contracts to western

27. Tanaka Shinji, "Tottori-han hinin seido no seiritsu," 12–14.
28. "Tōhoku," in Buraku Mondai Kenkyūjo, *Buraku no rekishi*, Higashi Nihon-hen, 219–34.
29. Takemura, *The Perception of Work in Tokugawa Japan*, 24–30.

lands, such as the island of Tsushima, which was thriving on its trade with Korea.[30] But as long as vagrants remained a real and recurring presence, the authorities needed to find more immediate ways to control them, and in this time period, the most common mechanism to do so was the occupation-based group. Although the Tokugawa authorities did not try to force villages and block associations to integrate homeless outsiders who had not previously been registered with them, they were comfortable with recognizing status groups composed entirely of outsiders if such groups made themselves useful in some way.

Especially in the beginning of the Tokugawa period, begging was still strongly associated with the itinerant arts, and throughout the period, the meaning of itinerant occupations was ambivalent and contested. On one hand, many people truly enjoyed the performances and rituals of wandering entertainers and clerics or observed them at least with amused curiosity.[31] Even artless beggars could be welcome because they helped givers accumulate merit for the afterlife, echoing the situation in medieval Europe, where beggars fulfilled a role as objects of Christian charity.[32] But there is evidence for a growing disenchantment with mendicancy and the itinerant arts by the late seventeenth century. Yokota Fuyuhiko has traced the rise of this new mentality by examining the genre of dictionaries and encyclopedia and their mode of classifying occupations. While medieval products of this genre used a broad rubric of "arts" (*geinō*) that included craftsmen, scholars, physicians, preachers, shamans, and entertainers, compilations from the late seventeenth century were much more dismissive about the spiritual and moral value of itinerant occupations. The *Illustrated Encyclopedia of Humanity* (*Jinrin kinmō zui*, 1690) lumped itinerant artists and monks together with ordinary beggars into a section called "Kanjin morai no bu" (literally: "Section on Religious

---

30. Morishita, "Tsushima no kakaekudashimono to toshi kasō shakai"; Tanaka Yoshio, "Kaga-han hiningoya-sei seiritsu no jijō ni tsuite," 58–63.

31. Ingrid Wenderoth describes the Tokugawa period as the golden age of itinerant entertainment; *Sekizoro*, 86–92. Also see the description of a scroll from the 1830s that depicts over 100 types of "mendicants" (*monomorai*) in Wakayama town; Fujimoto Seijirō, *Jōkamachi sekai no seikatsushi*, 176–89.

32. In medieval Europe, the idea of begging as a mutually beneficial transaction went hand in hand with a professionalization of beggar groups; see Geremek, *Poverty: A History*, 47–52.

Mendicants and Panhandlers"). It claimed that the religious meaning of their performances had been lost and depicted the itinerants as parasitical and cunning.[33] This perception might not have been entirely off the mark, considering that many mendicant groups had begun to perceive alms as a right rather than a favor as their relationships with benefactors matured into customary ties, and they could react with indignation when the expected amounts were not forthcoming.[34] In a case from around 1741, a shrine priest in the rural Shimo-Ina region used the terms "begging" (*kanjin*) and "base conduct" (*gesen no shosa*) to refer to certain itinerant performances (*ebisu-uta* and *haruta-uchi*) that were customary there. He dissociated himself from a group that engaged in them to protect his own social standing.[35]

Itinerants both benefited and suffered from urbanization and the gradual commodification of entertainment and ritual. By the seventeenth century, the complex outcaste communities of the Middle Ages had lost their inner coherence and disintegrated into independent groups of musicians, dancers, actors, and puppeteers, as well as leatherworkers, various types of artisans, and lepers.[36] Although some of these took advantage of the expanding market for entertainment and ritual and managed to shed their social stigma—for example, as theater actors or resident temple priests—the less successful ones suffered a loss of prestige. Others were interrupted in their aspirations when the new Tokugawa authorities began to define and register existing occupational groups to integrate them into the emerging status order. The commercial growth of the seventeenth century inspired a new self-confidence among commoners, especially townspeople, who tried to set themselves apart from both beggars and samurai by stressing their productivity and entrepreneurial skills.[37] Urbanization and commercialization thus had an ambivalent effect on the itinerant population. Although they fueled demand for

---

33. Yokota Fuyuhiko, "Geinō/bunka to 'mibunteki shūen'"; Wenderoth, "Von Straßenkünstlern, Scharlatanen und törichtem Volk." See also Minegishi, *Kinsei hisabetsuminshi no kenkyū*, 294–99; Wenderoth, *Sekizoro*, 321–38.

34. For an example, see Yokota Noriko, "'Monoyoshi'-kō," 22–25.

35. Yoshida Yuriko, "Manzai to haruta-uchi," 72.

36. Kuroda, *Nihon chūsei no kokka to shūkyō*, 393–97.

37. Yokota Fuyuhiko, "Geinō/bunka to 'mibunteki shūen,'" 29–48; Asao, "Kinsei no mibunsei to senmin."

entertainment of all kinds, they also bred contempt for lifestyles that did not conform to commoner values and brought little monetary gain. To avoid falling into disrepute, many groups of itinerant artists and clerics established loose ties of duty and privilege with temples, shrines, and families of courtiers that were prestigious enough to confer legitimacy on marginal occupations.[38]

The condemnation of beggars also involved moral judgments about poverty. In medieval Japan, the concept of karma and Buddhist sin served as an important medium for expressing such judgments. Eison, a Buddhist monk in the thirteenth century and avid promoter of beggar relief, considered beggars and lepers (the two core groups of medieval outcaste communities) to be even greater sinners than blood-stained fishermen and hunters because their very condition was punishment for misdeeds in a former life, and poverty had corrupted their minds with greed and desire. He found them to be in need of spiritual as much as material relief.[39] In the Tokugawa period, the idea of karma lingered on, but poverty became increasingly associated with a lack of secular virtues, such as familial harmony, filial piety, frugality, and hard work. As these values gradually filtered into the popular consciousness, people of all classes began to perceive poverty as a man-made condition.[40]

The reputation of particular occupational groups thus rose or fell in response to long-term changes in the values and structure of Japanese society. But when Tokugawa contemporaries sought to explain the existence of base groups, they usually reached for simpler explanations. For example, the idea that outcastes were of foreign origin (discredited today) enjoyed much currency among Tokugawa intellectuals.[41] In addition, many connected the exclusion of outcastes to the ancient Japanese custom of avoiding pollution (*kegare*).[42] The concept of pollution seems to

38.   Yoshida Yuriko, "Chiiki shakai to mibunteki shūen," 24–25; Yoshida Yuriko, "Manzai to haruta-uchi," 52–54.

39.   Taira, "Sesshō kindan to sesshō zaigōkan," 240–68. On Eison's charitable activities, see also Matsuo, *Chūsei no toshi to hinin.*

40.   Yasumaru, *Nihon no kindaika to minshū shisō,* 12–92.

41.   Uesugi, *Meiji ishin to senmin haishirei,* 9–19; Ooms, *Tokugawa Village Practice,* 302–5.

42.   Ooms, *Tokugawa Village Practice,* 298–301. Some Confucian thinkers of the early Tokugawa period were skeptical about the idea of outcastes as polluted because

have first emerged in the context of a death and blood taboo in Shinto worship and was later reinforced and modified by Buddhist teachings, which condemned the taking of life as a sinful act. Over time, pollution also evolved into a marker of social deviance.[43] In ancient Japan, pollution was a temporary condition befalling an individual that could be removed through purification rituals, but in the medieval period it became an attribute of particular occupational communities. To be sure, occupation-related pollution did not always translate into social stigma; the samurai, for instance, were not permanently tainted by their bloody pursuits. But it did marginalize people who were disadvantaged to begin with, such as itinerants, paupers, and deviants who had been excluded from their residential communities. The reputation of outcastes was further undermined by their frequent employment for removing pollution and disorder.

In the Tokugawa period, the fear of pollution seems to have lost much of its potency. Purification requirements grew less rigid over time, and people who interacted with outcastes in everyday life did not usually worry about contamination. Although there were cases in which commoners did play up the issue of pollution, they typically did so in the context of a conflict in which they hoped to gain a strategic advantage or defend their social status.[44] Even priests at the Ise shrines, one of the holiest Shinto sanctuaries that banned worship by "polluted people," tolerated worshipers of outcaste background for most of the Tokugawa period, and only became somewhat more restrictive in 1801 when shogunate officials suddenly brought it up as an issue.[45] Yet the stigma of outcaste birth did not fade. In the Tokugawa period, outcaste status became hereditary,

---

the concept was absent from the Chinese Confucian canon, but they condemned professional beggars on moral grounds; see Kinugasa, "Kinsei ni okeru mibunsei shisō to kisen jōe-kan," 18–24.

43. Klaus Vollmer, drawing on Mary Douglas's concept of pollution as disorder, has proposed to think about the idea of purity in Japan as an idealization of social harmony and perfect normality that could be undermined by deviant—and hence "polluted"—ways of life; see his "Reinheit und gesellschaftliche Ordnung in Japan."

44. For examples, see Ooms, *Tokugawa Village Practice*, 257–61, 272–78; Yoshida Yuriko, "Chiiki shakai to mibunteki shūen," 24–25.

45. Tsukamoto Akira, *Kinsei Ise jingū-ryō*, 141–68; Minegishi, "Kegare kannen to buraku sabetsu (ge)," 97–109.

probably because the ideal of the hereditary household was gaining ground and prejudice and lack of intermarriage were perpetuating each other. Outcastes thus remained associated with deviance, brutality, and filth, even though many of them did not actually engage in ritually polluting activities.

Ōno domain was home to several occupational groups that were either excluded from village or *chō* membership or in danger of being excluded: the Koshirō (and the village watchmen under their control), the *kawaya* leatherworkers, the fishermen of Kanazuka, blind performers, and the beggars in the beggar hospice. Of these, only the Koshirō and leatherworkers were ostracized by commoner groups and passed their stigma on to their descendants. The Kanazuka fishermen and the blind performers were not regarded as outcastes, neither by Ōno's commoners nor by the domain government. They intermarried with peasants and townspeople and were allowed to move into a village or a town block. However, their occupations and duties put them at a latent risk of falling into disrepute. The Kanazuka villagers made a living as hunters and fishermen and were responsible for cleaning up the jail after torture and executions, whereas the blind performers collected alms in a similar way as the Koshirō.[46] Although neither of these activities were stigmatizing by themselves, they could become a problem if played up by opponents. In Ōno, the danger of stigma by association with outcastes was probably greatest for the occupants of the beggar hospice and the village watchmen, who were both under the Koshirō's direct control. They were registered in the same population registers as the outcastes and could return to commoner status only if they had been commoners at birth. Apart from such cases, commoners seem to have interacted with outcastes in daily life without any damage to their reputation.

46. Yoshida Yuriko notes that the people of Iida domain drew a line between "base work," which included itinerant arts and watchman duty, and "base people," that is, outcastes with inheritable stigma. Whereas base work did not automatically translate into baseness as a personal attribute, it could become a problem if the mendicant in question seemed pauperized and frequently socialized with recognized outcastes; "Chiiki shakai to mibunteki shūen," 24–25, 27.

Relationships

Because the Koshirō were a guild of professional beggars, the alms they collected from commoner and warrior households were their most important source of income. It was thus in their best interest to cultivate long-term relationships with their givers. The Koshirō performed a variety of services for village and *chō* communities and some individual wealthy households. They also fulfilled duties for Ōno's domain government in return for permission to beg. Although these duties took up much of the Koshirō's time and were done without much direct compensation, the beggar bosses took them seriously because they wanted to make themselves seem indispensable in the eyes of the domain government and use these duties as leverage to ask for better treatment, including extensions of begging rights. The Koshirō particularly emphasized their police-related work because these activities had a relatively weak association with outcaste status and thus somewhat offset the stigma that came with mendicancy and some of the group's more despised duties.

With the exception of the exclaves of Anama and Nishikata, the castle town and villages of Ōno domain were all part of the Koshirō's begging territory. This meant that the Koshirō toured these communities twice a year to collect alms: once around New Year's and once at the time of the ancestor festival (*obon*) in the seventh month. In 1845, the seasonal offerings from the countryside amounted to 12.8 *koku* of rice a year, and if townspeople and vassals are included, the estimated total rises to at least 23.4 *koku*.[47] This was a substantial amount and probably represented the bulk of the Koshirō's income at the time. In addition to these seasonal alms, the Koshirō collected alms from households on life cycle–related occasions, that is, at times of celebration and bereavement, but the quantity of the seasonal alms was far greater.[48] The custom of giving alms on

---

47. If townspeople's contributions are calculated on the basis of almsgiving standards of 1845, town population figures of 1864, and a price of 25 *monme* per bale of rice, they equaled 10.67 *koku* of rice. For the countryside, see Ōjōya goyōdome 1845.12.20, YH 900, 663–64.

48. MT goyōdome 1796.8.11, YH 445, 310; MT goyōdome 1796, seventh month, YH 939, 692.

seasonal and life cycle–related occasions was widespread in Tokugawa Japan.[49] It seems to have derived from an older belief that itinerants were visitors from the netherworld who delivered blessings and expelled evil.[50] According to Buddhist precepts, the doing of good deeds (*sazen*) on occasions of funerals and death anniversaries also generated merit for the deceased and improved their prospects in the afterlife. In many well-to-do households, seasonal and life cycle alms as well as charity for the poor more generally were part of the family tradition and served to justify their social standing in the eyes of the community.[51]

At its core, almsgiving was a matter between the Koshirō guild and the giver's households. In theory each household could interact with the beggars on its own terms and negotiate appropriate amounts of donations. But in practice, most households negotiated with the Koshirō collectively through the framework of village and *chō* self-government. Most likely they preferred to interact with them in this way because it took considerable nerve to resist the beggars' solicitations. Although violence was unusual, the people of Ōno domain expressed trepidation about negotiating directly with the Koshirō, whom they perceived as "giving them a

49.   Tsukada, *Kinsei Nihon mibunsei no kenkyū*, 271–73, 315–16, 324; Tsukada, *Toshi Osaka to hinin*, 66–76, 91–92; Tanaka Shinji, "Tottori-han ni okeru 'zaichū' hiningashira," part 1, 26–29. Both the ancestor festival and the end of the year served as occasions for gift exchanges and as deadlines for settling debts and other financial transactions, but these payments must be distinguished from the alms that changed hands on such days. While gifts were given voluntarily or at least on a mutual basis, alms were only given on the beggars' request and often consisted of inferior items such as copper money, food leftovers, or grain crumbs. They rarely carried the same auspicious connotations as the delicacies commonly exchanged as seasonal gifts. Besides, most *hinin* associations begged on a far wider range of occasions than those reserved for gift exchanges. See Minegishi, *Kinsei hisabetsuminshi no kenkyū*, 130–32, 290–94; Ioka, "Hininban e no kyūmai."

50.   According to folklorist Orikuchi Shinobu's famous thesis of the centrality of the "visitor" (*marebito*) figure in Japanese folk belief; see, for example, "Kokubungaku no hassei (dai-san-kō)—marebito no igi." For a critical discussion of Orikuchi's thesis, see Wenderoth, *Sekizoro*, 54–67.

51.   For example, the house codex of Takinami Yoroku, a wealthy peasant in Ōno domain, warned family heads that they needed to avoid both extravagance and avarice and care about their tenants to prevent the household's downfall; "Daitsūin-sama eitai bungen kitei," undated (1841?), *Ōno shishi*, Shoke monjo-hen 2, 521–23. On wealthy commoners' motivations for providing charity, see also Drixler, *Mabiki*, 164–66.

hard time" (*karekore muzukashiku mō[su]*).[52] Only the wealthiest, most powerful households of the domain maintained individual ties with the Koshirō. This included the House of Doi—the household of the domain lord—which gave alms to the Koshirō and to male and female blind performers (*zatō* and *goze*) on family occasions such as weddings, funerals, memorial services for the dead, and coming-of-age rituals.[53] The lord gave these alms to the blind, who passed only a tiny share of them on to the Koshirō (see chapter 4). He also conducted seasonal rice gruel handouts for beggars and the Koshirō every winter (see chapter 5). In addition to the lord, there were a few wealthy peasant (and probably town) households that maintained independent ties with the Koshirō: in 1845, this included Kawase Shirōzaemon, Hanaguro Yosōzaemon, and "Zenbei" (Suzuki?).[54] All of these households were large landowners with special privileges from the domain.

The family journals of Hanaguro Yosōzaemon illustrate how a privileged rural household interacted with organized and unorganized beggars.[55] Hanaguro was one of Ōno domain's wealthiest and most distinguished peasant elites—a descendant of a vassal of the Asakura warrior house, which had flourished in the sixteenth century. In the late eighteenth century, at least for a while, the Hanaguro family distributed rice to beggars (*hinin*) in the so-called traditional auspicious handout (*karei no segyō*), held almost every year late in the first month. The journals record enormous numbers of recipients for these one-day occasions (see table 1), though most of these beggars were probably of commoner status. Each time, the Koshirō also received ten *monme* of silver in

---

52. For example, MT goyōdome 1786.5.6, YH 274, 204. In 1845, a village that had opposed a domain order on almsgiving gave up its resistance after domain officials "suggested" they directly negotiate with the beggars; see Ōjōya goyōdome 1845.12.26, YH 900, 666.

53. The tradition of rulers handing out alms to beggars on life cycle–related occasions was older than the Tokugawa period. One famous example is the mass handout conducted at the Toyokuni Shrine in 1604 in commemoration of Toyotomi Hideyoshi's passing; see "Toyokuni daimyōjin rinjisai nikki," in *Jizen kyūsai shiryō*, 345.

54. Ōjōya goyōdome 1845.12.20, YH 900, 664–65.

55. See Hanaguro's journal for official business (Goyōdome 1789.1.17, 1795.1.24, 1796.1.26, 1803.1.24, Hanakura-ke monjo); and the less formal daily record Nikki (1793.1.24, 1794.1.24, 1795.1.24, 1796.1.26, 1799.1.24, 1802.1.24, Hanakura-ke monjo). Apparently, the Hanaguro terminated their public beggar handouts in 1803.

Table 1
Number of recipients at the
"traditional auspicious handout"
of the Hanaguro household on 1/24

Year	Recipients
1789	730
1793	1,076
1794	1,043
1795	762
1796	981
1797	Unknown
1799	2,216
1800	1,302
1802	1,788
1803	2,536

Source: Goyōdome, 1789, 1796, 1797, 1803, and Nikki, 1793–96, 1799–1800, 1802, Hanakura-ke monjo.

"provisions" (*makanai-dai*) from Hanaguro as a guild, because they were beggars themselves and perhaps kept order on such occasions. In 1797, an exceptionally large number of important family ancestors needed to be commemorated, and the Hanaguro household used its auspicious handout in that year to distribute life cycle alms to the Koshirō and the guilds of blind performers, rice to all beggars, and millet money to 48 townspeople and almost 700 villagers who were suffering from unusually deep snow during that winter.[56] It also donated rice money to an individual Koshirō named Sōemon, who was identified as Hanaguro's "contact" (*deiri*). It seems that Hanaguro maintained a long-term relationship with Sōemon to get help with the panhandlers and thieves that such a wealthy household was likely to attract. Hanaguro's pattern of giving on the occasion of memorial services for the dead mirrored that of the lord and resembled the charity of large merchant houses in Osaka, Kyoto, and Edo, which had a semi-public character.[57]

Most households, however, bargained with the Koshirō collectively through their village or town community. The domain administration

---

56. Goyōdome 1797.1.24, Hanakura-ke monjo.
57. Tsukada, *Kinsei Osaka no hinin to mibunteki shūen*, 192–99.

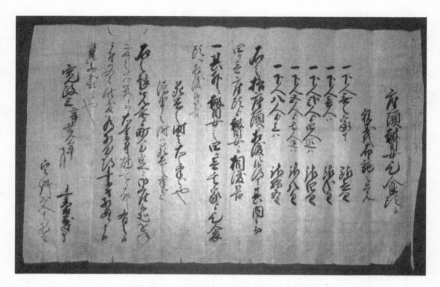

FIGURE 9 Zatō, goze, kojikigashira e shūgi fuse no oboe, 1791. *Source:* Mugiya monjo.

probably regulated the almsgiving of samurai households, though no
such records have survived. The townspeople of Ōno had concluded a collective agreement with the Koshirō and the blind that based amounts
of life-cycle alms on the number of servants a household employed
(see fig. 9). For seasonal alms, the townspeople were divided into three
classes: purveyor merchants, ordinary townspeople (*hira machiya*), and tenants.[58] The situation in the countryside is relatively well documented
thanks to a governmental survey of 1845. Each village had negotiated its
own precedent with the beggars, probably differentiating between ranked
peasants with the right of audience (*omemie*) and ordinary titled peasants.[59] Villagers had little choice but to respond to the beggars' demands

58. Zatō, goze, kojikigashira e shūgi fuse no oboe, 1791, Mugiya monjo. The standards for seasonal alms are mentioned in Yōroku, 1852, SSM.

59. Ōjōya goyōdome 1845.8.6, YH 893, 659. Almsgiving could serve as a barometer
of social status in the community. In one example from Shikoku, mendicants visited
the highest-ranking household of a village first, ended with the lowest, and refused to
visit some households altogether; see Kawato, "Kinsei hisabetsumin no seikatsu to
shisō," 155.

because the domain lord recognized the Koshirō's begging as an occupation. This meant that the authorities allowed the Koshirō to beg in the domain without concerning themselves too much with the particulars of their activity. They primarily expected the Koshirō to refrain from violence and collect alms "on the basis of mutual negotiation" (*aitai nite*), "appropriate to the giver's station" (*bungen sōō*), or "as much as the giver desired" (*kokorozashi shidai*).[60] The Koshirō had thus more or less free rein to demand alms from domain subjects.

Villages and block associations also used their ties with the Koshirō to ward off other beggars. Such protection agreements with beggar guilds were common across Tokugawa Japan and could range from oral compacts and informal notes to various forms of written pledges. They usually defined acceptable begging occasions and precedents for different kinds of households.[61] From the perspective of the donors, alms worked as protection money because the Koshirō reciprocated by helping the peasants and townspeople deal with vagrancy, crime, and other intrusions. In the case of life cycle alms, individual households inside the community were the beneficiaries of such protection. They often employed Koshirō on occasions of celebration and bereavement to keep unorganized beggars in check.[62] But the Koshirō performed their most important services for villages and block associations as a whole. Ōno's villagers summoned the beggar bosses to expel vagrants, identify and bury the bodies of unregistered mendicants, watch the crops, and expel peasants who had been convicted of stealing (in some cases after a mountain ascetic from the castle town had cast a lot to identify the culprit through divination).[63]

60. Expressions such as these appear in begging regulations from all over Tokugawa Japan; see Tsukada, *Kinsei Osaka no hinin to mibunteki shūen*, 35.

61. In Osaka and Sakai, some block associations in the 1770s and 1780s started to precollect alms on life cycle–related occasions and handed them over collectively to their local beggar watchman; see Uchida, "Osaka shikasho no soshiki to shūnyū," 93–101; Okamoto, *Ran/ikki/hinin*, 47–54; Tsukada, *Kinsei Osaka no hinin to mibunteki shūen*, 26.

62. See MT goyōdome 1796, seventh month, YH 939, 692. Compare to beggar associations in Qing China; Lu, *Street Criers*, 90–107; Schak, *A Chinese Beggar's Den*, 17–64.

63. Jisha machi goyōdome (Nojiri) 1781.3.21, YH 161, 127; MT goyōdome 1783.11.4, YH 173, 134–35; 1784.ii.28, YH 187, 144; 1787.5.21, YH 306, 225; 1837.11.6, YH 750, 541–42; 1847.3.26, YH 924, 679–80.

It seems that each village maintained a relationship with one particular Koshirō who regarded the village as his turf (*dannaba*) and showed up whenever his services were needed.[64] If a village desired protection around the clock, it could hire a beggar watchman (called *bannin* or *shitayaku*) in addition to its Koshirō contact and let him live right in or near the community of peasants. Alternatively, it could request the services of a beggar watchman who lived in a nearby village and allow him to collect alms from them in return.[65] In Ōno domain, the number of villages with watchmen was relatively small and fluctuated over time. In 1845 there were anywhere between two and five watchmen in the countryside of Ōno domain, and six in 1860 and 1864 (excluding Anama and Nishikata).[66] Most of them were based in valleys that took some time to reach from Ōno town. The Koshirō also claimed some villages of other domains as their territory and supplied some of them with watchmen, competing with the beggar bosses in Katsuyama, who also had ties to some villages in the Ōno area.[67]

Tokugawa peasants carried a much greater responsibility for their own security than townspeople because in most regions, warriors had stopped residing directly in the countryside—or, as in Hanaguro's case, had assumed peasant status. But peasants lacked the time and skills to pursue

64. This term appears in MT goyōdome 1783.11.4, YH 173, 134–35; 1787.5.21, YH 306, 225.

65. This phenomenon was not unusual. In the Kansai region, for example, the turfs of village beggar guards and town-based beggar bosses often overlapped, and some village guards answered to both domain-appointed bosses and a *hinin* association in a city administered by the shogunate; see Sakaguchi, "Izumi no kuni zaikata hinin-ban ni tsuite," 38–46; Asao, "Hiden'in to Ōmi no hininban"; Nobi, "Kōiki hininban-sei no tenkai to muramura no teikō."

66. In Izumi Province, for example, the density of village guards was higher; Sakaguchi, "Izumi no kuni zaikata hininban ni tsuite," 13. In Ōno, the distribution followed geographic expediency. In 1845, Kami- and Shimo-Daimon (and perhaps Koyato) in the northwest of the Ōno plain seem to have shared a guard, and Gojōhō and Sabiraki shared another one in the southeast. The Haniu, Ajimi, and Ashimi valleys and the "southern mountains" each had a watchman, at least for parts of the late Tokugawa period. See, for example, MT goyōdome 1741.6.26, 1841.2.1, SSM; 1837.11.6, YH 750, 541–42; Ōjōya goyōdome 1845.12.20, YH 900, 664–65; MT goyōdome 1860.3.12, NGM; 1860.10.21, YH 1208, 865; 1864.9.26, YH 1293, 916.

67. Morimasa-ryōke of Gujō domain is one example of a village under Koshirō control; MT goyōdome 1787.5.21, YH 306, 225. On watchmen controlled by Katsuyama's *hinin*, see, for example, *Heisenji monjo*, vol. 2, 52.

criminals effectively and welcomed the employment of beggars as an alternative. From the late seventeenth century onward, hiring outcaste village guards became common in many parts of Japan, perhaps because growing numbers of labor migrants and drifters were passing through rural communities.[68]

The relationship between village and watchman was contractual. It was thus more formal than the relationship with the Koshirō, which was merely based on precedent. The only surviving example of a watchman contract from Ōno domain is the one submitted to Hanaguro's home village Nakano in 1803. In that year, the peasants of Nakano decided to employ an outcaste guard, even though the village was conveniently located at the edge of the castle town and within close range of the Koshirō's settlement. The given reason was that the village had become "disorderly." The peasant community ended up hiring a man named San'emon, probably the former head of a Koshirō household.[69] San'emon submitted a written pledge to the peasants in which he promised to drive out masterless samurai, travelers who solicited money for straw sandals, drifters, and mendicant monks. He vowed to protect the village from theft, fire, and crop raiding; detect gamblers and their dens; and expel travelers who tried to camp on village territory. He also promised that he would be constantly on call to deal with local threats and provide an interim replacement if he fell sick, presumably in the person of his son and guarantor, Kichiemon. San'emon's remuneration included a stipend, money for a humble dwelling inside the village, and semi-annual begging rights, but he had to promise not to ask the peasants for alms on any other occasion.[70] Most village watchmen in eighteenth- and nineteenth-century Japan were compensated with a mix of alms and stipends. However, there were villages in some regions where *hinin* watchmen still collected their entire income in form of alms.[71]

68. Asao, "Hiden'in to Ōmi no hininban," 12–14, 22; Tanaka Shinji, "Tottori-han ni okeru 'zaichū' hiningashira," part 1, 19–25; Nobi, "Murakata hininban no seiritsu"; Leupp, *Servants, Shophands, and Laborers,* 11–28.

69. After 1773, there is evidence for a Koshirō household with heads named San'emon or Kichiemon.

70. Goyōdome (Matsuda) 1803.7.4, YH 554, 370.

71. For statements of support for village guards in other regions, see Tanaka Shinji, "Tottori-han ni okeru 'zaichū' hiningashira," part 1, 25–26; Mae, "Yamato ni

San'emon's contract suggests that the peasant community of Nakano uniformly welcomed his employment, but this might not have been the case. Nakano village included a very large number of landless peasants who rented land from Hanaguro and other wealthy landowners. In the years before 1803, the village had seen a few incidents of gambling and theft among youth of the tenant class, and in 1797, the titled peasants were officially reprimanded for letting a suspected local thief escape from their custody.[72] The presence of the watchman thus probably benefited all those residents, tenant or otherwise, who could be held responsible for the behavior of deviant youth in this large settlement on the borders of the town. Hiring a village guard could also have been a strategy for village elites to guard themselves against the lower peasantry or protect their crops from the poor. In 1793, the headman of another village in Ōno domain enraged his fellow villagers when he used the Koshirō against them in a private investigation of theft without first consulting the village elders.[73]

How did Ōno's domain government handle these relationships between the Koshirō and the commoners' self-governing groups? In principle, it tried to stay out of them as much as possible. At the same time, it had a vested interest in public safety and thus encouraged villagers' reliance on Koshirō and outcaste watchmen. A domain order dating from 1796 stipulated that if masterless samurai, beggars, and other dubious figures appeared in the village and extorted money or became violent, the peasants should expel them; if unable to do so, they should jointly overwhelm them and then call the nearest watchman or Koshirō to drive them away.[74] It is unknown whether Ōno's officials ever went as far as the government of Tottori domain in western Japan, which in the early 1700s

okeru 'hininban-kyū' shiryō," part 1; Ioka, "Hininban e no kyūmai," 10–18; Sakaguchi, "Izumi no kuni zaikata hininban ni tsuite," 23–24, 63–64. In the Ōno area, grain donations were usually part of the compensation package; see for example "Manpō kyūkichō," 1775, Ōbatake Seiemon-ke monjo (entry 1777?). Ōno's association of landowning townspeople once gave a beggar guard some land to farm, but officials regarded this case as exceptional; MT goyōdome 1847.3.26, YH 924, 679–80.

72.   Goyōdome 1797.4.2, 1797.6.6, 6.20, Hanakura-ke monjo.

73.   Issatsu no koto, 1793, twelfth month, Tsunewaki San'emon-ke monjo. On a similar tendency among village elites in Tottori, see Tanaka Shinji, "Tottori-han ni okeru 'zaichū' hiningashira," part 2, 22–25.

74.   Goyōdome (Matsuda) 1796.8.11, YH 445, 310.

began to install new watchmen in the countryside in consultation with village elites and forced all peasants to fund part of their stipends.[75]

The beggar guild performed a variety of duties for the domain in exchange for its begging privilege. These included the management of the beggar hospice, help with the seasonal rice gruel kitchens for beggars, burial of vagrants, torturing and expelling criminals, and guard duty under the supervision of the jail guard, who was a commoner of temporary samurai status. In 1852 the Koshirō even agreed to execute criminals through beheading. But the Koshirō's most important duty, from the domain's standpoint, was the daily running of town patrols. To be sure, there were other forms of patrols in the town such as fire vigils and samurai night watches, but the Koshirō specialized in the control of beggars and other unregistered strangers. In the second half of the eighteenth century, the Koshirō also began to be mobilized for criminal investigations, presumably to keep up with a gradual rise in vagrancy and crime. By the 1830s they had turned into a busy police force that investigated on behalf of the domain's criminal bureau (*tōzokukata*) and hunted criminals in cooperation with outcaste detectives from adjacent domains.[76] A similar transformation occurred with the beggar guilds of Osaka and Kyoto during roughly the same decades.[77] In Edo, by contrast, beggar bosses did not serve the shogunate as a citywide police force, but only patrolled their turfs to discipline beggars or expel them from the city.[78]

The domain government had one main motive for upholding the Koshirō's begging privilege: alms provided the beggars with sustenance and allowed them to discharge their responsibilities vis-à-vis the lord. At

75. Tanaka Shinji, "Tottori-han ni okeru 'zaichū' hiningashira," part 1, 19–29 and part 2, 11–12.

76. The town elders' journals from the 1740s to the 1830s strikingly illustrate the Koshirō's transformation from a beggar patrol into an experienced police force. See, for example, MT goyōdome 1740, 1741, 1834, 1836, 1837, 1838, 1840, 1841, SSM.

77. The shogunate's mobilization of *hinin* as policemen in Kyoto and Osaka can be traced as far back as the 1670s, but around the middle of the eighteenth century, these cities (and many domains) intensified their reliance on urban beggar guilds and village guards for patrols and investigations; Asao, "Hiden'in to Ōmi no hininban"; Sakaguchi, "Izumi no kuni zaikata hininban ni tsuite," 31–38; Nobi, "Kōiki hininbansei no tenkai to muramura no teikō," part 1.

78. Tsukada, *Kinsei Nihon mibunsei no kenkyū*, 259–70, 310.

the same time, officials needed to prevent almsgiving from becoming a drain on the givers and the domain economy, and by no means could they allow begging to interfere with patrol duty. In 1789, for example, the Koshirō made a routine request for temporary leave from their town patrols to go to the villages to "beg around New Year's," but the town governor rejected it because he was concerned about popular unrest and believed the domain could not do without the Koshirō's surveillance. Yet he was well aware that the Koshirō derived most of their income from their semiannual begging tours and came up with a compromise: why not take turns when going to the countryside?[79]

The domain strove to balance the Koshirō's need for alms with the interests of givers' households. In 1796, for example, after a series of disastrous fires in the castle town, the government informed the Koshirō that victims had been told to withhold seasonal alms for a period of five years.[80] The domain intervened again in 1852, when villagers from a nearby shogunal territory complained about alms the Koshirō were collecting from peasants who sold goods at Ōno's town market. The government probably acted to avoid trouble with a neighboring territory and make its town market more attractive. The collection of market offerings (*chūrōsen*) was an old custom in Echizen's castle towns, which probably explains why the domain continued to allow their semiannual collection "on the basis of mutual negotiation." The domain did, however, put an end to various demands the Koshirō had added over the years.[81]

The Koshirō strove to turn voluntary offerings into entitlements and move from the position of a "receiver" to that of a "taker."[82] To do so, they often cited the authority of precedent. The domain refrained from regulating almsgiving precedents as long as these did not run counter to its own

---

79.   MT goyōdome 1789.12.24, YH 376, 276.

80.   MT goyōdome 1796, seventh month, YH 939, 692. Two years later, the domain informed the monks of Eiheiji, a nearby Zen monastery, that town residents who had been impoverished by the fires had been encouraged to withhold alms; see MT goyōdome 1798, eleventh month, YH 472, 328.

81.   MT goyōdome 1852.10.28, YH 1020, 745–46, SSM; 1855.8.6, SSM. Market offerings were also customary in Katsuyama town; "Machidoshiyori-yaku kokoroeki," 1856, in *Katsuyama shishi*, Shiryō-hen 1 Hanchō/machikata, 766–67.

82.   Note the domain officials' careful distinction between the terms *morau* (receive) and *toru* (take) in MT goyōdome 1852.10.28, YH 1020, 746.

interests. In 1840, for example, the town governor refused to intervene in a conflict between the Koshirō and some townsmen who had organized a theater performance but failed to pay the customary gratuity (*osakete*) to the beggars "for patrols." According to the town governor, these offerings "were not an issue for the [domain] officials to decide, but because it was not right [*fudōri*] not to give something one had given before, we [i.e., the town elders] should investigate past precedent, and if the Koshirō's claim proved to be correct, it was advisable to give them something, no matter how much." In fact, the transaction in question was a thinly veiled form of solicitation, but the governor believed that precedent entitled the Koshirō to receive such payments, at least "as much as the giver desired."[83]

In 1845, the almsgiving customs of subjects suddenly became a matter of much deeper interest for the domain. Officials had noticed an imbalance in the triangular relationship between the lord, the Koshirō, and the villagers and townspeople. It turned out that the number of beggar boss households had dropped to a point where the guild's ability to fulfill its duties for the domain was at stake. The town and district governors were particularly concerned about the performance of the town patrols and blamed the villagers for this state of affairs: "These days, the town guards [*machi bannin*] receive only little alms in the countryside and have difficulty supporting themselves. Their number has gradually declined, and there are barely four of them still in residence."[84] The governors were right: as late as 1837, the town elders' journal noted a total of seven beggar bosses. The total population of the Eastern Village had also dropped from forty-five in 1815 to thirty-three in 1834, and shrank further in the 1840s (see table 2). It is likely that the Tenpō famine in the 1830s had something to do with this decline. Though it is unknown whether any Koshirō perished from hunger or epidemics, the famine almost certainly reduced their income because it impoverished the households of givers and eradicated some of them entirely.[85]

83. MT goyōdome 1840.8.3, YH 800, 575–76.
84. Ōjōya goyōdome 1845.8.10, YH 893, 659–60. The townspeople are not mentioned here because the quoted sentence was addressed only to the village group headmen.
85. During the Tenmei famine in the 1780s, the Koshirō did complain about fewer alms and seem to have suffered the temporary loss of two households; MT goyōdome 1784.3.2, YH 193, 151; 1784.4.10, YH 196, 152; 1786.4.26, YH 272, 200; 1789.12.26, YH

Table 2
Total number of Koshirō including household members

	First month	Twelfth month
(1734)	35	
1740	26	28
1741	28 (12 men, 16 women)	28
(1743)	28	
(1747)	28	
(year of bird)		28
1783		33
1815		45
1834		33
1835		30
1837		30
1838		29
1840		27
1841		27
1843		23
1847	30	
1852	34	33
1855	31	
1860	38	33
1861		37
1867		35

Source: MT goyōdome, SSM, AHM, NGM. For years in parentheses, see Ōno-chō yakuba no hokan ni kakaru yōdome-chū kyū-Ōno-han ni kansuru shorui, 12, Echizen Ōno Doi-ke monjo.

In the cities of Osaka, Kyoto, and Sakai, the membership of beggar boss organizations also suffered a marked decline in the late Tokugawa period—in underlings and in full hereditary members. In all three cities, the downward trend started as early as the eighteenth century and was much more gradual and drawn out than it was in Ōno.[86] The exact

377, 276–77. On a similar drop in Kaga domain, see Buraku Mondai Kenkyūjo, *Buraku no rekishi*, Higashi Nihon-hen, 30.

86. Tsukada, *Kinsei Osaka no hinin to mibunteki shūen*, 67–69; Sugahara, "Kinsei Kyoto no hinin," 96; Yamamoto, "Senshū no Sakai 'shikasho' chōri," 77–79. In Edo (1820s and later), beggar leader Zenshichi complained about absconding underlings; see Tsukada, *Kinsei Nihon mibunsei no kenkyū*, 273–82, 317–19. This trend contrasts with the population growth that has been observed for many leatherworker communities in

causes of this development are difficult to determine, but it coincided with the increasing mobilization of beggar bosses for police work and town patrols. Downturns in almsgiving could have been a factor, whether slowly and in the long run, or, as in Ōno, suddenly after a famine or other crisis. Beggar bosses with a declining income and growing duty burden might have looked for ways to make a living outside their guilds. To be sure, the authorities often granted the beggar bosses stipends in exchange for new duties—in Ōno, they gave them an annual bonus of three and later five bales (approx. 411 liters) of rice for the patrols[87]—but these stipends rarely grew in tandem with the labor burden.[88]

To reverse the Koshirō's loss of members, Ōno's town and county governor worked out an elaborate plan with the assistance of commoner officials. First, they asked the town elder on duty to estimate how many Koshirō would be needed for the patrols to be effective (the elder recommended an expansion by two). Next, the village group headmen asked four or five village headmen for their opinions, but the villagers showed little enthusiasm for the plan. As their leaders explained, they had been giving "according to precedent" and were not responsible for the decline. If the authorities forced them to give more, the headmen would have trouble distributing the burden fairly among the villagers and would meet with resistance from the ordinary titled peasants. Hearing this, the governors decided to have the peasant officials conduct a survey and "inquire roughly how much ordinary titled peasants gave to the Eastern Village throughout the year, converted into rice."[89]

Unfortunately, the results of this survey have not been preserved in detail, but according to the village headmen, there were precedents for the amounts to be given to the beggar guild, both for ranked peasants with the right of audience (*omemie*) and for ordinary full peasants. Until

the late Tokugawa period. In Echigo Province, where leatherworkers rather than beggars were used as policemen and guards, the population increase seems to have translated into rising numbers of village guards; see Buraku Mondai Kenkyūjo, *Buraku no rekishi*, Higashi Nihon-hen, 169–70.

87. MT goyōdome 1784.12.26, YH 242, 173; 1789.12.24, YH 376, 276.

88. In Ōno and Osaka, for example, payments from the government remained low despite a heavy increase in the amount of duty work; see Uchida, "Osaka shikasho no soshiki to shūnyū," 89–113.

89. Ōjōya goyōdome 1845.8.11, Fukui Daigaku Toshokan monjo.

1845, the domain had shown little interest in the details of those precedents and only issued vague reminders.[90] Now that the survival of the guild was at stake, the officials deployed their full bureaucratic potential. They concluded that the overall amount of alms had indeed decreased and that moreover the burden of alms was distributed unevenly among the villages. The county governor ordered the village group headmen to notify the peasants of the following solution: henceforth, each village would be collectively required to pay a fixed amount, half based on the village's productive yield (0.213 *gō* per 1 *koku* rice) and the other half on the number of titled peasant households (3.54 *gō* of rice per household). How they divided this burden internally would be up to them. But the offerings were to be gathered by the village headman, who would hand them over to the Koshirō. As before, half of the amount would be due at the ancestor festival and the other half at the end of the year. The bulk (8.5 *koku* out of 12.8 *koku*) was to be shouldered by the villages of the plain, whose rice acreage was more extensive than that of the "three valleys" Haniu, Ajimi, and Ashimi.[91]

The new mode of almsgiving resembled the old village-unit system of taxation, under which Tokugawa rulers imposed the annual rice tax on each village as a group and held village headmen accountable for the delivery of the full amount. The domain's motivation for employing this method seems to have been the same in both cases: using village self-government and peer pressure to ensure a stable and predictable yield. In 1845, domain officials were no longer willing to leave the level of the Koshirō's alms income to precedent and the discretion of villagers and townspeople. They now demanded formal guarantees that the communities would regularly deliver the appropriate amount.

Ōno's intervention of 1845 had parallels in other parts of Japan. A number of cases are known from the nineteenth century in which governments manipulated the beggar bosses' alms income, and beggar bosses discovered duty as a bargaining chip to extract more alms from givers with the help of the authorities. In Edo in 1821–22 and Kyoto in 1839 and

90. In sumptuary regulations, for example, the domain ordered subjects not to apply thrift to almsgiving for *hinin* because one was supposed to show compassion with the poor; MT goyōdome 1799.3.1, YH 480, 334; 1830, second month, YH 649, 467.

91. Ōjōya goyōdome 1845.11.26, YH 898, 661; Ōjōya goyōdome 1845.12.10, 12.14, 12.16, 12.20, YH 900, 663–66. On the townspeople's burden, see Yōroku, 1852, SSM.

1866, administrators simply gave beggar bosses permission to collect new types of alms, some of them temporarily.[92] Other interventions, such as those in Marugame domain (1796) and Sakai (1841), were more invasive and bureaucratic and thus more similar to Ōno's procedure. Although most of these measures seem to have favored the beggars' side, some of them were clearly intended to reverse a previous decline, and the authorities remained mindful of the impact these new offerings would have on givers.[93] There were places such as the hinterland of Osaka where the net burden of support for urban beggar guilds grew noticeably in the nineteenth century, but it is still far from clear whether this was also the case in other regions.[94] In Ōno, at least one village lodged a formal protest against the burden it was assigned in 1845, but some of the other villages possibly benefited from the measure.[95] In 1866, the townspeople of Ōno doubled their annual alms payment to the Koshirō, probably to adjust for inflation because their donations were in silver money.[96] The high inflation of the 1860s had a destabilizing effect on almsgiving agreements all over the country (see chapter 4).

How, then, should we describe these transfers—as alms, taxes, or compensation? They were all of the above, yet none of them exclusively. In the context of relations between the Koshirō and the domain, seasonal almsgiving constituted a police tax, but even in 1845, the domain officials only manipulated the amount of alms and left the

---

92. Tsukada, *Kinsei Nihon mibunsei no kenkyū*, 317–9, 334; Minegishi, *Kinsei hisa-betsuminshi no kenkyū*, 132–33. In 1866, for example, the beggar bosses of Kyoto asked for the right to collect semiannual alms in the provinces Yamashiro, Ōmi, and Tanba for a period of five years, arguing that high prices and fewer alms affected their ability to perform duty; Asao, "Hiden'in to Ōmi no hininban," 33–34.

93. In Marugame's case, the intervention concerned the semiannual alms collected by the local monkey trainers, who performed duty work for the domain; see Kawato, "Kinsei hisabetsumin no seikatsu to shisō," 145–50. On Sakai, see Sakaguchi, "Izumi no kuni zaikata hininban ni tsuite," 38–45. In Edo, the town governor mitigated the impact of the new alms by imposing restrictions on their collection. Earnings dropped considerably before 1839; see Minegishi, *Kinsei hisabetsuminshi no kenkyū*, 133.

94. Sakaguchi, "Izumi no kuni zaikata hininban ni tsuite," 36–52; Yabuta, *Kokuso to hyakushō ikki no kenkyū*, 298–306; Nobi, "Kōiki hininban-sei no tenkai to muramura no teikō," part 1, 5–9; part 2, 5–8; Uchida, "Osaka shikasho no soshiki to shūnyū," 101–3.

95. Ōjōya goyōdome 1845.12.26, YH 900, 666.

96. Yōroku, 1852, SSM.

customary relationships between Koshirō and peasants intact. This meant that the peasants of Ōno could continue to ask the beggars for services that benefited them exclusively and went beyond the Koshirō's duties for the domain. In the context of relations between the Koshirō and commoners, alms constituted a compensation for labor, most immediately in the case of the watchmen's stipends. Yet this evolution toward labor contracts was not straightforward either, because the Koshirō continued to solicit alms under various pretexts and treated the villages as begging turfs—a form of status property—without asking the villagers for permission.[97] Although the Koshirō had changed over time and their police duty now overshadowed their mendicant occupation, the status order accommodated this change by allowing the beggar bosses, the villages and block associations, and the domain to readjust and reevaluate their triangle of ties. The triangle itself remained in place and prevented each side from single-handedly dictating the terms of the Koshirō's presence in local society. Again, the episode shows that the domain government respected the precedents worked out between status groups and carefully researched them before making interventions.

By the 1840s, Ōno's domain authorities had thus come to rely on the Koshirō as a police force. Mobilizing the beggar bosses for police-related duties was relatively easy for the domain because the Koshirō themselves welcomed such work as a way to make themselves indispensable and distance themselves from their mendicant origins. But there were other assignments the Koshirō were more reluctant to perform. One example is the Koshirō's mobilization for "decapitation duty" (*kubikiri goyō*) in 1852. The Koshirō abhorred this duty because executions involved taking life, and they feared (for good reason) that engagement in killing and bloodshed would further tarnish their reputation. In 1815, for example, when the government ordered the Koshirō to kill stray dogs, the beggar bosses tried to resist, arguing that their actual trade was police work and that the leatherworkers were the more appropriate group for this undertaking. Their argument collapsed when

97.   On this point, see Minegishi, *Kinsei hisabetsuminshi no kenkyū*, 129–41; Minegishi, "Kinsei senminsei no kiso kōzō," 81–91.

domain officials located old records that showed the Koshirō had once killed dogs for the domain in the past.[98]

Up until 1852, executions in Ōno domain were the responsibility of the jail guard, a commoner of temporary samurai status, who seems to have done whatever he could to avoid decapitations by feigning illness, letting convicts escape, or encouraging suicide. The domain government tried to get the Koshirō involved, but for fifteen years, the beggar bosses staunchly resisted the proposal.[99] In 1852, an officer of the domain's criminal bureau finally came up with an offer that was too tempting to refuse: an additional annual stipend of six bales of rice and the title of "informer" (*meakashi*) for three designated executioners, plus permission to carry short swords and enter the halls of commoner houses while on police duty. The beggar bosses especially coveted the designation of informer because there were policemen of commoner background in other parts of Japan who served under that title.[100] The government was so desperate to get the Koshirō to accept the job that it overrode fierce resistance from the town elders and townspeople, who feared that the new title would elevate the beggar bosses above the lower-ranking townspeople and make them arrogant and defiant. Less than a year after the appointment, when they had completed their first few beheadings, the three executioner-informers regretted their decision and petitioned to be released from the assignment, but it was too late. The tables had turned, and the domain continued to mobilize the Koshirō for executions for the final years of the Tokugawa period.[101]

The negotiation over decapitation duty affected not only the two main parties to the agreement—the Koshirō and the domain's criminal bureau—but also several other status groups. Although the townspeople failed to make themselves heard in this case, there was another community that proved more difficult for the domain to ignore: the cormorant fishermen of Kanazuka village. These people had originally been in charge of cleaning up the site after an execution, but at some point before 1841,

98.   MT goyōdome 1815.6.20, YH 599, 422–23. See also MT goyōdome 1776.1.6, 1.7, 1.11, YH 97, 85–86.

99.   MT goyōdome 1838.5.9, YH 773, 553.

100.   Howell, "Kinsei shakai ni okeru shiteki bōryoku to kōteki bitoku," 125–26; Tsukada, *Mibunsei shakai to shimin shakai*, 52–54; Morishita, "Hagi-han no meakashi to autorō sekai."

101.   MT goyōdome 1852.12.18, SSM; 1853.5.21, AHM.

the Koshirō had started to fill in for them in return for an annual fee.[102] By 1841, Kanazuka had become too impoverished to pay that fee, but the domain decided for some reason that it needed to shield the Kanazuka people from the "handling of polluted people," as one of the town elders put it in his journal.[103] Instead of relieving Kanazuka from the duty altogether, the administration started to pay money to the Koshirō in the fishermen's stead, and Kanazuka reciprocated by offering sweetfish (*ayu*) to the lord. This convoluted arrangement expired in 1852—the same year the domain finally persuaded the Koshirō to undertake beheadings. This time, the beggar bosses were no longer satisfied with just the fee. In exchange for extending the agreement, they demanded access to Anama and Nishikata, the two parts of the domain that were not included in their begging territory. The government did not want to (and probably could not) grant this request because the villages in these exclaves had their own watchmen and were not prepared to give up their customary ties.[104] But there was a way of working around the problem. The domain offered to pay the Koshirō the sum of 2.02 *koku* (365 liters) of rice every year, which corresponded to the amount of alms the guild would theoretically have collected from these villages had they been allowed access to them. From 1852 onwards, the domain paid these substitute alms to the Koshirō every year for their willingness to fill in as execution assistants for Kanazuka, and the fishermen had to submit a written guarantee to the beggar bosses that they would renegotiate the agreement every ten years.[105]

In this manner, the domain government was often forced to consider several interlocking relationships at once before it could mobilize a status group for a new duty. The Koshirō made the most of the leverage they enjoyed over the domain and other self-governing entities, but ultimately they negotiated from a very weak position. The Koshirō remained the one

102.	For a more detailed discussion of this case, see Ehlers, "Executing Duty: Ōno Domain and the Employment of *Hinin* in the Bakumatsu Period." Also see Yōroku, 1852, SSM.

103.	MT goyōdome 1841.5.21, SSM.

104.	MT goyōdome 1852, i2.16, SSM; "Doi Noto no kami yōdomechō," in *Ota chōshi*, Shiryō-hen 2, 356; "Bannin sashidashi-jō," in *Ota chōshi*, Shiryō-hen 2, 273; MT goyōdome 1837.8.25, SSM.

105.	MT goyōdome 1852.6.4, 1855.12.16, 1860.7.11, 1865.1.11, SSM; MT goyōdome 1853.7.13, 1856.12.16, AHM.

group in domain society the government routinely turned to for unpopular duties because they were the most susceptible to minor increases in income and status. Although the Koshirō took on new obligations in the hope of lessening discrimination, they ended up breeding more resentment by performing new services for the domain. The status order thus provided the Koshirō with some room to better themselves, but it also entangled them in relationships that reinforced their marginal position.

Households

Towards the authorities and other status groups, the Koshirō acted as a collective that defended a shared set of interests. Internally, they were organized as a guild—a small community of privilege-holding, duty-performing households. The Koshirō's households mediated between the public and private identity of group members. In Tokugawa Japan, households not only structured the life of individuals but also constituted the basic units of most status groups because the privileges and duties of status groups were typically distributed among households. To study households and their functions, one would ideally turn to documents from inside the group, but such sources are relatively hard to come by for outcastes and did not survive in the Koshirō's case. Fortunately, the town elders' journals provide some insight into the guild's internal structure and even contain fragmentary information on particular Koshirō households, especially for the nineteenth century.

The almsgiving intervention of 1845 was successful in achieving its main goal: increasing the number of duty-performing Koshirō households. By 1847, the Koshirō population including family members and underlings had recovered from around twenty-three to thirty, and in 1852 there were at least five households (more likely six) instead of four.[106] By 1860, the guild had expanded to eight households with thirty-three residents, and six village guards were under their control.[107] Where did these new

---

106. MT goyōdome 1852.12.21, 4.21, 8.17, SSM. Chōemon, who appears in 1853, might also have been present in 1852; MT goyōdome 1853.5.21, AHM.
107. MT goyōdome 1860.10.21, YH 1208, 865; table 2.

households come from? It would have been quite unusual for the Koshirō to integrate outsiders into their group. Although the beggar bosses regularly accepted paupers into the hospice, they did not commonly turn them into household members because the job of underling or watchman (let alone beggar boss) required physical fitness and resilience. This might explain why the few outsiders who are known to have become affiliated with the Koshirō were recruited from the ranks of unregistered drifters and not from the hospice. Two village guards recorded in the 1780s were newcomers to Ōno domain, and one of them was a masterless samurai from Kaga domain. In 1837, an unregistered man from Kanazawa became the underling of a Koshirō boss and was later sent as a watchman to a village in a nearby shogunate territory.[108]

Village watchmen were ideal candidates for the position of beggar boss because they were experienced at serving duty and well versed in the customs of the guild. They often received visits from the Koshirō and frequently visited the Eastern Village in return, sometimes for extended periods of time.[109] Although it is unclear exactly how the guild expanded its ranks after 1845, the town elders' journals discuss a similar case from 1860 that can offer a clue. In that year, the Koshirō obtained permission to revive the household of Shirōbei because "duty had become heavier these days." Shirōbei's lineage had disappeared "a long time ago" and not even the homestead remained, so the Koshirō persuaded the outcaste guard of Otomi, a village in Ōno domain, to become the new Shirōbei.[110] Like most Tokugawa status groups, the Koshirō allocated rights and obligations among hereditary households, which might have made it easier to revive an old household than to establish a new one and upset the customary

108. Jisha machi goyōdome (Nojiri) 1781.3.2, YH 157, 125–26; MT goyōdome 1837.7.24, SSM. Once, in 1786, the domain government forced the group to integrate a thief who had been punished with degradation to beggar status, but the Koshirō protested this move and called it unprecedented; MT goyōdome 1786.4.26, 4.28, 5.2, YH 272 and 273, 200–201.

109. Jisha machi goyōdome (Nojiri) 1781.3.2, YH 157, 125–26. On the practice of mutual visits, see MT goyōdome 1834.4.21, 1834.8.16, 8.19, 8.20, 1834.10.6, SSM.

110. Shirōbei last appears as a beggar boss in 1789, but might still have been active in 1834; MT goyōdome 1789.12.26, YH 377, 276–77; MT goyōdome 1834.4.21; 1860.7.11, 7.21, SSM; 1860.3.12, 3.28; 1860.4.25, NGM.

structure of the guild.[111] It is likely that after 1845, the guild recovered by similar means—by turning watchmen, underlings, and younger sons into household heads.

At the end of the Tokugawa period, Ōno's beggar guild was growing in size and maintaining its income thanks to the government's reliance on its patrol and police duties. But there was at least one household in the Eastern Village that tried to overcome the limitations of *hinin* status and group membership by establishing an independent livelihood in the form of moneylending and introducing its children into commoner society. This household first appears under the name of Iemon, who was succeeded by his son Isuke and later his grandson Isaburō, an adoptee from Kyoto. On one hand, the story of this family illustrates the enormous hurdles outcastes frequently faced when acting beyond their station. On the other hand, it reveals that some people among the commoner class were willing to accept integration despite a generally strong popular aversion against intermarriage between outcastes and townspeople.

The first time a Koshirō named Iemon appears in the documents is in 1793.[112] In 1837, a year of acute hunger, Iemon was ordered by the domain to provide relief (*sukui*) to the beggars' "village," or "guild"; when he failed to obey that order, officials confiscated ten bales of rice from his storehouse and distributed them among the Koshirō, the beggars in the hospice, and even one of the leatherworkers ("*eta* Zenroku"). All Koshirō bosses except Iemon were given the same amount of rice.[113] In contrast to Iemon, who owned a plastered storehouse, the remaining Koshirō households were suffering from the famine; one even tried to steal to survive.[114]

---

111.   This is suggested by the fact that when Shirōbei's lineage was discontinued, the Koshirō made up for its share of the duty burden by temporarily dividing it up among the remaining households (*yonai itashi*). They also referred to the abandoned household as being "without resident" (*mujū*), a term often used for temples temporarily without a head priest.

112.   MT goyōdome 1793.5.29, SSM. Also see Horikane goyōdome, 1806, NGM.

113.   MT goyōdome 1837.4.6, 1837.8.12, SSM.

114.   Beggar boss Sōemon committed a burglary in 1834 and testified having acted out of poverty; see MT goyōdome 1834.4.21, 8.16, 8.19, 8.20, 10.6, SSM. The storehouse is mentioned in MT goyōdome 1837.7.24, 1852.12.21, SSM.

This incident is remarkable because unlike Danzaemon, the famous outcaste boss of Edo, Iemon was not the leader of his guild, let alone the outcaste population of Ōno. Had he been a proper outcaste leader, it would have been a matter of course for him to relieve his underlings and subordinate groups in times of need, in the same way as a privileged household in town or village society. Danzaemon, for example, provided aid to the monkey trainers under his control to rescue them from famine and destitution. In Kanazawa in 1829, one of the bosses of the *tōnai* beggar association helped the people inside his compound and was rewarded for his charity by the lord.[115] Even though Iemon was not the Koshirō's leader and clearly had no intentions of taking on that role, it made sense for the domain to force him to share some of his property in times of hunger because famished commoners could hardly be expected to support the Koshirō with more alms.[116] It is unclear how Iemon had obtained such an edge over the other Koshirō in the first place. In towns with larger beggar associations, the leadership was always wealthier than ordinary members because they received special allowances and begging rights from the authorities.[117] One hint can be gathered from a land register from the early Meiji period that lists Iemon's descendant as the only household in the village with agricultural land, and there are strong indications that Iemon was receiving annual payments from the domain for an unknown reason.[118] It is also possible that the family had a profitable turf that included many wealthy households.

Iemon seems to have died soon after this incident and was succeeded by his son Isuke, who appears repeatedly in subsequent town elders' journals. Isuke loaned money to townspeople, including those who engaged in shady business and would perhaps not have received loans

115.   Tsukada, *Kinsei mibunsei to shūen shakai*, 274; "Iburaku ikkan" 11, 538.

116.   Miwa Kiken, a Confucian scholar in Kyoto, suggested in 1713 that at times of famine, the beggar bosses of Kyoto, whom he suspected of having considerable reserves, should provide their starving underlings with relief instead of letting them beg in town; Miwa, "Kyūga taii," 452.

117.   Uchida, "Osaka shikasho no soshiki to shūnyū," 103; Asao, "Hiden'in to Ōmi no hininban," 24-29.

118.   Yokomachi yashiki tanbetsu shirabechō, 1872, Yokomachi kuyū monjo; MT goyōdome 1834.12.26, SSM; MT goyōdome 1835.12.23, fragment volume, SSM; Ōnohan jisha machikata goyōki, 1865.1.11, Echizen shiryō.

elsewhere. In 1838 he was placed under house arrest for transgressing status boundaries after he had done business ("settling sake accounts") with two townspeople whom the domain accused of violence and hosting prostitutes. In 1857 he was briefly jailed for taking profits from a gambling den and lending money to the players.[119] Once Isuke's "old mother" petitioned the town elders to enforce the repayment of a substantial loan she had made to a townsman. When the old mother died in 1864, her estate amounted to 3,082.5 *monme* of silver plus house and furniture, an impressive sum for an ostensibly penniless beggar family.[120] Interestingly, the old mother seems to have been the legal owner of the household's assets as long as she lived, while Isuke did duty as beggar boss. Perhaps this arrangement worked as a safeguard against further orders from the domain to share its wealth with the other Koshirō households.[121]

The family actively looked for ways to translate its money into social status and help its younger children escape the stain of their outcaste birth by living among townspeople. But it could not do so openly because it was technically illegal for an outcaste to move into a commoner district.[122] Isuke's nephew Heikichi, the product of a liaison between Iemon's eldest daughter and town doctor Matsukawa Shūsaku, was sent to Fukui as a child to be raised in a town household; in 1838, an Ōno townsman adopted him as his son-in-law and heir. It is possible that the adopting household was in fact one of Iemon's debtors. Heikichi's case offers some insight into town officials' views on the subject of outcaste discrimination. After receiving an anonymous hint, the two town elders began to argue over the handling of Heikichi's petition to be registered in Ōno. One of the elders supported the request. In a conversation, his son reasoned that "Heikichi may have come from a Koshirō daughter's womb, but this is no different from the lord of Fukui, who is the son of a cooper's daughter, but became lord because he is the honorable child of Fukui's previous

---

119. MT goyōdome 1838.6.1, 6.2, 6.3, 6.5, 6.6. SSM; 1857.11.21, AHM.

120. MT goyōdome 1853.5.2, 5.21, AHM; 1864.5.16, SSM. Even in the inflationary year 1864, this amount was still worth at least fifty bales of rice; see the appendix.

121. Many beggar households in Osaka in the early eighteenth century avoided their duty by installing widows or minors as family heads; Tsukada, *Kinsei Osaka no hinin to mibunteki shūen*, 67–69.

122. On this problem with regard to leatherworkers moving into the city of Osaka, see Hatanaka, *'Kawata' to heijin*, 109-68.

lord."[123] The second elder opposed Heikichi's admission because he feared the reaction of the townspeople in case word leaked out about the man's origins, which would have concerned him personally because he and Heikichi's adoptive father belonged to the same block association. His resistance grew when he learned that the domain administration had also been informed of the issue. Although the town governor gave the elders free hand to admit the man, he warned them that it was their responsibility to keep the matter secret: "When the son of a Koshirō marries into town, he will produce children, and if these children then go on to marry other people, the town will have plenty of people with Koshirō blood, which is a serious issue." The town elders began to worry that the domain would blame them if the matter became public, and they decided to deny Heikichi's request.[124]

One would need to know more about Heikichi's background to fully understand why his petition was supported by part of the town elite. Whatever their respective motivations, the two town elders argued their cases with reference to two different views of the nature of the outcastes' stigma. Heikichi's supporters interpreted the Koshirō's marginality as a problem of their relative social position, which could be superseded, for example, by the aura of a child's paternal ancestry. Some intellectuals at that time went further and advocated the abolition of outcaste status, thus building momentum for the legal emancipation of outcastes in 1871. According to these thinkers, baseness could be remedied through purification rituals and moral reform.[125] The second town elder and the town governor reflected (though not necessarily shared) the perspective of the lower townspeople, who took an absolute view of the Koshirō's stigma and dreaded the loosening of status discrimination, certainly because

123. It is unclear which lord of Fukui the town elder's son was referring to, but the lord of Fukui until 1835, Matsudaira Naritsugu, had a mother of lowly origins. According to the later lord Matsudaira Shungaku, who took care of this woman in her old age, she might have been a teahouse girl; see *Fukui shishi*, Tsūshi-hen 2, 553. I am grateful to Nagano Eishun for this reference.

124. MT goyōdome 1838.4.6, SSM.

125. Woldering, *"Eta wo osamuru no gi* oder 'Erörterung der Herrschaft über die Schmutzigen'"; McCormack, *Japan's Outcaste Abolition*, 53–58; Uesugi, *Meiji ishin to senmin haishirei*, 19–27.

some of them were also struggling to maintain their respectability.[126] Although the domain officials appeared more worried about public order than the purity of townspeople's bloodlines, this did not necessarily mean they were not invested in upholding the separation between townspeople and outcastes. For the government, discriminatory laws could deter the Koshirō from illegal activity and mollify the lower townspeople. In 1843, the domain issued a ban on Koshirō moneylending to townspeople, probably out of concern with Isuke's financial dealings, though it did not strictly enforce this prohibition.[127]

The second offspring of this family who sought his luck as a townsman was Isuke's younger brother Bunkichi. He went to Edo in 1841 after making a failed attempt to establish himself as a townsman in Ōno; the people of Lower Nibanmachi had gotten wind of his lineage and protested his admission to a tenement in an adjacent temple precinct.[128] After the death of the old mother, Bunkichi returned from Edo, where he had been living in a *chō* under a different name, and contested Isuke's inheritance.[129] A few Koshirō stepped in to mediate, and Bunkichi secured one third of the inheritance and Isuke and his two older sisters the remaining two thirds. In the course of this conflict, Bunkichi submitted a petition to ask the government for one of the following: either the authorities should force Isuke to retire from his position as beggar boss and confiscate the entire inheritance, or they should grant Isuke a surname to make him a proper domain official. The town elders returned the petition, stating that neither could be granted; Bunkichi probably did not expect a positive response anyway. He likely submitted it to undermine his brother's claims as beggar boss and get the town elders involved. Whatever Bunkichi's intentions, the case reveals two ambitious Koshirō who

126. Note the complaint about Koshirō attending a public bathhouse mentioned earlier in this chapter, and the protests against Bunkichi's admission mentioned below. In a conflict of 1852 that involved a leatherworker hoping to move into town, the carpenters refused to work on the Koshirō's behalf; MT goyōdome 1852.6.21, 8.6, 8.8, SSM.

127. Ofuredome 1843.7.12, YH 846, 626–27. This order threatened sanctions only in case the Koshirō were bold enough to have their debt quarrels adjudicated by the domain. When Isuke's "old mother" filed a petition against a townsman in 1853, the town elders simply asked both parties to solve their conflict through mediation; MT goyōdome 1853.5.2, 5.21, AHM.

128. MT goyōdome 1841.8.9, YH 818, 593–94.

129. MT goyōdome, 1864.5.16, SSM.

used different strategies to move up in society: one by performing duty for a privilege-granting authority, the other by bypassing his status group and reinventing himself as a townsman. Less than ten years later, the Meiji government issued the outcaste emancipation edict of 1871 and turned both Isuke and Bunkichi into ordinary town residents, at least in legal terms.

The dissolution of Ōno's outcaste order after the fall of the shogunate is not well documented, but it seems that during the first few years of Meiji, the Koshirō were still being used for police-related tasks.[130] The Koshirō continued to work as informers on behalf of the domain's criminal bureau until at least 1869.[131] In 1875, the Meiji government established a tax-funded police force composed of civil servants, but there was a transition period of several years in which administrators continued to rely on the manpower and expertise of former outcaste policemen. Many localities in Japan initially allowed these watchmen to gather alms while gradually abolishing their begging rights in favor of regular salaries and finally replaced them altogether.[132] In Ōno, one former Koshirō, Nihei, served in the police force as a detective (*tansakugata*) between 1873 and 1876 while the town was part of Tsuruga Prefecture.[133] In 1872, there were eight households in the so-called Koshirō-*chō*, and in 1877, the area of the former Eastern Village still had eight households of Koshirō background, though these were now integrated into one of the newly delineated town districts.[134] Apparently, the Koshirō had received titles to their residential land when the domain was abolished in 1871, but Isuke's successor Isaburō was the only household that also owned agricultural

130. On the dismantling of *hinin* guilds after the Meiji Restoration, see Porter, "Meiji shoki Osaka ni okeru hinmin no kyūsai to tōsei"; Porter, "Meiji shoki Tokyo ni okeru hinmin no kyūsai to tōsei"; Porter, "Tokyo no hinin shūdan no kaitai katei."

131. MT goyōdome 1869.7.21, NGM.

132. See, for example, Porter, "Meiji shoki Osaka ni okeru hinmin no kyūsai to tōsei," 325–30; Obinata, "Bakumatsu/ishinki ni okeru mibunsei no kaitai"; Kusayama, "Sonraku keisatsu-ri hininban ni tsuite," part 2, 18; Fukui-ken Keisatsushi Hensan Iinkai, *Fukui-ken keisatsushi*, vol. 1, 175–212.

133. Koseki, 1878. On *tansakugata*, see Fukui-ken Keisatsushi Hensan Iinkai, *Fukui-ken keisatsushi*, vol. 1, 182, 230; *Ōno shishi*, Tsūshi-hen (ge), 46–49.

134. Yokomachi yashiki tanbetsu shirabechō, 1872, Yokomachi kuyū monjo; Takuchi jūnanatō tōkyūchō, 1877, Ozaki Yaemon-ke monjo.

fields.[135] After the Meiji Restoration, mendicant outcaste groups were generally more likely to disintegrate than were groups of leatherworkers because they rarely gained ownership over their land and their two incentives for group cohesion—defense of begging privileges and performance of duty—disappeared. With their privileges and duties abolished, the Koshirō seem to have fallen back on the typical livelihoods of poor townspeople. In a register of 1878, four former Koshirō households, including Isaburō's, are marked as tobacco cutters and three as makers of straw sandals.[136] Their traces vanish after this point, and today, the Koshirō presence in Ōno is all but forgotten.

The Koshirō were outcastes, but they were also an important part of Ōno's domain society and structurally similar to the other occupational groups there. Once a band of penniless beggars, by the eighteenth century, the Koshirō had acquired the typical features of a recognized status group: an occupation, hereditary households, a family temple, self-government, duties vis-à-vis the authorities, and customary relationships with all the social groups in the domain. But such apparent normality came at the price of permanent, hereditary stigma. Not only did the beggar bosses have an occupation that associated them with home- and lawlessness, they were also forced to take on uncomfortable duties that confronted the harsh realities of crime, extreme poverty, and brutal law enforcement. Although the Koshirō exploited the mechanics of the status order to improve their material and social standing, they never reached a position of true respectability because the relationships they maintained with other status groups and the government were premised on their position as outsiders. Yet the Koshirō bargained hard and successfully redefined themselves over time, first as beggar bosses and later as policemen and informers.

Ōno's outcaste order represented one possible manifestation of the many ways occupations, privileges, and duties could be distributed among marginal groups. The outcaste hierarchy was configured differently in

135. It is unclear how affluent Isuke's household still was at that point because in 1869, a year of inflation and distress, the household applied for sales of cheap rice from the domain, together with other Koshirō and many town households; MT goyōdome 1869.7.21, NGM.

136. Koseki, 1878.

other towns and domains, even geographically similar ones such as Iida domain in Shinano Province or nearby ones such as Kaga.[137] Domains and the shogunate administered their territories by using the customary ties between their local status groups and manipulated them if necessary to stabilize their rule. To be successful at this task, officials needed to collect information on many kinds of precedents and carefully consider the implications of interfering with the interdependent network of relationships among their subjects. Status groups likewise had to build an institutional memory so they could defend their interests effectively and resist unwelcome government interventions. Although they responded primarily to local circumstances, they took advantage of their knowledge of the outside world and any ties they may have possessed with authorities and peer groups in other places. In that sense, the status order of Tokugawa Japan transcended local society.

137. Yoshida Yuriko, "Chiiki shakai to mibunteki shūen"; Yoshida Yuriko, "Manzai to haruta-uchi"; Yoshida Yuriko, "Shinshū Shimo-Ina chiiki ni okeru mibunteki shūen"; Tanaka Yoshio, "Kaga-han 'tōnai' no kenkyū."

CHAPTER 3

The Management of Mendicancy

Encounters with beggars have become quite rare in Japan today, but in the Tokugawa period they were a common occurrence. Some of these beggars were part of a recognized mendicant group and acted as beggar bosses rather than as ordinary panhandlers. But many people begged for alms casually without joining a beggar association. Some of these casual beggars were homeless vagrants; others were impoverished townspeople and peasants unable to support themselves through other means, either because they were old, sick, orphaned, or disabled, or because they were unemployed or had suffered a fire, crop failure, or other calamity. As discussed in the previous chapter, begging was not a respectable way of making a living, but it was not illegal either, and Ōno's domain authorities accepted that many of their poorer subjects depended on alms. They tolerated beggars—even begging strangers—within their territory and granted them a minimum of protection, provided that the beggars' presence did not interfere with the government's main goal: the control of vagrancy. This is not to say that unorganized beggars were treated particularly well in Ōno domain. They were often met with suspicion and had to survive on random acts of kindness.

To deal with these poor and abandoned people, the institutions of Tokugawa society engaged in what I call the management of mendicancy. This phrase refers to the mutually complementary systems and rules that governments and various status groups such as block associations, villages, and beggar guilds had worked out among themselves to relieve and control begging paupers. The self-governing groups enjoyed much latitude in handling such cases, although they often had to coordinate with government officials or with one another. This chapter examines the management of mendicancy in the social context of Ōno domain and surroundings. It explains how the domain government, *chō*, villages, and Koshirō interacted to provide beggars with relief and determined their placement in the social order. Within this cluster of relationships, each corner had its own set of interests. The domain authorities were primarily interested in beggar control but also emphasized beggar relief to prevent crime and unrest and uphold the lord's benevolent reputation. The villages and block associations shared the domain's concern with public safety and constituted units of mutual support, sometimes feeling compelled to abandon weaker residents to the streets to lessen the burden of providing them with aid. Mountain villages particularly depended on the townspeople for giving alms to poor villagers who begged in town during the winter. The Koshirō were in charge of managing the domain's institutions of beggar relief, which included seasonal rice gruel kitchens and a beggar hospice. They thus took care of beggars not out of a charitable impulse but because the management of mendicancy constituted an important aspect of their services for the domain, villages, and *chō* and justified their existence as a guild.

In the Tokugawa period, many documents, administrative and otherwise, did not make a clear terminological distinction between beggar bosses and casual beggars. The sources from the Ōno area are a case in point. As mentioned in chapter 2, shogunal edicts referred to the members of mendicant outcaste groups as *hinin*, and Ōno's town and domain officials sometimes used this term for the Koshirō as well. At the same time, *hinin* 非人 (also written 貧人) frequently appears in Ōno's town elders' journals with the meaning of "beggar," that is, a person begging on a casual basis. The characters 非 (*hi*, non-) and 貧 (*hin*, poor) seem to have been used interchangeably.[1] Another common term for beggars in the

---

1. The transcription of *hinin* as 貧人 was especially common during the first half of the Tokugawa period; see Tsukada, "Hinin–Kinsei Osaka no hinin to sono yuisho," 242; Kuroda, *Nihon chūsei no kokka to shūkyō*, 405–6. Some texts use the characters 疲人 (exhausted people). Another, somewhat less derogatory term for begging commoners was *kinin/kijin* 飢人 (starving person); Kikuchi, *Kikin kara yomu kinsei shakai*, 294–96, 308.

Ōno area and elsewhere was *kojiki* 乞食.[2] In the town elders' journals, *hinin* and *kojiki* were often used synonymously and could appear in combination as *kojiki hinin*—probably to differentiate street beggars from hereditary outcastes, who were sometimes called *eta hinin* in Tokugawa-era documents. In a few cases, the word *kojiki* also referred to the Koshirō.[3] The terminological overlap between mendicant outcastes and street beggars reflected the logic of the status order, which acknowledged begging as an occupation and held the organized beggars responsible for policing the casual beggars on the fringes of their group.[4]

To manage mendicancy effectively, beggar bosses needed to draw a line between suspicious vagrants and harmless beggars. The Koshirō were experts at making this distinction because they served as the vagrant police and were thus relatively familiar with the people of the street. Block associations and villages and their constituent households also played an important part in beggar classification and control. This chapter describes the various arrangements that existed between the status groups in Ōno domain and beyond to control and provide relief for begging paupers. In the eighteenth century, the elements of this system seem to have worked well together—at least well enough to make incarcerations or mass expulsions of itinerants appear unnecessary. By the 1830s, the customary mode of beggar management in Ōno came under strain because an increasing presence of criminal male drifters was tipping the balance from harmless beggars to suspicious vagrants. The domain government reacted to growing popular resentment against beggars by restricting the act of begging, paving the way for more rigorous bans after the Meiji Restoration.

Ōno domain seems to have been comparatively open to itinerant outsiders, perhaps in part because it was located in a region of scattered lordship. Because beggars were among the most unfettered and disorderly elements in Tokugawa society, most lords sought to keep them out of their lands and sometimes deported them, especially at times of famine.[5] On paper, Ōno's government also drove a hard line against mendicant

2. The original reading of this Buddhist term was *kotsujiki*, but during the early modern period it gradually changed to *kojiki*; *Nihon kokugo daijiten*.
3. Ōno machi ezu, 1730, SSM.
4. Tsukada, *Kinsei Nihon mibunsei no kenkyū*, 35–38.
5. Kikuchi, *Kinsei no kikin*, 223–33.

outsiders. But in practice, its officials usually tolerated the temporary presence of begging strangers, especially those from nearby mountain villages. The most likely reason is that the domain authorities acknowledged the economic interdependencies and social relationships that had developed between mountain villages and the settlements on the plain, and they did not see all forms of itinerancy as equally harmful. Ōno's lord probably benefited from showing lenience toward downtrodden outsiders because his own subjects depended on access to the towns and villages of neighboring domains, and the lord cared about his reputation as a benevolent ruler.

Winter Beggars

In Tokugawa Japan, poor people gathered alms in many different guises, and begging customs varied widely across regions. The Ōno area was known for the custom of seasonal begging, which was not practiced in many other parts of Japan. In the villages around Mt. Hakusan, poor mountain farmers endured the snowy winter months by collecting alms on the plains of Ōno, Fukui, Mino, and Kaga. Folklorists have labeled these people "Ushikubi beggars," after a cluster of villages where the phenomenon was particularly conspicuous.[6] "Echizen meisekikō," a gazetteer of 1815, offered the following explanation:

> Ushikubi is extremely deep in the mountains and a lot of snow falls during the winter months, which is why all the houses, beginning with the village's rich man Jūrōemon, have three floors and are sturdily built. . . . The poor, who lack reserves of firewood and food, lodge with the landlord, and the strong and healthy ones also go to Fushimi, Ōtsu and so on to work over the winter. Besides, among those who usually live in cabins in the mountains, the old and young ones and the women go to Fukui and beg for food, and wait for the snow to thaw before they return to their

6. Yanagita, "Mino Echizen ōfuku," 94–126; Yanagita, *Sanson seikatsu no kenkyū*, 72–73; Miyamoto et al., *Nihon zankoku monogatari*, vol. 1, 78–79; Miyamoto, "Shiramine sonki," 131–67; Chiba and Saigusa, "Chūbu Nihon Hakusanroku jūmin"; Yamaori, *Kojiki no seishinshi*, 65–85.

villages. Although this is true for all the mountain dwellers in the area of Uchinami and Anama and not limited to Ushikubi alone, in Fukui they are all referred to as "people from Ushikubi."[7]

According to this source, only the poorer residents of the mountain villages went away during the winter because they lacked sufficient reserves and had no houses to brave the heavy snow (fig. 10). Social hierarchies in mountain villages such as Ushikubi, Nagano, and Itoshiro were steep, with few wealthy landowner-traders on top, some smallholders in the middle, and many bond servants and landless tenants underneath. In 1850, 380 out of 480 households in Ushikubi worked as swidden farmers, lumberjacks, and charcoal burners, spending the summer deep in the mountains in makeshift cabins. Many of these went begging during the winter.[8] In Sunodani village, in the Meiji period, about 10 percent of the population practiced seasonal begging; in years of bad harvest, these numbers tended to increase.[9] The seasonal beggars were not necessarily the most miserable among the village poor. The truly downtrodden remained at home throughout the year, going around the village every day to ask for alms—a form of mutual aid within the community that was granted to children of poor families in Ushikubi and to widows in Ohara and Yokokura.[10] Still, the seasonal beggars typically belonged to the villages' underclass of tenant farmers (*jinago*), and peasants of a certain social standing refused to do it no matter how desperate their situation.[11]

The people of inner Echizen seem to have regarded winter begging as something akin to seasonal labor. In 1838, one of Ōno's town elders remarked that "extremely poor people from the countryside of this domain are going into town to beg, for winter earning [*fuyukasegi*] during the snowy season."[12] In 1807, a year of scarcity, the village community of

7. Inoue Yokushō, *Shintei Echizen no kuni meisekikō*, 338.

8. *Shiramine sonshi*, vol. 2, 436–37; Imanishi, "Bunmeika to 'Ushikubi kojiki,'" 353–58.

9. Chiba and Saigusa, "Chūbu Nihon Hakusanroku jūmin," 278. On seasonal begging in bad years, see also Kikuchi, *Kikin kara yomu kinsei shakai*, 294–95.

10. Saku, *Echizen no kuni shūmon ninbetsu on-aratamechō*, vol. 2, 1025; Chiba and Saigusa, "Chūbu Nihon Hakusanroku jūmin," 262, 266–69, 277.

11. Chiba and Saigusa, "Chūbu Nihon Hakusanroku jūmin," 277.

12. MT goyōdome 1838.10.6, SSM.

FIGURE 10 Uchinami village buried in snow, 1963. Courtesy of Ōno-shi Shōgai Gakushū Center.

Kami-Uchinami (Gujō domain) in a remote branch of the Anama Valley, wrote in a petition that "among the extremely poor in this village, the strong-bodied go away for work or begging, but old people and those who cannot walk find it difficult to survive."[13] In practice, mendicancy and casual labor often overlapped because villagers who left as laborers over the winter begged while out of work, whereas those who begged sometimes repaid their benefactors by doing little favors around the house.[14] Unlike the Koshirō, the mountain farmers practiced begging as a temporary livelihood, not as a status-relevant occupation. They did not maintain turfs, even though many of them developed personal ties with particular households of givers. In the Kansai region, where Ushikubi's geographical location was completely unknown and the name was associated with cattle (Ushikubi literally meant "ox head"), the seasonal

13.   Osukui hiedai kudasare-jō, 1807, Oka Nioji-ke monjo. Yanagita Kunio's field report of 1937 also includes a brief reference to the situation in this valley; *Sanson seikatsu no kenkyū*, 72–73.

14.   Chiba and Saigusa, "Chūbu Nihon Hakusanroku jūmin," 265–66, 270, 282.

laborers had an outcaste-like reputation,[15] but in Fukui, givers tended to empathize with their difficult lot. "Ushikubi-mono" (on the Ōno plain also "Uchinami-mono" after the name of the branch valley in Anama) had become something of a trademark here, and there even were impostors who tried to take advantage of the mountain people's good name.[16] Folklorists have been struck by the fact that people on the plains of Echizen, Mino, and Kaga were willing to give alms to seasonal beggars who did not reciprocate by performing rituals, dances, or songs,[17] but this does not necessarily mean reciprocity was completely absent. Givers might have understood their handouts as a meritorious act, and many merchants in Ōno town did business with mountain villagers and thus had an economic stake in the survival of these communities.

Land-Based Communities and the Loss of Registration

The Ushikubi beggars were an unusual phenomenon even by Tokugawa standards, but they were not the only commoners who begged for alms in Ōno domain. The domain government took for granted that some of the poorer villagers and townspeople gathered alms to support themselves through tough times. Sometimes, officials even recommended begging to reduce expenses for hunger relief. In the winter of 1767–68, for example, Ōno's government repeatedly disbursed relief loans to starving villagers, but toward the spring, when the weather improved and reserves started to run low, it denied these loans to "people who were capable of going begging et cetera," and reserved them for "sick and old people who could not walk."[18] Ōno was not alone among domains to issue such specific

---

15.   Ibid., 265–66, 269–70.

16.   Ibid., 266.

17.   Yamaori, *Kojiki no seishinshi*, 81–85; Chiba and Saigusa, "Chūbu Nihon Haku-sanroku jūmin," 270, 296–305.

18.   This case is included in the precedent manual for town governors, meaning that administrators used it as a guideline; see Tsutomekata oboegaki Tamura-hikae, 1810, TKM. For another example, see MT goyōdome 1741.2.3, SSM.

orders.[19] To be sure, no self-respecting lord would have wanted his peasants to turn into beggars on a mass scale because such a phenomenon would have been interpreted as a sign of economic and administrative collapse.[20] But Ōno's government tolerated and recommended begging in ordinary times, too. Begging could be beneficial for the domain if it enabled poor households to overcome a temporary crisis and retain their viability as taxpayers. The domain did not take issue with almsgiving either and only restricted it when it saw the need to enforce frugality. But even Ōno's standard set of sumptuary regulations for peasants and townspeople in the nineteenth century included the following item: "It goes without saying that mutual help among relatives and old friends is important, but almsgiving to widows and orphans, blind people, and beggars is also a most virtuous act. It is therefore not an issue on which thrift should be applied. Taking pleasure in almsgiving according to one's station is appropriate."[21]

Domain and commoner officials seem to have shared an understanding that poor people could be expected to help themselves through begging. At least this is suggested by a number of materials from the late eighteenth century. In 1789, for example, the headmen of the town's branch village Kanazuka submitted the following petition to request relief for the starving family of a man called Okubei:

> Okubei of Kanazuka village has been able to survive until today thanks to the relief granted to him by the lord after our earlier petition [about ten days ago], and we are very grateful. As we also reported the other day, he is sick and hence completely unable to work, and as he cannot even walk he is not capable of begging in town either. His son has barely turned ten this year, and the family has been lying sick since the tenth month of last year for inexplicable reasons. We therefore agreed among the villagers to each provide them gradually with a little bit of mutual aid [*gōriki*]. But we

19.   Fukaya, *Hyakushō naritachi*, 56–57; Kikuchi, *Kikin kara yomu kinsei shakai*, 305–6.

20.   Kikuchi, *Kikin no shakaishi*, 58–63; Kikuchi, *Kinsei no kikin*, 168–72, 223–33; Namikawa, *Kinsei Hokuō shakai to minshū*, 107–15, 237–82; Kurihara, "Kinsei bikō chochiku no keisei to sonraku shakai," 30–31.

21.   1799, reissued in 1830; MT goyōdome 1799.3.1, YH 480, 334; 1830, second month, YH 649, 467.

have been a poor village to begin with, and have now reached a point at which we cannot take care of them any longer. So we have no choice but to appeal to the lord's benevolence once again, and ask him to provide them with relief.[22]

This petition, which was granted, suggests that both villagers and domain officials would have found it perfectly natural to see Okubei beg for alms in the town had he been physically fit enough to do so. Kanazuka as a whole struggled during those years, and begging had emerged as a survival strategy because mutual aid in the community was faltering. According to a journal entry from the summer of 1777, all Kanazuka villagers were "extremely poor," had no food, and four or five of them were going begging.[23] In a similar case of 1786, this time from one of the central *chō* of the town, a man described as "extremely poor" petitioned to be released from the obligation to feed a female relative, whom the authorities had placed in his custody for supervision. But the town governor had a different idea. He told the town elder that if the man was poor, the *chō* headman should allow him to walk around the neighborhood and beg for alms.[24]

The town governor's word choice in the latter case is significant. He used the verb *minogasu* (to overlook), suggesting that although the poor man was not in a position to behave like a beggar, he could still be allowed to collect alms in the town with the tacit permission of his local headman. If even the town governor encouraged such arrangements in some cases, it seems safe to assume that the informal overlooking of begging townspeople was fairly common. Officially, the only people who were permitted to beg in the town were persons of beggar status and members of legitimate mendicant associations, including monks and nuns. Ōno's authorities also acknowledged that some poor townspeople "became [monks or nuns] in order to survive [through begging]," and allowed

22. MT goyōdome 1789.2.5, 2.14, 2.17, SSM.
23. Goyōki 1778.7.26, Miyazawa Yoshizaemon-ke monjo (probably a town governor's journal).
24. MT goyōdome 1785.12.15, 1786.3.11, SSM. On temporary begging permits in Kaga domain, see, for example, Tanaka, "Kaidai," in *Teihon: Kaga-han hisabetsu buraku kankei shiryō shūsei*, 684.

such people to collect alms while remaining on the town register.[25] This phenomenon is well documented for Osaka, where the status of lay monk or nun (*dōshinmono*) provided townspeople who did not want to join a temple community with the option to live and beg as observant Buddhists.[26] For townspeople who hoped to gather alms for only a limited period of time, such a profound change of persona and demeanor must have appeared inconvenient. They benefited more from being "overlooked."

Despite such exceptions, street begging does not appear to have been regarded as an acceptable long-term solution to a poor townsperson's problems. When prospects of recovery were dim and the burden of support became overwhelming, landlords, relatives, and neighbors in Ōno town could decide to reject their caretaking responsibilities altogether and remove individuals and even entire households from the population register. The cruelty of such a decision was obvious to everyone involved, but sometimes households believed they had no choice if they wanted to maintain their standing as full hereditary members of their status communities. Although status groups could subsidize weak households and tenants temporarily, they could not allow such assistance to destabilize the other households within the group. In the Tokugawa period, the institution of the hereditary household was no longer limited to warriors, imperial aristocrats, and other elites; many peasants and townspeople tried to build them and sometimes made great strides to perpetuate them over time.[27] Yet established hereditary households remained elusive for many members of the urban underclass. As research on Osaka has shown, urban back-alley tenants were especially vulnerable to common blows of fate, such as illness or the death of the main income earner. They moved frequently and were ready to break up or reconfigure their households in

25. Ōno's domain administration asked prospective lay monks or nuns to report their change of status to the town elders informally, but continued to treat them as townspeople on paper and also required them to pay taxes on their houses; see MT goyōdome 1787.3.26, SSM.

26. Tsukada, "Mibunteki shūenron—Kanjin no heizon o tegakari to shite," 195–208.

27. In 1853, the household of a tenant in Ōno town was reestablished by a relative seventeen years after it had been wiped out during the Tenpō famine; see Shoganshodome 1853, fourth month, SSM.

order to secure a tenancy, support a relative, or gain some other temporary advantage.[28]

A removal from the population register was a major intervention, one the town officials did not undertake lightly. The town elders' journal of 1740 includes the case of townsman Kichisaburō, who was described as extraordinarily impoverished. He had been forced to sell his house, which stood on another person's piece of land, and his wife had left him to live with another man from the same *chō*, taking one of their two sons with her. Although Kichisaburō had asked around for a place to rent, his efforts had been unsuccessful, and as the time of the annual registration check was approaching, his former landlady filed a petition to have him deleted from the register. The town elders hesitated to transmit the petition to the town governor, hoping that Kichisaburō might be able to return to his native village, but the *chō* headman informed them that the man could not go there because he was "extraordinarily poor, and did not have food even for a day." Eventually, the officials of the block association removed both Kichisaburō and his son from the register as beggars in a procedure called "beggar deletion" (*kojikibarai*).[29]

Kichisaburō's case gives some insight into the situation of extremely poor households in Ōno town, especially those of tenants, who were probably the most vulnerable to such abandonment. For a family unit in distress, the first step was to pawn or sell its belongings. But if the family owned a house or land, it often held on to them until the bitter end, even though tenancy would have been a feasible alternative. Once it became clear to the family that it could no longer survive as a unit, it broke up, and its members moved into the households of different relatives or went into service.[30] One can see this pattern play out in another case from the 1740s. A poor widow with two children tried to keep herself afloat by sending her daughter into service, but she eventually lost the ability to pay the tax on her house and reached the verge of starvation. Only then did she decide to sell her house, but not without confronting fierce objections

28. Tsukada, "Kinsei kōki Osaka ni okeru toshi kasō minshū no seikatsu sekai," 94–98.

29. MT goyōdome 1740, third month, 4.3, SSM.

30. On the temporary disintegration of impoverished households, see also Saitō Hiroko, "Kinsei Izumi no sonraku shakai ni okeru 'konkyūnin' kyūsai," 311–17.

from her relatives and daughter and fighting off her own fears that the loss of her house might result in her turning into "a beggar."[31]

Cases of this kind were recorded in the petition books of the town elders, because to move into another household or take in relatives from outside, townspeople needed to submit a petition for changing the household's entry in the population register. So-called registration requests (*ninbetsunegai*) went up from the landlord to the headman of the block association and from there on to the town elders and town governor. The complete loss of registration was tantamount to a transition from townspeople status to the status of an unregistered person, which was associated with begging and vagrancy and described by terms such as *hinin, mushuku* (person without a home), or *muninbetsu-mono* (person without a registration).[32] As Kichisaburō's case illustrates, the town elders did not transmit such petitions to the town governor unless they had confirmed that every material and social resource had been exhausted to keep the person on the books. Getting approval for a beggar deletion was not easy. Unlike other registration issues, it needed to be approved by the Council of Vassals (*retsuza*), the highest decision-making body in the domain.[33] If the person in question had absconded, petitioners needed to let some time pass and state that they had undertaken a careful search. Villagers who begged in the castle town during the winter did not usually have their registration deleted, and the town officials and Koshirō were quite suspicious of villages claiming to have deleted a resident who appeared to be begging only on a casual basis.[34] Villages in the Ōno area practiced beggar deletions as well, and here, too, the domain expected

31.   MT goyōdome 1741, first month, SSM.

32.   These terms could refer to the same person, but *hinin* emphasized the act of begging, whereas *mushuku* emphasized the lack of a permanent home and registration. Not all people labeled *mushuku* begged for alms; see Tsukada, *Kinsei Nihon mibunsei no kenkyū*, 300-4.

33.   According to the town governor's precedent manual, where poverty deletion is clearly distinguished from disinheritance; see Tsutomekata oboegaki Tamura-hikae, 1810, TKM.

34.   MT goyōdome 1784.4.24, 4.25, YH 197, 152–53; MT goyōdome 1785.7.12, SSM; MT goyōdome 1789.2.2, 2.3, YH 343, 255.

communities to exercise strict oversight to ensure that taxpaying peasants did not abandon their land.[35]

Petitions for beggar deletion were submitted by the headman of the block association, meaning that by the point they reached the town elders, the *chō* had already decided to reject its responsibility for the pauper in question. The town elders served as a buffer. They could urge *chō* members and relatives to reconsider their decision and resume the search for solutions. In the famine year of 1837, a town elder reminded a man: "They say that [this orphan] is your wife's niece, and because she is becoming a beggar now, it would be truly inhuman [*jingai*] of you to look on as you abandon her."[36] The elders ordered landlords and headmen to contact relatives for support and sometimes appointed caretakers from the family with the backing of the town governor, although the latter was reluctant to be drawn into such town-internal matters.[37] They also tried to de-escalate critical situations by making certain exceptions for people suffering from poverty. For example, once Ōno's town elder on duty obtained tacit permission from the town governor for a day laborer under house arrest to leave his home clandestinely to go to work. On another occasion, he provided a small loan from his own pocket to a man who needed more aid than the government was willing to provide.[38] The deletion of a townsperson from the register often came after town officials had tried but failed to mobilize the pauper's personal safety net. In most of these cases, the relatives were either too poor to take in additional mouths to feed or they had dissociated themselves from their care-taking obligations by formally breaking off relations through divorce (*rien, ribetsu*) or, between blood relatives, through a legal procedure called *gizetsu* (literally: cutting the bond of obligation).[39] There seems to have been

---

35. See, for example, MT goyōdome 1787.1.21, SSM; Murayaku shoyōdome, 1810.10.20, Komori Seibei-ke monjo.

36. MT goyōdome 1837.10.27, SSM.

37. MT goyōdome 1740, third month/3.16; 1837.10.27, 11.9, 11.14, 11.18, SSM; MT goyōdome 1784.11.16, 11.21, YH 237, 171–72.

38. MT goyōdome 1785.2.5, 1838, 14.16, SSM.

39. MT goyōdome 1740, third month/4.3; 1837.11.9, SSM. On impoverished or overburdened caretakers, see MT goyōdome 1786.3.11, 1837.10.27, 11.14, 11.18, SSM; MT goyōdome 1853.7.21, AHM.

little the town elders could do besides persuasion when relatives had resorted to cutting bonds.

The following petition is a typical, highly formulaic example of a request for poverty deletion (*hinkyūbarai*) or beggar deletion (*kojikibarai, monogoibarai*) by an Ōno townsperson:

Written Petition Submitted in Fearful Deference

Item: My tenant Yoemon, his wife, and his sons Onomatsu and Ukichi, four
   people in total, have always been poor, but in recent years they have
   fallen on extremely hard times. They left the house in the late second
   month of this year and have not returned. I subsequently searched
   for them everywhere but do not know their whereabouts. I believe
   that they have probably become beggars, and for the future would like
   to remove them from the population register and the town. I would
   be grateful if the authorities would mercifully order as I requested.

Petitioner: Gisaburō, resident of

1852, fourth month   Gobanmachi and landlord in
                          Sanbanmachi
                  Yohei, headman of Sanbanmachi

To the [town] governor[40]

The precedent manual of the town elders' assistants included a template for petitions for beggar deletion and offered a helpful menu of set phrases for inexperienced administrators, such as "my son so-and-so has suddenly left home," "he went into service at this and that place in such-and-such year and has disappeared from there," or "he has gone on a pilgrimage."[41] By the time this manual was created, the procedure of beggar deletion in Ōno could apparently be applied to many different kinds of absconding. It also resembled other forms of removal (*ninbetsubarai*) from the population register such as disinheritance (*kandō*) and expulsion as punishment.[42] In all of these cases, relatives, landlords, and neighbors

---

40.   Shogandome 1852, fourth month, SSM; MT goyōdome 1852, 4.16, SSM. See also Shoganshodome 1853, fourth month, SSM.

41.   Yōroku, 1852, SSM.

42.   On disinheritance, see Ooms, *Tokugawa Village Practice*, 43–49. In Ōno, punishments of expulsion included expulsion from town or village (*machibarai* or *muraba-*

were simultaneously released from their responsibility for supervision and their responsibility for economic support. While disinheritance and expulsions were undertaken on the premise that the excluded ones might commit a crime, beggar deletions were primarily a safeguard against the possibility that they got sick or died on the road and became a financial burden on their community. The distinction mattered when absconders returned home and asked to be reentered into the register. For people who had been expelled for a misdemeanor, and to a lesser extent also for those who had been disinherited, readmission was a difficult process that usually required a pardon from the lord, preferably on the occasion of a public amnesty.[43] But people who returned to Ōno after a beggar deletion were immediately readmitted if they disclosed the itinerary of their travels and convincingly stated that "they had persevered without committing any crimes abroad." It did not matter that in some of these cases years had passed since the removal of the name.[44]

Beggar Hospices and Their Internees

The domain government showed its goodwill toward beggars in the castle town by maintaining two charitable institutions: a beggar hospice and rice gruel kitchens during the winter months (the latter is discussed in chapter 5). Beggar hospices were the most common institution of indoor relief in Tokugawa Japan. There were precursors as early as the time of the ancient Ritsuryō state (seventh century and later), and some Tokugawa Japanese associated their contemporary hospices with these ancient antecedents. The beggar guilds of Osaka, for example, invented a founding

---

rai), expulsion from the domain (*ryōbunbarai*), and expulsion from the province (*kunibarai*). *Kunibarai* also banned entry to the "three metropolises" Edo, Kyoto, and Osaka.

43. On amnesties, see MT goyōdome 1740, several petitions from the fifth month; 1855.12.16, SSM; MT shogandome 1852, second month, SSM; Hiramatsu, *Kinsei keiji soshōhō no kenkyū*, 1023–55.

44. MT shogandome 1852, fourth month; MT goyōdome 1852.4.21, and twelfth month; MT goyōdome 1855.8.16, SSM; MT goyōdome 1853.9.16, AHM. Several townspeople who had left during the Tenpō famine returned a few years later and were reinscribed into the register; see MT goyōdome 1838.i4.26, 1841.2.6, 2.26, SSM.

narrative for themselves that placed one of their compounds in the tradition of one of the country's oldest and most prestigious relief facilities. According to legend, Prince Shōtoku (574–622), an imperial regent renowned for his Buddhist piety and Confucian benevolence, set up four charitable halls inside the precinct of Shitennōji temple, on the margins of what later became part of the city of Osaka: the Keiden'in, a place of prayer; the Seyakuin, a dispensary of medicinal herbs; the Ryōbyōin, a medical hospital for people without kin; and the Hiden'in, a hospice for paupers, orphans, and widows. Although there is no reliable evidence of Prince Shōtoku's involvement, the emperors of the seventh and eighth centuries did indeed operate institutions of this kind, and the beggar bosses of Osaka's Tennōji beggar compound claimed to be the successors of Prince Shōtoku's Hiden'in. They maintained that the prince had asked their ancestors living in the hospice to help with distributing alms to unorganized beggars at yet another charitable hall at the temple and to serve as "beggar rulers" (*hinin tsukasa*) in the two provinces around Osaka in return for regular compensation.[45]

In reality, there was no institutional continuity between the Tennōji beggar compound and Prince Shōtoku's ancient hospices. Through Shōtoku, the beggar bosses hoped to associate themselves with the nearby Shitennōji temple, which had been founded by the prince and was sufficiently grounded in tradition to help the beggar bosses defend their independence against Osaka's powerful community of leatherworking outcastes. Although the narrative was a fiction, it must have sounded persuasive because Buddhist temples had been leaders of beggar relief throughout the Middle Ages. In the Heian period, temples gradually stepped in for the declining imperial state and expanded their charity for beggars. Eison and Ninshō, two monks of the Ritsu sect, constructed large hospices for beggars and lepers and organized self-governing beggar associations on behalf of the Kamakura shogunate. Many medieval beggar groups sought the protection of temples and shrines to benefit from their political power.[46] The main *hinin* settlement

45. Ikeda, *Nihon shakai fukushishi*, 62; Tsukada, "Hinin–Kinsei Osaka no hinin to sono yuisho," 237–53.
46. Matsuo, *Chūsei no toshi to hinin*; Amino, *Chūsei no hinin to yūjo*, 64–84; Shinmura, *Nihon iryō shakaishi no kenkyū*, 1–46; Ikeda, *Nihon shakai fukushishi*, 81–86.

of early modern Kyoto and some of Osaka's and Sakai's beggar compounds were named Hiden'in or Hidenji after medieval temples that operated relief hospices for beggars in those areas.[47] It also seems likely that some of the early members of Osaka's beggar guilds had been affiliated with relief institutions of Christian missionaries in the late sixteenth century.[48] The beggar hospices of the Tokugawa period, however, were not usually run by temples but by warrior and town officials as well as beggar bosses.

The exact founding date of Ōno's hospice—the so-called *hiningoya* (beggar hut)—is unknown. But the building already appears on a town map of 1730 in a location in northern Shibanmachi (see fig. 11).[49] Unlike in the neighbor domain Katsuyama, the hospice was not also the residence of the hereditary beggar bosses, and it was located outside the Eastern Village.[50] As suggested in the previous chapter, it was probably established in an earlier hunger year to feed and control beggars who had come to the castle town in search of alms. The lord paid for the thatching and other repairs to the building, and there are instances of the hospice being referred to as *osukuigoya*, "seigneurial relief hut."[51] Yet the hospice was more than a product of the lord's benevolence because the townspeople and the Koshirō also contributed to its operation. Its function was quite narrow and must be understood in the larger context of Ōno's management of mendicancy.

47. Yamamoto, "Senshū no Sakai 'shikasho' chōri," 71; Sugahara, "Kinsei zenki Kyoto no hinin," 179–83.

48. Seventeenth-century registers reveal an unusually high number of former Christians in at least two of Osaka's beggar compounds; see Tsukada, *Osaka no hinin—Kojiki/Shitennōji/Korobi-kirishitan*, 25–74. On Christian charity in sixteenth-century Japan, see, for example, Ikeda, *Nihon shakai fukushishi*, 86–88; Tsuji, *Ōita-ken no shakai fukushi jigyōshi*, 1–29. On Christianity in a beggar community in Wakayama, see Fujimoto Seijirō, *Jōkamachi sekai no seikatsushi*, 322–25.

49. Ōno machi ezu, 1730, SSM. Many urban beggar hospices were founded in the last three decades of the seventeenth century, such as in Wakayama (1697), Iida (1675–76), and Kanazawa (1670).

50. Katsuyama town had two very large beggar households, referred to as *hiningoya*, which also took in sick beggars; see "Nedoshi shūmon on-aratame iekazu hitokazu oboe," 1756, *Katsuyama shishi*, Shiryō-hen 1, 630–31.

51. MT goyōdome 1784, second month, SSM; 1853.7.21, 7.26, AHM.

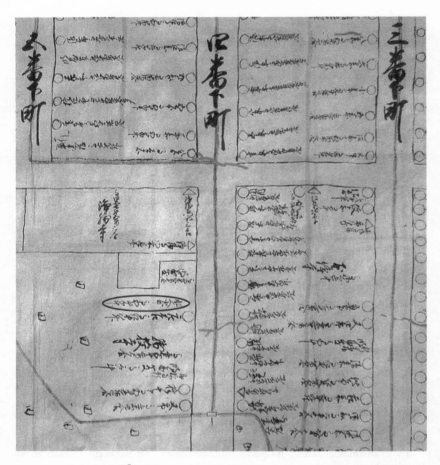

FIGURE 11 Location of Ōno's beggar hospice (*hiningoya*), circled, in Shibanmachi on the map "Ōno machi ezu," 1730. *Source:* SSM.

The beggar hospice of Ōno belonged to a spectrum of mostly urban institutions that went by a variety of names and were intended to control and rescue people without community ties.[52] This spectrum included

52. The permanent beggar hospices of Edo and Osaka, which also interned sick prisoners, were known as *tame* (gathering place). Other typical names for institutions on this spectrum were *segyōgoya* (hut for almsgiving, Morioka), *kaihōgoya* (nursing hut, Edo), and *(on)jihigoya* (compassionate hut, Tottori); see Kikuchi, *Kikin kara yomu kinsei*

everything from facilities that confined and rehabilitated vagrants to hospices for the sick and disabled, workhouses, group residences for beggars, and temporary famine shelters. The emphasis of each facility could shift over time. Ikeda Yoshimasa has described this type of relief as *yōmin* (literally: "nourishing the people"), following the terminology of Yamaga Sokō, a Confucian thinker of the late seventeenth century. Sokō argued that the ruler was responsible for providing three types of relief, which corresponded to three different stages of destitution: relief loans (*shintai*) for poverty prevention, relief grants (*shinshi*) for poverty relief, and *yōmin*, the relief of uprooted people.[53] The ultimate goal of nourishing the people was the reintegration of paupers into a status group, preferably as a productive commoner, not a mendicant. But there were always some internees who could not be rehabilitated, and over time, many temporary shelters developed into permanent hospices to provide such helpless people with a home.

The preference for rehabilitation is clearly reflected, for example, in the history of Kanazawa's beggar hospice, one of the largest institutions of this kind. The Kanazawa hospice (*hiningoya*) was established in 1670 with the explicit goal of putting uprooted commoners to work and preparing them for resettlement as peasants. It did not accept the sick and abandoned, who were placed under the rule of the beggar bosses to permanently live as beggars. By the late eighteenth century, however, the old hospice had developed into an institution of relief for helpless people without relatives, and an additional hospice (*osukuigoya*) was set up for poor commoners with prospects of rehabilitation as member of a village or block association.[54] Ōno domain, by contrast, did not have more than one shelter, which thus had to serve a variety of purposes: caring for temporary beggars from within the domain, nursing sick vagrants until they could be expelled, and permanently housing helpless commoners without kin.

---

shakai, 289–312; Tsukada, *Kinsei Nihon mibunsei no kenkyū*, 244–46, 288–89; Tanaka Shinji, "Tottori-han ni okeru 'zaichū' hiningashira," part 1, 20. See also Fujimoto Seijirō, *Jōkamachi sekai no seikatsushi*, 143–72, 251–79, 337–42.

53. Ikeda, *Nihon shakai fukushishi*, 96–105; Yamaga, "Yamaga gorui," 62–69.

54. Tanaka Yoshio, "Kaidai," in *Teihon: Kaga-han hisabetsu buraku kankei shiryō shūsei*, 679–88; Tanaka Yoshio, "Kaga-han hiningoya-sei seiritsu no jijō ni tsuite," 45–67; McClain, *Kanazawa*, 127–29.

In Ōno's case, the domain lord seems to have played a leading role in founding the hospice in the castle town. According to an order of 1847, "the lord's intention was to build a shelter to relieve those among beggars who are sick or of old or young age, and thus suffer exceptional distress."[55] On the other hand, much of the relief provided at the hospice was actually funded by townspeople. One major purpose of the facility was to take care of sick beggars who had collapsed in the castle town. While these beggars were recovering inside the hospice, they received rice gruel, paid for by the owner of the land on which they had been found, and sometimes collectively by all townspeople.[56] For example, in 1784, the townsman Masuya Mokichi paid for the board (and later burial) of a beggar in the hospice, a young boy who had been lying on his field.[57] In another case of the same year, townsman Manjūya Kiemon discovered a sixty-year-old male beggar lying sick under the eaves of his house, accompanied by a daughter and toddler grandson. Domain officials ordered Kiemon to feed the sick man and transfer him to the beggar hospice in case the Koshirō classified him as a beggar, and he appears to have remained in the facility until the Koshirō brought in two men from his home village to pick him up.[58] If sick beggars were discovered on temple, shrine, domain, or vassal land, the domain seems to have paid for their care.[59]

Townspeople's payments on behalf of hospice occupants suggest that the town community was directly involved in the facility. In fact, Ōno's hospice was a typical example of collaboration between the lord and various status groups, in this case the block associations and beggar bosses. Despite the hospice's role as a site of seigneurial compassion, it also was a communal institution in the sense that it helped the townspeople fulfill their collective obligation of providing aid to sick travelers. According to laws first issued by Shogun Tsunayoshi in 1687/88 as part of his larger

55.   MT goyōdome 1847.8.21, YH 939, 693.

56.   In 1860, sick beggars in the hospice received rations of three *gō* rice a day; see MT goyōdome 1860.7.21, SSM.

57.   MT goyōdome 1784.7.27, YH 217, 164.

58.   MT goyōdome 1784.11.28, YH 186, 144. See also MT goyōdome 1784.2.30, YH 192, 149–50.

59.   MT goyōdome 1784.5.28, YH 201, 155; 6.2, YH 203, 155–56; 6.26, YH 207, 159; 1784.8.15, YH 221, 166; 1784.12.26, YH 242, 173; 1786.11.9, SSM.

agenda of promoting compassion, village and town communities were required to look after sick travelers and, if the strangers so requested, send them home via village or post station relay and share the cost of transportation.[60] Communities of house-owning commoners were also obliged to take care of unregistered sick travelers unless they had a beggar hospice to accommodate them.

In Osaka, a city under direct shogunal control, the city governors decided in 1773 to ease the townspeople's burden by establishing a new hospice for "unregistered beggars who had fallen sick." The new infirmary, which was in addition to an earlier facility catering to unregistered people and sick prisoners, was operated by members of Osaka's four beggar associations, and its costs were split between the shogunate and the townspeople. The townspeople paid for the initial construction of the hospice, equipment such as stretchers and straw mats, and compensation for the outcaste-supervisors. The shogunate funded subsequent repairs, rice gruel, lamp oil, and medicine.[61] Before the creation of this hospice, the block associations had taken care of sick beggars on their own, though they could transfer them to the beggar guilds for a negotiated fee.[62] The intervention of 1773 thus formalized the respective obligations of shogunate, *chō*, and outcastes and integrated them in a jointly operated, public institution of beggar relief.

In Ōno, the respective burdens of lord, townspeople, and beggar guild were distributed somewhat differently. Here, the domain was responsible for "miscellaneous expenses" with regard to the hospice building and medical treatment for unregistered travelers, whereas the townspeople paid all other items pertaining to sick travelers without a registration.[63] Neither the townspeople nor the domain government seem to have owed the Koshirō a regular amount of money for their work at the hospice. Probably the Koshirō ran it as part of their duty toward the lord and

---

60. Tsukamoto Manabu, *Shōrui o meguru seiji*, 213–15. For detailed studies of assistance mechanisms for sick travelers in the Tokugawa period, see Kouamé, *Pèlerinage et Société*, 115–39; Naitō, "Bakuhanki shomin ryokō to sono hogo shisetsu." Tsunayoshi also turned foundling care into a collective responsibility of the *chō*; see Sugahara, "Kinsei Kyoto no chō to sutego."

61. Hotatsubure 139, 1773.6.20, in *Osaka shishi*, vol. 3, 821–22.

62. Hotatsubure 26, 1734.1.7, in *Osaka shishi*, vol. 3, 341.

63. Yōroku, 1852, SSM.

the townspeople compensated them on a case-by-case basis. Like in Osaka, townspeople treated the hospice as a supplement to the relief practiced through their block associations and used it to outsource the care of unregistered people. Seigneurial relief and urban community relief thus came together in this facility.[64]

From the domain government's point of view, the hospice was an important instrument of orderly and benevolent rule because it sheltered and helped repatriate sick beggars who would have been abandoned otherwise. The townspeople also welcomed the hospice because it released them from the obligation to take care of sick beggars found on their land and spread at least part of the cost to the town community as a whole. The hospice also served the more sobering purpose of hiding human suffering from the public eye. In 1784, a dead beggar woman was rushed into Ōno's hospice because the lord's son was about to pass through the area where she was lying. The town elders ordered the landowner to throw some salt on the spot to cleanse it (probably from death-related pollution), but the case serves as a stark reminder that the beggar hospice helped the townspeople maintain an orderly facade by concealing the bodies of dead and ailing beggars.[65]

Ōno's beggar hospice interned not only travelers from within and without the domain but also local townspeople. The facility served as a form of poorhouse, a space where local paupers could be sent to live as mendicants. In 1852, for example, a widow in Ōno town asked to be admitted to the hospice because she was old and frail and had no relatives to support her.[66] Normally, elderly townspeople were expected to rely on their families, and if they had none, on their block associations, particularly the five-people's groups within it, at least until another caretaking

---

64.   Fujimoto Seijirō describes the beggar hospice of Wakayama both as an "urban caretaking and support system transcending the boundaries of individual *chō*," and a "seigneurial social welfare policy undertaken by the lord that was located outside the urban community and supplemented it"; see Fujimoto Seijirō, *Jōkamachi sekai no seikatsushi*, 266, 277. In Ōno, the *chō* remained in principle responsible for beggar care and still had to act on this responsibility in certain cases; see MT goyōdome 1838.1.10, SSM.

65.   MT goyōdome 1784.7.17, YH 213, 163.

66.   MT goyōdome 1852.12.1, SSM.

arrangement had been found.[67] The need for a caretaker in old age was a frequently cited reason people in the Ōno area asked for permission to move from one household to another and why they petitioned the lord to pardon their expelled or disinherited children.[68] Sometimes, impoverished old people worked as night watchmen on behalf of their block association.[69] But if the *chō* and the family were unable to provide care in the long run, they could force such people to move into a local temple as a disciple or into the beggar hospice.[70] Poor households in the mountain villages could send their relatives to the hospice in the castle town if they were subjects of Ōno domain.[71]

Ōno's domain authorities made a clear and categorical distinction between relief for poor townspeople and relief for beggars. Townspeople who were admitted to the hospice gave up their eligibility for townspeople relief and became recipients of beggar relief. In the case of the widow of 1852, domain officials warned the woman that if she "became a beggar," she would not be able to simultaneously collect starvation aid from the domain, as she requested at the time. Because grants of starvation aid were limited to townspeople, the woman needed to choose whether she wanted to take advantage of the care and begging opportunities in the hospice or remain on the town register and live on starvation aid. The record does not mention which option she chose.[72] The acceptance of townspeople and villagers into the hospice was rarely documented in the town elders' journals, making it difficult to determine how common

67. For cases of old and sick people and orphans receiving support from household groups or villages or *chō*, see Tenmei hachi tomeki, 1783, third month, AHM; MT goyōdome 1784.11.16, YH 237, 171; MT goyōdome 1789.2.5, SSM. A lack of relatives was sometimes cited as the reason a pauper had to resort to aid from the five-people's group; see MT goyōdome 1852.12.21, SSM.

68. MT goyōdome 1740, several petitions from the fifth month, SSM; 1741, fourth month, fifth month, 12.11, SSM.

69. For two cases of poor old men working as neighborhood watchmen, see MT goyōdome 1740.3.5 and third month/3.16, SSM.

70. MT goyōdome 1740, twelfth month; 1769.4.6, 1860.7.4, SSM.

71. MT goyōdome 1784.7.5, YH 209, 160. Two teenagers found dead in 1741 might also have been hospice dwellers; at least they had both been begging in the town for several years; MT goyōdome 1741.10.13 and 11.7, SSM.

72. Compare with a case of 1853, in which officials admonished a poor townsman who asked to send his wife's sick brother to the hospice that if he did so, the brother-in-law would "become an outsider to him"; MT goyōdome 1853.7.21, 7.26, AHM.

this practice might have been. But there were other towns whose beggar hospices also functioned as a community poorhouse and might shed light on Ōno's situation.

Fujimoto Seijirō's study of the beggar hospice in the castle town of Wakayama introduces a number of cases from the eighteenth century in which townspeople asked for admission to the institution themselves or were placed there by relatives and neighbors who could no longer take care of them.[73] Many of them were orphans, poor widows, and elderly people, and often (but not always) they suffered from illnesses, mental conditions, disfiguring ailments, and handicaps such as blindness—chronic and (especially in the case of leprosy) stigmatizing conditions that prevented sufferers from making a living in their communities and posed a major burden on their caretakers.[74] To be sure, none of these health problems invariably resulted in an internment in the hospice. In the Tokugawa period, lepers were more likely to live at home with their families than in segregated leper colonies under the control of beggar bosses.[75] But hospices such as Ōno's and Wakayama's offered an alternative. They eased the burden on households and status groups by forcing the handicapped to support themselves through begging or by stepping in as paid caretakers to relieve family members. To prevent abuse of the system, admission to the hospice required official approval. In Ōno, domain and town officials tried to persuade and sometimes forced reluctant households to look after their orphaned, disabled, and widowed relatives, though the solutions they imposed were not always more charitable because some of the appointed households were clearly too poor to take in more mouths to feed.

The beggar hospice thus reduced the burden on families and block associations. The question is whether it also benefited the internees. Beggar hospices had little in common with medical hospitals. Ōno domain and other domain governments such as Kaga's mobilized town doctors to treat prisoners and travelers (including beggars) as part of the doctors'

---

73. Fujimoto Seijirō, *Jōkamachi sekai no seikatsushi*, 251–79. See also Shōji, "Tenpō no daikikin to Kubota (Akita)-machi ni okeru osukuigoya."

74. On the rejection of lepers as marriage partners and the stigmatization of "leper lineages," see Suzuki Noriko, "Kinsei raibyōkan no keisei to tenkai," 91–96.

75. Suzuki Noriko, "Kinsei raibyōkan no keisei to tenkai," 137–38; Kujirai, "Sendai hanryō no 'raijingoya' ni tsuite," 12–14.

official duty but seem to have limited such treatment to occupants who suffered from acute conditions.[76] Ōno's hospice functioned primarily as a shelter to ensure basic survival. It provided begging opportunities to abandoned townspeople and rice gruel to beggars who were so sick that they could no longer walk and collect alms. During Ōno's long and snowy winters, access to fire was also an important concern, which is why the sources sometimes mention beggars asking townspeople to let them sit by their fires for a while.[77]

No matter how miserable life was inside the hospice, it was preferable to sleeping on the street. Most beggars who gathered around Ōno town appear to have slept beneath verandas, bridges, eaves, or in wooden sheds; often they seem to have done so with the owner's tacit approval.[78] They tended to seek out places located just outside the town settlement because the town's wooden gates were closed overnight. Temple and shrine grounds attracted beggars as well, but there is no reason to assume that religious institutions treated beggars more compassionately than did ordinary peasants or townspeople. For example, the regulations for the caretaking Buddhist priest of the Hakusandō shrine, issued in 1729 most likely by Nakano village, strictly prohibited him from letting "beggars [*kojiki hinin*] or any other polluted rascals and suspicious people" into the shrine. In 1770, the priest of Tokuganji, a temple in the town, complained about beggars (*hinin kojiki nado*) camping on a field next to the temple compound. He tried to acquire this field from the domain so he could expel them more effectively and reduce the risk of fire.[79]

76. "Hiningoya ishi no rōya ishi kennin," in *Teihon: Kaga-han hisabetsu buraku kankei shiryō shūsei* II, B71, 551; McClain, *Kanazawa*, 128. In Ōno, at least one (and perhaps all) of the town doctors were obliged to treat prisoners and sick travelers; MT goyōdome 1784.2.13, 3.11, 3.26, 12.26; 1789.1.3, SSM. On the hospices of Edo, see the entry "Tame," in *Burakushi yōgo jiten*, 196–98.

77. MT goyōdome 1783.12.17; 1785.5.11; 1786.11.9, SSM.

78. Although the townspeople of Ōno were not allowed to host unregistered persons overnight, the town elders' journals mention cases in which they invited them inside; see MT goyōdome 1783.12.17, 1784.4.10, 1785.5.11, 5.12, SSM. On the custom of sleeping outside, see Chiba and Saigusa, "Chūbu Nihon Hakusanroku jūmin," 274–75.

79. "Jōyō gūan sho-dōguchō," *Ōno shishi*, Shaji monjo-hen, 470; Tokuganji monjo, *Ōno shishi*, Shaji monjo-hen, 519–20.

With a capacity of thirty, the hospice appears to have been too small to accommodate all the beggars in the town, and it is unclear to what extent it served them as a winter shelter. Once, in the autumn of 1784, Ōno's town leaders discussed the construction of a new shelter for the homeless to protect them from the cold. It was a famine year, and the castle town had been filled with beggars in the spring and summer months, but after the harvest most of the survivors had returned to their home villages, and only a handful remained. The town elder on duty turned to the town governor and suggested building an additional hospice with funding from the townspeople because he was concerned that these beggars might freeze to death. In the end, no new shelter needed to be erected because the old one turned out to be spacious enough for the number of homeless people still left in town.[80]

The Identification of Beggars and Vagrants

Because beggar relief was different from commoner relief, officials needed to identify beggars before they could provide them with aid. But the identification of beggars was a difficult process. On the one hand, administrators upheld the principle that a beggar was a rootless person without a registration. They assumed that people who begged had been abandoned by their community and could therefore be sent to the beggar hospice or otherwise treated like beggars without compromising their reputation or that of their relatives or neighbors. They also assumed that villages and block associations would not want to pay for the care or burial of an unregistered person. If a dead stranger turned out to be registered, town or village officials had to notify relatives or officials in the home community to let them take the remains back. They also had to honor requests of sick travelers who wished to be sent home via the village relay system (*muratsugi, muraokuri*) mandated by the shogunate.[81] On the other hand, administrators were perfectly aware that many

80. MT goyōdome 1784.9.21 and 10.4, YH 227 and 230, 169.
81. For a detailed discussion of the village relay system on the island of Shikoku, see Kouamé, *Pèlerinage et Société*, 115–39. Examples from Ōno include MT goyōdome 1784.7.1, YH 209, 159–60; MT goyōdome 1834.4.16, 6.11; 1837.4.26, SSM.

beggars did in fact have a registration, and they did not want to withhold aid from people who were obviously suffering. They usually dealt with this dilemma pragmatically: assigning provisional beggar status to people in need and tackling the registration question later.

Ōno's town officials faced the problem that many visitors to the town, especially those from villages in the surrounding area, were not required to carry travel documents, even if they came from another domain. Unlike travelers from far away, these villagers did not need to ask for permission to stay in town overnight. If such visitors fell sick or died in the town, the process of confirming their registration could be costly and time-consuming. Domain and town officials therefore classified dead or ailing travelers on the basis of superficial appearance. They assumed that everyone who looked and behaved like a beggar could temporarily be treated like one. Because they were not usually familiar with the begging strangers in the town, they relied on the judgment of the Koshirō, who kept a sharp eye on the local mendicants and were often quite well informed about their personal background.

In many cases the Koshirō were the first to discover a dead or sick beggar. They were summoned whenever the leader of the town corps, the town elders, or *chō* or village headmen undertook an inspection of an unidentified body. For the town officials of Ōno, identifying a stranger as a beggar and checking his or her registration were two entirely separate procedures. In a case from the Tenmei famine in the 1780s, the town elder gave the Koshirō the following instructions regarding a dead beggar who had been discovered in the castle town: "If you are sure that the man is a beggar, go to Hōkyōji [the man's home village] and let them know. If it turns out there that the man has been excluded from the village community and has no registration, take a written guarantee [from the village officials] before you return."[82] First, the town elder had the Koshirō evaluate physical appearance and past behavior to establish whether they were dealing with a beggar (*hinin, kojiki*) and not some other kind of traveler. In Ōno, the main criteria were whether the person in question carried a bowl or bag to collect alms, wore old or ragged travel clothing, had been observed soliciting alms, and camped outside. These were fairly

---

82. MT goyōdome 1784.4.2, SSM.

universal markers that were also relied on in Kyoto and Shikoku.[83] Second, if the Koshirō knew the name of the home community, the officials had them go there in person and check whether the beggar thus identified was included in the population register. For villages within Ōno domain, officials also established contact through the rural intendant bureau (*daikansho*) and sometimes by sending the owner of the land where the body had been found.[84] If the village officials persuasively declared that the person in question was not on the register, the town officials had little choice but to accept that response.

Officials took identification very seriously and were careful not to make any mistakes. In 1784, the time of the Tenmei famine, a sick woman who had been found on the street was initially denied admission to the beggar hospice solely on the grounds that she was staying with a relative in town and did not camp outside like other beggars.[85] Whenever town elders and governors had any doubts about the identity and registration status of a dead beggar, they ordered a provisional burial (*kariume*) and did not give permission to cremate the body unless they had obtained a written pledge from the deceased's current or former home village that it would not "bring up any objections in the future."[86] For the same reason, officials also insisted the townspeople properly take care of every beggar body. In 1837, during the Tenpō famine, when many beggars were dying in the town, the town elders warned house owners not to neglect reporting dead beggars on their land: "Beggar or not, human life is

83.   See MT goyōdome 1784.4.24, 5.12, YH 197, 152–54; 1784.2.30, YH 192, 149–50; 1784, ii.28, YH 187, 144, and many other examples. For similar procedures in other parts of Japan, see, for example, Sugahara, "Kinsei Kyoto no hinin," 73–75; Murakami, "Kinsei ni okeru kyūsai no sōgo fujoteki seikaku."

84.   MT goyōdome 1784.ii.28, YH 186, 144; 1784.4.24, YH 197, 152–53; 1784.6.2, YH 203, 155–56; 1784.7.5, 7.8, YH 209, 160–61; 1784.7.30, YH 217, 164–65; 1784.8.19, YH 221, 166; 1784.9.4, YH 223, 167; 1784.9.8, YH 224, 167; 1789.2.2, 2.3, YH 343, 255; 1838.1.10, 1.14, SSM.

85.   MT goyōdome 1784.7.1, YH 209, 159–60.

86.   See, for example, MT goyōdome 1784.4.24, YH 197, 152–53. In cases of suspected murder, officials had the body placed in a wooden tub filled with salt; MT goyōdome 1840.10.4, SSM. But unidentified beggars who appeared to have died a natural death probably received a shallow burial; see MT goyōdome 1785.4.6, SSM. Beggar remains were interred on different graveyards or sections of graveyards than were commoners, but these areas were avoided for provisional burials; MT goyōdome 1837.9.4, 1838.1.14, SSM.

extremely precious, and if these were people from another domain who had a registration, we, the town elders, would be accused of misconduct."[87]

Landowners had an incentive for ignoring sick or dead beggars on their land because they were responsible for paying for care and burial in case the person did not have a registration. It seems, though, that at some point the townspeople started to split the cost of beggar burials among themselves, probably to distribute the burden more fairly. The domain government only paid for removals of beggars who had died on vassal or other domain-administered land.[88] Part of the money went to the Koshirō, who were usually the ones to remove beggar bodies, but even landowners who did not wish to hire the Koshirō were expected to pay them money, probably because the Koshirō had monopolized the job and felt entitled to the resulting income.[89]

The responsibility for sick and dead beggars could become a source of tension between Ōno town and the mendicants' home communities. The most contested point was the cost of repatriation. Villagers often lacked the resources to travel to town, pick up their kin, and pay for food or funeral or, alternatively, reimburse the townspeople for their expenses. After all, most beggars had gone to town precisely because their families and communities were unable to provide for them. The town elders' journals of Ōno, especially in years of famine, contain many examples of villagers pleading for a burial in town, of sick beggars trying to prevent officials from contacting their impoverished families, and of village officials pretending that their begging residents no longer had a registration.[90] In one case of 1837, the home village of a deceased beggar was presented with a bill of 11.07 *monme* of silver for burial, six days of care at the hospice, and a fee for the messenger, an amount that could have bought half a bale of rice in the years before the famine.[91]

87.   MT goyōdome 1837.7.28, SSM.

88.   MT goyōdome 1837.4.20, 6.21, 7.1, 7.11, 7.21, 7.25, 7.30, 9.6, 9.16, 9.21, 9.26, 10.22, 11.6, SSM. On the definition of town and village land with regard to beggar burials, see also MT goyōdome 1838.2.1, SSM.

89.   MT goyōdome 1784.6.5, YH 203, 156; 1837.11.6, SSM.

90.   For examples, see MT goyōdome 1784.4.24, 5.26, YH 197 and 200, 152–55; 1789.2.2, YH 343, 255; 1837.7.24, 1838.1.14, SSM.

91.   MT goyōdome 1837.7.24, SSM.

Benevolence and Repression

As these examples show, begging strangers were able to enter Ōno's castle town and receive care when they fell sick. This seems surprising because on paper, Ōno domain did not suffer the presence of mendicant strangers on its territory. A domain order first promulgated in 1717 and reissued in 1847 in no uncertain terms called for the immediate expulsion of peddlers, fortune-tellers, beggars (*monogoi*), and itinerant entertainers.[92] The government was concerned that begging strangers might drain people's pockets and undermine public safety. Beggars from outside the domain seemed especially dangerous because there was no community nearby that could have been held accountable for their behavior. Most domains in the Tokugawa period issued begging bans and expulsion orders against mendicant strangers at some point or another, and at face value these documents convey the impression that begging and itinerancy were being rigorously suppressed.

The actual treatment of begging strangers, however, was much more complex. There was, first, a great deal of local variation. The travelogue of Noda Senkōin, a mountain ascetic (*yamabushi*) from Kyushu, commented on the rigidity of begging policies he encountered as a mendicant pilgrim between 1812 and 1818.[93] Although his account confirms that begging itinerants were controlled more strictly than local beggars, it also reveals that official attitudes and almsgiving customs varied greatly from place to place. After his descent from Mt. Hakusan, Senkōin—a respectable and highly educated pilgrim—also visited the Ōno area, where he seems to have been able to collect alms completely undisturbed.[94] The second point to consider is that most begging bans only addressed aggressive begging and did not deny the collection of alms "on a mutual basis," nor did they cover all modes and types of begging. To be sure, domains occasionally did issue bans that prohibited every kind of

92.   MT goyōdome 1847.8.21, YH 939, 690. The edict the first Doi lord Toshifusa issued on his arrival in Ōno in 1682 also prohibited hosting mendicants and suspicious people; "Tenna ninen machi gōchū e ōsewatasare gojōmoku," *Ōno shishi*, Shoke monjohen 2, 535.

93.   Rotermund, *Pèlerinage aux neuf sommets*, 228–41.

94.   Noda, "Nihon kubu shugyō nikki," in *Ōno shishi*, Shiryō sōkatsu-hen, 756–61.

mendicancy and almsgiving, but most of these were temporary interventions at times of crisis. Most territories tolerated itinerant clerics, entertainers, and paupers if they did not linger and refrained from fraudulent and violent behavior.[95]

Ōno's policy was draconian on paper, but in practice the domain was willing to differentiate between harmless beggars and suspicious vagrants. Although the government would probably have preferred to see no begging strangers at all on its territory, it was inclined to tolerate the presence of beggars from other domains as long as they were truly needy and did not pose any obvious threat. Informal overlooking was characteristic for the domain's approach to mendicancy as a whole. But this strategy could only work because the Koshirō served as an institutional cushion between the beggars and the domain administration. The beggar bosses regulated the beggars' access to the lord's benevolence. They were allowed and even expected to decide who among the begging strangers should be expelled and who could safely be overlooked. At the same time, the bosses would have taken the blame if people they had overlooked later turned out to be harmful criminals or if subjects of other lords complained about repressive treatment.[96]

The beggar bosses were in charge of distributing food to beggars at the annual rice gruel kitchens and could also admit beggars to the hospice, although domain officials claimed final jurisdiction. The Koshirō had clear instructions that beggars who were not subjects of Ōno domain were not acceptable as occupants of the hospice. In 1771, domain officials criticized the guild for hosting an elderly and sick man for several months without checking his travel document, which showed that his home village was in another territory.[97] Nor was the hospice open to people

---

95. See, for example, Nathalie Kouamé's conclusions on the treatment of mendicant pilgrims on the island of Shikoku, *Pèlerinage et Société*, 95–139, 158–60, 185–86; Kouamé, "Shikoku's Local Authorities and Henro"; Kouamé, "Le pèlerinage de Shikoku pendant l'époque d'Edo."

96. Such complaints were quite rare. In one example from 1838, a visiting shamisen player from Kyoto was injured in a fight with townspeople, and the government forced him to leave without granting him medical care or the right to collect compensation. When an envoy arrived to accuse the domain of maltreatment, officials became very defensive and argued that they had mistaken the man for someone "no different from *eta* or *hinin*"; MT goyōdome 1838.6.1, 6.2, 6.3, 6.5, 6.6, 6.7, 6.9, 6.11, 6.12, 7.6, 7.7, SSM.

97. MT goyōdome 1771.12.18, YH 65, 57–58.

without registration. Although unregistered people were allowed to stay in the hospice while sick, the Koshirō had orders to expel them from the town as soon as they regained the ability to walk.[98] This left only abandoned paupers from within Ōno domain as potential long-term residents of the beggar hospice.

The beggar bosses apparently decided at their own convenience whether to overlook an illegal beggar, and they got away with it in most cases. One example is the sad story of a beggar boy who died in Ōno town in 1785, during the Tenmei famine. The boy's body was found outside the gate of Tokuganji temple, and the headman of Gobanmachi was able to identify the child as Shirō, son of a widow in a village deep in the eastern valleys that was part of Gujō domain. Shirō's mother had taken (or perhaps sent) the boy to Ōno town and put in a "request" with a local *chō* headman, who might have been acquainted with her or got involved because his *chō* was adjacent to the mother's family temple.[99] For some of the begging mountain villagers, family temples seem to have served as bridgeheads into Ōno town.[100] The headman testified that he "asked the Koshirō to let the boy beg in town. When the Koshirō told him that they could not do such a thing for a person from another domain, he asked them to please overlook him." The beggar bosses allowed the child to stay.[101]

The Koshirō might have tolerated Shirō in part because he carried a note from his mother, in which she stated that she did not mind having her son buried in town in case he died. This meant that the Koshirō were spared the trip to the boy's home village to notify the relatives. The beggar bosses perceived travels on behalf of sick or dead beggars as a nuisance, particularly if the home community failed to take responsibility. During the Tenmei famine (1783–88), the Koshirō complained about a mountain village in Ōno domain that produced "large numbers" of beggars

98.   MT goyōdome 1784.5.28, YH 201, 155; 1847.8.21, YH 939, 693; 1786.11.9, SSM.

99.   The mother was registered at Chōshōji, a temple of the True Pure Land sect, which served as a head temple of many prayer halls in mountain villages.

100.   When a beggar woman from Kadohara village (Gujō domain) died in Ōno town in 1784, town officials also turned to her family temple Chōshōji for identification; MT goyōdome 1784.3.1, SSM.

101.   MT goyōdome 1785.8.4, SSM. For a comparable case involving a domain "insider," see MT goyōdome 1784.7.5, YH 209, 160.

FIGURE 12 Beggars at the door, as depicted by Kawamura Kihō, *Kafuku ninpitsu*, 1809.

but refused to take them back when they collapsed or died in town.[102] Not all beggars who were tolerated by the Koshirō had the endorsement of a headman or carried documents on burial procedures, and it is quite likely that the Koshirō took money from such people. In 1847, after the government had introduced a tag system for beggars, it reprimanded the beggar bosses for selling these tags to newcomers.[103] But the government rarely found fault with the practice of overlooking—in Shirō's case, domain officials were notified but did not criticize the Koshirō for their transgression.

Still, the management of beggar relief often caused friction between the domain government and the beggar guild. Domain officials complained about corruption, negligence, and brutality against beggars. The Koshirō were indeed prone to such behavior because they were not proper officials of the domain and received very little direct supervision. At the

102.   Otomi village; see MT goyōdome 1785.7.12, SSM. See also MT goyōdome 1784.3.2, YH 193, 151.

103.   MT goyōdome 1847.8.21, YH 939, 693.

same time, the beggar bosses could hardly afford to alienate the government, which was the source of their privilege and power.

The Tenmei famine provides a good illustration of the dynamic between the domain, the town elders, and the Koshirō. In the fourth month of 1784, domain officials noticed a growing number of beggars in the town who rested near the entrances of houses. The domain leadership was bothered by their presence and repeatedly admonished the beggar bosses "to patrol without neglect, and if they saw any evil people, expel them." If patrol discipline did not improve the situation, they threatened to withhold the Koshirō's annual rice allowance. The beggar bosses took the domain's message to heart. They apologized for their misconduct and justified it with the fact that several of their members were lying sick from an epidemic.[104] Two months later, the Koshirō were again reprimanded, this time for patrolling too strictly. It seems that the bosses were taken by surprise by this turnabout. When asked by the town elder whether the domain had ever ordered them to shut out beggars from other territories, the representatives of the beggars replied: "We have not received any such command so far, but this year the beggars are dying all over the place, which is why we are trying to drive out weakened people from other domains in order not to inconvenience the authorities. However, we are not quite able to keep up because there are so many of them."[105] The Koshirō anticipated being accused of negligence, but instead, the town elder told them to be more lenient. The town elder was particularly concerned by the behavior of a Koshirō nicknamed "limping Toramatsu," rumored to be beating up and injuring beggars from other domains and bragging about his status as an "official" (*yakunin*). As the elder explained, it was not acceptable for the Koshirō to beat and injure people, not even if they were "lawless."[106] Domain officials were not involved in this particular exchange, but it is still remarkable that despite the insistence on proper patrolling, the domain had not given any orders to close the castle town to incoming beggars. In the eighth month of 1784, when the situation had deteriorated further, the town governor finally instructed the Koshirō to keep out beggars from other domains, but even then, the governor

104.   MT goyōdome 1784.4.2, 4.10, YH 194 and 196, 151–52.
105.   MT goyōdome 1784.6.29, YH 208, 159.
106.   Ibid.

stressed that "this was not being ordered strictly, but the town elders should tell the Koshirō unofficially [*nainai*]."[107]

The events of 1784 reveal a government wavering between toleration and containment in its policy vis-à-vis nondomestic beggars. Despite their initial hard line, the officials avoided harsh crackdowns and continued to tolerate harmless beggars from other domains. When the domain leadership was finally forced to back down from this position, it did so clandestinely and made it appear as if the Koshirō alone were responsible for the repression. The Koshirō thus shielded the lord from cracks to his benevolent facade.[108] The downside of this approach was that the Koshirō could use their power in ways that ran counter to the interests of the domain. One example is the violent behavior of limping Toramatsu, who relished his authority as an "official."

A complete rejection of outsiders would have been risky to implement in this territorially fragmented region. The small domains of inner Echizen could not afford to be harsh on their neighbors if they wanted to protect their subjects from receiving similar treatment elsewhere. Any measures that facilitated or restricted access to the castle town were likely to create a ripple effect within the region. In 1860, for example, a carpenter from a nearby shogunal territory reacted to protectionist measures by Ōno domain by asking his own government to retaliate and ban Ōno's carpenters in return. Ōno's officials tried to mollify the man by granting him special rights of access.[109]

The Crisis of Managed Mendicancy

Ōno's system of beggar control belonged in a particular historical context. It served the needs of a society that was wary of vagrants and intolerant of idlers, but also took for granted the presence of beggars and regarded many of them as worthy of compassion. This ambivalence

107. MT goyōdome 1784.8.9, YH 220, 166.
108. Daniel Botsman has identified a similar dynamic with regard to the employment of outcastes as executioners, which had the effect of protecting the authorities' benevolent reputation; *Punishment and Power*, 41–58.
109. MT goyōdome 1860.9.21, 9.23, SSM.

echoes attitudes toward beggars in early modern Europe, where local governments tolerated begging often well into the nineteenth century and developed mechanisms to regulate it, provided that the beggars were local and "deserving."[110] With regard to begging strangers, early modern European governments were notably more repressive than Japan. During the sixteenth century, municipalities all over Europe, both Catholic and Protestant, centralized and bureaucratized their systems of poor relief and intensified the suppression of vagrancy and begging. Some established houses of correction to intern vagabonds and beggars, punish them for their idleness, and reeducate them through forced labor, a trend that gained further momentum in the seventeenth century and persisted until the beginning of the nineteenth.[111] By contrast, Tokugawa authorities acknowledged the begging rights of a wide variety of groups. Even though the shogunate and some domains built stockades to put vagrants and petty criminals to work, workhouses remained few in number and were intended not as places of punishment but of rehabilitation. Edo's Stockade for Laborers of 1789, for example, was reserved for sturdy vagrants (*mushuku*) and did not admit beggars, who continued to be sent to the beggar hospice.[112] Conversely, deviant vagrants in Ōno did not enter the beggar hospice either but were held briefly in the town jail or in the Koshirō's village before being banished from the domain.

In the eighteenth century, Ōno town seems to have been able to accommodate begging itinerants without major problems, except during times of famine, when masses of small peasants and townspeople took to the streets. In Ōno, mendicancy followed a seasonal rhythm, with numbers swelling during the winter months. But in the nineteenth century, the region developed a chronic vagrancy problem that changed the perception of mendicancy as a whole. This trend affected the whole

110.   See, for example, Hüchtker, *"Elende Mütter" und "liederliche Weibspersonen,"* 26–82.

111.   Jütte, *Poverty and Deviance in Early Modern Europe*, 100–142, 165–77; Foucault, *Madness and Civilization*, 38–64. On parallels and differences between Europe and Japan, see also Pons, "Ordre marginal dans le Japon moderne," 1159; Pons, *Misère et Crime au Japon*, 89–90; Leupp, *Servants, Shophands, and Laborers*, 155–57; Botsman, *Punishment and Power*, 111–12.

112.   Botsman, *Punishment and Power*, 85–114; Hiramatsu, "Ninsoku yoseba no seiritsu to hensen," 83–132.

country, though the timing differed by region. In Edo, the shogunate was considering the construction of a vagrant camp as early as the 1720s.[113] In Ōno, it took until the Tenpō famine (1833–34 and 1836–38) for vagrancy to be perceived as a serious crisis.

During the Tenpō famine, begging strangers in the town became a major source of disruption. At the time of the Tenmei famine fifty years earlier, beggars had been much tamer, even though their number had been very high. The town elders' journals from the 1780s do not note any significant rise in crime. They show that the vast majority of beggars who fell sick or died in the town were children and elderly people from mountain villages, as well as mothers and fathers who accompanied their offspring.[114] During the Tenpō famine, by contrast, public safety deteriorated dramatically. The town elders' journal of 1837 recorded at least forty-six counts of theft—an extraordinary number for such a small town.[115] The majority of these crimes were committed by unregistered vagrants and beggars. According to the testimonies of suspects included in the journals, many offenders were habitual criminals with far-flung networks of collaborators.[116] Almost all of them were natives of the Ōno plain and surroundings and had been expelled from their home communities for some previous crime or misdemeanor. They had relatives and friends in the area and relied on them for lodging as well as pawning and selling their contraband. Many of them engaged in casual labor, and some were on familiar terms with the beggar bosses of Ōno and Katsuyama and testified to having spent time in their hospices and villages. Although the eighteenth century had of course not been free from deviant vagrants either, there had not been a criminal underworld of this scale.

Complaints about beggars abounded during the Tenpō famine. In 1837, after a case of arson, the town elder proposed expelling the entire beggar population from the castle town but was vetoed by the town governor, who worried that repression might upset the beggars and make

113. Minami, *Edo no shakai kōzō*, 69–72.
114. Ehlers, "Mibun shakai no hinmin kyūsai," 314–15. For instances of theft in those years, see MT goyōdome 1784.2.26, 10.11; 1785.1.26, 12.28; 1786.2.5; 1787.1.25, 4.2, SSM.
115. MT goyōdome 1837, SSM. This trend continued into the following year.
116. See, for example, MT goyōdome 1837.4.11, 6.26, 7.3, 7.22, 7.24, 7.28, 10.8, SSM.

them even more lawless.[117] In the same year, a crowd of about eighty beggars appeared at the gates of rich peasant houses on the Ōno plain to extort rice gruel, and Ōno's government mobilized troops and prepared money to appease the rioters.[118] This event must have been particularly unsettling because it happened in the aftermath of Ōshio Heihachirō's rebellion in Osaka, an uprising conducted in the name of the poor that inspired unrest in other parts of the country.[119] In Echizen, there were several instances of such violent begging (*oshigoi*), which blurred the boundary between misbehaving mendicants and protesting peasants.[120] As usual, the hungry also stole directly from the fields. In 1837 and 1838, around harvest time, the landowning "town peasants" of Ōno petitioned for signposts, more Koshirō patrols, and a nighttime curfew to protect their crops.[121]

The domain government rejected some of the townspeople's more extreme demands, but gradually became more exclusionary in its policy toward beggars. The Tenpō famine seems to have undercut the tacit consensus among administrators in Echizen Province that beggars from other jurisdictions were to be mutually overlooked. In 1838 the domain authorities introduced a system of begging licenses. The idea had been raised by one of the town elders, who had heard that "all the neighbor domains were expelling beggars from outside jurisdictions," and believed that "if this was the case, they would probably all come here."[122] To protect the town from the impending invasion, he proposed expelling nondomestic beggars. But the plan only targeted newly incoming beggars; it advocated tolerating the existing ones on the condition that they wore waist tags (*koshifuda*) for easy identification. The domain leadership adopted the proposal, probably because the plan allowed shutting out incoming beggars

---

117.   MT goyōdome 1837.6.6, SSM.
118.   Yōdome (Suzuki) 1837.3.26, YH 728, 529; "Tori nikki," 51–53.
119.   Yōyōdome (Nojiri) 1837, YH 726, 524–29.
120.   See the journal of the shogunate's outpost in Honbo; "Tori nikki," 4, 7, 24, 25, 28–30, 35, 60. See also Sippel, "Popular Protest in Early Modern Japan," 294–307.
121.   MT goyōdome 1837.8.6, 8.7; 1838.7.21, SSM.
122.   MT goyōdome 1838.9.11, SSM. Around the same time, a similar chain reaction unfolded on the island of Shikoku, where Tosa domain banned mendicant travelers from entering its territory; see Machida, "Kinsei kōki Awa ni okeru 'takoku mukitte/ uronmono' tōsei to Shikoku henro."

without provoking the ones who were already there. The town elder took eighty wooden tags from the town office equipment, asked the Koshirō to distribute them to the beggars in town, and ordered them to expel all newcomers. The number eighty was chosen because it represented the current beggar population in Ōno town as estimated by the Koshirō.

Beggar tags were a conventional tool of Tokugawa beggar control and were widely adopted from the seventeenth century onward, but in Ōno, officials introduced them only during the Tenpō famine.[123] In the winter of 1836–37, the rice gruel kitchens began to limit their handouts to those who carried cards of eligibility (*tefuda*) issued by village officials. This measure was probably intended to stretch thin resources by excluding certain groups from the pool of recipients—unregistered vagrants, for example, or townspeople who were already collecting other types of aid. Subjects of other domains, however, continued to be eligible for the handouts.[124] In the autumn of 1838, the town elders also proposed that "very poor" villagers of Ōno domain who begged in town in winter should be asked to carry a letter from their village officials for better identification.[125] The domain leadership took up this idea, probably because the town elders experienced great difficulty identifying the dozens of beggars who had died in town the previous year.[126] The famine had clearly overwhelmed the beggar bosses' capacities. Normally, the Koshirō gathered information on newcomers informally and confirmed with villages only in case of illness or death, but during a famine of this magnitude they were no longer able to keep up.

After the famine the beggar problem subsided somewhat, but it did not go away. In 1841, the town elder reported to the town governor that

123. In Kanazawa in 1691, administrators required unlicensed mendicants who lived in town permanently to wear tags and later recognized the "tag-holding beggars" as an association with formal duties; see Tanaka Yoshio, "Kaga-han hiningoya-sei seiritsu no jijō ni tsuite," 47; McClain, *Kanazawa*, 130–31.

124. MT goyōdome 1836.11.2, SSM. This system of identification seems to have been in place for at least two more years. The cards were collected by the Koshirō and circulated back to the villages through the rural intendants; see MT goyōdome 1838.2.6, SSM.

125. MT goyōdome 1838.10.6, SSM.

126. The town elders' journal of 1837 recorded seventy-six dead beggars (the actual number was higher), only three of whom carried documents and could be identified without problems.

the attitude of the local beggars had worsened. He complained that they were resting beneath the eaves of townhouses, committing petty thefts, picking fights with children, berating people who refused to give alms, and molesting vendors on the market. After consulting with domain officials, he ordered the Koshirō to expel all male beggars. For the future, he urged the townspeople to beat and expel every beggar who misbehaved, if necessary with the Koshirō's help, and overlook only those who "really, really looked like beggars."[127] In 1847, the town community submitted a joint petition asking for permission to set up signposts that banned "various kinds of mendicancy" (*sho-kanjin*) in the castle town.[128] Two years later, Nojiri Gen'emon, a wealthy peasant, remarked in his journal that "in recent years the beggars are spoilt and accept only white rice as alms. For this reason, villages in both shogunate and domain territories have erected signposts against various kinds of mendicancy, though they continue to donate unpolished rice."[129] These examples suggest that the behavior of beggars had become a widespread concern in the 1840s, and communities in the region began to respond by prohibiting or at least limiting access to mendicant strangers. The expression "various kinds of mendicancy" (*sho-kanjin*) reflected the fact that the vagrancy crisis did not manifest itself in a generic mass of unregistered people but in an imitation and expansion of existing groups with formal begging privileges.[130]

The domain leadership was initially reluctant to abandon its old and more informal approach. In 1847 it declined the townspeople's request for signposts due to the "novelty" of the measure and simply reminded them to be more discriminatory in their almsgiving.[131] Shortly thereafter the domain issued a decree, worked out in consultation with the town elders, that implicitly blamed the Koshirō for the presence of vagrants in the castle town.[132] The decree criticized the Koshirō for taking money from

127.   MT goyōdome 1841.8.21, YH 819, 594.
128.   MT goyōdome 1847.7.11, YH 931, 684.
129.   Kōshi yōdome (Nojiri) 1849, twelfth month, YH 969, 711.
130.   The term *kanjin* originally referred to the collection of donations on behalf of Buddhist temples, but in the Tokugawa period the word came to be widely used for many forms of begging.
131.   MT goyōdome 1847.7.11, YH 931, 684.
132.   MT goyōdome 1847.8.21, YH 939, 690–93.

incoming beggars in exchange for supplying them with waist tags. Under these circumstances, the edict went, "the Koshirō would regard [the tags] as a source of profit and neglect the expulsion of those who needed to be expelled." It emphasized that the tags were intended for use by "the sick, the old, and children, that is, people who are begging out of necessity," and not by suspicious elements. The government also found fault with the Koshirō's management of the beggar hospice. Instead of reserving the shelter for the sick and helpless, they admitted greedy vagrants who dressed beyond their station and accepted only white rice and coins from their benefactors. The town elders in particular repeatedly condemned the Koshirō for sheltering criminals and stopped short of denouncing them as a band of criminals in their own right.[133] In principle, there was nothing new to these allegations because the Koshirō had always maintained connections to the world of vagrants; these very connections made them so valuable in the authorities' eyes. But the proliferation of deviant vagrants made it increasingly difficult for officials to overlook such behavior.

The domain's hesitation to abandon the traditional system suggests that it did not see a viable alternative to managing mendicancy at the time. Territorial fragmentation made it impossible to follow the example of Tosa domain, which occupied an entire province on the island of Shikoku and reacted to the vagrancy crisis of the Bakumatsu era by sealing off its borders against begging itinerants.[134] In retrospect, however, Ōno's response reads like a prelude to the bans on mendicancy that many local governments adopted soon after the Meiji Restoration. The domain gradually hardened its stance during the 1850s, and a few years before the Restoration of 1868 instituted a major change to its policy on begging. In 1860, it abolished the seasonal rice gruel kitchens for beggars after more than 130 years of continuous operation. According to the town elders' journal, the lord took this step because he wanted to concentrate on supporting his subjects and prevent aid from going to outsiders. From that point on, the domain continued to give rice to the Koshirō and the occupants of the hospice every winter but no longer funded kitchens that were accessible to itinerants in and around the castle

133.   MT goyōdome 1852.4.21, 4.22, YH 999, 732–34.
134.   See note 122.

town.[135] Public health was probably another concern. In 1860, Ōno town reported a case of suspected cholera, and the authorities ordered the Koshirō to expel begging strangers who were suffering from smallpox.[136] Ōno's beggar hospice, however, continued to operate in some form until the abolition of outcaste status in 1871.[137]

In 1869, one year after the Meiji Restoration, Ōno's domain authorities issued an order to recall and record unregistered people. This measure, which put an effective end to the practice of beggar deletion, was part of the new imperial government's plan to repatriate the unregistered and reenter them into the population register. In Ōno, the text of the decree was promulgated as follows:

> There have been repeated orders from the imperial court with regard to people outside the register [*chōgaimono*]. Therefore, people who thus far have been disinherited or turned into beggars et cetera upon request shall be recalled if their destination or place of residence is known, and they shall be instructed warmly and made to improve their character. As for people whose destination is unknown, and even those who have been expelled from the domain as a punishment, they shall be understood as registered residents of their respective *chō* or village.[138]

The initiator of this measure was the new Meiji government, which perceived vagrancy as a source of political instability, an administrative headache, and a drain on the country's resources.[139] The repression of begging gained further momentum after the formal abolition of mendicant status groups around 1871 and was reinforced by a new national discourse about civilization, self-reliance, and popular hygiene that condemned mendicancy and almsgiving as an obstacle to Japan's progress as a modern nation. The emerging newspapers of the 1870s welcomed the resettlement

135. MT goyōdome 1860.11.26; 1861.12.6, SSM; MT goyōdome 1860.12.1, YH 1221, 872–73. On expulsions in the 1850s and beyond, see, for example, MT goyōdome 1853.6.6, AHM; 1855.4.21, 5.15; 1861.4.14, SSM.

136. MT goyōdome 1860.6.13, 11.6, YH 1162 and 1214, 832, 867.

137. The beggar hospice is listed as tax-exempt in an early Meiji register; Shohikidaka ni tsuki moto-Ōno-ken todoke, Echizen Ōno Doi-ke monjo.

138. MT goyōdome 1869.11.7, YH 1382, 976.

139. Yokoyama, *Meiji ishin to kinsei mibunsei no kaitai*, 62–87.

of vagrants as a milestone of civilization and celebrated the all-embracing benevolence of the emperor, who welcomed even drifters and outlaws back into society's fold. In Echizen, an "enlightened" public of government officials, village elites, and journalists began to denounce the seasonal begging customs of mountain villagers as a threat to the popular work ethic and a disgrace to modern civilization.[140]

In 1873, bureaucrats of the newly created Asuwa Prefecture, which included Ōno's former domain territory, issued a decree that ordered not only the repatriation and resettlement of beggars but for the first time prohibited giving alms. As a local newspaper reported: "Even though the proposals . . . differed in length and content, there was broad consensus that it would be necessary to send beggars [*kikkai no mono*] from each district back to their original place of registration; to do all one could to care for and relieve the old and young; and to make the strong ones work diligently or employ their labor."[141] This decree drew on suggestions the new district and village headmen had submitted to the prefectural administration—most likely the same village and town elites who had petitioned for a tougher stance on begging in the Bakumatsu years. Of course these policies did not succeed at eradicating mendicancy overnight. Many local administrations of the early Meiji period initially mitigated the consequences of these bans by distributing beggar tags to those they considered truly needy,[142] and for many decades, begging and vagrancy remained widespread partly because the development of social welfare did not keep pace with the extent of destitution, partly because customs of almsgiving survived despite legal prescriptions. Yet the Meiji Restoration profoundly changed the parameters of mendicancy because the authorities refused to manage it and completely denied its legitimacy not only as an occupation but as a method of obtaining relief.

In Ōno, the crime and unrest that surfaced during the Tenpō famine damaged the core premise of managed mendicancy—that one could and should distinguish between suspicious vagrants and harmless

---

140.   Imanishi, "Bunmeika to 'Ushikubi kojiki'," 364–68. A similar discourse developed in other regions; see Imanishi, "Bunmei kaika to sabetsu," 134–42.

141.   *Satsuyō Shinbun* 9, 1873, first month.

142.   See, for example, Kusayama, "Sonraku keisatsu-ri hininban ni tsuite," part 2, 13.

beggars. Beggar guilds, beggar hospices, open rice gruel kitchens, beggar deletions, and beggar tags belonged in a society that in principle acknowledged mendicancy as an occupation, a spiritual exercise, and a form of self-help for the poor. These institutions also depended on self-governing status groups, which supported the poor and enjoyed much leeway in their decisions on whom to admit and keep as members. Although Ōno's domain government was concerned about its tax income, benevolent reputation, and safety of its territory, it exercised only light supervision over the villages and block associations that were in charge of registering, relieving, and rejecting poor people, and it worked with these groups and with the beggar guild to fund and run institutions of beggar relief. Ōno's mode of managing mendicancy was particular to this domain, but most territories and castle towns performed the same theme with minor variations. Because of the status groups—autonomous but interconnected—administrators were able to manage extreme poverty without extensive reliance on indoor relief institutions.

In the nineteenth century, administrators and educated elites in many parts of Japan developed an interest in indoor institutions of social welfare that addressed noncriminal vagrants and emphasized medical care, vocational training, and saving.[143] These institutions differed from earlier workhouses such as Edo's Stockade for Laborers in that they confined not only sturdy vagrants but also weak, "deserving" beggars and gradually moved away from the logic of managed mendicancy. In the years around the Meiji Restoration, many new beggar hospices sprang up across Japan that put beggars to work and either limited begging for alms or prohibited it entirely. Kyoto's new beggar hospice of 1868, for example, still employed a limited form of begging license, but no longer relied on the local beggar guild for its administration. It forced beggars to engage in various types of work with the goal of enabling them to stand on their own feet.[144] In Tokyo, the new Meiji government established a combined poor and workhouse (*kyūikusho*) for homeless beggars in 1869 and had it

143.   For two such proposals from Edo, see Minami, "Bakumatsu Edo chōnin no fukushi shisetsu setsuritsu negai."

144.   Ikeda, "Ryūmin atsumesho kara kyūmin jusansho e"; Imanishi, "Bunmei kaika to sabetsu," 137–41. A person from Ōno died there in 1869; see MT goyōdome 1869.7.18, NGM.

managed by Tokyo's beggar organization.[145] As Daniel Botsman has shown, Western writings served as an important inspiration for nineteenth-century intellectuals and reformers interested in penal reform.[146] The Western phenomenon of orphanages and poorhouses also aroused their curiosity. After first encountering such institutions in Dutch writings, Japanese reformers were able to observe them firsthand during the shogunate's first embassy to Europe in 1862, for example, in the Netherlands.[147]

However, contact with the West was not the main reason reformers insisted on prohibiting begging. Rather, the Western model fell on fertile ground because by the time of the Meiji Restoration, many Japanese commoners were already convinced that the Tokugawa system of managed mendicancy had spiraled out of control. One such commoner was Nojiri Gen'emon, the wealthy landowner on the Ōno plain mentioned before. At the end of 1873, Gen'emon reflected on the reforms he had witnessed in recent years. He applauded the demise of the authoritarian warrior regime and rejoiced that under the benevolent rule of the emperor, talented commoners were being appointed to governmental office and allowed to thrive. Even the useless warriors, he noted with glee, were beginning to engage in productive trades and crafts. But the entire final third of his journal entry was devoted to a condemnation of managed mendicancy:

> As for the common folks—no more beggars and poor people are wandering about, calling at their houses for alms; no people of monk or nun appearance, no masterless samurai and gangsters; all solicitation has ceased. The system of imperial bureaucrats is reaching into the farthest corners, and there is no gambling and fighting at all among the people in towns and villages; absolutely no one stealing the crops from the fields in the summer; and the people are all whispering among themselves that in over two hundred years of rule by the Tokugawa House, governmental

---

145.   Porter, "Meiji shoki Tokyo ni okeru hinmin no kyūsai to tōsei." For other examples, see Yoshida Kyūichi, "Meiji ishin ni okeru kyūhin seido," 64–81.

146.   Botsman, *Punishment and Power*, 117–29.

147.   Ibid., 119; Miyanaga, *Bakumatsu ken'ō shisetsudan*, 114–16, 165–67, 178, 184, 193–94.

control had never been as effective as it is now. The fundraising campaigns of shrines and temples have also stopped.[148]

These words sound exaggerated, even sarcastic, if one considers that 1873 was the same year the Ōno plain exploded in a massive popular uprising against the religious reforms of the Meiji government and reformist local elites. But they must probably be taken seriously because in those same years, Gen'emon repeatedly glorified the achievements of imperial rule in his journal and contrasted them with the shortcomings of the House of Doi as well as the "stupid people" who launched the protests in 1873. His entry powerfully conveys the vision of the Meiji Restoration he had constructed: a triumph of productive, talented, enterprising commoners, and a release from ceaseless exploitation and solicitation through warriors from above and beggars from below. Behind his perception was the specter of the vagrancy problem in the final decades before the Meiji Restoration, which the domain government and the status order had failed to contain.

148.   Shoyōdome (Nojiri) 1873, December, YH 1405, 990–91.

CHAPTER 4

The Guilds of the Blind

Besides the Koshirō, Ōno domain had another small community that collected alms on a regular basis: blind healers and entertainers. Such blind professionals were fairly common in the Hokuriku region along the Sea of Japan and were entitled to various kinds of material support at home and when traveling. As elsewhere, they organized along gender lines into a guild of blind men (*zatō*) and a guild of blind women (*goze*), the latter subordinated to its male counterpart. All of them lived in Ōno's castle town. In the eighteenth century, the total number of blind professionals in Ōno town was around ten,[1] and at the end of the Tokugawa period, in the 1860s, it still hovered between seven and nine.[2]

The guilds of the blind may have been small, but they belonged on a diverse and colorful spectrum of occupation-based groups that structured the underclass in Japan's early modern towns and cities. Urban tenant populations encompassed a stunning variety of occupations—from

1. Six men in 1740; see MT goyōdome 1740.2.10, YH 5, 4; at least five women in 1815; see MT goyōdome 1815.2.7, YH 587, 410–11; 1815.2.12, 2.13, 2.19, SSM.
2. 1855–57: five men, two women; 1861: seven men, two women, 1871: four men, four women; Sō-ninbetsu yosechō, 1855, 1856, 1857, 1861, 1871, SSM. These figures might have excluded apprentices because a list of town households of 1860 indicates a total of fourteen "individuals" (*nin*); MT goyōdome 1860.10.21, YH 1208, 865. Ōno's numbers of *zatō* and *goze* were fairly typical for a castle town of this size. By comparison, the capital of Edo had a population of 1,000 *zatō* in 1722 and 1,283 in 1743. A figure from 1837 (8,697) was probably a countrywide total, though its reliability is unclear; see Katō, *Nihon mōjin shakaishi kenkyū*, 67–70.

hairdressers and textile workers to maidservants, construction laborers, porters, fish hawkers, paper scrap collectors, noodle vendors, itinerant storytellers, diviners, dancing monks, prostitutes, and many more. Although these people rarely owned any land, some operated their own small shops or backroom shrines, and others worked on the streets or for outside employers. All of them were indirectly integrated into the status order through their households and landlords that were part of a block association, and many also belonged to occupational groups that transcended the block associations or they were under the control of labor bosses or professional guarantors who maintained guilds among their own kind. Governments used occupation-based groups like these to control small townspeople and protect their livelihoods by investing them with privileges. They regarded blind professionals as especially deserving of compassion because of their disability and allowed their guilds to collect alms on a regular basis. The occupational groups among the urban poor long attracted more attention from folklorists than from historians, but in the 1980s, scholars in Japan began to recognize their significance for understanding the structure of Tokugawa urban society more generally.[3] This chapter discusses the organized blind as part of an assertive underclass that used occupational groups as vehicles for its aspirations, even if their top leaders were not of a lower-class background.

Among town residents, the blind professionals were marginal in the sense that they were physically impaired and did not engage in productive labor. Administrators did not regard them as common townspeople and governed them as a status of their own. The Tokugawa authorities highly valued productivity and endorsed the neo-Confucian ideal of the "four estates" (samurai, peasants, artisans, and merchants) that excluded entertainers and condemned them as "idlers" (*yūmin*) and a threat to

---

3. For seminal studies on the structure of the urban underclass, see Yoshida Nobuyuki, *Kinsei toshi shakai no mibun kōzō*; Yoshida Nobuyuki, *Mibunteki shūen to shakai=bunka kōzō*; Tsukada, Wakita, and Yoshida, *Mibunteki shūen*; Tsukada, "Kasōmin no sekai"; Tsukada, "Mibunteki shūenron—Kanjin no heizon o tegakari to shite"; Minami, *Edo no shakai kōzō*. On guilds of professional guarantors, see Nishimura, "Kinsei Osaka sangō ie ukenin nakama ni tsuite"; Nishimura, "Kinsei Osaka sangō ie ukenin nakama no tenkai katei." In Western languages, see Leupp, *Servants, Shophands, and Laborers*; Pons, *Misère et Crime au Japon*; Stanley, *Selling Women*; Stanley, "Maidservants' Tales."

public morals.[4] Beyond that particularity, however, the guilds of blind performers had a lot in common with the other occupational self-governing groups, especially in town society. They wrote and enforced their own law codes, they asserted privileges by invoking precedent and the legacy of semi-mythical founders, they cultivated relationships with multiple power centers, and they took on roles of public responsibility by controlling the behavior of their members.

Because the guilds of the blind had a countrywide organization, they possessed an extraordinary amount of leverage that belied their members' physical limitations. In the Tokugawa period, it was common among certain types of occupations, such as artisans, artists, scholars, and clerics, to seek the protection of temples, shrines, or families of court nobles, which were in most cases based in or around the old imperial capital of Kyoto.[5] Ōno's guild of blind men was affiliated with the so-called *tōdōza*, an organization with medieval roots that maintained its headquarters—the Council of Elders—in Kyoto and a loose affiliation with a family of the imperial aristocracy. The name *tōdōza* meant "guild of our way." In medieval times, the term "our way" (*tōdō*) had been used by a variety of craftsmen and performers, but in the Tokugawa period, it came to refer exclusively to the national organization of blind men. The leaders of the *tōdōza* were quite wealthy, and some made great contributions to the musical arts, historical scholarship, and medicine. But the majority of members, especially outside the large cities, consisted of humble and often destitute people who scraped by as itinerant healers and entertainers. Scholarship on the guilds of the blind, which spans the disciplines of history, literature, musicology, anthropology, and folklore studies, has shown a strong preference for examining the situation in Edo and other metropolises. Only recently has a fuller picture begun to emerge, thanks to new research on small-town guilds[6] and Gerald Groemer's rich work

---

4. Asao, "Kinsei no mibun to sono hen'yō," 22–24. For a nineteenth-century polemic against idlers from the perspective of a samurai, see *Lust, Commerce, and Corruption* (1816).

5. For one example (bronze-casters), see Yokota Fuyuhiko, "Imoji–Tsuji-mura imoji to Matsugi-ke."

6. Examples include Asao, "Ikoma-ke to zatō/goze nakama"; Matsumoto Eiko, "Kinsei shakai ni okeru zatō/koze [*sic*] no kōsatsu"; Yamada, "Matsushiro hanryō no

on female blind performers.[7] These studies offer important background for Ōno's case.

Because the *tōdōza* enjoyed many official protections, scholars have often studied it in the context of social welfare. This interest was especially strong before World War II, when Japanese conservatives searched for indigenous alternatives to the costly welfare systems they observed in the West. The guilds of the blind feature prominently in Inoue Tomoichi's first historical survey of Japanese welfare, published in 1909.[8] As a Home Ministry bureaucrat specializing in welfare policy, Inoue skimmed the Japanese past for distinctly "Japanese" approaches to social welfare. Somewhat surprisingly, he concluded that the *tōdōza* was the closest indigenous approximation of a "normal system of poor relief." He cited the guild's longevity and continuity, which set it apart from most other welfare institutions in Japanese history.[9] Second, Inoue and many of his contemporaries erroneously assumed that the guild had been established in an imperial act of compassion in the ninth century and enjoyed privileged treatment under subsequent rulers.[10] In other words, he envisioned the *tōdōza* as a uniquely Japanese institution that thrived under imperial benevolence. Although the Home Ministry did not actually favor a revival of blind privilege, the government eventually yielded to intense lobbying by blind activists and in 1911 restored part of the professional protections for blind people as acupuncturists and masseurs, which the blind had lost when their guild was disbanded in 1871.[11]

---

mōjin"; Nakagawa Miyuki, "Junzai zatō no katsudō o meguru chiiki shakai no ichi dōkō"; Nakagawa Miyuki, "Zatō shukusen o meguru chiiki shakai no dōkō."

7.   Groemer, *Goze to goze-uta no kenkyū*, 2 vols.

8.   Inoue Tomoichi, *Kyūsai seido yōgi*. On Inoue, see Garon, *Molding Japanese Minds*, 40–43.

9.   Inoue Tomoichi, *Kyūsai seido yōgi*, 104–8. On Inoue's concern with Japan's lack of distinct, continuous welfare institutions, see Ikeda, "Nihon zenkindai ni okeru shakai fukushi no kōzō." See also Taniyama, *Nihon shakai jigyōshi*, 476–78.

10.   The old legend that Emperor Kōkō had established the guild in the ninth century to provide for his blind brother and help his blind subjects continued to be propagated in anthologies of blind biographies from the 1890s onward for the purpose of blind education; see Monbushō Futsū Gakumukyoku, *Honchō mōjinden*.

11.   The new regulations made it easier for the blind to obtain, for example, a license by passing a simplified examination; see Namase, "Hoshō: Kin-gendai no 'shikaku shōgaisha' o megutte," 223; Sugino, "Shōgaisha undō no soshiki to nettowāku," 92–93.

In the postwar era, the guilds attracted attention from historians of disability, such as Katō Yasuaki, whose groundbreaking 1974 study on the blind in Tokugawa society has offered the most persuasive interpretation of the guild's character thus far.[12] In Katō's view, policy vis-à-vis the *tōdōza* was determined by the shogunate's desire to use the guild for controlling and relieving blind itinerants. As a result, the organization developed from a professional association of blind performers into what Katō calls "a distribution guild [of alms and rank money]" (*haitōza*).[13] The glue that held the early modern *tōdōza* together was its ability to extract funds from the rest of society and distribute them among its members. These funds could take the form of so-called rank money, which was collected from new and upcoming members and divided among high-ranking members in the entire country, or of alms, which were shared among the low-ranking blind on the level of the local associations. In addition, *zatō* and *goze* received support in form of room, board, and pocket money whenever they traveled through the countryside.

In the Tokugawa period, the guild thus developed a hybrid character and no longer functioned primarily as an association for protecting and transmitting professional skills. Its monopolies on particular kinds of healing and entertainment nevertheless continued to be important for the livelihood and identity of the blind. The shogunate also protected moneylending by the blind to a certain extent by exempting the members of the guild from some restrictions on filing lawsuits against debtors, because it acknowledged that the blind needed to save substantial amounts of money to rise within their organization.[14] One might also expect the *tōdōza* to have functioned as an institution of mutual aid because it included richer and poorer individuals, and it is true that some sharing of resources took place. But generally the *tōdōza* did not distribute wealth from richer to poorer members; on the contrary, it had a tendency to shift funds from the bottom to the top.

---

12. Katō, *Nihon mōjin shakaishi kenkyū*. See also Namase, *Kinsei Nihon no shōgaisha to minshū*; Namase, *Nihon no shōgaisha no rekishi*, Kinsei-hen; Sugino, "Shōgaisha undō no soshiki to nettowāku."

13. Katō, *Nihon mōjin shakaishi kenkyū*, 154–60, 231–35; Katō, "Kinsei no shōgaisha to mibun seido," 158–63.

14. Katō, *Nihon mōjin shakaishi kenkyū*, 127–32, 320–24; Groemer, "The Guild of the Blind," 357.

The character of the *tōdōza* in the Tokugawa period was complex and should not be reduced to its material aspects, but the protection of livelihood was indeed central to the workings of this organization. The guilds of the blind played similar roles as some of the other occupation-based associations that protected and controlled the urban poor. They negotiated privileges, regulated begging, and allowed households and residential communities to transfer the burden of supporting unproductive kin to society at large. This chapter situates the guilds of the blind in Ōno in the context of both local society and blind self-rule countrywide. The case of Ōno town offers a framework for contrasting the blind with the Koshirō as another example of an officially recognized mendicant group. The blind did their utmost to distinguish themselves from the beggar bosses, who were heavily stigmatized and not allowed to live among the townspeople.

The Blind in Society and the Role of the Guilds

Because the *tōdōza* and the female *goze* guilds admitted only certain types of professionals, they did not represent the blind in their entirety. Most people with visual handicaps pursued mainstream occupations such as farming and tried as hard as they could to compensate for their loss of eyesight. Blind peasants, for example, wove straw mats, ground millstones, cultivated vegetables, and collected horse fodder for their own households or on behalf of their employers.[15] Tokugawa authorities were not interested in disability as long as it was contained and handled within households, villages, and block associations. They only intervened when a household appeared too weak to fulfill its tax and corvée obligations. Many domains openly encouraged peasants to replace family heads who were physically or mentally disabled, although such encouragement was often unnecessary because popular custom tended to exclude them from hereditary succession.[16] Often, disabled people continued to live in their

15.   Katō, *Nihon mōjin shakaishi kenkyū*, 32–34.
16.   Ibid., 27–32; Katō, "Kinsei no shōgaisha to mibun seido," 126–31. As Katō shows, blind peasants during the Tokugawa period were not exempt from land tax or corvée.

native households, and their formal social status remained unchanged. Although Tokugawa governments were generally opposed to reducing the size of the agriculturally productive population, they allowed blind peasants to enter the guilds of the blind if doing so helped alleviate the burden on taxpaying households. Aside from the guilds of the blind, Tokugawa society offered few protections specifically for people with disabilities. Concerned families could try to apply to the authorities for ordinary poor relief, an option that was not altogether unpromising because illness and disability were considered acceptable grounds for requesting assistance.[17]

For most families in the Tokugawa period, the loss of eyesight was first and foremost an economic problem. From the seventeenth century onward, most households were made up of stem families, consisting of only one married couple in each generation; for them, the burden of feeding a blind relative could quickly become overwhelming.[18] A good illustration is the compilation *Kōgiroku* ("Record of Filial Behavior"), published by the shogunate in 1801 to honor paragons of virtue among the common people. The biographies of hardship and sacrifice that make up the bulk of this publication suggest that blindness was not only quite widespread but debilitating enough to push some households into desperate poverty.[19] Among 480 cases of officially rewarded virtue among subjects in late eighteenth- and early nineteenth-century Osaka, illness was the most common cause of poverty, and eye conditions were by far the most common sort of poverty-inducing illness, resulting in blindness in thirty-six of the cases.[20] Katō estimates that the incidence of blindness in Japan's total population in the Tokugawa period was higher than 0.25 percent—two or perhaps three times as high as in postwar Japan.[21]

17. Namase, *Nihon no shōgaisha no rekishi*, Kinsei-hen, 105–6; Inaba, *Kyūmin kyūjo seido no kenkyū*, 101–2, 116–18. For isolated examples of relief systems specifically for the blind, see Katō, *Nihon mōjin shakaishi kenkyū*, 446–47; Tsuji, *Ōita-ken no shakai fukushi jigyōshi*, 42–53.

18. Namase, *Nihon no shōgaisha no rekishi*, Kinsei-hen, 55–74.

19. See, for example, *Kankoku kōgiroku*, vol. 1, 87, 132, 149–50, 333–34; vol. 2, 134–35, 246; vol. 3, 62–63.

20. Tsukada, "Kinsei kōki Osaka ni okeru toshi kasō minshū no seikatsu sekai," 78–80, 95.

21. Katō, *Nihon mōjin shakaishi kenkyū*, 70–71; Mori, *Nihon mōjinshi-kō*, 104–6. This is a very rough estimate because the surveys Katō relied on differed in their goals

The primary causes of blindness and other eye conditions were external damage (often caused by harsh labor environments), smallpox, measles, leprosy, malnutrition, sexually transmitted diseases, and afflictions inside the womb. Foreign observers between the sixteenth and nineteenth century were struck by the high incidence of blindness among the Japanese and often blamed it on unhealthy lifestyles and low-quality medical care.[22] In fact, Japanese ophthalmology in the early modern period was quite sophisticated, and cataract surgery was practiced with considerable success. Eyeglasses came into use from the eighteenth century onward, especially in the cities, but they were too unwieldy to benefit those engaged in physical labor,[23] and the poor were left with few choices besides folk remedies and prayers.[24]

The abandonment of blind children was a common trope in premodern Japanese folk tales, though it is questionable to what extent such tales reflected actual social practice. The birth of a blind child could be interpreted as karmic punishment for sins of a previous life or misdeeds of the parents.[25] But poverty probably played a much greater role in compelling some households to abandon or kill their disabled offspring. Most disabled beggars, including blind ones, ended up under the wing of an outcaste beggar organization.[26] Begging lepers, who had once constituted one of the core groups of outcaste settlements in the Japanese Middle Ages, sometimes formed their own small communities in the Tokugawa period under the oversight of beggar bosses.[27] The blind

---

and local foci, and their definition of blindness is often unclear. Generally speaking, authorities were likely to allow admission to the *tōdōza* and *goze* guilds only to people whose eyesight was so weak that they could no longer meaningfully engage in productive labor.

22. Mori, *Nihon mōjinshi-kō*, 98–101, 243–89.

23. Ibid., 89–96; Chiba, "Edo jidai no ganka shōshi"; Mishima, *The History of Ophthalmology in Japan*, 129–207; Screech, *The Lens Within the Heart*, 166–94.

24. Some eye doctors such as the Takeuchi of Suwa treated poor patients free of charge; Nakaizumi, "Meiji-zen Nihon gankashi," 281. On folk remedies, see Yanagita, "Tabemono to shinzō," 365–511.

25. Fritsch, "Blindheit in Japan: Stigma und Charisma," 427–32.

26. Katō, "Kinsei no shōgaisha to mibun seido," 146–49; Katō, *Nihon mōjin shakaishi kenkyū*, 41–43; Karen Nakamura, *Deaf in Japan*, 36–40.

27. Yokota Noriko, "'Monoyoshi'-kō"; Suzuki Noriko, "Kinsei raibyōkan no keisei to tenkai," 106–28; Miyamae, "'Raijingoya' no kanjin to chiiki shakai"; Burns, "From 'Leper Villages' to Leprosaria."

were the only subset among the disabled that formed autonomous organizations outside the purview of outcaste rule. Blindness was a necessary but not sufficient condition for joining these associations. Sufferers also needed to be able and willing to practice one of the arts on which the blind held a monopoly: the performance of a musical instrument such as the koto, a long zither with thirteen strings, and the shamisen, a three-stringed banjo; or a healing skill such as massage, moxibustion, or acupuncture.

The life of blind professionals in small towns, including Ōno, must be pieced together from fragmentary evidence. One especially illuminating case is the story of Onoichi, one of two leaders (*zamoto*) who headed Ōno's *zatō* guild in the 1770s.[28] He owned a house in the central neighborhood of Gobanmachi, which he shared with his wife and four children. In the spring of 1777 he developed symptoms of mental illness, and because he was a heavy smoker, the other guild members who looked after him began to worry that he might set his own house on fire. Initially, the blind men shared the task of watching Onoichi with his brother-in-law Matabei, a tenant farmer who also owned a house in Gobanmachi. Before long, the two parties felt overwhelmed by the task of supervising the deranged man around the clock. The *zatō* argued that their blindness prevented them from keeping him in check, and Matabei claimed to be "living just for the day" (*sono higurashi no tei*) and not having the means to support Onoichi's family members, who were "starving." Onoichi had relatives in his home village Kami-Kurodani on the western rim of the Ōno plain, some of whom were living in his parental home (see map 5). Although they agreed to take him in at first, they sent him back to the castle town only a short while later.[29]

At this point, the *zatō* guild and Matabei decided to petition the authorities for mediation. They suggested that Matabei could take in Onoichi's wife and two daughters if the relatives in the village could be made to accommodate Onoichi and his two sons. The domain officials agreed to enforce this proposal under the condition that the wife continue

28. In some documents the guild leaders are tagged as *sōdai*, whereas others carry the signatures of a *zamoto* and a (*shūbun*) *sōdai*. The difference between these positions is unclear, but the guild appointed at least one *zatō* who represented it vis-à-vis the town elders; MT goyōdome 1838.i4.24, YH 772, 553.

29. MT goyōdome 1777.8.i, SSM (both journal and petition book).

to meet the tax obligations on the house. The village relatives had no choice but to comply with the order, but they tried to make the best of the situation by asking for permission to keep Onoichi's furniture because they were "people of small means." As it turned out, Onoichi did not have any property to speak of except for a wheeled chest, which he had pawned to his guild for forty *monme* of silver.[30] The new leader of the guild, a man named Tamiichi, agreed to give up the chest but only "on the basis of mutual negotiation," meaning he hoped to recover at least part of the loan from the relatives. After a few months of suffering, Onoichi eventually passed away, probably to the relief of his caretakers.

Onoichi's story provides a useful introduction to Ōno's *zatō* guild. First, the man's background suggests that the guild recruited its members from the local peasants and townspeople. This was true for all the *zatō* and *goze* for whom we know the place of origin. Kichiya, an apprentice who joined the guild in 1777, was from Shōbuike, a village adjacent to Ōno town,[31] and Sennoichi was a peasant son from Fukai village.[32] Onoichi had married a townswoman and lived as a house owner among the townspeople, which would have been unthinkable for the members of outcaste associations but was common for *zatō* and their children.[33] All of Ōno's guild members seem to have resided in the castle town, probably because they hoped to benefit from urban demand for the blind arts. Although Onoichi's relatives might have exaggerated their poverty for strategic reasons, their claim must have appeared sufficiently persuasive. Matabei was a tenant farmer who, like many of his peers in Ōno town, was in the possession of a house but was said to be "living just for the day," meaning that he did not have any reserves. Although there is no information on the family background of other *zatō* and *goze* in Ōno, it is significant that one of the highest-ranking guild members hailed from the class of impoverished house owners.

The economic circumstances of Onoichi's family were fairly typical for a blind performer in a town in central Japan. In Takayama in 1819, a

30. The two entries on the case do not mention whether and when Onoichi's house was sold.

31. MT goyōdome 1777.4.26, SSM.

32. Tenmei hachi tomeki, 1783.3.6, AHM.

33. For more examples, see MT goyōdome 1740.3.14; 1777.3.16, SSM; Tenmei hachi tomeki, 1783.2.26, AHM.

somewhat larger mountain town in Hida Province not far from Echizen, there was only one well-to-do and high-ranking *zatō*, who was the son of a wealthy merchant. All the other members of the guilds, including nine blind men, eight blind women, and thirty-four apprentices, lived alone or in units of twos and threes in a neighborhood on the margins of the town, surrounded by day laborers, porters, and lumber workers.[34] In Ōno, the residential concentration was not quite so extreme, but many *zatō* and *goze* lived on the northern end of Shibanmachi, one of the town's poorest areas that was home to many laborers and included the beggar hospice and the jail. There were three houses in that neighborhood that were held by the blind continuously through several generations and by the mid-nineteenth century had been exempted from the land tax.[35] The blind women occupied one of them, and the men held the remaining two. The houses of the guild leaders (*zamoto*) might have doubled as meeting places for the group. In 1837, a *zatō* whose time had come to serve as guild leader passed the job on to one of his comrades "because his residence was extremely small."[36]

Goze often lived in households composed of one master and several apprentices because they did not marry and never established their own families (fig. 13). Due to their ability to form all-female households, the *goze* guilds were the only status groups in Tokugawa Japan (aside from nunneries) that were entirely made up of and controlled by women.[37] The *goze*'s law codes prohibited marriage with *zatō* and in general.[38] Although the reasons for this ban are unclear, the heads of hereditary households in early modern Japan were generally imagined as male, and blind men had a vested interest in living with a sighted wife who could help them run a household. In Ōno, blind women do not seem to have formed units

34. Katō, *Nihon mōjin shakaishi kenkyū*, 387–90.

35. See, for example, the maps in Sakata, *Ōno machi ezu*. On the land tax exemption, see "Uma on-mononari kaisai mokuroku," 1847, in *Ōno shishi*, Shoke monjo-hen 2, 529–30.

36. MT goyōdome 1837.6.26, SSM.

37. On the relationship between gender and status, see Nishida, "Miko"; and Yokoyama Yuriko's statement in Gotō et al., *Mibunteki shūen o kangaeru*, 236–39.

38. Groemer, *Goze to goze-uta*, Kenkyū-hen, 2–4, 366–67; Katō, *Nihon mōjin shakaishi kenkyū*, 247–48, 252–53. On the composition of *goze* households, see the population registers of Hida Takayama reprinted in Groemer, *Goze to goze-uta*, Shiryō-hen, 301, 326, 400–402.

larger than two. In 1838, a *goze* named Yotsu, who had been living with her father until that point, purchased a house in Shibanmachi whose previous owner, a *goze* named Mie, had recently passed away.[39] During the transition, the house was managed by a third blind woman who was living as a tenant in another neighborhood. It seems that the *goze* guild was keen on keeping the house within the guild and preventing it from being taken over by Mie's relatives. In some instances, "blind" houses appear to have been transferred among guild members without any money changing hands.[40]

Onoichi's case also shows that there were limitations to the help blind performers could expect from their guild. The guilds allowed the blind to gain independence from their families and establish themselves as house owners and household heads in town society, but they were not caretaking institutions or associations of mutual relief. In the event of infirmity and other disabilities, the relatives, wives, and children continued to play an important role.[41] In fact, Onoichi's story is comparable to many of the cases cited in chapter 3 in which commoner families shared (and evaded) the burden of supporting their poor kin. Although the relatives of impoverished peasants and townspeople had few resources to begin with, they took in people from in- and outside their immediate lineages, sometimes voluntarily and sometimes under pressure from domain officials and town elders. Commoner households did not permanently cut their bond to family members who had joined a guild of blind professionals, as they would have done with a relative who entered the beggar hospice. To be sure, many local *zatō* associations set aside part of their collective income to maintain funds (so-called *kōmotsu*) for guild members in distress; perhaps the money Onoichi had borrowed from the guild originated from such a fund. In old age, when they were unable to work, *zatō* were still entitled to a share of the guild's collective alms income.[42] But they also maintained kinship ties that could serve them as a safety net.

39. MT goyōdome 1838.i4.ii, SSM.

40. MT goyōdome 1777.3.16; 1780.5.2, SSM.

41. In 1860, the wife of a *zatō* received a reward from the lord for dedicating herself to the care of her sick husband; MT goyōdome 1860.8.26, NGM.

42. Katō, *Nihon mōjin shakaishi kenkyū*, 188, 195.

FIGURE 13 *Goze* in Kanazawa, as depicted in Jippensha Ikku, *Muda shugyō kane no waraji*, vol. 19, 1813–34.

Finally, Onoichi's case highlights the importance of mutual control as a public responsibility of the guild. When the blind men supervised their sick comrade, they acted on the basis of laws requiring them to discipline their fellow guild members. Madness was an extraordinary condition and certainly not what the Tokugawa authorities had in mind when they charged the guilds of the blind with mutual supervision in exchange for autonomy. The issue at stake was Onoichi's ability to start a fire and disrupt the public peace. In 1776 the guild expelled a member who was suspected of theft,[43] and in 1815 scolded and then expelled another man for "violence."[44] Like other status groups in Tokugawa Japan, the *zatō* had their own body of laws, the so-called guild law (*zahō*), which in their case consisted of a central statute for blind professionals around the country and local codes adopted by the local associations in coordination with domain governments. At the same time, they also had to abide by the laws of the block associations in which they lived. Each *chō* issued a code under the overarching framework of domain and shogunate law and excluded people for whom it did not want to assume responsibility.

Within the *tōdōza*, the blind men of Ōno formed a distinct local guild with its own officers and laws and its own relationship to the domain government. This local guild affected the daily lives of its members much more immediately than did the decisions of the Council of Elders in Kyoto. The *tōdōza*'s internal structure was almost as complex as the structure of feudal rule itself and mirrored it to a certain extent. Aside from the headquarters in the imperial capital, there was a sub-boss (*sōroku*) in Edo, who oversaw the guild's affairs in the Kantō region and served as a liaison to the shogunate; for a few decades around 1700, the guild's highest leader was required to live in Edo.[45] The territories of local *zatō* associations often roughly coincided with the territories of domains but could easily extend over several fiefs in regions of scattered lordship.[46] The *zatō* and *goze* of Ōno and Katsuyama seem to have regarded the villages of inner Echizen as their joint territory. There were independent groups of blind professionals in Ōno, Katsuyama, Fukui, and Tsuruga

43.   MT goyōdome 1776.8.10, SSM.
44.   MT goyōdome 1815.2.7, YH 587, 410–11; 2.12, 2.13, 2.19, SSM.
45.   Katō, *Nihon mōjin shakaishi kenkyū*, 213–15.
46.   On the delineation of *zatō* jurisdictions in Yamato Province, an area of scattered lordship, see Nakagawa Miyuki, "Zatō shukusen ni kansuru kenkyū nōto," 115.

and in Fuchū, the castle town of a prominent rear vassal of the lord of Fukui.[47] Except for Fuchū, which had been the seat of Echizen's provincial administration until the sixteenth century, these guilds were based in castle towns that had come into existence in the late sixteenth century.

Despite this territorial fragmentation, the *zatō* groups of Echizen seem to have had neither a province-wide umbrella organization nor a regional leader (*shiokiyaku*), which existed in some provinces to oversee the affairs of *zatō* in one or more than one domain.[48] Ōno's guild did not rely on any intermediaries when communicating with the headquarters in Kyoto.[49] To be sure, Echizen's blind men held an annual convention every autumn that was attended by about twenty to forty guests, but according to a source of 1776, this gathering was a cheerful party with music and song and not an administrative meeting.[50] The handful of *zatō* from Ōno who participated in it did not even include the guild's leaders. Still, the fact that they attended it at all shows that the *zatō* of Ōno were integrated into an informal regional network of blind professionals who were in regular contact with one another.

The law code of Ōno's *zatō* guild also covered the female blind. It thus subordinated the *goze* to their male peers, even though no such hierarchy existed between the blind women and the *tōdōza* on the national level. The *goze* guild had its own leaders, who could be quite assertive in defending the blind women's interests against the *zatō*, but generally, its members were required to obey the *zatō*'s orders in matters pertaining to guild law.[51] The other area in which the *goze* depended on the *zatō* was

47. There is no previous research on blind professionals in Echizen Province except for a very brief account in Groemer, *Goze to goze-uta*, Kenkyū-hen, 124–26. The following sources provide some leads on blind guilds in towns other than Ōno: MT goyōdome 1777.4.26, SSM; MT goyōdome 1797.5.10, YH 450, 314; "Goyō shoshikimoku," in *Fukui kenshi*, Shiryō-hen 3, 81; Shiryō-hen 6, 252; *Katsuyama shishi*, vol. 1, 1026–27.

48. Katō, *Nihon mōjin shakaishi kenkyū*, 215–16. Echizen was not the only province that lacked an intermediate layer of supervision; see Yamada, "Matsushiro hanryō no mōjin," 217.

49. MT goyōdome 1769.2.16, 2.26, SSM, YH 59, 54–55; 1776.8.10, 1777.4.26, SSM.

50. MT goyōdome 1776.8.10, SSM.

51. MT goyōdome 1815.2.7, YH 587, 410–11; 1815.2.12, 2.13, 2.19, SSM. The law code of Ōno's guild of blind women has not been preserved, but one of the most common versions, used by *goze* guilds between the Kantō region and Echigo Province, included

the collection of alms. Whenever domain subjects provided the blind with alms, they handed them over to the leaders of the male blind, who then distributed part of the money to the rank and file and to the *goze*, whose share was smaller than that of the men (though in Ōno this was partly compensated by the *goze* guild's smaller size).[52] On one hand, the blind women might have benefited from their affiliation with the blind men because the latter could bring greater bargaining power to bear on the givers.[53] On the other hand, there is some evidence that the centralization of the *tōdōza* and its transformation from a professional guild into an organization for the collection of rank money and alms had a marginal-izing effect on female blind performers. As Asao Naohiro has shown for the Nagoya area, by the 1670s the local *goze* guild still belonged to a tri-partite "comprehensive guild" (*sō-nakama*) made up of male and female blind performers operating in that area, but was pushed out of it soon thereafter as the comprehensive guild was being absorbed by the *tōdōza*. The *goze*'s share of alms sank as a result.[54]

Blind Arts and Itinerancy

The subordination of the *goze* with regard to alms collection suggests that questions of livelihood had a great impact on the structure of the guilds of the blind. There were two major aspects to the livelihood of the blind: the performance of arts and the collection of alms. In addition, many higher-ranking *zatō* engaged in moneylending, but there is no evidence of any moneylending by the blind taking place in Ōno. The guild func-tioned partly as a professional association that provided training to its

---

some variation of the following rule: "Proviso: If order cannot be established, we will, being women, settle conflicts by accepting directions from the local *tōdō(za)*" (cited after "Goze no engi," 1843, from *Sunkoku zasshi*, in Groemer, *Goze to goze-uta*, Shiryō-hen, 909–10). See also Groemer, *Goze to goze-uta*, Kenkyū-hen, 10–18.

52.   Zatō, goze, kojikigashira e shūgi fuse no oboe, 1791, Mugiya monjo.

53.   Groemer, *Goze to goze-uta*, Kenkyū-hen, 14–16, 24. Guilds of female blind performers might also have depended on the *zatō* for the transmission of certain musi-cal skills.

54.   Asao, "Ikoma-ke to zatō/goze nakama," 88–91.

members and defended its monopoly on blind occupations, but it was also a mendicant group that asserted begging rights, negotiated alms, and controlled blind mendicancy within a particular territory. In Ōno, both of these aspects were well developed.

The *zatō* of Ōno practiced massage and acupuncture and probably played the string instruments koto and shamisen. Nothing is known about the skills of Ōno's *goze*, but it is unlikely that they were any different from those of *goze* in other towns in central Japan, who performed popular songs and narratives accompanied by the shamisen.[55] It was not uncommon for a rural *zatō* to be trained in both healing and musical entertainment. In 1797, a *zatō* from Etchū Province appeared in Ōno to perform massage, shamisen, *kouta* (a genre of popular song), and *hachiningei* (a noisy one-man impersonation of a musical band).[56] The fields of healing and music were similar in that they could be practiced by people without eyesight and suited the *zatō*'s itinerant lifestyle.

The *tōdōza* had its roots in groups of blind minstrels in the medieval period that specialized in reciting epic narratives such as the Tale of the Heike on the *biwa* lute. But in the late fourteenth century, the phenomenon took on a new quality when a countrywide guild, the *tōdōza*, began to emerge with headquarters in Kyoto and eventually won the approval of the imperial and shogunate authorities.[57] The western and northeastern peripheries of Japan were the only areas that retained some independent blind groups of a more religious character—shamans, exorcists, and diviners.[58] By the early seventeenth century, the *tōdōza* constituted a powerful guild under the leadership of highly respected artists who rubbed shoulders with mighty warriors and court nobles. When Tokugawa Ieyasu came to power, he confirmed the *tōdōza*'s autonomy as

55. For a detailed discussion of *goze* songs, see Groemer, *Goze to goze-uta*, Kenkyūhen, 378–470. The archive of Honda Okuemon, headman of Kamiarai village in Ōno domain, includes the copy of a *goze* recital that narrates the circumstances of an 1828 earthquake in Echigo Province: "Goze kudoki jishin no mi no ue," copied in 1839, Honda Okuemon monjo.

56. MT goyōdome 1797.5.10 and 5.30, YH 450 and 452, 314–15.

57. Katō, *Nihon mōjin shakaishi kenkyū*, 134–38; Katō, "Kinsei no shōgaisha to mibun seido," 134–36, 152–54; Taniai, *Mōjin no rekishi*, 26–57.

58. Nagai, "Chikuzen/Chikugo no mōsō shūdan to sono shūhen"; Nakai, *Nikkan mōsō no shakaishi*; Katō, *Nihon mōjin shakaishi kenkyū*, 79–99, 256–81; Katō, "Kinsei no shōgaisha to mibun seido," 136–39.

he did for other self-governing groups, and his successors Iemitsu and Tsu-nayoshi confirmed the guild's law code with some modifications (the Shikimoku in 1634 and the Shin-Shikimoku in 1692).[59] Although the *tōdōza* nominally remained under the control of a family of imperial court nobles (the House of Koga), it rejected any interference from these aris-tocrats and emphasized its link to the imperial court only when it found it opportune to do so: when asserting its right to collect alms, for exam-ple, and after the Meiji Restoration, when the guild faced the threat of elimination.[60]

During the Muromachi period (1336–1573), the *tōdōza* developed a hierarchy of ranks (*kan*) that grew increasingly complex over time. By the seventeenth century, the guild had four ranks—*kengyō, bettō, kōtō,* and *zatō* (*zatō* was also a generic label for all organized blind men)—which were subdivided into sixteen steps (*kai*) and seventy-three increments (*kizami*). Originally, these distinctions probably correlated with artistic skill and were conferred by the guild's aristocratic patron, who collected a fee in return. But by the fifteenth century, there were already cases of lords purchasing rank for their favorite performers, and as the authority of the House of Koga declined, the fees began to be collected by the guild itself. By the early Tokugawa period, the hierarchy of ranks had lost its artistic meaning and become entirely mediated by money. Even the very lowest increment required the payment of at least 4 *ryō* of gold, and the price for the highest rank of *kengyō* was 669 *ryō* or more.[61] Obviously, only blind men with wealthy families or sponsors could afford to pay these exorbitant amounts.

The privileges that came with high rank were considerable. For example, only a *kengyō* could serve on the Council of Elders. Rank also determined the share of so-called rank money (*kankin*) a member was entitled to receive. Whenever a *zatō* purchased rank, the compensation was transmitted to the headquarters in Kyoto and distributed among the upper

---

59.   Katō, *Nihon mōjin shakaishi kenkyū*, 146–52, 160–67.

60.   After a conflict in 1657, the shogunate ordered the *tōdōza* to submit at least 100 *ryō* of gold as an annual tribute to the Koga, but the Koga wielded no power over the guild aside from such financial exactions; Nakayama, *Nihon mōjinshi*, vol. 2, 67–112; Katō, *Nihon mōjin shakaishi kenkyū*, 167–71, 469.

61.   According to data compiled in Katō, *Nihon mōjin shakaishi kenkyū*, 180–81. As a general rule of thumb, 1 *ryō* was equivalent to 1 *koku* (about 180 liters) of rice.

echelons (fourth-level *zatō* or higher) of the guild's membership, with the dividend increasing with rank. The system reproduced inequality within the guild and guaranteed power and an adequate lifestyle to the blind sons of samurai and rich commoners, mirroring the distinctions in society at large.[62] In this respect, the *tōdōza* resembled a monastic order rather than a professional guild. The Buddhist orders of the Tokugawa period were composed of nonhereditary members who attained rank within their organization through their social status at birth as well as significant monetary transfers.[63] The main difference was that in the case of the *tōdōza*, internal stratification was achieved entirely through redistributing money. In smaller towns such as Ōno, and especially in the case of the semi-independent *goze* guilds, differences in rank tended to correlate with instructional relationships between master and apprentice, but in more urbanized areas there was often a gap between the two.[64]

The blind men of Ōno had names that situated them at the very bottom of this hierarchy of rank. When a blind man first joined the guild as an unranked apprentice, he took on a novice name, such as Keiya, Shun'ya, Kichiya, Shunmatsu, or Keizō.[65] After his promotion to the preliminary rank of *uchikake*, he was allowed to adopt a name either starting with Jō- (城) or ending with -ichi (一・市・都).[66] Most of the blind men who appear in Ōno's sources had obtained a Jō- or -ichi name, and one or more of them must have climbed from *uchikake* to *zatō* because only *zatō* were treated as full-fledged guild members (*shūbun*) and allowed to hold office.[67] The next major status leap was the promotion to fourth-level *zatō*, which came with the right to use a surname and participate in the distribution of rank money. It seems that none of the blind men of Ōno were able to reach this still comparatively humble position. There was an enormous gulf in status and wealth between the *zatō* of Ōno and blind

62.   Groemer, "The Guild of the Blind," 357.

63.   See, for example, Takebe, "Jiin ryōshu to chiiki shakai," 251.

64.   Katō, *Nihon mōjin shakaishi kenkyū*, 208–9.

65.   All these names appear in the journals of Ōno's town elders; MT goyōdome 1769.2.26, YH 59, 54–55; MT goyōdome 1777.4.26, SSM.

66.   Whether a blind man received a Jō- or an ichi-name depended on his master's lineage, which had originally been associated with a particular style of performing the Tale of the Heike; see Katō, *Nihon mōjin shakaishi kenkyū*, 212–13.

67.   Ibid., 196–98.

elites in large cities such as Kyoto, Edo, or Kanazawa. The vast majority of the *tōdōza* membership (around 90 percent) never crossed the threshold to fourth-level *zatō* to enter the guild's top ranks and never obtained the concomitant right to receive rank money.[68] A miscellany from Obama, a castle town in Echizen's neighbor province Wakasa, stated in 1757 that the local blind men lacked the means to make it beyond the status of ordinary *zatō*.[69] The same was probably true for other associations in smaller-sized towns, but even among *zatō* in the capital of Edo, high rank was clearly the exception. According to a survey conducted four years after the Meiji Restoration, low-ranking *zatō* made up 83.3 percent of the guild membership in the capital, and 60.6 percent of these lived in "poverty."[70]

The initial cost of entering the guild, which included payments to one's master, could be an insurmountable barrier for blind men from poor backgrounds.[71] Lacking proper instruction in the blind arts, they often ended up begging on their own or sold their labor as masseurs, itinerant performers, and in other low-skilled trades.[72] In Ōno, the *zatō* insisted that only guild members professionally engage in massage. In 1864, for example, the headman of Sanbanmachi approached the town elders about a poor widow who had become sick and saw the "massage trade" (*anma shōbai*) as her only option for making a living. He complained that the *zatō* would not let her work as a masseuse unless she entered the guild, and he asked whether the authorities could not grant her special permission.[73] It is unknown whether the government granted this request, but the case shows how jealously Ōno's *zatō* guarded their monopoly on this marginal livelihood. It also raises the question of whether and in what form the *zatō* would have been willing to integrate a female (and possibly

68. Ibid., 187–88.

69. Kizaki Tekisō, "Shūsui zatsuwa," vol. 16, 253-54.

70. The Meiji authorities assumed (falsely, as it turned out) that impoverished *zatō* would not suffer from the dissolution of the *tōdōza* because they did not receive any rank money; Katō, *Nihon mōjin shakaishi kenkyū*, 461–63, 471–72; Tokyo-to, *Tokyo shishi-kō*, Shigai-hen, 596, 612–13.

71. Even induction into a *goze* guild, where the system of rank money was less developed, could be quite costly because novices had to submit payments to their masters; see Yamada, "Matsushiro hanryō no mōjin," 214–15.

72. Katō, *Nihon mōjin shakaishi kenkyū*, 394–97, 406–7.

73. MT goyōdome 1864.3.3, SSM.

sighted) masseuse into their guild. By comparison, in Osaka it seems to have been quite common for blind townspeople and their female relatives among the urban underclass to work in massage, acupuncture, or the performance of string instruments without affiliating themselves with the *tōdōza*, even after the shogunate had reaffirmed the *tōdōza*'s monopoly in 1776.[74]

There are plenty of examples of families of small means that did manage to save the necessary amounts to join the guild, either through their own hands' labor or with the help of relatives. A poor man also had the option of joining the guild as an apprentice and then gathering his rank money on extensive begging tours (*junzai kange*).[75] It took the poor blind many years, sometimes decades, to collect the money necessary for promotion to *zatō*, if they ever achieved it at all. Wealth and family background also determined the quality of the master a *zatō* could choose as his teacher and thus influenced his chances of achieving professional success.[76] Although the *tōdōza* helped reproduce social inequality among the blind, it remained an attractive option because it provided them with access to education, work, and alms. Especially in rural areas, life as a blind professional outside the framework of the local guild would have been daunting because the market for blind skills was small there. Moreover, as we shall see, the local guilds enjoyed various protections from domain authorities. Matsushiro domain intervened in 1847 on behalf of poor blind women to lower the admission fee for the local *goze* guild. Officials called this measure a "token of benevolent government," benefiting the "blind [who] cannot perform in the same way as ordinary members of society" and who were "a status that indulges in people's pity," even "[gathering] alms at times of celebration and bereavement" from lord, vassals, townspeople, and peasants.[77]

---

74.   Tsukada, "Kinsei kōki Osaka ni okeru toshi kasō minshū no seikatsu sekai," 117–21.

75.   Katō, *Nihon mōjin shakaishi kenkyū*, 406–15; *Kankoku kōgiroku*, vol. 3, 62–63. See also the petitions from the 1830s cited in Nakagawa Miyuki, "Junzai zatō no katsudō," 14; Nakagawa Miyuki, "Chiiki shakai to junzainin," 94.

76.   Katō, *Nihon mōjin shakaishi kenkyū*, 410.

77.   Yamada, "Matsushiro hanryō no mōjin," 218–24. This study also introduces the case of a blind woman whose father entrusted her to the *goze* guild because he was too poor to support her; Yamada, "Matsushiro hanryō no mōjin," 200.

The *tōdōza* successfully navigated the massive economic and cultural changes of the seventeenth century and developed new livelihoods to survive the waning popularity of the Tale of the Heike. In the Tokugawa period, oral performances of the Tale of the Heike were relegated to a fringe existence as an elite diversion and rarely staged except during memorial services for the dead.[78] In the seventeenth century, however, some prominent blind leaders revolutionized the musical scene as performers, teachers, and composers for the new string instruments koto and shamisen.[79] Acupuncture attracted fresh interest in the seventeenth century after the transmission of new medical knowledge from Korea. Along with some sighted doctors, a number of blind guild members received training in the new technique. Toward the end of the century, shogunal acupuncturist Sugiyama Waichi established his own school of acupuncture and massage and used his political clout to promote his particular method of acupuncture among the blind. His guild gained a monopoly on these skills in the sense that all blind acupuncturists and masseurs had to submit to the control of the *tōdōza*.[80] Massage developed a mass appeal among affluent townspeople in search of health and relaxation, and blind masseurs became a fixture of pleasure quarters and inns.[81] In the Genroku period (1688–1704) and thereafter, shamisen and koto play became popular hobbies among townspeople and opened up a new livelihood for *zatō* and *goze* as musical instructors. By the late

78. Katō, *Nihon mōjin shakaishi kenkyū*, 102–3. For an example of a household that had the Tale of the Heike performed during funerals and memorial services, see Asao, "Ikoma-ke to zatō/goze nakama," 79, 84. Members of the *tōdōza* did, however, instruct growing numbers of sighted amateurs in performing the tale; see Tan, "The Careers of the Blind in Tokugawa Japan," 112–72.

79. Groemer, "The Guild of the Blind," 362–63; Katō, *Nihon mōjin shakaishi kenkyū*, 99–106.

80. Katō, *Nihon mōjin shakaishi kenkyū*, 119–23, 531–48. As Tan argues, the acupuncture school established by Sugiyama Waichi was not fully controlled by the *tōdōza*, but it became a hereditary institution led by the descendants of one of its first heads and as such began to accept sighted students as well; see "The Careers of the Blind in Tokugawa Japan," 179–207, 226–29.

81. Jippensha Ikku, *Shank's Mare*, 55, 160–64; Koikawa Harumachi, "Kinkin sensei eiga no yume," 321–35; Kuriyama, "Fukushin: Some Observations on Economic Development and the Imagination of the Body"; Tan, "The Careers of the Blind in Tokugawa Japan," 207–26.

eighteenth century, even townspeople in remote areas such as Ōno were learning the shamisen.[82]

Considering the growth of these markets, it is not surprising to find sighted people making inroads into blind occupations. In the seventeenth century, prostitutes and dramatic storytellers began to perform on the shamisen, and sighted townspeople started to offer musical instruction. Massage was an especially attractive livelihood for the poor because it did not require much training. In big cities, demand for blind arts was so large and instruction so accessible that practitioners no longer needed to rely on the guild for training and protection. But even Ōno's *zatō* struggled with the presence of the so-called lay blind (*mōjin* or *zoku-mōjin*)—unlicensed blind professionals—who competed with them for apprentices and clients throughout the eighteenth and nineteenth centuries.[83] The shogunate did not do much to stem this tide, although it issued an edict in 1776 to force blind commoners who practiced blind livelihoods under the oversight of the *tōdōza*.[84] During the Kansei reform in the 1790s, shogunate elder Matsudaira Sadanobu briefly considered taking the medical monopoly away from the blind entirely and instead expanding their jurisdiction over entertainers. When shogunate and domains cracked down on entertainers in the context of moral reform, they often made an exception for the blind, most likely because they wanted to avoid undermining their livelihood.[85]

Little is known about the musical skills of Ōno's *zatō* and *goze*, but the townspeople of Ōno seem to have appreciated the blind men's medical treatments. For example, *zatō* could be called alongside town doctors

82. Nakagawa Sugane, "Utajamisen no shūhen"; MT goyōdome 1799.8.2, YH 494, 339–40.

83. MT goyōdome 1769.2.16, 2.26, 3.11, 1777.4.26, SSM. In 1844, a high-ranking blind leader from Kyoto came to Ōno to force three local lay blind into the guild, and in 1850, the domain government ordered four lay blind to join the *tōdōza* under threat of punishment; MT goyōdome 1844.4.17, YH 875, 648; 1850.5.25, Ōno-han yōdome bassui eisei shokusan kōgyō, Echizen Ōno Doi-ke monjo. In the 1850s, the Yoshida School, which taught massage and acupuncture primarily among the sighted, tried to establish itself in Ōno; MT shogandome 1853, fourth month, YH 1033, 761.

84. *Ofuregaki Tenmei shūsei* no. 3191, 955; Groemer, "The Guild of the Blind," 365–66.

85. Katō, *Nihon mōjin shakaishi kenkyū*, 339–44, 400–403.

to assist with childbirth.[86] In 1740 the lord upset the town doctors by employing one of the local *zatō* as his personal acupuncturist. The physicians complained that the *zatō*'s methods were inferior to the internal medicine (*hondō*) they were practicing. The town doctors' objections were directed not so much against the *zatō*'s high-level employment, which was fairly common among daimyo, but against the disrespect the lord had shown for their own autonomy and occupation. He had chosen the man almost at random from among the local blind mendicants, turned him into a town doctor without the doctors' consent, and even promoted him to a rank higher than theirs. This case, and the way the town elders wrote about it in their journal, suggest that the *zatō* were not considered proper physicians and their status in town society was low.[87]

Especially in rural areas, where market demand was less concentrated, blind men and women continued an itinerant lifestyle throughout the Tokugawa period. Some *zatō* traveled widely in search of opportunities to perform. In 1834, two blind apprentices from Fukui came to Ōno, accompanied by a woman from the Noto Peninsula who was serving as their guide.[88] In such cases, the domain seems to have allowed the strangers to practice their arts on its territory if they carried letters of introduction from blind leaders in other towns and practiced arts that fell within the range of blind men's occupations. The local guild members hosted them and vouched for their conduct vis-à-vis the authorities. The *zatō* and *goze* of Ōno, too, often traveled through the countryside of inner Echizen and left traces in the documents of local villages. In Imai, a village on the Ōno plain, the headman kept a record of blind visitors from 1851 to 1871.[89] His register noted only the blind who stayed overnight: small groups of *zatō* from Ōno (two to six people each) and Katsuyama (two to five people), who were assigned to different peasant households. The

86. MT goyōdome 1787.4.16, SSM. From the late eighteenth century onward, massage won popularity as a gynecological and obstetrical treatment; see Tan, "The Careers of the Blind in Tokugawa Japan," 221–24.

87. MT goyōdome 1740.2.10, YH 5, 4; MT goyōdome 1740.3.15, 5.20, 12.26; 1741, first month, 1.11, 7.1, 12.27, SSM.

88. MT goyōdome 1834.4.16, SSM. See also MT goyōdome 1797.5.10 and 5.30, YH 450 and 452, 314–15.

89. Sairei kamaban narabi ni zatō goze tomariyado oboe-chō, 1851, Yamada Saburōbei-ke monjo.

village received two to five such visits each year; only once there were nine. *Goze* groups from Ōno and Katsuyama also stayed overnight on occasion.

The register shows that Imai village regularly lodged blind men from Katsuyama and Ōno even though it belonged to neither of these two domains. Apparently, blind itinerancy in Echizen was not regulated very tightly, not even in the vagrant-plagued Bakumatsu years, and domain borders were crossed with ease. The blind guilds of the two castle towns toured the countryside at least twice a year, preferably in the spring and autumn, and they did so separately from each other. Many villages on the Ōno plain and surrounding mountain valleys produced annual records of blind visitors to share the cost of hosting and feeding them. Yokomakura, the only village of Ōno domain for which such records have survived, divided the cost among the full peasants, half of it by landholdings and the other half by household, possibly as part of a larger redistributive formula that covered several villages.[90] Villages of other domains in the area worked out other amounts and modes of cost sharing.[91] In addition, the townspeople community of Ōno supplied *zatō* and *goze* with guides for their travels, and villagers probably did so as well.[92]

As itinerants, the blind shared the road with pilgrims, mendicant monks, and wandering entertainers. All these travelers relied on the hospitality of villages and towns along the road to fund their journeys, but they offered something in return. Itinerant clerics, ascetics, and pilgrims commanded spiritual powers; by hosting them, villagers could indirectly participate in their austerities and acquire merit for themselves and the

90. Uma no toshi mura sashihikimaichō, 1774, Mura sashihikichō, 1775, Saru mura sashihikichō, 1776, Nojiri Kiheiji-ke monjo; Gōchū shoshiki warikata oboe, 1725, Yasukawa Yozaemon-ke monjo.

91. See, for example, On-nengu sashihikichō etc., 1714–1871, Kose Norio-ke monjo (Nagano village); "On-kōgi kakarimono sono hoka issai warichō," 1782, in *Ōno shishi*, Shoke monjo-hen 2, 992–96 (Tsuchiuchi village); Aikime-mōsu shōmon no koto, 1771, Matsumura Toshiaki-ke monjo (Rokuroshi village); "Mura sōdan aikime-mōsu jōmoku no koto," 1743, in *Fukui kenshi*, Shiryō-hen 7, 189–91 (Warabyō village); "Bunka jūsannen hachigatsu murakata ken'yaku no gi sadame oboe," 1816, in *Heisenji shiyō*, 304 (Heisenji village).

92. Yōroku, 1852, SSM.

community.[93] Traveling performers brought songs, tales, and news from the wider world. *Goze* and *zatō* belonged to this latter category of itinerant entertainers. In Takada in Echigo Province, where the custom of blind itinerancy survived into the twentieth century, *goze* told interviewers that they went from door to door during the day and performed songs for their host villages at night.[94]

Travel assistance for itinerants existed in a gray zone of mutual benefit, hospitality, and aggressive solicitation, but it was endorsed at the highest political level. In the 1760s and 1770s, the shogunate issued a number of decrees that prohibited the extortionist practices of a variety of itinerants: masterless samurai (1769 and 1774), mendicant flute-playing priests of the Fuke sect (*komusō*; 1774), and "traveling monks, mountain ascetics, *goze*, *zatō*, and other similar mendicants" (1774).[95] It conceded that all these travelers, with the exception of the masterless samurai, had the right to collect contributions "as much as the giver desired," and to ask for lodging "on a mutual basis." Only in case they went too far and extorted alms, complained, pretended to be sick, or beat people did the decrees order apprehending them and handing them over to authorities. These shogunal edicts also applied to the domains of Echizen Province, but as long as the blind itinerants behaved appropriately, they were able to roam the countryside relatively undisturbed. Domains in that area do not seem to have made any prescriptions to the villages regarding the proper amount of travel support.

Blind Mendicancy

Assistance for the blind can be broken down into three categories: (a) room, board, guides, and pocket money for traveling performers; (b) alms on life cycle–related occasions such as weddings and funerals (known as

93. Kouamé, *Pèlerinage et Société*, 175–84; Kouamé, "Le pèlerinage de Shikoku pendant l'époque d'Edo," 221–28.

94. *Jōetsu shishi*, Tsūshi-hen 7, 341–45; Groemer, *Goze to goze-uta*, Shiryō-hen, 621–24.

95. *Ofuregaki Tenmei shūsei* no. 3097, 922–23, no. 3104, 925–26, no. 3105, 926.

haitō, shūgi, fuse, etc.);[96] and (c) donations to assist with the purchase of rank (*junzai kange* or *kaizai kange*).[97] The differences between these types might seem insignificant to a modern observer, but the blind and their benefactors took them very seriously. Because the blind were neither monks nor ascetics, they could not claim to be collecting alms as an austerity. On what grounds did they assert the right to request such assistance? The shogunate never made an official proclamation regarding the begging rights of the blind,[98] but the *tōdōza* justified them with imperial and shogunal compassion. The best way to understand the rationale is by examining cases in which the blind were forced to defend their begging privileges.

Like the Koshirō and other mendicant outcastes, the blind collected life-cycle alms from local villagers, townspeople, and vassals on the basis of precedent and long-term agreements (fig. 14). In Ōno domain, there was a regulation for vassals dating from 1803 that determined the amounts of life-cycle alms for the blind down to the third decimal place and tied them to the amount of warriors' stipends.[99] A house elder with a stipend of 400 *koku* was expected to donate 15.624 *monme* of silver on a wedding, whereas a foot soldier had to give only 1.5 *monme*. For townspeople, the amount correlated with the number of servants employed by the household.[100] No written agreement has survived from the peasantry, but in 1818, the *zatō* submitted a list of almsgiving precedents in the

96. *Haitō* had two meanings in the context of blind mendicancy: (a) the life cycle alms themselves, and (b) the act of redistributing alms and rank money within the organization. *Shūgi* denoted alms on auspicious occasions, *fuse* those on occasions of funerals and memorial services for the dead.

97. See note 75. The law code of 1634 cited in the Tōdōyōshū included a (probably unenforced) provision that the guild would execute members who begged for rank money but never applied for promotion; "Tōdōyōshū," 237.

98. Namase and others point out that the law code "Tokugawa seiken hyakkajō" stipulated that the shogunate should provide leatherworking outcastes, beggars, and the blind with relief as a part of benevolent government; Namase, *Nihon no shōgaisha no rekishi,* Kinsei-hen, 95. But according to legal historian Hiramatsu Yoshirō, this text is unlikely to have been produced by the shogunate and probably dates from the latter half of the Tokugawa period; see Hiramatsu, "Kinsei-hō," 335.

99. A copy of this agreement is included in the town governor's precedent manual, Tsutomekata oboegaki Tamura-hikae, 1810, TKM.

100. Zatō, goze, kojikigashira e shūgi fuse no oboe, 1791, Mugiya monjo; Yōroku, 1852, SSM.

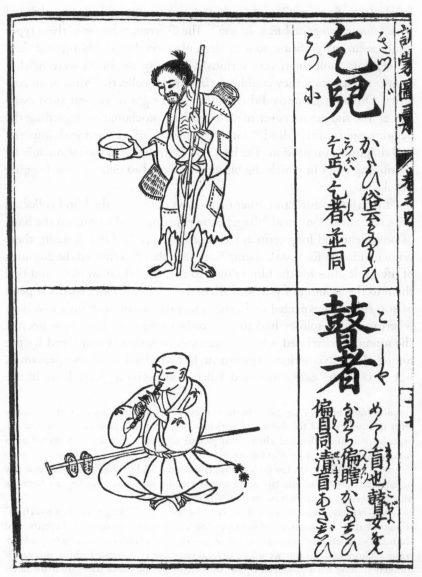

FIGURE 14 The items "beggar" and "blind man" are paired in Nakamura Tekisai's illustrated Chinese-Japanese encyclopedia *Kinmō zui* of 1666.

countryside that based donations on a household's "rank" (*kaku, iegara*) and exempted landless full peasants and hereditary tenant farmers entirely. The greatest donors on the list were Hanaguro and Nojiri, the two wealthiest peasants of Ōno domain; some of the others were powerful peasants in neighboring fiefs. The offerings were differentiated by rank and occasion. In Ōno, almsgiving to the blind was limited to weddings, funerals, and memorial services for the dead, and the full amount was due only on weddings. Funerals were worth half as much as weddings, and services for the dead half as much as funerals.

Ōno's blind guilds defended their begging rights by emphasizing their poverty. In 1818, the two leaders of the *zatō* guild wrote in a petition to the domain government that "we have never been able to live only from massage and acupuncture to begin with; we are a status that survives by the support of society [*sejō no fujo o motte tachiyuki-sōrō mibun*]."[101] The support they were referring to in this appeal was the collection of life-cycle alms. A similar argument appeared in a much earlier petition of 1769:

> Item: We get no alms at all here on the occasion of changes of household headship and coming-of-age ceremonies, neither from the vassals nor from town and villages. Hence we are suffering, poor as we are. However, [these alms] do exist in other domains, and we would thus be grateful if you could relieve us poor people by compassionately issuing orders so that in this place, too, we will receive celebratory alms appropriate to the giver's station.[102]

The main objective of this petition was to persuade the domain to crack down on local lay blind healers who refused to join the guild. It seems that the *zatō* brought up the alms issue to raise the specter of aggressive solicitation in case the domain refused to act against the lay blind. Although the domain eventually rejected this petition, the interaction shows that the blind considered their government capable of interfering with

101.   MT goyōdome 1818.7.26, YH 615, 438. For the full text of the petition, see MT shogandome (fragments), SSM. This was a credible claim; Katō estimates that the daily income of a masseur did not even match that of an unskilled day laborer; *Nihon mōjin shakaishi kenkyū*, 398–99.

102.   MT goyōdome 1769.2.16, SSM.

local almsgiving customs—a reasonable expectation, considering that the domain did intervene in 1845 to increase almsgiving for the Koshirō, as explained in chapter 2.

   In other regions, blind associations had more success negotiating begging rights with the samurai authorities. In Yamato Province, for example, the blind were forced to defend their privileges against an increasingly skeptical peasantry. In 1842, the Yamato Province guild overseer presented the shogunate governor in the city of Nara with a founding narrative (*yuisho*) that attributed the guild's privileges to an emperor in the ninth century who sought to provide for his blind brother,[103] and explained the origins of life-cycle alms as follows:

> During the reign of Shijōin, the eighty-sixth of human rulers, the emperor felt pity with the people of our way having no means of sustenance and bestowed upon them the taxes he collected from the various professions on occasions of celebration and bereavement. Tradition has it that this is the origin of the alms privilege. . . . Tōshōgū-sama [Tokugawa Ieyasu] . . . announced that he would preserve the rules of our way according to the precedent of the past. He ordered that as a matter of course, he would eternally grant people of *kengyō* and *kōtō* rank the rank money from within the guild, and would endow members ranked *zatō* or lower with the taxes from the various professions according to precedent.[104]

   This passage drew on the guild internal record *Tōdōyōshū* and probably reflected the position of the guild leadership.[105] The historical basis of these claims was extremely questionable. Although it is true that Tokugawa Ieyasu confirmed the guild's body of precedents when he came to power, influential critics of the *tōdōza*, such as Tokugawa Mitsukuni and Ogyū Sorai, rejected the references to imperial lineage and privilege. In the final years of the Tokugawa period, Shirai Hirokage, a phonologist

---

103. See note 10.
104. Nakagawa Miyuki, "Junzai zatō no katsudō," 9–11.
105. "Tōdōyōshū," 240. Katō tentatively dates this record to the 1740s; *Nihon mōjin shakaishi kenkyū*, 152–54; Nakayama, *Nihon mōjinshi*, vol. 1, 26–29, 250, 321–23. On the founding legend of the *Tōdōyōshū* and alternate versions, see Fritsch, *Japan's blinde Sänger*, 78–140; Nakagawa Miyuki, "Kinsei ni okeru tōdō soshin denshō no hen'yō"; Nakagawa Miyuki, "Kinsei ni okeru tōdō soshin denshō no hen'yō (sono ni)."

and scholar of national learning, used careful philological analysis to expose the historical inconsistencies in the *Tōdōyōshū*.[106] Yet the tale of imperial compassion remained an important tool for the *zatō* in defending their begging privilege.[107] Officials in the shogunate and domain administrations never openly denied its veracity even though they might have doubted privately. Most likely they did so because many social groups, including the warrior houses, relied on similarly dubious legends to obtain official recognition. The reference to imperial benevolence was especially compelling because it reminded critics that the blind were helpless and deserving of relief. Last, the tale had an uplifting effect on the blind because it enhanced their pride and collective identity.[108]

Although there is no evidence for the shogunate explicitly conferring begging rights on the *tōdōza* as a whole, many domain governments concluded almsgiving agreements with the local blind in the second half of the seventeenth century. Fukui domain, for example, issued one in 1661–62 on behalf of its vassals.[109] Between the 1660s and 1680s, Japan experienced a wave of blind mendicancy for which there are two different explanations. According to Katō, many of the small peasant households that had gained independence within villages in the seventeenth century proved unable to care for their disabled dependents and abandoned them when faced with famine in the 1670s. Blind performers struggled during those years because the popularity of the Tale of the Heike had already declined, whereas the market for music, massage, and acupuncture had not yet sufficiently developed.[110] Groemer, on the other hand, argues that strong economic growth during the late seventeenth century probably

106. Katō, *Nihon mōjin shakaishi kenkyū*, 234–35; Nakayama, *Nihon mōjinshi*, vol. 1, 26–47.

107. See, for example, Matsumoto Eiko, "Kinsei shakai ni okeru zatō/koze [*sic*] no kōsatsu," 65. In 1766, the guild headquarters distributed copies of yet another version of the legend to guilds across the country; see Fritsch, *Japans blinde Sänger*, 117; Yamada, "Matsushiro hanryō no mōjin," 180–82. Even the author of "An Account of What I Have Seen and Heard" (1816), who was a harsh critic of blind begging and moneylending, accepted the legend as true; see *Lust, Commerce, and Corruption*, 193–208.

108. On this point, see Sugino, "Shōgai no bunka bunseki."

109. "Goyō sho-shikimoku," in *Fukui kenshi*, Shiryō-hen 3, 81. In Katsuyama domain, an agreement covering vassals was concluded in 1692; *Katsuyama shishi*, vol. 1, 1027.

110. Katō, *Nihon mōjin shakaishi kenkyū*, 158–60.

improved the situation of many commoners and allowed more blind people to leave their families and get by on alms.[111] Considering the unevenness of economic growth between regions, it is likely that both of these explanations have some validity and that these trends unfolded at the same time.

Without the prestige of the *tōdōza*, most of these blind beggars would probably have ended up under the wing of one of the emerging outcaste beggar organizations. Instead, the authorities chose to entrust the control of blind beggars to self-governing groups of blind performers and forced all these groups to submit to the *tōdōza*. Asao Naohiro has traced the formalization of blind begging in the 1670s and 1680s through the case of Owari domain.[112] In Owari, the conclusion of almsgiving agreements went hand in hand with a centralization of the local guilds. Existing confraternities of *zatō* gradually coalesced into a domain-based organization under the control of the blind in the castle town of Nagoya. Whereas *zatō* and *goze* had previously needed to go directly to the givers' houses to request alms, they now received them from the guild leaders, who distributed them according to rank. This transition was strikingly similar to the introduction of centralized stipend payments for vassals, who had been moved from their fiefs to the castle town. The result was a disciplined and hierarchical association of blind performers whose territory roughly coincided with the territory of the domain. During the same years, the *tōdōza* transformed from a professional guild into what Katō has called a *haitōza*—an organization that supervised blind beggars and guaranteed the orderly collection and distribution of rank money and alms. The *tōdōza* benefited from this development because it could extend its power over local guilds, but the guild's structure now reflected the interest of Tokugawa rulers in controlling blind mendicancy.

In Ōno, the surviving documentation on the blind only goes back to the middle of the eighteenth century, and by that time, the male blind leaders were collecting predetermined amounts of alms from the lord on behalf of the whole group. Each time the lord's family experienced an event of celebration or mourning, one of the guild leaders was summoned to the office of the town elders, who handed out the lord's alms (usually

---

111.   Groemer, *Goze to goze-uta*, Kenkyū-hen, 93–96.
112.   Asao, "Ikoma-ke to zatō/goze nakama," 79–93.

silver money) in exchange for a receipt. The leader distributed the money to the other guild members and the *goze*. Initially, the blind men also seem to have received life-cycle alms on behalf of the Koshirō, but in 1740, the guild leaders suddenly refused to issue a receipt for the outcastes' share and pushed the town elder to accept a compromise. After collecting the full amount of alms and submitting the receipt, they would return the Koshirō's portion to the town elder on duty and ask him to hand the money over to the beggars in their stead. Over time, this informal compromise developed into a precedent in its own right.[113] The incident shows that the blind were uncomfortable serving as the representatives of outcastes in an official setting.

The status anxiety of the blind was not unfounded. Some prominent critics of the *tōdōza* such as Tokugawa Mitsukuni, the lord of Mito domain, and Ogyū Sorai, scholar and shogunal adviser, maligned even the highest-ranking guild members as beggars,[114] and Edo's outcaste boss Danzaemon was rumored to have tried to bring the *tōdōza* under his control.[115] The *tōdōza* countered by refusing membership to people of outcaste origin and avoided asking outcastes for alms.[116] Especially for the lower rungs of the guild, however, the distancing from outcastes remained a balancing act. Although they depended on the collection of alms economically, they had to obfuscate the fact that they were begging at all. In Ōno, for example, the blind did not try to compete with the Koshirō for the same kinds of alms. Whereas the beggar bosses derived the bulk of their income from seasonal begging, the blind did not engage in such begging and instead collected much higher amounts than the Koshirō on life cycle–related occasions.[117] This phenomenon can be observed in many parts of Japan, although one could argue that the blind did in fact

113. MT goyōdome 1740.1.28, 1855.6.12, SSM.

114. Nakayama, *Nihon mōjinshi*, vol. 1, 30–31; Katō, *Nihon mōjin shakaishi kenkyū*, 234; *Ogyu Sorai's Discourse on Government (Seidan)*, 285–86.

115. Groemer, "The Guild of the Blind," 352–55.

116. Ibid., 352–55; Matsumoto Eiko, "Kinsei shakai ni okeru zatō/koze [*sic*] no kōsatsu," 62–67; Yamada, "Matsushiro hanryō no mōjin."

117. Matsumoto Eiko does not interpret the collection of life-cycle alms as begging ("Kinsei shakai ni okeru zatō/koze [*sic*] no kōsatsu," 62, 64), but this argument seems to be based on the impression the *tōdōza* itself wished to convey. Begging in the Tokugawa period was especially common on seasonal and life cycle–related occasions. On this problem, see also Fritsch, *Japans blinde Sänger*, 77.

engage in seasonal begging when they toured the countryside in the spring and autumn.

Like the Koshirō, the blind of Ōno appear to have had some difficulty maintaining their level of alms income in the second half of the Tokugawa period. For example, the *zatō* and *goze* were affected by the domain's fiscal problems. In 1741, when his heir married, the lord gave out fewer alms than usual and justified the decision with the need to save money.[118] In 1803, the domain government lowered almsgiving standards for vassals because it had borrowed a significant part of the vassals' stipends.[119] There is no indication that the domain ever raised almsgiving standards on behalf of the blind, as it did for the Koshirō in 1845. In 1818, the officials made an inquiry into customs of almsgiving for the blind in the countryside, apparently with the intention of standardizing them, but the blind suspected that the domain was planning to decrease the amounts and threatened that if the lord went ahead with the plan, they would need to ask for compensation, for example, by expanding the pool of givers to landless peasants and tenants.

Most likely, the domain was less interested in the *zatō*'s income because the blind were not as useful as the Koshirō in maintaining public order. Whereas the Koshirō served as a vagrant police and helped protect the castle town from crime, the *zatō* were primarily responsible for controlling their own members. The complaints about deviance of the blind that appear in local sources were of a rather harmless nature: lay blind who refused to join the guild and local *goze* who did not follow the blind men's orders.[120] When it came to blind professionals who were not part of their organization, the *zatō* were relatively powerless and needed help from the authorities to enforce their monopoly.

This is not to say that the domain did not appreciate the blind's contributions to public order. After the Tenpō famine in the 1830s, Echizen Province experienced a surge in unregulated blind begging, and in 1845,

118. MT goyōdome 1741.12.11, SSM.
119. Tsutomekata oboegaki Tamura-hikae, 1810, TKM. By contrast, the shogun's household increased alms for the blind of Edo in the late eighteenth century, probably because it wanted to strengthen the declining *tōdōza*; Katō, *Nihon mōjin shakaishi kenkyū*, 445–46.
120. MT goyōdome 1769.2.26, YH 59, 54–55; 1815.2.7, YH 587, 410–11; 1815.2.12, 2.13, 2.19, SSM.

Heisenji, a village near Ōno but part of Katsuyama domain, obtained the following promise from the blind guilds of Ōno and Katsuyama:

> Since the past, the members of our guilds have been visiting your and other honorable villages and have entrusted ourselves to your care, and for that we are very grateful. Yet, we have heard that these days, lawless people are going around pretending [to be *zatō*], and we deeply regret this. We have now examined our stamps and asked our members to carry one, and we therefore request that from now on you compare them [with those on the stamp register we have provided to you] and continue to support us. Besides, please do not accommodate people who do not carry matching stamps, not even for a single night, let alone allow them to beg.[121]

It seems there were fraudulent *zatō* in the region, and the local blind associations tried to preserve the villagers' goodwill by distributing stamp registers to help them identify the pretenders. In 1850, Ōno domain forced four unorganized lay acupuncturists to join the *zatō* guild, even though it had largely ignored their presence until that point.[122] This might be a sign that the government was taking disorder among the blind more seriously and tried to strengthen the local guild.[123] The problem was not limited to Echizen Province. In nineteenth-century Yamato, villagers complained about rising numbers of blind mendicants who collected alms under the pretext of gathering rank money, and they began to formalize their payments to local guild leaders. The *zatō* chose to call these transfers "rank money arrangement fees" (*kanmotsu torihakarawase-ryō*), whereas the villagers referred to them as protection money (*torishimari-ryō*).[124]

121. *Heisenji monjo*, vol. 2, 356–57. For another example of a *zatō* guild distributing stamp registers, see Matsumoto Eiko, "Kinsei shakai ni okeru zatō/koze [*sic*] no kōsatsu," 63–64.

122. Ōno-han yōdome bassui eisei shokusan kōgyō, 1850.5.25, Echizen Ōno Doike monjo.

123. In 1856 or earlier, a group of villages in Ōno's neighbor domain Sabae also began to make semiannual protection payments (*shikiri-gin*) to an unidentified group of *zatō*; Zatō shikiri-gin muramura wappuchō, 1856, 1858–65, 1867–69, Oka Fumio-ke monjo. On the role of village groups in managing collective payments to mendicants, see Yabuta, *Kokuso to hyakushō ikki no kenkyū*, 312–22.

124. Nakagawa Miyuki, "Chiiki shakai to junzainin"; Nakagawa Miyuki, "Bakumatsu/Meiji shoki no junzai zatō."

The most thorough effort of institutionalizing and territorializing blind mendicancy unfolded in southwestern Japan. In the seventeenth and early eighteenth century, several southwestern domains decided to replace travel support with stipends (called *ibuchi*, etc.) that minimized confrontations between the blind and their givers and excluded the subjects of other jurisdictions.[125] In Uwajima domain on the island of Shikoku in 1698, the blind asked for the introduction of stipends, arguing that travel in mountainous territory was arduous and that hosting itinerants distracted peasants from their work in the fields.[126] In Tokuyama, in 1724, peasants joined the blind in petitioning for a stipend system to free themselves from the inconvenience of having to guide and feed blind travelers. Other examples include Matsuyama (1702), Iwakuni (1717), Chōshū (1734), Hiroshima (1757), and Takamatsu (1845).[127] Often, the process seems to have started with travel restrictions, which forced the local blind to move within a narrow strip of land and increased frictions with the peasantry. This created a situation in which the introduction of stipends became almost inevitable. Interventions like these also seem to have triggered chain reactions in surrounding domains because they prevented the blind there from traveling through territories other than their own.

One domain that tried to territorialize blind mendicancy was Tosa, a large, contiguous fief on the island of Shikoku.[128] According to a document produced by Tosa's *zatō* guild, in the 1670s the domain had limited blind travel within its borders to the domestic blind and excluded all outsiders.[129] But because the *zatō* insisted on their right to travel countrywide, the domain was forced to negotiate with the *tōdōza* in Kyoto and eventually granted the privilege of *jige makanai* (literally: "provision by

125. Katō, *Nihon mōjin shakaishi kenkyū*, 429–36; Groemer, *Goze to goze-uta*, Kenkyū-hen, 92–123.

126. Katō, *Nihon mōjin shakaishi kenkyū*, 430; Groemer, *Goze to goze-uta*, Kenkyū-hen, 100–104.

127. In all these domains, the giving of life-cycle alms was organized separately from the stipends but was also strictly regulated; Groemer, *Goze to goze-uta*, Kenkyū-hen, 105, passim.

128. Matsumoto Eiko, "Kinsei shakai ni okeru zatō/koze [*sic*] no kōsatsu"; Hiroe, "Kinsei goze zatō-kō," 1–7.

129. Dated 1720; *Kenshōbo*, vol. 5, Mōjin no bu, 495–97, 516, 533; Matsumoto Eiko, "Kinsei shakai ni okeru zatō/koze [*sic*] no kōsatsu," 54–55.

the local people") to its local blind, who in turn agreed to remain within the fief. As a result, the organized blind of Tosa began to live as officially protected itinerants and eventually as passive recipients of stipends. Whenever *zatō* or *goze* passed through a village, peasants were obliged by domain law to supply them with pocket money, food, shelter, guides, and (in the case of higher-ranking *zatō*) even horses for the next leg of their journey. The institutionalization of travel aid did not stop there. In the 1780s, around the time of the Tenmei famine, some villages complained that they had to host about 300 *zatō* and *goze* a year, about 200 of whom stayed overnight. After the famine, the government restricted blind travel further and instead granted substantial stipends of rice and money (one *koku* or more) that were entirely funded by the peasantry on the basis of a standardized formula.[130] Even then, villages remained responsible for supplying the blind with guides, as Tosa never prohibited blind travel entirely.

Stipends for the blind had advantages for everyone involved. They minimized confrontations with the peasantry, improved public order, and allowed the blind to make a living without doing any actual traveling. They also created their own set of problems. On one hand, the stipends were vulnerable to cuts at times of fiscal crisis and famine; on the other hand, they could make membership in the guilds too attractive. Tosa domain was forced to impose strict criteria for admission: young age (fourteen or lower) to ensure that applicants were serious about learning a blind art or a poor background.[131] Apparently these limitations did not suffice to prevent the guilds from substantially growing after the stipends had been instituted. In the 1860s, high inflation finally foreclosed any possibility of reconciling the interests of the blind with those of the peasants, as the blind demanded higher stipends while the peasants petitioned for tax relief. This dilemma seems to have been the main reason Tosa eventually abolished blind privilege in 1870, one year before the new Meiji government decided to take a similar step.[132]

130. *Kenshōbo*, vol. 5, Mōjin no bu, 499–501.

131. Ibid., 509, 517–18, 532.

132. Matsumoto Eiko, "Kinsei shakai ni okeru zatō/koze [*sic*] no kōsatsu," 59–60; Hiroe, "Kinsei goze zatō-kō," 6–7. In other parts of Japan, too, the inflation of the 1860s had a destabilizing effect on travel support for the blind and other forms of almsgiving; see Groemer, *Goze to goze-uta*, Kenkyū-hen, 269.

In this way, travel support for the blind transformed from a customary system of village hospitality into a domain-wide tax, which served the purpose of control and relief and resembled a modern, tax-funded welfare scheme. At the same time, the tax only benefited a small subset among the blind, namely, those who had begging privileges. It thus remained firmly anchored in the framework of the status order.[133] In a territorially fragmented region like Echizen, domains would have found it much more difficult to confine the blind within their fiefs, but some of the western domains that introduced stipends were not particularly large either. Katō speculates that systems of this kind could only develop in regions that were so agriculturally advanced that the peasants could afford to shoulder these taxes, but not developed enough to provide sufficient begging opportunities and markets for the blind arts.[134] These conditions could have applied to parts of Echizen Province.[135] Tosa's case shows that *zatō* and *goze* perceived countrywide travel as a right and used the authority of the *tōdōza* to defend it. Although the custom of hosting blind itinerants in the Ōno area remained more informal than in the southwest, it could potentially have evolved into a more centralized and formal mechanism of support.

After the Meiji Restoration, the welfare function of the guilds of the blind was a much-discussed subject among the officials of the new government who were charged with deciding the fate of the *tōdōza*. A document of the Kyoto regional authorities stated: "Because blind people constitute part of the poor, of course they would support themselves by receiving

---

133.   Katō, *Nihon mōjin shakaishi kenkyū*, 435–36; Matsumoto Eiko, "Kinsei shakai ni okeru zatō/koze [*sic*] no kōsatsu," 68. See also Yabuta, *Kokuso to hyakushō ikki no kenkyū*, 320.

134.   Katō, *Nihon mōjin shakaishi kenkyū*, 436.

135.   The presence of groups of blind monks (*mōsō*) in western Japan could have been another factor. In Kyushu and western Honshu (though not in Tosa), villagers received regular visits from these monks, who had their own, Kyoto-based status organization and specialized in performing hearth rituals after the *tōdōza* had pushed them out of the entertaining professions; see Nagai, "Chikuzen/Chikugo no mōsō shūdan"; Katō, *Nihon mōjin shakaishi kenkyū*, 79–99, 256–81; Katō, "Kinsei no shōgaisha to mibun seido," 136–37.

alms from various constituencies."[136] But when blind privilege was abolished in 1871, the government provided hardly any safety net and forced the blind to get by without official protection. When Tosa domain dismantled its stipend system in 1870, it announced that former beneficiaries should henceforth be provided for by their families and if necessary apply for general types of poor relief; those who had no relatives should enter a so-called poorhouse (*hin'in*).[137] One of the most prominent poorhouses of the late Meiji period, the Ono Jizen'in in Kanazawa (which still operates today), started out in 1873 as a private shelter for blind people who had lost their support after the dissolution of the *tōdōza*.[138] Well into the Meiji period, relief petitions submitted on behalf of blind people deplored the loss of begging privileges.[139]

The eventual fate of the *zatō* and *goze* of Ōno is unknown. After the Meiji Restoration, some of them might have been accomplished enough to stand on their own feet as musicians or healers, but they would have had to cope with growing competition from sighted musicians and acupuncturists. They would also have faced new restrictions imposed on their medical livelihoods by the Medical Regulations of 1874, which established modern standards for medical practice and education.[140] Perhaps some of Ōno's *zatō* and *goze* participated in the nascent movement for blind rights, which until the 1910s focused primarily on reinstituting the massage monopoly.[141] It is also possible that Ōno's blind continued to collect support informally while traveling the countryside as itinerant masseurs

136. Katō, *Nihon mōjin shakaishi kenkyū*, 455. See also Tokyo-to, *Tokyo shishi-kō*, Shigai-hen, 586–620; and Yokoyama, *Meiji ishin to kinsei mibunsei no kaitai*, 218–23, on Tokyo officials debating the consequences of dissolving the *tōdōza*.

137. Matsumoto Eiko, "Kinsei shakai ni okeru zatō/koze [*sic*] no kōsatsu," 59–60; Hiroe, "Kinsei goze zatō-kō," 6–7.

138. Ikeda, "Ono Jizen'in no seiritsu," 24–26.

139. Katō, *Nihon mōjin shakaishi kenkyū*, 390.

140. The Medical Regulations (Isei) of 1874 stipulated that acupuncturists must practice under the supervision of a licensed medical doctor. A licensing system for acupuncturists was introduced in 1885; Namase, "Hoshō: Kin-gendai no 'shikaku shōgaisha' o megutte," 221–23.

141. Sugino, "Shōgaisha undō no soshiki to nettowāku," 92–94.

and performers.[142] Whatever donations they now received were based on informal custom rather than institutional protection.

The guilds of the blind were a typical product of how the Tokugawa state governed and protected poor and itinerant people. The authorities did not address disability itself but focused on the problem of abandonment. They applied the principle of rule by occupation and transferred the burden of support from families and residential communities to mendicant guilds, and through them to society at large. Although the blind had to acquire skills to make a living, they depended heavily on the official protection of their livelihoods and begging customs. From the perspective of administrators, the organized blind were less useful than the beggar guilds because they did not perform major public duties; their only significant duty was the control of other blind itinerants. Yet the powerful leadership of the *tōdōza* provided the blind with an influential voice in government circles. Many of the funds the guild extracted from society were channeled upward to back up the prestige of these leaders. But the powerful headquarters helped assert the interests of poorer members vis-à-vis the shogunate and domain authorities and protected them from falling under outcaste rule. Ultimately, blind performers were only one of many types of groups within the urban underclass that used occupation-based collective action, myths of ancient privileges, appeals to benevolent rule, and the logic of vagrant control to carve out some autonomy and defend their monopolies on marginal and mendicant occupations.

142. Nakayama, *Nihon mōjinshi*, vol. 2, 150–51.

CHAPTER 5

Benevolence, Charity, or Duty?

Hunger Relief in the Castle Town

In the fifth lunar month of 1783, the people of Ōno were startled by a roll of thunder that returned over several weeks and reminded them of giant drums or cannon shots.[1] The source of this menacing noise was Mt. Asama, a large volcano in Shinano Province, which erupted later in the summer. Ōno was too far away to be directly affected by the eruption, but the noise proved an unlucky omen nonetheless. After a cold and rainy summer in 1783, the peasants of the Ōno plain suffered what they called a "crop failure" (*fusaku*). This came in the wake of a meager harvest the previous year and was followed by two more years of dearth in 1784–85 and 1786–87.[2] Ōno, together with many other parts of eastern and central Japan, had entered one of the worst and longest food crises of the Tokugawa period: the Tenmei famine.[3]

In a famine, the mechanisms that contained poverty in normal times reached their limits. When masses of people took to the streets to survive, authorities needed to intensify the management of begging and step in more forcefully to prevent starving subjects from abandoning their

1. According to the journal Tenmei hachi tomeki, 1783.7.7, AHM.
2. MT goyōdome 1783.12.2, SSM; *Fukui kenshi*, Tsūshi-hen 4, 486–94.
3. One important indicator of food scarcity, especially for townspeople who bought their food on the market, is the price of rice. Although in Ōno domain this remained well below the levels of the hard-hit areas in the northeast, by the summer of 1784 one bale cost roughly twice as much as the 18.9 *monme* silver price average for 1782; see the appendix. In Ōno, one bale (*hyō*) of rice equaled 4.56 *to*, that is 82.26 liters = 0.456 *koku*.

communities and land and dying. During the Tenmei famine, Ōno's domain government had to experiment with new ways to deal with this extreme situation and, in doing so, again relied heavily on the capacities of
self-governing groups. In the castle town, domain officials consulted and
coordinated with various occupational associations in urban society and
mobilized the charity of wealthy townspeople as a form of duty on behalf
of the lord. The relief measures in Ōno town during this famine not only
reveal how the castle town dealt with the problem of mass hunger but also
help reconstruct the shape of castle town society and trace the reciprocal
relationships linking warrior rule to townspeople self-government.

This chapter explores the character and interplay of three different
schemes of hunger relief that kicked into gear in 1783–84, the worst year
of the Tenmei famine. The first was a system of domain-sponsored seasonal rice gruel kitchens (*osegyō*) for beggars. The second was mutual
relief within block associations, which in 1784 was extended into a town-
wide collection of rice donations (*sukui*) for the starving. The third took
the form of a domain-funded grain loan program (*osukui*). Subjects were
involved in all three schemes through their self-governing communities,
and many participated in them as a duty to the domain lord. In Ōno,
the groups most active in the context of hunger relief included the sake
brewer guild, the purveyor guild, the beggar guild, and the block associations. The town elders worked closely with these groups and the domain government to coordinate the schemes and negotiated precedents
for the future that respected the interests of all parties relevant to the process. Although the domain and the wealthier part of the town's merchant
population were eager to reduce their respective share of the burden, they
shared a fear of food riots and thus had a strong incentive to overcome
disagreements to mitigate class tensions in town society.

There are two advantages to anchoring this chapter in 1783–84. First,
a snapshot of one particular year can clearly reveal how different measures worked together in their social context. Second, the Tenmei famine
represented a turning point within a longer process of welfare institution-
building in Japan that affected different regions at different times.[4]
Throughout the eighteenth century, already before the famine, samurai

---

4. Yamaguchi Keiji, *Sakoku to kaikoku*, 177–78; Garon, *Molding Japanese Minds*,
30; Drixler, *Mabiki*.

officials and wealthy commoners in most parts of the country were starting to see a need for new systems of hunger aid that were more organized
and centralized than the existing ones. During the first half of the
Tokugawa period, the predominant form of hunger relief in towns and
cities had been mutual relief within block associations, with rice gruel
kitchens for beggars as a fallback option at times of severe hunger. The
Tenmei famine spurred almost all affected administrations to make significant changes to their mechanisms of hunger relief. In Edo, where the
famine triggered urban unrest, the shogunate established a citywide relief endowment in the 1790s, the so-called *machi kaisho*, which drew on
grants from the shogunate and periodic contributions from the city's block
associations and was managed by ten purveyor merchants.[5] In Ōno, too,
the Tenmei famine was the catalyst for developing new institutions.
One of the most conspicuous features of this new trend was the increasing involvement of wealthy commoners in urban poverty relief. Because
charitable townspeople tended to collaborate closely with the warrior authorities, their activities did not herald the rise of a civil society in the
Western sense.[6] Nor did they signify a revival or growth of traditional
community spirit within block associations and villages, because the
greatest contributions to the new relief schemes came not from ordinary
townspeople but from representatives of big merchant capital.[7] The existing structures of townspeople self-government provided a framework
for institutionalizing hunger relief and were in turn modified and strength-
ened by such mobilization.

Each town developed its own mechanisms of hunger relief that reflected the local social structure. Whereas most previous research on
urban famine relief has focused on the big cities of Edo, Osaka, and

5. Yoshida Nobuyuki, *Kinsei kyodai toshi no shakai kōzō*, 3–38.
6. Some scholars have proposed variations of the concepts of civil society and the
"public sphere" (*kōkyōken, ryōshuteki kō*) to describe the increasing involvement of commoner elites in poor relief in the late Tokugawa period; see Yamasaki, *Kinsei kōki no
ryōshu shihai to chiiki shakai*. These concepts, however, do not seem to adequately describe samurai governments' heterogeneous relationships with multiple status groups
under their control. If a civil society did take shape at that time, it did not do so in the
sense of an autonomous force that opposed or challenged the power of the state; see
Garon, "From Meiji to Heisei: The State and Civil Society in Japan," 42–62.
7. Community spirit is emphasized, for example, by Kurihara, "Kinsei bikō chochiku no keisei to sonraku shakai," and Najita, *Ordinary Economies in Japan*.

Kyoto, Ōno's case sheds light on the situation in a small castle town.[8] The town elders' journals constitute a rich source on matters of hunger relief because the elders channeled all relief petitions submitted to the domain government and coordinated the activities of status groups. Missing from Ōno's archives for those years is a detailed account of the decision-making process within the domain government—information that can be reconstructed only insofar as the town elders mention it in their journals. This makes it impossible to discuss the government's policies in anything but impersonal terms, but prevents us from replicating the tendency of commentators of the time to relate famine policies to the personal vices or virtues of individual lords or officials. Although high-level political choices were obviously important, Ōno's case forces us to shift attention away from the decisions of government leaders and toward the local social context in which famine relief as a manifestation of benevolent rule was designed to function.

The decades before the Tenmei famine were a challenging time for Ōno domain. The domain government tried to remedy its chronic fiscal deficit by reducing vassals' stipends and repeatedly borrowing money from wealthy commoners. In 1775 and 1780, fires destroyed large parts of the castle town and on one occasion the castle itself.[9] In the 1750s and 1760s, the province of Echizen experienced several incidents of popular upheaval, the greatest of which, the Great Meiwa Uprising of 1768, stirred up more than 20,000 people in Ōno's neighbor domain Fukui. Such unrest was partly a response to long-term economic and social changes in the region. The people of Echizen were reacting to the consequences of participating in an increasingly integrated commercial economy where prices fluctuated according to supply and demand, wealthy merchants

---

8. The two most significant points of comparison for this study are Yoshida Nobuyuki, *Kinsei kyodai toshi no shakai kōzō*, and Kitahara, *Toshi to hinkon no shakaishi*. For detailed studies of mid-sized castle towns, see, for example, Matsuzaki, "Kumamoto jōkamachi ni okeru kyūmin no kyūsai," and Shōji, "Tenpō no daikikin to Kubota (Akita)-machi ni okeru osukuigoya" and "Tenpō no kikin-ka no Akita Kan'onkō," and so on. Saitō's case study examines the interplay of various types of seigneurial relief and internal donation schemes in village society; see Saitō Hiroko, "Kinsei Izumi no sonraku shakai ni okeru 'konkyūnin' kyūsai." On Bakumatsu-era Kyoto, see Kobayashi, "Bakumatsu ishinki no toshi shakai."

9. *Fukui kenshi*, Tsūshi-hen 4, 100–110.

hoarded grain at times of scarcity, and domains tried to solve their fiscal problems by imposing new taxes on the rich and the poor and intervening in the market.[10] The developments in poor and hunger relief discussed here represented one aspect of a larger transformation that affected the regions along the Sea of Japan in the eighteenth century.

In Ōno domain, the Tenmei famine fell into the latter half of the sixty-year reign of Lord Toshisada (r. 1746–1805). A laudatory chronicle of 1812 praised Toshisada's time as an age of benevolent and wise government, noting that he had promoted poor relief as early as the 1770s.[11] But the chronicle particularly emphasized his initiatives taken after the Tenmei famine: a new relief granary, winter relief grants for people without kin, and the appointment of two part-time relief officials to help the poor throughout the domain. The chronicler observed that he did not have any information on relief-related activities from before the 1770s, adding that the same was probably true for other domains and villages in Ōno's vicinity. He pointed out that building welfare institutions in general seemed to be a recent trend inspired by the shogunate's Kansei reform around 1790. The journals of Ōno's town elders confirm that the domain had already begun to improve relief procedures prior to that reform, and they paint a far richer picture than the chronicle of the process by which Toshisada expanded hunger relief in collaboration with wealthy merchants.

The crop failure in the autumn of 1783 triggered the events described in this chapter. But the extent of the grain shortage only became apparent in the beginning of the twelfth month, when the domain government opened kitchens to distribute rice gruel to beggars. These kitchens were held every winter, usually for two months, with handouts occurring every two or three days. In a normal year, they would have attracted between 60 and 150 people a day, but in 1783, the number of recipients attended to on a single day was already up to almost 600 by the day kitchens opened early in the twelfth month, then rose to over 800, and finally climbed to

10. Motokawa, "Jūhasseiki Echizen ni okeru hōkensei no tenkan"; Mikami, "Hyakushō ikki no shitsuteki tenkan ni tsuite." On the link between famine and economic change in eighteenth-century Japan, see also Walker, "Commercial Growth and Environmental Change," and Kikuchi, *Kinsei no kikin*, 71–81.

11. Ishikawa, "Shinchō kazenroku," 339, 357.

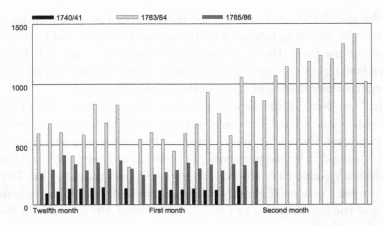

FIGURE 15 Number of recipients (including Koshirō) at the rice gruel kitchens per day of operation in the winter of 1783–84, with the winters of 1740–41 and 1785–86 added for comparison. The only nonfamine winter in the eighteenth century for which a complete data set is available is 1740–41. The year 1785–86 was one of relatively good harvest between two famine years. Fragmentary data for other years, including the nineteenth century, suggest that there were fewer than 200 recipients in most nonfamine winters. *Sources:* MT goyōdome 1740–41, 1783–84, 1787, SSM and AHM.

over 1,000 after the beginning of the new lunar year (see fig. 15).[12] By the twelfth month, townspeople also began to submit so-called starvation petitions (*katsumei onegai*), which were channeled through the headmen of the block associations and the town elders and addressed to the lord of the domain. The domain government was initially reluctant to take them up, but eventually responded by ordering wealthy townspeople to pool charitable donations for their poorer neighbors. About three weeks later, the domain finally began to provide aid from its own coffers in form of starvation loans. These three forms of relief—rice gruel kitchens, mutual aid within block associations, and starvation loans—operated according to their own logic and historical precedent. This chapter introduces them separately while emphasizing their mutual connections.

Hunger relief in Ōno town was anything but generous and not designed to secure more than bare survival. In 1784, for example, the domain government terminated its loan program in early April with the

12.   MT goyōdome 1784.2.2, SSM.

excuse that the snow had thawed, even though the crisis was far from over—the price of rice remained high well into the summer, and there was almost no spring harvest of barley.[13] The domain, however, presumably held to the same argument that had been made in a relief petition presented by tenant farmers from Ōno town in the winter of 1777: once the snow was gone, the poor could go out and gather roots and plants and bring in the barley.[14] Begging and day labor also became easier in the spring. Yet hunger relief in Ōno did not stand out as particularly low by Tokugawa period standards either, and the aid Ōno's poor townspeople received in 1783–84 was more substantial than what they could have expected during previous crises.

Seasonal Rice Gruel Kitchens for Beggars

Since the early eighteenth century or even sooner,[15] Ōno's domain lord funded rice gruel kitchens every winter to help beggars survive during the cold months. Some of the gruel recipients were town residents, but many were poor mountain villagers who descended to the castle town to beg during the snowy season. At first, the kitchens were in operation only seven times a month, but halfway through the eighteenth century the frequency increased to nine and finally ten times a month (by 1765) and remained at that level until the handouts were abolished in 1860.[16] Although the

13.   MT goyōdome 1784.2.18, SSM; Kaidō, "Ōno-machi yōdome ni miru beika no hensen," 33.

14.   MT goyōdome 1777, second month, YH 123, 100–101. See also Tsutomekata oboegaki Tamura-hikae, 1810, TKM.

15.   The earliest known reference to the kitchens dates back to one of the first surviving entries of the town elders' journals in 1734, so the practice might have been older than that; Ōno-chō yakuba no hokan ni kakaru yōdome-chū kyū-Ōno-han ni kansuru shorui, sono 12, Echizen Ōno Doi-ke monjo. Saitō Shūsuke assumes that the kitchens were introduced under the Matsudaira lords of Ōno, that is, before 1682, but does not cite any evidence; see *Ōno chōshi*, vol. 3, 129. Although no town elders' journals have been preserved from the period before 1740, some earlier entries have survived in copied form.

16.   MT goyōdome 1740, 1741, 1765, SSM; Ōno-chō yakuba no hokan ni kakaru yōdome-chū kyū-Ōno-han ni kansuru shorui, sono 12, Echizen Ōno Doi-ke monjo (1734, 1743, 1747).

reasons for this expansion are unclear, it could well have been a reaction to a growth in the number of beggars roaming the castle town during the winter.

In Ōno the rice gruel kitchens were known as *osegyō*. *Segyō* was a Buddhist term translatable as "almsgiving," and Ōno's *osegyō* was a prime example of what historian Ikeda Yoshimasa has called "benevolent relief" (*jikei kyūsai*), meaning that the kitchens were entirely financed from the domain budget and were presented as an expression of the lord's benevolence.[17] The domain set the amount of rice to be used for the gruel, usually ten bales per winter, and paid for the rice and other expenses. The honorific "o" crowning the name of these operations made clear that they were a lordly gift. Although the domain financed the seasonal kitchens and had the final say in disbursing the funds for them, the central figures in planning the distribution of the gruel were the two town elders, who kept in touch with the self-governing associations in the castle town.

The town elders' journals are the only substantial source that has survived that discusses the operation of the kitchens. They demonstrate that almost every detail was meticulously regulated by precedent, facilitating the involvement of various parties. Every year, the kitchens were open on the same dates of each month, in intervals of two or three days.[18] Rules determined how much money should be expended on firewood, which domain and town officials would be present at the scene of distribution, in what order they were to be seated, on what day the costs would be reported to the domain officials, and in what style of writing the reports should be made. Whenever an exception was made, the town elders carefully noted it in their journals to transmit the information to their successors, but most items of the procedure remained essentially unchanged over a period of more than 100 years. Under famine conditions, when the number of beggars was extraordinarily high, domain officials could grant a higher amount of rice than the normal ten bales or order an exten-

---

17.   See, for example, Ikeda and Ikemoto, *Nihon fukushishi kōgi*, 15–42. Other scholars use the term *osukui*, which, following Vlastos (*Peasant Protests and Uprisings in Tokugawa Japan*) can be translated as "seigneurial relief." In the Tokugawa period, the term *osukui* could refer to particular types of aid granted by lords or the shogunate and to policies that ensured the economic well-being of subjects in a broader sense. In Ōno, as discussed later, *osukui* usually referred to a domain-funded loan program distinct from *osegyō*. Here, the term *osukui* is reserved for that program rather than seigneurial relief in general.

18.   Tsutomekata oboegaki Tamura-hikae, 1810, TKM.

sion of the kitchens' operation.[19] Heavy snow that stayed on longer than usual might also spur officials to extend the kitchens.[20] In 1783–84, the domain provided reimbursements for the 28 *koku* of rice ultimately used for the gruel handouts—an expenditure far exceeding the reimbursements paid in more ordinary winters, when the quantity of rice used by the kitchens was generally only 4.56 *koku*, or ten bales.

How unusual was Ōno's provision of hunger relief through rice gruel kitchens? Within Echizen Province, Ōno seems to have been the only domain that distributed rice gruel on a yearly basis, and therefore it attracted beggars from villages outside of its territory as well.[21] But rice gruel handouts were one of the most common methods of hunger relief in Japan and other parts of East Asia. When served as gruel, rice could be stretched with large quantities of water and feed more people than it could when cooked in the usual way. Moreover, the Japanese famine prevention manual *Minkan bikōroku* of 1755 recommended salted rice gruel for people suffering from extreme starvation because it was easily digested and its salt content was believed to have a detoxifying effect.[22] In Beijing and other Chinese cities during the Qing dynasty, rice gruel kitchens operated every winter and constituted one of the pillars of urban poor relief.[23] In Japan, many towns organized them only sporadically in response to a food crisis, but there were places such as Kyoto and Ōno where they were regularly set up during the cold season. In Kyoto in the late 1600s, the shogunate began to operate rice gruel kitchens at times of famine, but between 1735 and 1871 there were annual kitchens as well, funded not by the warrior authorities but by big merchant houses such as the Mitsui, who set them up every winter in the Kamogawa riverbed with the help of the local beggar bosses.[24] In Kyoto, Buddhist temples

---

19. Ibid.

20. There were extensions in 1785, 1809, 1836, 1837, 1838, 1841, and 1855.

21. Beggars from other nearby domains were not turned away but were treated as legitimate recipients of relief from Ōno's rice gruel kitchens; MT goyōdome 1836.11.2, SSM.

22. Tatebe, "Minkan bikōroku," 112, 114.

23. For example in Beijing, Tianjin, and Shanghai; see Li, *Fighting Famine in North China*, 158–61, 228–29; Takahashi Kōsuke, *Kikin to kyūsai no shakaishi*, 91–92.

24. Tsukada, "Shiryō shōkai: Mitsui Bunko shozō," 151–54. For more examples of rice gruel kitchens in Kyoto that were funded by townspeople, see Mueller, "Documenting Disaster in Japanese Painting."

were another major provider of rice gruel aid during famines,[25] whereas in Ōno, temples do not seem to have played any organized role in poor relief at all. This latter difference probably reflected the power, wealth, and long charitable tradition of many of the temples in the imperial capital, with roots in the medieval period.[26] In Ōno, at least one wealthy peasant—the Hanaguro household mentioned in chapter 2—followed the lord's example and distributed uncooked rice to beggars almost annually in the 1790s on one day in the first month. Because the surviving town elders' journals from the 1790s do not mention Hanaguro's event, which was easily accessible from the town and attracted hundreds of people (see table 1, chapter 2), it is possible that other handouts by town and peasant elites also went unmentioned and that there were regular opportunities for beggars to collect aid in Ōno town during the winter.[27]

Handing out cooked rice was an effective first-aid measure for beggars and starving townspeople living in the immediate vicinity, but it had the disadvantage of requiring the hungry to walk long distances and line up at the distribution site. The resulting chaos has been vividly described by Miwa Kiken, a Confucian scholar, who in a tract of 1713 lobbied for reorganizing shogunal famine relief in Kyoto.[28] Kiken argued that gruel kitchens were wasteful, chaotic, and ultimately did more harm than good: "Because [the shogunate] gathers people from all over Kyoto in only one or two shelters, there is horrible pushing and shoving, and starving people are sometimes unable to bear this in their weakened condition and die." The kitchens' potential for disorder and the growing danger of urban unrest could have been reasons the shogunate promoted new systems of hunger relief for commoners to reduce the numbers of townspeople who

25. See Motojima, *Getsudō kenmonshū* (1733), 248–49, 255, 257; Kitahara, *Toshi to hinkon no shakaishi*, 28–30. Temple grounds could also be borrowed as distribution sites by other donors, including domain administrations; see Kikuchi, *Kikin kara yomu kinsei shakai*, 296–303, 308–9.

26. See, for example, Ikeda, *Nihon shakai fukushishi*, 85–86; Takahashi Bonsen, *Nihon jizen kyūsaishi*, 192–96.

27. See, for example, Goyōdome 1789.1.17, Hanakura-ke monjo. Suzuki, another wealthy peasant in Nakano village, distributed rice gruel to beggars during the Tenpō famine and copper coins in normal years; Yōdome (Suzuki) 1837.8.6, YH 736, 534–35.

28. Miwa, "Kyūga taii," 449–58. On Miwa Kiken (Shissai), see Yoshida Kyūichi, *Nihon shakai fukushi shisōshi*, 248–51; Najita, *Visions of Virtue*, 63–73.

depended on aid from rice gruel kitchens.[29] In Ōno, too, as discussed in the context of the vagrancy problem in chapter 3, the government eventually decided to abolish the seasonal kitchens, although it waited to do so until 1860, the eve of the Meiji Restoration.[30] In 1860 the Japanese economy was suffering from high inflation, and authorities anticipated the outbreak of violent protests in the castle town. It seems that the kitchens were never revived after this point.[31]

Although Ōno's domain government financed the rice gruel kitchens, it depended on various groups in town to carry out distribution. As noted already, the two town elders played a key role in the kitchens' overall operation, but the members of the sake brewer guild and the beggar guild also oversaw different parts of the distribution process and exercised a fair amount of discretion. The elders' job was to coordinate and supervise the activities of the groups that were involved in the rice gruel kitchens. One of the elders was always present at the site of the kitchens, together with their assistant (*gachigyōji*). The headmen of the block associations were required to join whenever a kitchen was set up in their *chō*. Also in attendance was the leader of the town corps (*machigumi*), a low-ranking vassal in service of the town governor, who was accompanied by two of his underlings.[32]

As might be expected, the different types of officials who met at the site of distribution were extremely rank-conscious. In 1815, the leader of the town corps challenged the town elders' right to withdraw from the distribution setting before him and his underlings. The town elders fought back, asserting that "in any case, with regard to the relief kitchens we are the masters [*nushikata*], and because the leader of the town corps and its members are only standing by [*tachiai*], we believe that we should come first in every respect."[33] The town governor settled the matter in the town elders' favor by referring to precedent. In their journals the town elders avoided the term *tachiai* for their attendance at the kitchens and instead spoke of "going on duty" (*shutsuyaku*). The episode illustrates that the relief operation as a

29. Kitahara, *Toshi to hinkon no shakaishi*, 11–12, 24–25, 37–38, 49; Sugahara, "Kinsei Kyoto no hinin," 75–79.

30. MT goyōdome 1860.11.26, SSM.

31. MT goyōdome 1860.12.1, NGM; 1861.12.6; 1867.12.11, SSM; Yōroku, 1852, SSM.

32. MT goyōdome 1815.12.2, 1852.1.22, SSM.

33. MT goyōdome 1815.12.2, SSM.

whole had been entrusted to the townspeople, with low-ranking domain vassals attending the scene as mere witnesses and bystanders.

The actual operation of the rice gruel kitchens was handled by members of the sake brewer guild, who most likely set the kitchens up in front of their own premises (see fig. 16). Running the kitchens constituted one of the guild's duty obligations vis-à-vis the domain, a service (among several others) they performed in return for the lord recognizing their guild and protecting them from unlicensed competition.[34] To carry out this service, they procured rice, salt, and firewood and hired workers (two each day), although in reality they might have been using their own servants. They advanced the requisite funds from their own resources. In the spring, when operation of the kitchens ceased, the town elder on duty submitted to the domain a statement summarizing the brewers' expenses for rice, salt, firewood, and workers.[35] Upon receiving the money granted against these costs, he divided it up among the brewers. He had their stamps of confirmation taken in a special register, which he kept in the official chest in the town office.[36]

The duty of serving as "hunger relief host" (*osegyō-yado*) rotated among the guild membership in an order worked out each year by the town elders on the basis of precedent. For example, the brewer who had joined the guild most recently was put in charge of the first kitchen of the season. When a new guild member made his debut as host, he treated all participating officials (except the beggar bosses) to a meal of sake, fish, and rice.[37] While this feast must have presented a stark contrast to the rice gruel offered to the beggars, it underscores how deeply the seigneurial relief scheme of the kitchens was rooted in the society of the town, in this case as a seasonal event in the life of the brewer guild.

As a guild service, taking charge of the rice gruel kitchens was incumbent on all in the brewing business with certain exceptions. Most notable were brewers of tax-exempt (*gomenchi*) rank.[38] This privilege was granted only to a few elite among the townspeople who had made par-

34. See, for example, "Shuzō-kabu kariuke ni tsuki torikime issatsu," in *Ōno shi-shi*, Shoke monjo-hen 2, 300.
35. See, for example, MT goyōdome 1838.4.1, 1843.2.6, SSM.
36. MT goyōdome 1801.2.6, SSM.
37. MT goyōdome 1837.11.16, 1852.1.22, SSM.
38. MT goyōdome 1837.11.16.

FIGURE 16 Illustration of a rice gruel handout in *Hinin Taiheiki*, 1688.

ticularly generous contributions to the domain budget. It freed them from all duties imposed on parts of their town land and apparently from guild-based duties such as hosting the gruel kitchens. Because sake brewing was a business of the affluent, six of the town's eleven "tax-exempt" in 1784 were active as brewers but exempted from the rotation of hosting the kitchens. Members who retreated from the brewing business were also released from this duty, as happened to one man who declared his withdrawal immediately after the extension of the kitchens was announced in 1784 (his turn was going to come up).[39] On the other hand, from the late eighteenth century onward we even see brewers from the rural parts

39.   MT goyōdome 1784.1.26, SSM.

of the domain serving as kitchen hosts via deputy brewers in the castle town. The guild in the town had persuaded the government to force these new and unwelcome competitors under their wing, and they were expected to undertake the hosting duty as well.[40]

Various factors suggest why among the town guilds the sake brewers were mobilized for the rice gruel kitchens. Thanks to its fine-tasting water, Ōno was one of the centers of sake brewing in Echizen Province, and the local sake brewer guild counted twenty-five members in 1784, a remarkable number for a town of Ōno's size.[41] Perhaps the domain relied on the brewers because they were likely to hold major rice reserves due to the requirements of their trade and the fact that they tended to be among the wealthiest merchants. At times of dearth, brewers were often ordered to curtail production and frequently became targets of popular resentment. The desire of lords and the shogunate to regulate the price of rice was the main reason why in 1657 sake brewers became one of the first trades in Tokugawa Japan to be placed under a governmental licensing system.[42]

Another possible (but not mutually exclusive) explanation is that sake brewers possessed the tools needed to cook rice gruel for a large number of people. Big iron pots (*ōkama*, with a diameter of about one meter or more) were used at several stages during the brewing process.[43] When the Mitsui in Kyoto set up rice gruel kitchens for poor townspeople during the Tenmei famine, they also relied on local sake brewers to undertake the cooking. In Morioka (Nanbu domain), some of the pots used in the domain's famine shelters during the Hōreki famine (1755–56) were borrowed from sake brewers.[44]

The Koshirō also played an important part in the organization of rice gruel relief. In return for their begging privilege, much like the sake brewers, the Koshirō had to fulfill duty obligations as beggar bosses, and no

40. MT goyōdome 1780.2.16, 1783.10.16, 1836.11.10, SSM.

41. According to a reconstruction of guild membership based on "Shuzōmai kokusū no oboe" in MT goyōdome 1786.10.26, YH 290, 215–17; and the data in the town elders' journals concerning the rice gruel kitchens for 1783 and 1784, SSM.

42. Yunoki, *Nihonshu no rekishi*, 47–72, 79–85.

43. For cooking the rice, for boiling water, and for heating and sterilizing the freshly brewed sake; see Yunoki, *Nihonshu no rekishi*, 181–89.

44. Yoshida Nobuyuki, *Kinsei kyodai toshi no shakai kōzō*, 265; Kikuchi, *Kikin kara yomu kinsei shakai*, 299.

other site in town was in greater need of their services than the rice gruel kitchens, where hundreds of beggars stood in line for a meager bowl of warm food (see fig. 17). The Koshirō were also in charge of handing out the rice gruel to the beggars in a so-called *mossō*, a mold for measuring rice.[45] They must have been well suited to this task because in nonfamine years the Koshirō were familiar with almost all the beggars in the castle town and could confirm their eligibility. Because the Koshirō were professional beggars themselves, they also counted as recipients of relief. In the town elders' journals, their number was included in the recipients' total for each distribution day, and like the other beggars, they received a set amount of rice for each member of their households, probably in uncooked form.

The mobilization of beggar bosses for famine relief was not uncontroversial. After all, many of the people who lined up for rice gruel were not relying on alms permanently but were townspeople or peasants desperate enough to resort to begging.[46] In Kyoto, where beggar bosses were also in charge of policing the distribution sites for the shogun- and merchant-funded rice gruel kitchens,[47] Miwa Kiken, the author of the tract on famine aid mentioned before, was particularly disturbed by how the kitchens enhanced the authority of the beggar bosses. He blamed them for various abuses and suggested entrusting the kitchens to temples—some of which already had a tradition of feeding beggars, were in the possession of large pots, and could break down the crowds into smaller groups to make them more manageable.[48] The leader of the Ōno town corps in 1838 accused the Koshirō of favoring the occupants of the beggar hospice when distributing rice gruel.[49] The Koshirō asserted their innocence, and the town elder on duty came to their rescue by pointing out that officials had previously agreed that "beggars who helped should receive two *shaku* per person."

45. Each beggar received 1 *gō*=10 *shaku*=0.18 liter; MT goyōdome 1784, second month, 1838.1.19, SSM.

46. In nearby Fukui, many townspeople begged during the Tenmei famine, but only at night and with disguised faces; see Tachibana Sōken, "Denrai nenjū nichiroku," 581. See MT goyōdome 1785.1.26, SSM, for a reference to an Ōno townswoman seeking a handout at a rice gruel kitchen.

47. Sugahara, "Kinsei Kyoto no hinin," 69–104. On the involvement of beggar bosses in merchant-funded kitchens, see Tsukada, "Shiryō shōkai: Mitsui Bunko shozō," 151–54.

48. Miwa, "Kyūga taii," 450, 452–53.

49. MT goyōdome 1838.1.19, SSM.

FIGURE 17 Illustration of a rice gruel handout in Tatebe Seian, "Minkan bikōroku," 1755. Courtesy of Tōhoku Rekishi Hakubutsukan.

Apparently, subordinate beggars from the beggar hospice were also helping out at the rice gruel kitchens in exchange for a bonus.[50]

These transactions demonstrate that Ōno's rice gruel kitchens were a collaborative effort of the guild of sake brewers, the beggar guild, the town elders, and the domain government. The domain supplied the funds, while the town officials, the sake brewers, their employees, and the beggar bosses organized the kitchens and became the public face of the relief operation that was visible to the beggars at the site. At the same time, the two guilds followed the principle that determined their relationship with the domain government in general: they provided their services as a duty loosely connected to their particular trade. Moreover, both guilds and the town elders accepted their roles as conduits of seigneurial benevolence and actively incorporated them into their social identities—whether it was the town elders proudly referring to themselves as the "masters" of the relief operation, new members of the brewer guild celebrating their debut as kitchen hosts with the town officials, or

50. It is unclear whether in this context, "two *shaku*" meant an additional 2 *shaku* (1 *shaku* = 0.1 *gō*) to the standard ration of 1 *gō*, or simply a "second helping."

the Koshirō cementing their role as bosses of the world of mendicants by disciplining and feeding beggars in an official setting.

Extraordinary Famine Relief for Townspeople: Pooled Donations and Loans

During the Tenmei famine, the lord's rice gruel kitchens operated in combination with several other mechanisms of hunger relief specifically for townspeople. The most basic form, and that with the longest history, was charitable mutual relief within block associations, provided to the needy by their more well-to-do neighbors. Chapter 3 introduced a number of examples of poor townspeople relying on such aid for certain periods of time. Mutual assistance of this sort was a premise of the Tokugawa system of local administration and was encouraged by rulers as one of two major responsibilities of the *chō*, and especially the five-people's groups within them. The second was mutual supervision and control.[51]

Obviously, mutual relief functioned best if there were a number of wealthy people within the community. As research on other Tokugawa towns and cities has shown, it was typical for wealthy merchant households to provide assistance to neighbors within their block association, and they distributed aid to their own tenants, employees, clients, and subcontractors in other parts of the town as well as to beggars at the door.[52] There were plenty of motives for the rich to voluntarily open their pouches for the poor: a need to deflect violence, a desire to show off prestige and economic success, and of course genuine compassion or at least a sense of moral reciprocity. The dominant value systems of the time rewarded charitable behavior: most Buddhist schools, including the True Pure Land sect, which prevailed in Ōno, extolled almsgiving as a good deed, and Confucian thinkers regarded compassion for suffering neighbors as a major

51.   Hozumi, *Goningumi seidoron*; Ikeda, *Nihon shakai fukushishi*, 114–15; Inaba, *Kyūmin kyūjo seido no kenkyū*, 103–5.
52.   Consider Yoshida Nobuyuki's research on the giving habits of the merchant house Mitsui in Edo; *Kinsei kyodai toshi no shakai kōzō*, 181–228. A similar pattern prevailed in the charity of the merchant house Sumitomo in Osaka; Umihara, "Toshi Ōsaka ni okeru shōka hōkōnin."

virtue as long as it was practiced in moderation.[53] In reality, these lofty ideals often intermingled with more mundane considerations of economic give-and-take. For example, wealthy donors preferably helped subordinates on whose labor and timely rent payments they depended. Many of Ōno's rich would probably have agreed with the merchant house Mitsui, which, in an internal communication of 1733, justified its charitable donations as "thanksgiving for a flourishing business" (*shōbai no myōga*).[54] In Ōno town in 1783–84, voluntary donations by the well-to-do were substantial, amounting to about three-quarters of the relief total of over seventy *koku* of rice provided by townspeople in that year.[55] Records of such donations are fragmentary but show that almost all providers of voluntary charitable aid during the Tenmei famine resided in Ōno's traditionally wealthy neighborhoods.[56]

This kind of unregulated charity was not sufficient, however, to meet the challenges posed by conditions on the scale of the Tenmei famine, because most of it went to townspeople who had some sort of relationship with a wealthy household.[57] Limitations were already becoming apparent several decades before the Tenmei famine, but Ōno's domain officials initially showed great reluctance to address them with governmental handouts. In the snowy winter of 1740–41, for instance, many townspeople applied for hunger relief, but the domain was fiscally hardpressed in that year and tried to keep relief grants to the absolute minimum. The town elders' journal explicitly stated that only people who had not eaten for two or three days and were pallid and swollen were eligible

53. For a survey of Tokugawa Confucian thinkers and their ideas regarding the practice of compassion and benevolence, see Yoshida Kyūichi, *Nihon shakai fukushi shisōshi*, 185–301.

54. Yoshida Nobuyuki, *Kinsei kyodai toshi no shakai kōzō*, 237. The idea that wealth should be kept in circulation to benefit society and help the needy was a central tenet of Tokugawa merchant ethic; Najita, *Ordinary Economies in Japan*, 20–59; Najita, *Visions of Virtue*, 49–50, 62–70.

55. The total of townspeople donations in 1783–84 was 69.83 *koku* of rice, 0.68 *koku* of unhulled rice, and 267.64 *monme* of silver money. This figure includes both voluntary donations and ordered donations, the latter of which will be discussed below.

56. See the excerpt preserved for 1785; MT goyōdome 1785.3.16, SSM.

57. For a discussion of this problem with regard to Hirosaki domain during the Tenpō famine, see Namikawa, *Kinsei Hokuō shakai to minshū*, 113, 139.

for help from the domain. Those townspeople who were still strong enough to go out on the streets were expected to beg for alms instead.[58]

The townspeople expressed their requests for hunger relief through so-called starvation petitions (*katsumei onegai*). Although the wording of such petitions in Ōno has not been preserved, it appears that townspeople addressed these requests to the domain and channeled them upward via the *chō* headmen and town elders. Generally, relief petitions in the Tokugawa period referred to one of two different levels of deprivation.[59] The first major threshold for seigneurial relief was life-threatening starvation (*katsumei, ue*, etc.), and the second the loss of viability (*naritachi*) of a taxpaying household. Either way, government officials insisted that community members help each other first before applying for seigneurial relief. Subjects therefore had to convince officials in their petitions that their entire community was impoverished (*konkyū, hinkyū, nangi*, etc.) or otherwise deserving of external support. The petitioning skills of an experienced village or *chō* headman could make all the difference here.[60]

In addition to starvation petitions, the townspeople of Ōno tried other petitioning formats, depending on what residential communities or other occupational groups they belonged to. The cormorant fishermen of Kanazuka, for example, sometimes petitioned the domain for special loans to support the feeding of their cormorants, including in 1783 and 1784 (see table 3).[61] The so-called town peasants (*machibyakushō*) or landowners (*takamochi*)—townspeople who owned agricultural land—had an organization with officers to represent their interests and could petition for the same production support rice (*sakujiki*) and extensions on tax deadlines that were also granted to the rice-growing villagers of the domain.[62] The

---

58. MT goyōdome 1741.2.3, SSM.

59. Fukuda Chizuru, *Bakuhanseiteki chitsujo to oie sōdō*, 137–39; Fukaya, *Hyakushō naritachi*.

60. For an example of strategic petitioning during the Tenmei famine, see Saitō Hiroko, "Kinsei Izumi no sonraku shakai ni okeru 'konkyūnin' kyūsai," 303–10.

61. Tenmei hachi tomeki, 1783.4.6, AHM; MT goyōdome 1784.3.26, SSM.

62. On petitions for tax extensions in 1783–84, see MT goyōdome 1783.12.2, 12.11, 1784.6.11, 12.6, SSM. In one case of 1777, townspeople who worked as tenant farmers tried to obtain relief in addition to what they received through starvation petitions by petitioning on an agricultural rationale, but their request was denied; see MT goyōdome 1777.2.5, YH 123, 100–101.

Table 3
Key events related to famine relief in the town of Ōno, 1783–84

Date	Event	Details
1783		
Twelfth month	Operation of rice gruel kitchens (ten times)	311–835 recipients per day
12.26	Pooling of donations within Sanbanmachi	33 recipients
1784		
first month	Operation of rice gruel kitchens (ten times)	445–1,056 recipients per day
1.13	Pooling of donations within Shibanmachi	76 recipients
1.26-1.29	Town-wide pooling of donations (excluding Goban-machi and Yokomachi, where pooling was *chō*-internal)	617 recipients (+22 in Gobanmachi, 27 in Yokomachi)
Intercalary first month	Extension of rice gruel kitchens' operation (ten more times)	862–1,413 recipients per day
i1.19	First disbursal of domain grain loans	Worth 3 *shō* of barnyard millet per person; 92 recipients (7 in Shibanmachi, 7 in Noguchi, 78 in Kanazuka)
i1.21	Second disbursal of domain grain loans (applicants from many *chō*)	267 recipients
2.2	Third disbursal of domain grain loans (applicants from Shibanmachi)	56 recipients
2.11	Fourth disbursal of domain grain loans (applicants from many *chō*)	231 recipients; reduction in worth of loans to 2 *shō* of barnyard millet per person for third-time applicants; 127 were first- and second-time applicants and 104 were third-time applicants
2.18	Cutoff of acceptance of starvation petitions	Ended due to thaw
3.16 and 4.2	Report to the town governors' office of instances of mutual relief and alms for beggars	3.16 report included ordered and voluntary donations for the 1.26 pooling and for *chō*-internal relief in Sanbanmachi and Shibanmachi; 4.2 report provided additional information specifically on millet donations

Date	Event	Details
3.26	Disbursal of domain loans to Kanazuka (for cormorant food)	250 *monme* of silver
4.9	Reward ceremonies for town donors held	At the domain bureau and the town office
5.21	Disbursal of domain loans to Kanazuka due to epidemic	Worth 3 *shō* of barnyard millet per person; 78 recipients
6.11	Submission of petition by town peasants for another extension of the deadline for part of last year's tax payment	Declined?
8.29	Repayment by Kanazuka of previous year's loan (for cormorant food)	3 *ryō* of gold

Source: MT goyōdome 1783–84, SSM.

boundaries between these relief categories were not easily crossed. In 1860, for example, a conflict broke out among the townspeople over whether a domain relief loan for the owners of agricultural land could also be distributed to the owners of residential land, who had not participated in the petition for the loan.[63] In 1789, when the domain distributed aid after a fire, the headmen of the block associations had to submit a follow-up petition on behalf of the owners of shops (perhaps market stalls) operating within their blocks, whom they had neglected to include in the text of their original petition.[64]

In the hunger winter of 1783–84, the domain authorities initially tried to deal with starvation petitions by ordering *chō* communities to collect donations among themselves. Sanbanmachi and Shibanmachi were the first block associations to submit petitions for starvation aid, and around the new year, the town governor ordered them to collect and distribute pooled donations within their borders.[65] But the Tenmei famine brutally

63. Ōjōya goyōdome 1860.11.16, YH 1218, 870; MT goyōdome 1860.11.21–24, YH 1218, 870–72.
64. MT goyōdome 1789.7.23, SSM.
65. MT goyōdome 1783.12.26, 1784.1.13, SSM.

exposed the inequalities that existed within each *chō* and between the *chō* in different parts of the castle town. The presence of wealthier residents was not a guarantee that a block association was actually fulfilling its function as a mutually supportive community. In the spring of 1784, the domain government declined an aid petition from a starving family in Shibanmachi. The household had been receiving help from its five-people's group, but they were too impoverished to help the family out for long.[66] Here and in other similar instances, solidarity was intact at least among neighbors and relatives, but it was of limited value because the neighbors or relatives were often not much better off themselves. By rejecting the Shibanmachi family's petition for direct aid, the domain authorities indicated that the headman should search for resources within the block association first. Only after being pressured by the domain did the headman turn to the richer residents in the southern part of the *chō*.

By the end of the first month of 1784, so many petitions for hunger aid had accumulated that the domain and town officials decided it was time to share resources on a town-wide scale. The government ordered the town elite to collect and distribute relief donations from well-to-do townspeople: "According to precedent, relief should first be provided by the purveyors and by people within the block associations who are living comfortably."[67] In the wake of this order, the town elders organized a big grain collection that raised 16.7 *koku* of rice, which amounted to roughly one fourth of the total of donations made by townspeople during that winter, which were equally distributed among the 617 people who applied for starvation aid. In their journal, the town elders referred to this collection as *sukui* (relief) or *sukuimai* (relief rice).[68] *Sukui* was a system of ordered donations by better-off townspeople in which resources were pooled and distributed to townspeople who had applied for hunger aid to the domain. This form of relief built on the old tradition of mutual aid within block associations and

66. MT goyōdome 1784.2.20, SSM.

67. MT goyōdome 1784.1.26, YH 179, 137.

68. The number of applicants was already known when the collection of donations began. The amounts of aid per recipient for each year of the Tenmei famine are similar enough to suspect that a specific collection target was set. In 1784 those who petitioned for relief received 2.7 *shō*, in 1785 they received 2.9 *shō*, and in 1787 they received 3.1 *shō* (1 *shō* is equivalent to 10 *gō*, or 0.01 *koku*—or 1.8 liters).

extended it by leveling economic disparities between the *chō* and enabling the poor to receive aid regardless of where they resided.

The introduction of this collective donation scheme in Ōno happened at a time when solidarity within the town's block associations was showing signs of decline. This was the case also in Osaka and Kyoto, although these cities encountered the problem a bit earlier than Ōno did. In Osaka and Kyoto, merchant capital had started to alter the communal structure of block associations as early as the seventeenth century, and during the Kyōhō famine in 1732–33, the shogunate initiated collections by wealthy commoners and sent out urgent reminders to the *chō* to provide mutual relief and keep the poor from the streets.[69] The block associations of Ōno were never dominated by wealthy merchant landlords to the same extent as some of those in the "three metropolises," but in the late eighteenth century, Ōno's society was becoming more polarized. The ratio of tenants to house owners was rising, and more merchants and temples began to operate tenements for profit (see chapter 1).

The Tenmei famine was not the first time a town-wide pooling was undertaken in Ōno town, but the system went back no further than 1769 and was still fairly new when tested by the famine.[70] The town elders appear to have introduced it in consultation with other merchants,[71] although domain officials probably also had a hand in the matter. In 1769, the town poor submitted a flood of petitions for millet aid to the domain authorities, and the town elders might have proposed the new system in anticipation of the domain's reluctance to take on an additional financial burden. Or the elders might have received orders from the domain to work out a solution. No matter who took the initiative, there is little doubt that the new model was advantageous for both sides. In 1768, the Great Meiwa Uprising had swept through Fukui domain, and the rich and powerful

69. See the documents in *Osaka shishi*, vol. 3, 322–25. On the transformation of *chō* communities, see Yoshida Nobuyuki, *Kinsei kyodai toshi no shakai kōzō*, 229–79, 308–22.

70. The event of 1769 is mentioned in a journal entry of 1777; MT goyōdome 1777.2.1, YH 122, 98–99.

71. This is suggested both by the journal entry of 1777 and by the town governor's manual of 1810 (Tsutomekata oboegaki Tamura-hikae, TKM). According to the manual, the new system was introduced in the summer of 1768, right after the Great Meiwa Uprising, not in 1769.

were scrambling for ways to prevent the violence from spilling over to Ōno.[72] Although the wealthy merchants were responsible for funding the new system, it is unlikely that they required much persuasion in the face of popular unrest.[73] By that time, the domain had already begun to re-think its former reluctance to provide relief for starving subjects. In the 1740s or 1750s, the domain increased the frequency of the annual rice gruel kitchens from seven to ten times a month and from the end of the 1760s onward implemented two innovative practices: the town-wide donation scheme mentioned above, and a system of interest-free loans for starving townspeople.

The loan program first appeared in the town elders' journal in 1777. Under it, the domain government loaned barnyard millet (or a monetary equivalent) to starving townspeople without interest, repayable in three annual installments. The town elders referred to the loans as *osukui* (sei-gneurial relief) or *katsumei osukui* (seigneurial starvation relief), the honorific prefix "o" again indicating that the domain was the source of the funds.[74] Food loans of this type belonged to the standard toolkit of Tokugawa administration,[75] but they had not been granted to Ōno's townspeople before because the domain regarded them as a rural form of aid. The decision to overlook the lack of precedent and make grain loans available to starving townspeople came in the wake of a devastating fire in 1775 that annihilated almost the entire town.[76] When poor townspeople petitioned for relief in 1777, the town elders briefly considered calling on

72.　Motokawa, "Jūhasseiki Echizen ni okeru hōkensei no tenkan, 68–71;" Mikami, "Hyakushō ikki no shitsuteki tenkan ni tsuite."

73.　On the link between merchant charity and popular unrest, see also Yoshida Nobuyuki, *Kinsei kyodai toshi no shakai kōzō*, 229–30, 254–55, 270–77; Kitahara, *Toshi to hinkon no shakaishi*, 60–63.

74.　How the loans were financed is unclear, but after the fire the domain had received a 4,000 *ryō* reconstruction credit from the shogunate—one of those rare in-stances in which the shogunate extended financial help to domain lords who faced ex-traordinary disaster; Goyōki (machibugyō) 1775.6.16, YH 94, 82; *Ofuregaki Tenmei shūsei* no. 2706, 776–77; *Fukui kenshi*, Tsūshi-hen 4, 105. Ōno's lord gradually repaid the loan in the subsequent years, incurring new debt in the process.

75.　They appeared as *bujikigashi* (food loans) in handbooks of rural administra-tion such as Ōishi Kyūkei's *Jikata hanreiroku*. On *bujikigashi*, see also Ikeda, *Nihon shakai fukushishi*, 99; Fukaya, *Hyakushō naritachi*, 39–48.

76.　Various sources, YH 94, 72–84.

their more well-to-do fellows to make pooled donations in the same way as in 1769. The idea was dismissed, however, because as the town elders remarked, "in this year, it did not seem that even the purveyor merchants would donate when asked for surplus rice."[77] By disbursing starvation loans in 1777, the domain demonstrated its readiness to help the townspeople when their collective capacities of self-help had been exhausted and wealthy merchants also needed to focus on their own reconstruction.

These two types of extraordinary relief—pooled donations by townspeople and loans by the domain—were thus initially employed separately as alternative measures. Pooled donations took place for the first time in 1769 and again in the winters of 1782–83, 1783–84, 1784–85, and 1786–87. The grain loans from the domain were given only once before the Tenmei famine, in 1777, and once during the famine, in 1783–84. In the hunger winter of 1783–84, circumstances were so severe that both types of aid came to be implemented in conjunction. By taking a closer look at how this was done, we can get a fuller picture of the nature of such extraordinary relief measures.

The Collection of Pooled Donations

The town-wide charitable collection in the first month of 1784 was an organized public effort mediated by the collective bodies in town society. The funds for this distribution were collected in four different ways.[78] First were contributions from "people who are leading comfortable lives within the block associations" (*chōchō nite sōō ni kurashi-sōrō mono-domo*), in other words, well-to-do townspeople of middling fortunes who had reserves to give away.[79] In the entry in the town elders' journal, their contributions were listed summarily for their respective *chō*, indicating a close connection with the practice of mutual relief within block associations. The list of donations by people in the *chō* also shows that the town-wide

77. MT goyōdome 1777.2.1, YH 122, 98.
78. MT goyōdome 1784.1.26–29, YH 179, 137–40.
79. Other entries on pooled donations referred to this group as "the well-off ones" (*shinjō yoroshiki mono*; MT goyōdome 1777. 2.1, YH 122, 98) or "the prominent ones" (*omodachi-sōrō mono*; MT goyōdome 1785.2.6, SSM).

Table 4
Number of recipients of *sukui* and *osukui* during the Tenmei famine

	1783	1784		
	Sukui	Sukui	Sukui	Osukui
Upper Ichibanmachi		2	19	
Lower Ichibanmachi				
Upper Nibanmachi	12	8	76	
Lower Nibanmachi	29	21	126	
Temple precinct				
Sanbanmachi	47	46	110	
Shibanmachi	45	4	117	7
Gobanmachi	6	13	(22)	
Bikunimachi	18	12	88	
Yokomachi	1	3	(27)	
Shichikenmachi (West)				
Shichikenmachi (East)				
Daikumachi		5	30	
Kajimachi				
Noguchi	4		3	7
Kanazuka			48	78
Total	162	114	617	92

Source: MT goyōdome 1784–85, 1787, SSM; Tenmei hachi tomeki, 1783, AHM.

pooling achieved some redistribution between the richer and poorer areas of the town (see table 4). Donations were obtained, for example, from Lower Ichibanmachi and Eastern and Western Shichikenmachi, the most affluent *chō* along the Mino Highway, which cut right through the heart of Ōno town (see map 4).[80] There were no beneficiaries of relief in any of these *chō* on this occasion. Instead, recipients were heavily concentrated in Upper and Lower Nibanmachi, Sanbanmachi, Shibanmachi, and Bikunimachi, and in two of the town's branch villages, Noguchi and Kanazuka. These locations included the town's most impoverished areas; some of them did not produce any contributions to the donations pool at all.

80.　Residents of these block associations were also subject to the highest tax rates in town; see Ōno-machi danmen ezu, 1743, copy of 1775, TKM.

Osukui	Osukui	Osukui	1785 Sukui	1787 Sukui
		.14	33	.18
5			3	.1
.41		.10	.82	.49
.50		.61	.104	.63 (+5)
				5
76		.84	.88	.58
.31	56	.21	.98	.69
.22			.24	.20
.25		.25	.103	.89
.15		4	.28	.2
			.27	
				.6
.2		.12	.18	.11
			.60	.29
.267	56	.231	.668	.420

The second source of pooled donations was rice collected from the *chō* headmen and the two town elders. These may also be considered as an extension of relief within block associations, because headmen were likely to play a leading role whenever resources were shared within a *chō*. The proportion of rice gathered from these first two sources was small, however: out of the total of 16.7 *koku* distributed, only 1.22 *koku* came from the wealthy people in the block associations and a mere 0.68 *koku* from the town officials. A much greater part, almost 5.5 *koku*, derived from a third source: the guild of purveyor merchants (*goyōtashi nakama*). The first two sources were extensions of mutual relief within block associations, but the donations from the purveyor guild had a somewhat different character: they represented a duty to the lord, delivered by an association of merchants with special privileges. This was also the case for the fourth source—contributions by exceptionally wealthy individuals, which made up the balance of the donations and are discussed later.

Ōno's purveyor guild, which existed since at least 1741, differed from the brewer guild in that it was not based on a shared trade of any kind. Instead, it was organized around a shared duty. Like most other guilds in town, it had officers who rotated on a monthly or yearly basis, and it also had specific obligations vis-à-vis the domain. To this end, in 1799 it started to keep its own record of official business.[81] The twenty-three merchants in the purveyor guild (in 1784) were united by the fact that they all held the rank of "purveyor" (*goyōtashi*), which also included the tax-exempt mentioned before. This meant that they had made significant contributions to the domain budget, mostly in form of loans, and the lord continued to call on them for financial assistance. A related function was to cooperate in the acquisition of loans and donations on behalf of the domain.[82] Other guild tasks were merchant-specific. The purveyors supervised the guild of wholesalers (*toiya*) and the guild of brokers (*suainin*), who engaged in brokering rice, wax, rapeseed, and other commodities on behalf of local vendors. They might have overseen the pawnbroker guild as well and were collectively responsible for shielding the castle town economy from financial damage by making members keep monetary reserves and covering losses caused by speculative trading.[83]

Compared to these tasks, which coincided with the merchants' own business interests, another guild duty strikes the modern observer as somewhat peculiar: lending out silken nightgowns, futons, mosquito nets, bathtubs, bathrobes, and vases. These items and more were collectively supplied by the purveyor guild every time the domain hosted official visitors, for example, shogunate envoys or out-of-domain creditors. In fact, this seemingly marginal duty seems to have been the main reason the

81. Goyōdome, 1799, AHM.

82. MT goyōdome 1741, eleventh month, YH 24, 20–23; 1785.11.16, 11.17, 11.21, YH 260, 190–91; 1786.1.22, YH 263, 192–93; Tenmei hachi tomeki, 1783.4.12, 5.17, AHM. Ōno domain used various methods to impose extraordinary levies on the town population, not all of which depended on the purveyor guild.

83. MT goyōdome 1741.2.6, YH 16, 15, et al., SSM; 1785.2.16, 4.21, 5.1, SSM; Goyōdome, 1799, fifth month, AHM; *Ōno chōshi*, vol. 2, 1202–21.

guild started to keep a journal in 1799.[84] Prominent townspeople accommodated the guests in their houses, and the purveyor guild provided the items needed to outfit the guest rooms. Entries in the journal specify exactly how many nightgowns, futons, and so on were supplied by each guild member. Whenever the domain announced an official visit, the guild held preparatory meetings at a member's house. The town elders and the two guild officers supervised and directed the preparations and maintained close contact with domain officials.

Government financiers were an indispensable part of Tokugawa society, but not everywhere did they form permanent associations. Often, they were appointed individually and on a case-by-case basis to provide financial support to their lords in return for substantial privileges. However, if a service also required insider knowledge of commercial transactions, governments were more likely to turn to professional guilds. For example, guilds of moneychangers helped with loans and money transfers, and guilds of grain dealers undertook price interventions.[85] Yet there were equivalents to Ōno's purveyor guild also in other towns. One example are Edo's "purveyors of the shogunal accounting bureau" (*kanjōsho goyōtashi*), established in 1788 during the Kansei reform period to serve the shogunate as a quasi bank. The ten men appointed to that body were extremely wealthy moneylenders and merchants of various trades. Their tasks included shogunate financing, price intervention, and backup and control of rice agents (*fudasashi*) who served as bankers to lower-ranking shogunal vassals.[86] They were also put in charge of managing an important Edo relief institution: the *machi kaisho*, an emergency fund for townspeople started as part of the Kansei reform, whose stocks were lent out in good years to struggling house owners for low interest.[87]

The shogunate established the purveyors of the shogunal accounting bureau to control and exploit the money and financial expertise of a new class of Edo merchants who had risen to prominence in the eighteenth

84. Goyōdome, 1799, fifth month, AHM.

85. Takeuchi, "Kansei kaikaku to 'kanjōsho goyōtashi,'" part 1, 24; Crawcour, "Changes in Japanese Commerce," 193–97; Yokoyama, "Meiji ishin to kinsei mibunsei no kaitai," 136–38.

86. Takeuchi, "Kansei kaikaku to 'kanjōsho goyōtashi,'" part 1, 23–32, part 2, 49–56.

87. Yoshida Nobuyuki, *Kinsei kyodai toshi no shakai kōzō*, 3–178.

century. In Ōno's case, we do not know what circumstances prompted the establishment of the purveyor guild, but perhaps the town's small size was a factor. There were relatively few wealthy merchants to begin with, and not many occupations developed enough to form guilds that could have been mobilized for specific duties. For the lord of Ōno, it must have been convenient to have an organized body of financially stable merchants who could shoulder some of the responsibilities commonly taken on by a wider range of townspeople associations.

How did the purveyor guild enable the collection of the 5.5 *koku* they contributed to the donation pool in 1783–84? As with the responsibility for guestroom duty, the guild structure helped spread the burden and exert peer pressure on merchants who were reluctant to contribute. Nineteen purveyor merchants made a donation—almost the entire membership of the guild.[88] The amounts given by individual purveyors varied considerably and did not match their respective rank within the group. Giving was voluntary, at least on paper: an order of 1787 instructed the purveyors to provide "as much [relief] as they desired" (*shinnai shidai*).[89] At the same time, the purveyors were usually singled out as the primary contributors to the pooled donations in domain orders and in townspeople's petitions, showing that as a group, they were expected to guarantee the successful conduct of the fundraising campaign. When the domain later rewarded the donors, it referred to the contributions to the pooled donation scheme as "ordered" donations. The guild structure probably helped the purveyors set donation targets and collect amounts deemed appropriate for each member's economic situation.

The fourth component of town-wide pooled donations in 1783–84 consisted of contributions from two exceptional merchants who chose to deliver their "ordered" donations as individuals rather than through the collective framework of the purveyor guild: Nabeya Seizaemon and Kameya Moemon. Both men were members of that guild, but the quantities

88.   The journal lists the names of nineteen individuals, all of whom can be identified as merchants of either *goyōtashi* or *gomenchi* rank. A comparison of this list with the lists of *goyōtashi* and *gomenchi* compiled for the lord's New Year audiences of 1784 shows that of the twenty-five merchants who held these titles, only two did not participate in the collection and distribution of pooled donations (the town elders and Nabeya and Kameya were also purveyors but donated in a separate capacity).

89.   MT goyōdome 1787.2.21, SSM.

they donated far outstripped anything the other purveyor merchants were able or willing to contribute. Nabeya gave 6.17 *koku*, more than the entire purveyor guild together, and Kameya supplied exactly half of Nabeya's amount.[90] Both donated a set amount per applicant, and the starving owed it to them alone that the rice grants they ultimately received amounted to 2.7 *shō* instead of just 1.2 *shō* (1 *shō*=1.8 liters). Nabeya and Kameya apparently also took the lead in individual charity: the "voluntary donations" listed for their block associations, Gobanmachi and Eastern Shichikenmachi, surpassed all the others by a large margin.[91]

Nabeya and Kameya were moneylenders and sake brewers whose fortunes had risen in the eighteenth century (see chapter 1). "Ōno machizukushi," a humorous song that surveyed the qualities of the town's various neighborhoods, hailed them as the two rich men of Ōno town: "If I had my own household, I would build a home like Kameya's in Shichiken; I would have money like Nabeya and let my servants run the business for me."[92] These men likely tried to excel as givers of pooled donations and other money for the domain because they aspired to higher ranks and needed to win the favor of the domain government. The year 1784 was the first time Nabeya and Kameya made per capita donations to all the starving townspeople at once,[93] and in 1785 and 1788, respectively, they were promoted above the other purveyors and placed under the direct rule of the town governor, the highest rank a townsman could attain at the time.

Pooled relief donations in Ōno thus consisted of two separate layers: donations from townspeople of middling fortune collected through the block associations, and donations from very wealthy and privileged merchants collected through the purveyor guild or provided by them individually.

90. This amount excludes the donations they made to the fundraising campaigns within Gobanmachi and Yokomachi, which took place in conjunction with the town-wide pooling of donations, but includes their contributions to the earlier fundraising campaign within the block association of Shibanmachi.

91. MT goyōdome 1785.3.16, SSM.

92. Ōno machizukushi, Yasukawa Kaibutsu-ke monjo; Nagami, "Echizen Ōno no kadozuke geinō," 78–80.

93. During the collection of pooled donations in the winter of 1782–83, the two were already by far the most generous contributors; see Tenmei hachi tomeki, 1783, second month, AHM.

This structure had much in common with the city-wide charitable collections taken up in Osaka and Kyoto during times of crisis in the eighteenth and nineteenth centuries. Modern scholars have labeled them "town-wide almsgiving" (*sōchō segyō* or *machikata segyō*).[94] In these two cities, the shogunate called up all well-to-do townspeople simultaneously to donate to the starving, either on the level of the *chō* or the entire town. The main difference was that neither Osaka nor Kyoto had a purveyor guild. In Osaka, wealthy and privileged merchants made individual donations to the scheme, which were then distributed to the poor via the framework of town administration. In Kyoto, some powerful merchant houses such as Mitsui also participated in "city-wide almsgiving" by distributing aid through their own channels, for example, by approaching the block associations directly.[95]

As suggested, a key factor behind the willingness of the wealthiest merchants to participate in town-wide relief was probably fear—they wanted to deflect the possibility of violence directed toward them. Many of the purveyors were engaged in moneylending (pawn brokering) and sake brewing, two occupations that easily attracted the ire of poor townspeople when rice prices were high. The moneylenders of Ōno accumulated agricultural land from unredeemed collateral and worked it by employing the town's large population of tenant farmers and laborers.[96] They also held major rice reserves, part of which they had collected as pawns or deposits from peasants in the villages.[97] The sake brewers were often criticized by townspeople of small means for hoarding and export-

94. The term *sōchō segyō* is used by Yoshida Nobuyuki, *machikata segyō* by Ikeda Yoshimasa. Neither of these terms was common among contemporaries, who often simply spoke of *segyō*—not to be confused with alms for beggars, which is how *segyō* was used in Ōno and represented the older meaning of the term; Yoshida, *Kinsei kyodai toshi no shakai kōzō*, 249–51; Ikeda, *Nihon shakai fukushishi*, 117–28, Kitahara, *Toshi to hinkon no shakaishi*, 14.

95. Yoshida Nobuyuki, *Kinsei kyodai toshi no shakai kōzō*, 262–69.

96. See, for example, *Ōno chōshi*, vol. 3, 433–35; Tenmei hachi tomeki, 1783, second month, AHM.

97. This is indicated by an emergency survey undertaken in the spring of 1783 to estimate the amount of rice reserves in the town. Of the 8,700 bales of rice stored by townspeople, pawned rice and "rice in custody" (*azukarimai*) amounted to more than 3,200 bales each. See Tenmei hachi tomeki, 1783, fourth month, AHM; MT goyōdome 1787.2.16, SSM; *Ōno chōshi*, vol. 3, 434.

ing rice and sake.[98] Last and most important, many purveyor merchants engaged in exporting rice and other goods to the mountainous hinterland of Ōno, a business model that became enormously problematic whenever a part of the town population was suffering from high food prices.

During the Tenmei famine, uprisings and violence were no more than a hair's breadth away. In 1783, 1784, and 1787, Ōno's townspeople successfully petitioned the domain for export bans on rice, but in 1783 the movement almost escalated into open protest when some called for an assembly at a local shrine.[99] In 1787, riots and peasant conspiracies in other domain territories on the eastern rim of the Ōno plain threatened to spread to the town, and domain officials and town elders reacted by punishing rice dealers accused of illegal exports.[100] The looming threat of unrest might explain why Nabeya, Kameya, and the other purveyors felt compelled to aid the whole population of starving townspeople, not just their own neighbors, tenants, subcontractors, and employees.

The Link between Seigneurial Relief and Townspeople Charity

The domain government tried to encourage townspeople charity through both orders and positive incentives. One measure was ceremonies held at the castle to reward townspeople who had given aid to the hungry. Such ceremonies for charitable givers were widespread in the Tokugawa period.[101] In Ōno in the fourth month of 1784, givers received a letter of praise from the lord, which was read aloud to them.[102] Those who enjoyed the

---

98. In 1783, for example, most *chō* participated in a petition movement that succeeded at imposing various restrictions on sake sales; MT goyōdome 1783.10.1, 10.11, SSM.

99. Tenmei hachi tomeki, 1783.4.13–26, AHM.

100. MT goyōdome 1787.6.24–29, 7.2, YH 320 and 324, 233–42, 244.

101. Kikuchi, *Kikin kara yomu kinsei shakai*, 408–9; Ikeda, *Nihon shakai fukushishi*, 122; *Fukui shishi*, Tsūshi-hen 2, 665; Kalland, *Fishing Villages in Tokugawa Japan*, 262–64, 294–97.

102. MT goyōdome 1784.4.9, YH 195, 151–52; 1785.3.28, SSM. The journals of 1783 and 1787 do not mention such ceremonies, even though pooled donations were distributed in those years.

right of audience, such as purveyor merchants and headmen of block associations, proceeded into the domain bureau (*gokaisho*) within the castle moat to hear the letter read. For donors of lesser status, the town elder read the letter at the town office. The ceremony was not open to the public and was not meant to create publicity but to encourage givers to repeat their generosity on future occasions. The domain tried to achieve this goal by extolling the virtue of those who had given, while shaming those who had not and thus were not invited to the ceremony.[103]

To prepare for the ceremony, the domain asked the town elders to submit registers of all donations made by townspeople during the winter: large and small; rice, millet, silver, and copper money; alms (*segyō*) for beggars (*kojiki*) and mutual relief (*gōriki*) for poor townspeople (*konkyū no mono*).[104] These data, gathered from the headmen of the block associations, have survived only in small fragments, but they allow us some insight into the dynamics of the reward process and the actualities of who gave what.

Although the ceremony might have been intended partly to soften the imposition of ordered donations, it also shows a desire on the part of the domain to shore up the traditional practice of mutual relief within block associations. The invited donors were divided into two groups: those who had given "upon orders" only, in other words, participated in the domain-ordered town-wide pooling at the end of the first month, and those who had given both "upon orders" and "voluntarily," that is, to beggars and people within their *chō*.[105] After the first part of the ceremony was over, the former group was asked to leave, and only the donors who had given voluntarily remained to listen to a second letter addressed specifically to them. Not all voluntary donations thus recognized were large. For 1784, the town elders' journal contains a list of all donations made in millet, and some of them were no higher than two *shō*.[106] We do not know precisely where the domain officials and headmen were drawing the line, but they obviously tried to reward even relatively minor acts of charity. In terms of quantity, voluntary charitable contributions substantially outweighed those ordered and made through the pooling

---

103. In 1784, there was only one person, the headman of Bikunimachi, who failed to give while expected to do so; in 1785, there were two.
104. MT goyōdome 1784.3.11, SSM.
105. *Osetsukerare-sōrōte aisukui* and *jibun hodokoshi*.
106. MT goyōdome 1784.4.2, SSM.

mechanism. In 1784 and 1785 the voluntary donations were more than twice as large as the ordered ones.

As this process shows, Ōno's domain authorities encouraged voluntary giving and were overall quite reluctant to replace mutual relief inside block associations with a more formal town-wide system. Eventually, the severity of the Tenmei famine forced them to permit the town-wide pooling of *chō* and purveyor donations, and even then they were not ready to abandon the idea of the block association as a self-supporting status community that took care of its poorer members. Rather than replacing solidarity within block associations permanently with a completely integrated system of town-wide relief, the domain tried to use the redistributions of 1784 and 1785 to revive it.

The domain's preference for mutual relief within the *chō* was evident throughout the winter of 1783–84. As mentioned, domain officials initially ordered the block associations of Sanbanmachi and Shibanmachi to support their own petitioners instead of providing them with help from outside. Later, they included Sanbanmachi and Shibanmachi in the common pool of donations to allow them to benefit from the resources of other, richer *chō*, but at the same time, they ordered two other *chō*, Gobanmachi and Yokomachi, to stay out of the town-wide scheme for the moment. As the town governor put it, "Gobanmachi and Yokomachi should provide mutual relief only within their blocks because their economic situation is comfortable." The structure of these communities can be described as balanced: they had a certain number of starving residents but also enough wealthy house owners to support them.[107] In 1785, the town governor insisted again, against the objections of the town elders, that internal collections must be held in the block associations before town-wide pooled donations could be allowed to take place. He backed down from this position only when the headmen protested that some *chō* were simply too poor to collect sufficient donations.[108]

In this fashion, the domain tried to reinforce the traditional system even as it allowed town-wide collections to overcome the limitations of community relief during the Tenmei famine. In Osaka and Kyoto, too, town-wide donation schemes did not override the block associations as

107. MT goyōdome 1784.1.26, YH 179, 137–40.
108. MT goyōdome 1785.2.6, 2.11, SSM.

units of mutual relief but were designed to strengthen and supplement them. In these cities, the schemes had a two-layered structure, but the donations of the first layer that came from the ordinary well-to-do townspeople were not pooled and were distributed solely within each *chō*. Only very few privileged merchants made large contributions for the entire town community.[109] That no town-wide pooling of resources from block associations took place in Osaka and Kyoto may have been partly due to logistical reasons: redistributing rice among the whole town population would have been impractical in cities of this size. In many cases, richer *chō* were instead required to pass on leftovers of their fundraising campaigns to poorer *chō* in their vicinity.[110] In Ōno, on the other hand, the town's smaller size made it easier to gather donations at the town elders' office and pick them up from there.

The domain's emphasis on mutual relief within block associations as a condition for a town-wide pooling also went hand in hand with an insistence on making the provision of domain relief loans contingent on a prior collection of donations among townspeople. As mentioned before, 1783–84 was the first year when domain loans and town-wide pooling took place during the same winter. At the end of the first month of 1784, when the domain ordered the purveyors and well-to-do townspeople to collect and distribute donations, the representatives of the purveyor guild requested that the domain also step in and provide some relief to the hungry. The reaction of the government officials is revealing. They responded that "in light of this year's circumstances, the lord will have to provide relief as well, but only if there is another round of petitions. He will not do it at this point because the two would become mixed up."[111] In other words, the domain officials did not categorically rule out disbursing relief loans from the domain, but they were concerned with timing and precedent: the purveyors and people who were "leading comfortable lives within the *chō*" should act first. If the year were sufficiently bad, the domain would also intervene, but only after these people had given their share.

109.	Yoshida Nobuyuki, *Kinsei kyodai toshi no shakai kōzō*, 249–51; Kitahara, *Toshi to hinkon no shakaishi*, 15–21.

110.	Kitahara, *Toshi to hinkon no shakaishi*, 22.

111.	MT goyōdome 1784.1.28, YH 179, 139.

Most likely domain officials insisted on this division so as to establish an order of subsidiarity and maintain seigneurial relief as a separate category. In 1777, the domain officials warned the town elders that the application of village food loans to the town was exceptional and they were not allowed to invoke it as precedent in the future.[112] In 1784, the town governor emphasized once more that the domain would not again grant starvation loans: the authorities never gave such loans to townspeople; 1777 had been an exception and 1784 would be treated as an exception, too. He stressed that loans were being granted only because the crisis was so severe.[113] Although relief loans for townspeople were obviously just a step away from evolving into precedent, the town governor kept denying this fact to prevent the townspeople, rich and poor, from developing a sense of entitlement. Domain loans would complement wealthy commoner donations when the situation was serious, but there could be no guarantee. This needed to be clarified not only to defend the domain's negotiating position and protect its budget but also to leave the lord with an opportunity to display his "extraordinary" benevolence. Indeed, the loans remained extraordinary for a while. Ordered donations by townspeople took place four times during the Tenmei famine (1783, 1784, 1785, and 1787), but only in 1784, the worst year of the famine, were they supplemented by loans from the lord.[114] In the 1790s, finally, the domain made a more explicit commitment by instituting hunger relief loans for townspeople as a permanent system.

In the spring of 1784, following one round of pooled donations, the domain began to issue starvation loans (see table 4). It supplied them in response to the same kind of starvation petitions poor townspeople had been submitting since the beginning of the winter, and which to that point had been addressed only with pooled relief from wealthy townspeople. Applicants received a visit from an inspection team of domain officials. If deemed "starving" (*katsumei*), each person in the household received a monetary loan worth three *shō* of barnyard millet from the rural intendant's office, interest-free and repayable in three annual installments.

---

112. MT goyōdome 1777.2.1, YH 122, 98.
113. MT goyōdome 1784.ii.19, YH 184, 142.
114. In 1783, when no loans were given, pooled donations were given out twice to bridge the period of need; Tenmei hachi tomeki, 1783, second month, AHM.

If a recipient proved unable to repay, relatives and officials of block associations were ordered to step in.[115] There is little information on how a person needed to look to be classified as "starving," but the criteria were hopefully a bit looser than those specified in 1741, when only people with pallid and swollen bodies had been deemed eligible (see the second section of this chapter). In any case, the fact that inspectors were used suggests that the domain officials were interested in the applicants' physical condition.

In 1784, the domain disbursed starvation loans on three separate occasions (in intervals of roughly ten days) whenever a certain number of petitions had accumulated, eventually providing a total equivalent to 18.7 *koku* of barnyard millet (see table 4).[116] Many people needed to apply more than once because three *shō* of millet were not sufficient to feed a person for longer than about ten days (for third-time recipients, the loans were reduced to two *shō*).[117]

In 1783–84, the starving townspeople of Ōno thus received relief both in the form of outright grants from their fellow townspeople and loans from the domain, but they did not receive both simultaneously. The two kinds of relief were carefully timed to ensure the survival of the town poor over the longest possible period of time. Domain loans were granted about three weeks after the distribution of the town-wide donations. Whether they applied for donations or loans, townspeople used the same petition format (see table 3).[118] Officials included grants of pooled donations when they counted the frequency of applications, a sure sign that they saw the types of relief as constituting a sequence.

Ōno was not the only town in eighteenth-century Japan where commoner and seigneurial relief were aligned in a sequence. A similar arrangement had been observed for Osaka and Kyoto during the Kyōhō famine

---

115.   See, for example, MT goyōdome 1785.7.6, 1786.6.26, SSM.

116.   The total number of applications was 646, which seems to have roughly coincided with the number of eventual recipients.

117.   MT goyōdome 1784.2.11, SSM. In the Tokugawa period, five *gō* of rice were considered the standard daily ration for an adult male, but Miwa Kiken estimated that survival was already possible on two *gō* of rice gruel a day; "Kyūga taii," 454. In Kyoto and Osaka, the size of relief grants during the Kyōhō famine was two *gō* of rice per day for men, and one *gō* for women and minors; see Kitahara, *Toshi to hinkon no shakaishi*, 26.

118.   MT goyōdome 1784.2.11, SSM.

(1732–33), but there, seigneurial relief came first.[119] After a certain point, rich merchants or (in Kyoto) temples began to fill in for the shogunate, sometimes using the same distribution channels. Shogunal administrators were responsible for regulating the sequence and timing of these various sources of relief.[120] Why the warrior authorities gave first is unclear, but it should be noted that these two cities did not have purveyor guilds. In Osaka and Kyoto, the absence of an organized and permanent body of wealthy purveyors made it impossible for the shogunate to approach "the rich" collectively. Instead, it was forced to solicit donations by issuing edicts, publishing donor rankings, conducting surveys to identify potential givers, and contacting them individually. Such methods were far more persuasive if the shogunate had already gone ahead and provided help to the poor. During later famines, seigneurial relief could come second.[121] In urban communities such as Osaka and Ōno, commoner charity usually surpassed the amount of seigneurial relief, whereas the situation in villages could be the reverse. In Ikegami, a village near Osaka, seigneurial relief—loans and grants—was given first and constituted the bulk of hunger aid for villagers during the Tenmei famine and later.[122] Perhaps this balance reflected the villagers' importance as taxpayers and the financial weakness of the elite, at least in comparison with town merchants.

Hunger Relief and Townspeople Autonomy

Did the introduction of pooled donations in Ōno represent a step toward greater townspeople autonomy? Some of the evidence at first glance seems to point in this direction. Ōno's domain officials, for example, clearly considered the scheme to be a town-run system. Although they issued orders regarding the collection and distribution of donations and interfered with

119. *Osaka shishi*, vol. 3, no. 1500, 323–25; Kitahara, *Toshi to hinkon no shakaishi*, 15, 21–25, 37, 42–43, 53. In these cases, seigneurial relief consisted of rice grants, not loans.

120. Kitahara, *Toshi to hinkon no shakaishi*, 22, 26–30. See also Maehara, "Kyōhō kaikaku-ki Kyoto ni okeru haraimai to beika seisaku," 32–37.

121. Kitahara, *Toshi to hinkon no shakaishi*, 10–12, 37, 45–49; Ikeda, *Nihon shakai fukushishi*, 123.

122. Saitō Hiroko, "Kinsei Izumi no sonraku shakai ni okeru 'konkyūnin' kyūsai."

the scheme's operation, they always asked the town elders for their opinion before making any decisions. In 1787, for example, townspeople residents of an area attached to the precincts of a temple (*monzen*), and thus outside the jurisdiction of the town elders, asked to be included in the distribution pool. Before reaching a decision, the domain officials confirmed with the elders whether a precedent for this existed and whether they had any objections against establishing one for the future.[123]

Moreover, the first layer of pooled donations, their collection through the block associations, had a communal character because it was an extension of townspeople mutual relief. When implemented on this larger, town-wide scale, it is possible that—as Ikeda Yoshimasa argues for Osaka and Kyoto—pooled mutual relief might have become a source of empowerment for the community, because it would have given the town leadership the authority to distribute resources from the rich to the poor.[124] As mentioned, the domain was not eager to move away from mutual sharing within block associations and replace it with a more centralized and impersonal redistribution system.

Innovative as the town-wide pooled donations scheme was, however, it was essentially a product of the old, reciprocal style of town government in which samurai authorities collaborated with self-governing groups. In Osaka and Kyoto, *chō* contributions to town-wide aid collections were not pooled in the first place. Whether in these two cities or in Ōno, the donations from the purveyor merchants were the most significant part of these schemes, not the donations from the block associations. The fact that these merchants donated to the entire town did not have any implications for townspeople autonomy—it neither expanded nor eroded it. Ōno's purveyor guild was already well established when it began to shoulder this burden, and it entertained a symbiotic relationship with the domain government—providing services to the lord, controlling the town economy, and enjoying privileges of various kinds. The town-wide donations of wealthy purveyor merchants were not a communal affair

---

123. The town elders responded that although there was no such precedent, they were in favor of the inclusion for humanitarian reasons; MT goyōdome 1787.2.23, SSM. Also see table 4.

124. Ikeda, *Nihon shakai fukushishi*, 114–28; Ikeda, "Ryūmin atsumesho kara kyūmin jusansho e," 71.

but a reflection of their financial power (which was itself of a town-wide scale) and of their close relationship with the samurai authorities.

On its part, the domain mobilized the wealthy for "relief duty," so to speak, because it wanted to avoid paying for the relief itself, even though the starvation petitions were submitted to the domain and not the purveyors. The domain tried to limit its help to instances when the townspeople had run out of reserves collectively. This does not mean that the lord had given up on his claim to rule with benevolence or dropped the burden of relief onto his subjects. In the latter half of the eighteenth century, the domain increased the frequency of the rice gruel kitchens, provided swift help after the fire of 1775,[125] and granted starvation loans to the town for the first time. Without the status order and its institutionalized relationships of duty and privilege between status groups and their ruler, most of the new relief schemes would have been unable to function and probably would not have existed in the first place. The status order continued to structure poor and famine relief even as the commercial economy was altering the fabric of castle town society and required new modes of redistributing wealth among townspeople.

Ōno's domain authorities applied pressure on the merchants to organize their charity and made it quasi-mandatory, but the merchants benefited from this particular arrangement as well. Unlike outright taxation, it left them with the flexibility to determine the amount of their donations and allowed them to be openly recognized for their "generosity." The domain lord did not need to worry that the mobilization of merchants would diminish his aura of benevolence, as long as he could convince his subjects that he was still capable of fulfilling their requests for relief.[126] Consider, for example, the way Ōno's town poor interacted with the domain in the latter years of the Tenmei famine. In 1787, the fifth year of the famine, more than 300 poor townspeople submitted starvation petitions to the government. This time, however, they let the officials know that they were no longer interested in starvation loans because

---

125. Various sources, YH 94, 72–84. In 1780, the government also granted aid to 1,192 townspeople who had lost their houses in a fire; Goyōki (machibugyō) 1780.3.19, YH 156, 123–24.

126. That this was not always the case is amply demonstrated by the case of Sendai domain, whose government badly mismanaged two big famines in the eighteenth century; see Kikuchi, *Kikin kara yomu kinsei shakai*, 375–422.

the length of the famine had made it difficult to repay them.[127] They wanted the domain to order a town-wide collection. In other words, the poor rejected the help from the domain and demanded more aid from wealthy townspeople, but asked the domain to make them provide it.

The domain was unable to grant more than the unpopular starvation loans, but it did have the authority to put pressure on the purveyors. The poor, although not ignorant about the source of these grants, were clearly aware that they owed them to the intervention of the domain. This might explain why in their journal the town elders twice used the term *osukui* (seigneurial relief) to refer to petitions for relief in the form of pooled donations (*sukui*), even though none of the rice was coming from the domain.[128] It would be a gross mischaracterization to portray Lord Toshisada as a shining example of a virtuous ruler, considering the deaths, misery, and discontent his people suffered during the Tenmei famine. Whatever relief the town poor were given was barely enough to ensure their physical survival, and it was granted only under threat of popular unrest. The available help did not prevent the spread of an epidemic among the weakened population in the early summer, nor did it keep dozens of beggars from dying on the streets.[129] But the lord granted the town poor the minimum of what they expected in this situation and successfully preempted the popular unrest that plagued so many other towns in those years.[130]

In the winter of 1783–84, three formal schemes operated to relieve people in the town of Ōno from hunger: domain-funded rice gruel kitchens, town-wide pooled donations, and starvation loans provided by the domain.

127.   By then, the *chō* headmen had indeed reported a number of cases in which townspeople proved unable to repay their starvation loans; see MT goyōdome 1785.7.6, 1786.6.26, SSM.

128.   MT goyōdome 1785.2.6, 1787.2.21, SSM.

129.   No population data have survived for these years, but the town elders' journal for 1784 mentions twenty-nine beggar deaths in the town. On the epidemic in the fifth month of 1784, see MT goyōdome 1784.5.21, SSM. For neighboring Katsuyama domain, population records indicate a drop in population of roughly 10 percent between 1783 and 1786; *Fukui kenshi*, Tsūshi-hen 4, 493.

130.   In his journal, Tachibana Sōken, a doctor in nearby Fukui, included the lord of Ōno in his list of local lords who had provided aid (*teate*) to their subjects in 1784; "Denrai nenjū nichiroku," 1784.11.18, 582.

Although they differed in their sources of funding, their circle of beneficiaries, and other terms and conditions, these schemes involved close collaboration between domain officials, town officials, and various associations within town society. In Ōno, the block associations, the sake brewer guild, the purveyor guild, and the beggar guild were deeply involved in the funding and management of hunger relief. The town elders played a pivotal role in these systems. They provided the channel of communication between the domain and the *chō* and three guilds; all orders, petitions, and reports pertaining to the relief schemes went through their hands.

The rice gruel kitchens represented a case of an established and entirely domain-funded form of relief that relied heavily on commoner services. The system of pooled donations, on the other hand, was exclusively funded and run (and probably also invented) by townspeople but functioned on the basis of status obligations vis-à-vis the domain government and was closely coordinated with domain-funded relief. The distinction between commoner and seigneurial relief was by no means irrelevant—the domain government did what it could to maintain it—but the relationship between lord and commoner elites in poor and disaster relief is better characterized as one of collaboration and shared responsibility, not contestation over the control of town society. When it came to relieving the poor, the conflict of interest between wealthy merchants and hungry laborers and tenant farmers was far more consequential than the social gap that separated rich townspeople from domain officials.

It is undeniable, however, that the involvement of commoners in famine relief in Ōno domain changed over time. Of course it made a difference whether wealthy merchants were asked to donate substantial amounts of rice and money on behalf of the domain or whether they were merely mobilized for cooking rice gruel. The implementation of town-wide pooled donations was the first case in which Ōno's domain authorities systematically interfered with the redistribution of wealth among the townspeople. Although the town elders' journal of 1784 betrays some reluctance on the part of the purveyor guild, the domain's order did not meet with any sustained opposition, in part probably because the merchants were rewarded for their participation and also in part because they stood to gain from a system that reached farther than their own limited charitable efforts.[131] Pooled donations were an application of old rules to a new situation: for the first time, the funding of relief among townspeople was openly drawn into the relationship of duty and privilege between the lord and his wealthier subjects. As long as the domain authorities were seen to be doing their part, Ōno's wealthy merchants and peasants seem to have been willing to take on the duty of relieving the poor. A far greater problem, in the eyes of the town elite, seems to have been the domain's growing inability to repay its forced loans, as well as its propensity for using the wealthiest households as intermediaries for acquiring loans in other towns. This kind of mobilization increased around the end of the eighteenth century and drove one of Ōno's town merchants to the verge of bankruptcy.[132]

On one hand, there were striking structural similarities between the famine donation schemes of Ōno, Osaka, and Kyoto. On the other hand, some castle towns never developed semivoluntary donation schemes of this kind and instead adopted other solutions. One alternative approach, seen in cities as far apart as Edo and Kumamoto, was to establish relief granaries that were largely funded through tax-like contributions from the block associations but were also supported by purveyor merchants and samurai authorities.[133] It is still unclear why some towns and cities developed certain systems and not others, and more case studies are needed to identify and compare patterns of famine relief in their social context. But famine relief in Japanese towns does seem to have become more organized toward the end of the Tokugawa period and often resulted in the creation of permanent aid schemes. Many of these new schemes were explicitly designed to overcome the inequalities that ensued when wealthy,

131.   On this point, see, for example, Howell, "Hard Times in the Kantō," 357–68; Kalland, *Fishing Villages in Tokugawa Japan*, 262–64, 294–97; Makihara, *Kyakubun to kokumin no aida*, 59–68; and Drixler, *Mabiki*, 159–66.

132.   *Fukui kenshi*, Tsūshi-hen 4, 100–111.

133.   Matsuzaki, "Kumamoto jōkamachi ni okeru kyūmin no kyūsai," 59–83. On the establishment of relief funds in a rural area (Harima Province) at the time of the Kansei reform, see Yamasaki, *Kinsei kōki no ryōshu shihai to chiiki shakai*, 98–104. On Fukuoka, see Kalland and Pedersen, "Famine and Population in Fukuoka Domain," 64. Typically, a lord or the shogunate would contribute a certain sum to such a fund, frame it as an expression of benevolence, and demand that the wealthier subjects reciprocate the favor and follow the ruler's good example; see, for example, Yamasaki, *Kinsei kōki no ryōshu shihai to chiiki shakai*, 59.

charitable townspeople chose to channel their donations to their own employees, subcontractors, and neighbors. Such programs were a response to the increasingly ruinous effects of famines and grain shortages on town residents and the economic polarization of urban society.

In Tokugawa Japan, seigneurial relief and commoner charity expanded hand in hand. The reason for this development must be sought in the structure of the status order. Although the status order encouraged self-rule and mutual help within occupation-based associations, it simultaneously forced these groups to take on public roles by fulfilling duty obligations toward their lords, reflecting their professional expertise. Self-rule and duty continued to be central to the provision of poor and hunger relief in the latter half of the Tokugawa period. Samurai authorities not only tried to fix the cracks in mutual relief within block associations, they also used the promise of privilege to channel the wealth of new groups of rich townspeople, without whom none of the new relief mechanisms would have been able to function. Although Ōno's pooled donations were not a permanent institution like the *machi kaisho* granary in Edo, both cases display a close link between big merchant capital, duty obligation, and the management of townspeople relief. It would be meaningful to compare these trends in Japan to the development of famine relief in late Chosŏn Korea, where the central government reacted to commercialization and the resulting social changes by increasingly mobilizing the local wealthy for funding relief while trying to stabilize the traditional social hierarchy.[134]

After the Tenmei famine, Ōno's domain leadership finally put seigneurial relief for the poor on a more solid footing, despite its deepening fiscal crisis. The domain established an additional granary—the so-called *okakoimomi* (enclosed rice)—specifically as a precaution against food crises. In doing so, it responded to a new initiative by the shogunate, which in 1789 had ordered all lords and bannermen in the country to establish granaries in their fiefs and save 50 *koku* of rice a year for every 10,000 *koku* of productive land they governed.[135] Ōno domain entrusted the management of this granary to two vassals who served as part-time

---

134. Karlsson, "Famine Relief, Social Order, and State Performance in Late Chosŏn Korea."

135. Kikuchi, *Kinsei no kikin*, 178–92; Ishikawa, "Shinchō kazenroku," 339, 357.

"relief officials" (*osukuikata*)—a newly created position. These relief officials were also in charge of distributing three new types of seigneurial relief to townspeople and villagers: the previously mentioned millet loans for the starving; so-called seigneurial relief grants during the snow season (*yukichū osukui*; grants for elderly and other poor townspeople without kin to help purchase grain); and "monthly seigneurial relief" (*tsukizuki osukui*) for people completely incapable of working.[136] These measures showed the government's determination to support its weakest subjects and reduce the pressure on villages and block associations.

The lord's reputation appears to have improved as a result, if we believe the chronicler of 1812, who celebrated the wisdom and benevolence of Lord Toshisada's reign. What did not change was the mobilization of commoners for managing and funding poor and hunger relief, especially with regard to wealthy townspeople and peasants of the purveyor class. During the Tenpō famine in the 1830s, wealthy merchants once again bore the brunt of the burden of hunger relief for townspeople.[137] Even the new enclosed rice granary was primarily stocked by two privileged peasants of Nakano village, Hanaguro Yosōzaemon and Takinami Yoemon. In 1787, the lord granted these wealthy landowners some marshy land near the castle, asked them to bring it under cultivation, and made them reciprocate the favor by paying an annual contribution from these fields to the new relief granary in lieu of land tax.[138] Ōno domain thus entered the nineteenth century with plenty of precedents for domain–commoner collaboration in the area of hunger relief.

136. Ishikawa, "Shinchō kazenroku," 357; MT goyōdome 1809.12.27, SSM (fragments); Goyōnin-yaku yōyō tehikae, 1852, sections 23 and 24, Kōbara-ke shūshū monjo. On *yukichū osukui* and "monthly [*tsukizuki*] osukui," see Osukuikin narabi ni momi hie oboe, 1821; Oboe, 1808, TKM.

137. See, for example, Chōnai yōdomeki (Honmachi kuyū) 1831, first month, YH 660, 481–82; MT goyōdome 1834.6.26, 6.28, SSM; Goyōtashi goyōdome 1837, SSM. See also MT goyōdome 1837.4.21, YH 730, 530–31.

138. Goyōdome 1787, Hanakura-ke monjo. In ordinary years, Ōno domain seems to have lent out part of these reserves to villagers in the spring to refresh them; see, for example, Goyōdome 1805.3.14, Hanakura-ke monjo; Goyōnin-yaku yōyō tehikae, 1852, section 24, Kōbara-ke shūshū monjo.

CHAPTER 6

Growth through Gratitude

Welfare in a Mercantilist Domain

Late in the fourth month of 1842, Ōno's seventh Lord Toshitada (r. 1818–62) assembled all his vassals in the white audience room in the castle and ordered one of his house elders to read a declaration marking a new departure in domain politics. The text concerned nothing less than the survival of the domain. Toshitada stated that in recent years, the fiscal situation had deteriorated to a point that even frequent loans and stipend cuts no longer sufficed to finance his core obligations toward the shogunate, his retainers, and subjects in need. He announced his intention to implement a radical financial restructuring and encouraged his vassals to submit suggestions and criticisms to facilitate the reform. The young lord promised to do his own part by cutting personal expenses and abandoning his costly ambitions for higher office in Edo. He ended his speech on a dramatic note: "I plead you to exert your true and loyal energies. If not, I am extremely worried that my House might not continue."[1]

Ōno's retainers were reportedly moved to tears by Toshitada's earnest address and later referred to it as the "order for a new beginning" (*kōshi no rei*),[2] which initiated a "reform for the survival of the House" (*o-ie go-sonbō no go-kaikaku*).[3] The early 1840s were a time when many lords in Japan, including the Tokugawa shogunate, implemented reforms to

---

1. Yoshida Setsuzō, "Ryūin kiji," 364–65. Former vassal Yoshida Setsuzō compiled "Ryūin kiji" in 1883 as a chronicle of Toshitada's rule.

2. Ibid.

3. Goyōtashi goyōdome 1844.12.3, YH 886, 652.

address their chronic fiscal and social problems in the aftermath of the catastrophic Tenpō famine in the 1830s. Ōno domain had been experimenting with mercantilist policies since 1830, and the reform order of 1842 represented an intensification of those efforts. Initially the reformers focused on conventional mercantilist measures, such as export promotion, import controls, austerity, and the renegotiation of loans. But soon, especially after the forced opening of the country in 1854, they began to experiment with knowledge from overseas and explored the possibility of international trade.[4] The project was carried forward by a dynamic, talented group of vassals who enjoyed the lord's unequivocal backing and were thus protected from conservative backlashes. They sustained the reforms over almost three decades and eventually succeeded in putting the domain budget on a solid footing. Today, the decades before the Meiji Restoration are etched into local memory as Ōno's golden age—a rare progressive interlude in the history of an often backward and remote region.

The reforms brought a paradigm shift to the domain's response to poverty. Mercantilist rulers had a strong incentive for caring about the poor because they sought to harness their subjects' labor power and experienced disabled, unmotivated, and defiant peasants and workers as an obstacle to their goals. Lord Toshitada clearly saw a connection between the domain's fiscal health and an obedient, productive workforce. To fight depopulation and poverty, he particularly emphasized public health measures, such as smallpox vaccinations and medical care. He also sought to foster productivity, frugality, and self-reliance among the poor and unemployed through village reform, emergency granaries, and the promotion of new industries. The reforms were also a reaction to the vagrancy crisis described in chapter 3. Mercantilism made the government more reluctant to expend resources on unproductive and potentially diseased outsiders and thus hastened the demise of managed mendicancy.

This chapter examines how the domain's new mercantilist orientation changed its political interactions with subjects in the field of poor relief. On one hand, the government had to continue providing status groups with incentives because it needed to persuade subjects to cooperate with its reforms, as seen, for example, in the Koshirō's mobilization

4. *Fukui kenshi*, Tsūshi-hen 4, 635–36, 718–26, 813–61.

for executions in the 1850s. The government had come to administer society through reciprocal relationships with occupational groups, and as long as domain society remained organized into such groups, the government had to implement its reforms through them. The new welfare policies the domain introduced in the 1850s and 1860s led to a variety of new collaborations with self-governing groups, such as physicians and purveyor merchants, and changed the government's relationships with villages and block associations. On the other hand, the lord of Ōno also played up the idea of benevolent rule, which had always served to legitimize his government. He used rhetoric and actual relief and public health measures to persuade the domain population (especially the poor) that his House was worth their sacrifice because it was governing on behalf of the people. This chapter emphasizes the ideological dimension of reciprocal governance. It looks beyond the Meiji Restoration to show how the legacy of the domain reforms shaped social welfare in the region up until the end of the nineteenth century. The influence of the reforms manifested itself both on the ideological level—through a preoccupation with public health and self-reliance—and on the level of concrete social structures. Some of the social constellations that had supported the reforms continued to facilitate the organization of social welfare even after the status order and the domain had been abolished.

The marriage between mercantilism and benevolent rule was an uneasy one because under a mercantilist regime, economic standards of success were more important than the personal virtue of the lord, who was to protect the polity by maintaining harmony between Heaven and Earth through enlightened behavior.[5] Mercantilism posed a challenge to the Tokugawa moral economy because subjects could not easily accept the premise of a profit-seeking, self-interested government. Late Tokugawa proponents of mercantilist thought, such as Satō Nobuhiro and Yokoi Shōnan, were aware of this dilemma and tried to resolve it by arguing that a prosperous populace was synonymous with a prosperous domain: neither could exist without the other.[6] But this idea, so persuasive in principle, was difficult to put into practice because prosperity could not

---

5. Roberts, *Mercantilism in a Japanese Domain*, 152–53.
6. Yamazaki, *Yokoi Shōnan no shakai keizai shisō*, 100–103; Yokoi, "Kokuze Sanron: The Three Major Problems of State Policy," 157–64; Satō, "Yōzō kaikuron," 106–8.

be achieved overnight, and governments had to convince their subjects that hardships in the present would pay off in the future.[7] According to intellectual historians Ogawa Kazunari and Koseki Yūichirō, domain governments chose to modify rather than discard the idea of benevolent rule to make state strengthening palatable to subjects. The deeper Japanese domains got involved in mercantilist reforms, the more heavily they propagated the trope of the enlightened lord (*meikun*) and the need for harmony between high and low.[8] Mercantilist reform was thus not just a problem of economic policy but also one of rhetoric and communication. The events described in this chapter illustrate the importance of effective communication for the performance of benevolent rule.

With regard to mercantilism, Ōno domain was a comparative latecomer. Many other domains had already started in the eighteenth century to implement extensive mercantilist programs to overcome financial difficulties.[9] Because mercantilism prioritized the lord's fiscal poverty over the poverty of subjects, most reforms involved repressive measures such as price controls, monopsonies, sumptuary restrictions, and taxes, which exploited land and people to generate as much revenue as possible for the state. Accordingly, historians have been slow to recognize the links between domain mercantilism and the development of social welfare in Japan. For example, most of the research done on charity in the final decades of Tokugawa rule has concentrated on grassroots activism outside the purview of the state, especially the charitable initiatives of medical doctors, the Confucian-inspired charity of learned samurai and

7. The reconceptualization of benevolent rule was a challenge all East Asian states faced to a certain extent in the nineteenth century. In the 1870s, when leading Chinese officials at the Qing court debated whether to divert funds for projects of military modernization and spend them on famine relief in northern China, proponents argued that imperial benevolence did not conflict with the goal of national self-strengthening because the beleaguered country was in dire need of unity between high and low; see Edgerton-Tarpley, "From 'Nourish the People' to 'Sacrifice for the Nation,'" 453–55.

8. The classic study of benevolent government as economic thought is Fujita Teiichirō's *Kinsei keizai shisō no kenkyū*. For recent intellectual histories of political thought in Tokugawa Japan that are mindful of the ideas of domain reformers, see Ogawa, *Bokumin no shisō*; Koseki, *"Meikun" no kinsei*. See also Ravina, *Land and Lordship in Early Modern Japan*, 89–93.

9. Roberts, *Mercantilism in a Japanese Domain*; Ravina, *Land and Lordship in Early Modern Japan*; McClain, "Failed Expectations."

merchants, and communal loan societies in towns and villages.[10] Although these studies have greatly advanced our understanding of charity in nineteenth-century Japan, they have tended to underestimate the engagement of domains and shogunate in poverty relief. As scholars of Japanese mercantilism have pointed out, mercantilism could not succeed by exploitation alone. According to Mark Ravina, Yonezawa domain learned this lesson the hard way in the late 1600s when it tried to address its fiscal problems through coercive monopsonies and tax policies, which angered producers and resulted in depopulation from famine and peasant flight. The domain economy only recovered in the 1790s when the government began to work with incentives, easing restrictions on popular economic activity while fostering population growth through child-rearing subsidies and preventing infanticide.[11]

Without doubt, Lord Toshitada's promotion of medical science and public health and his concern with productivity, frugality, and self-reliance benefited many of his subjects. At the same time, these measures represented an attempt to discipline the people. In the context of Western history, Michel Foucault has introduced the concept of biopolitics to describe a similar constellation—a change in the strategy of rule that replaced sovereign power with a discourse of science and reason and allowed state power to penetrate deeply into people's lives and bodies through diffuse processes of discipline and control.[12] Foucault located the roots of biopolitics in the European mercantilist states of the eighteenth century, but at least in some parts of Japan, the rise of mercantilism likewise resulted in policies that intensified state control over people's productive bodies—decades before the Meiji government decided to adopt Western models of statecraft and public hygiene for rapid self-strengthening in an imperialist world. Tokugawa rulers also grappled with the legacy of paternalist governance and looked for ways to make it compatible with their mercantilist reforms.

As many scholars have noted, domain mercantilism anticipated the self-strengthening efforts of the Meiji state, and the same can be said about Toshitada's mercantilist approach to poverty. The focus on Ōno reveals

10. Najita, *Ordinary Economies in Japan*; Konishi, "The Emergence of an International Humanitarian Organization in Japan"; Maus, "Rising Up and Saving the World."
11. Ravina, *Land and Lordship in Early Modern Japan*, 71–114. On infanticide prevention and child-rearing subsidies in the late Tokugawa period, see also Drixler, *Mabiki*.
12. Foucault, *The Birth of Biopolitics*.

breaks and continuities in local society's responses to poverty before and after the dismantling of the Tokugawa order. The abolition of the domain and the status order in 1871 constituted a major break, and yet the legacy of Ōno's domain reforms continued to influence social welfare in Echizen's interior for the rest of the nineteenth century. Local elites, no matter what background, remained convinced that poor relief should be achieved by helping the poor acquire healthy bodies and become self-sufficient through productive labor. They retained some of the social structures that had supported the domain reforms. The most important was the so-called Ōnoya trade company, launched by domain vassals in the 1850s. In the Meiji period, this company remained in the possession of Toshitada's son and became the region's greatest charitable donor and employer of former domain vassals. Second, Ōno's wealthy town merchants continued to use their social ties as former members of the purveyor guild to organize poor relief and many other forms of philanthropy, and they revived the domain's public health institutions in collaboration with physicians and former samurai involved in Toshitada's reforms. Third, local elites showed a preference for self-perpetuating endowments and loan societies, which had been popular among commoners in the area since at least the late 1700s and also served domain reformers as a financial tool.

The chapter begins with a discussion of Ōno's mercantilist reforms and highlights the domain's initiatives in public health and creating emergency granaries in the 1860s. The second part introduces Ōnoya, the domain's trade enterprise, and outlines the philanthropic initiatives of Ōnoya and Ōno's local elites from the Meiji Restoration until the 1890s. Together the two parts show how social welfare operated within the reciprocal relationships between high and low in one particular region, both with and without the domain lord as a "benevolent" authority and privilege-granting center.

Domain Reform and Public Health

The promotion of smallpox vaccinations was the earliest and most innovative part of Toshitada's welfare agenda. In 1850, Ōno's lord obtained the smallpox vaccine from doctors in nearby Fukui domain, who had brought it to the region shortly after its introduction to Japan in 1849 through the Dutch trading company in Nagasaki.[13] In doing so, the lord relied on the expertise and professional connections of his own physicians, Hayashi Unkei and Tsuchida Ryūwan, as well as town doctor Nakamura Taisuke, all of whom specialized in Dutch medicine. Toshitada had personal motives for acquiring the vaccine. He was an avid student of Dutch learning, having trained with the prominent scholar Sugita Seikei in Edo, and shared his doctors' ethical commitment to saving life.[14] The death of his oldest son from smallpox in 1849 probably reinforced his determination to eradicate the illness.[15] But the fight against smallpox also suited Toshitada's mercantilist policies. One of the earliest domain edicts advertising the benefits of the vaccine began with the statement that in "Holland," not a single life had been lost to smallpox since the commencement of the vaccinations, and the population was increasing every year.[16] In 1858, the domain government proudly pronounced its vaccination program a success, claiming that in the past seven or eight years the population of the domain had increased by 2,000.[17] It seems that Toshitada saw the program both as a benevolent policy and a way to boost the economy. According to domain records, the domain had lost at least 4,900 people (out of a population of approximately 29,000) during the Tenpō famine.[18] In addition, many villages in the area were experiencing a gradual population drain as poorer peasants gave up agriculture and moved to castle towns as laborers.[19]

In Japan, smallpox vaccinations constituted the first substantial attempt of rulers to standardize and control medical treatment and make it mandatory for all subjects. Until recently, however, historians have not read them as part of the history of public health. According to the

13. Jannetta, *The Vaccinators*, 139–43.

14. The vaccinators' humanitarian ideals are expressed in an oath of 1849; Fukui-ken Ishikai, *Fukui-ken igakushi*, 545–52.

15. Iwaji, *Ōno-han no yōgaku*, 69.

16. "Shutō shōrei ni tsuki furegaki," 1851, in *Fukui kenshi*, Shiryō-hen 7, 458–59. "Holland" was probably a reference to England, the vaccinations' country of origin.

17. Shoyōdome (Nojiri) 1858, third month, YH 1119, 804–5.

18. *Fukui kenshi*, Tsūshi-hen 4, 499. See also Yōdome (Suzuki) 1837.8.6, YH 736, 534–35.

19. Fukai, *Kinsei no chihō toshi to chōnin*, 58–61.

standard narrative, modern ideas about public health and hygiene entered Japan from the West and were implemented only after the Meiji Restoration, for example, during the fight against cholera in the 1870s.[20] This interpretation seems persuasive enough because the shoguns and lords of the Tokugawa period, who saw public health as part of their responsibility as benevolent rulers, focused more on sponsoring research and the distribution of medicinal herbs and self-help manuals than on building an infrastructure for medical treatment.[21] In her book on the transmission of the smallpox vaccine to Japan, Ann Jannetta emphasizes physician initiative and their social networks and portrays the Tokugawa authorities primarily as a barrier to those efforts.[22] But Jannetta recognizes that some lords supported the doctors' activities and notes that the shogunate conducted a large vaccination campaign on Ezo (Hokkaido) in the 1850s, which was intended to assimilate the Ainu, prevent them from interacting with the Russian empire, and strengthen their labor power.[23] Ōno's case shows that state-led vaccination programs such as the shogunate's were not limited to the northern periphery but also occurred right in the heart of Honshū for the benefit of mercantilist reform.

In Ōno, the introduction of smallpox vaccinations was a governmental initiative. Although the domain would not have been able to obtain the vaccine without the connections of its local physicians, it was used to seeking common ground with the doctors, who pursued their own agenda, slightly different from that of the domain. Ōno's first vaccinators formed a chapter of a regional professional society (*shachū*) founded by specialists of Dutch medicine in Ōno's neighbor domain Fukui for the purpose of promoting the vaccine and preventing it from going extinct. All members of this society swore an oath to accept proper instruction in admin-

20.   For recent critiques of this interpretation, see Kōzai, "Yobō sesshu to iu 'eisei,'" and Fujimoto Hiro, "Kinsei iryōshi kenkyū no genzai."

21.   See, for example, Umihara, *Kinsei iryō no shakaishi*, 138–39; Hübner, "State Medicine and the State of Medicine in Japan," 12–36. An important exception is the Yōjōsho, a permanent public hospital for poor townspeople established in Edo in 1722 by Shogun Yoshimune; see Minami, *Edo no shakai kōzō*, 295–341.

22.   Jannetta, *The Vaccinators*.

23.   Ibid., 135–39, 161–62. See also Walker, "The Early Modern Japanese State and Ainu Vaccinations." Kōzai Toyoko interprets the shogunate's Ainu vaccinations as a coercive form of public health; see "Ainu wa naze 'yama ni nigeta' ka?"

istering the lymph and not pass it on to uninitiated individuals, to prevent a loss of faith in the new technique and retain a monopoly on it.[24] Ōno's domain government, however, was primarily intent on getting its subjects vaccinated as quickly as possible. This discrepancy between the domain's and the physicians' interests surfaced a few years after the start of the program. In 1853 or later, a domain official in the distant Nishikata exclave encouraged a local medical practitioner named Koyama Yōju to vaccinate subjects in that area, even though the man had no connections to the vaccinators' society and had obtained the lymph clandestinely from a nearby doctor, probably by "tapping" a freshly vaccinated child. When the organized physicians complained about this transgression, Ōno domain had to put all vaccinations in Nishikata on hold and remove the responsible official from his post. In 1857, Ōno's physicians eventually allowed Koyama to conduct vaccinations in Nishikata under the condition that he received instructions and abided by the society's rules.[25]

This incident shows that Ōno domain could not implement vaccinations without respecting the interests of its practitioners of Dutch medicine, who participated in a regional professional network of specialists in their field. On one hand, the vaccinators reinforced domain rule because they formed associations with domain-based subchapters and relied on their lords' coercive power over subjects to achieve their medical goals. On the other hand, the logic of lymph transmission led them to act autonomously across domain borders, like many other occupational groups in this region. In 1857, for example, the leading vaccinator in Fukui domain decided to elevate Koyama's clinic in Nishikata to the status of an "extension clinic" (*bekkan*) of Ōno domain, because he wanted to remove bureaucratic hurdles for physicians in nearby fiefs such as Fuchū and Sabae in case they needed to resupply Koyama with the vaccine.[26] The vaccinators thus built their own organizational structures that suited the needs of their profession and had only a limited stake in helping domain governments assert authority over their scattered territories.

Initially, Ōno domain conducted vaccinations on a voluntary basis, but soon ran into difficulties due to the limitations of the new technique.

24.　"Jotōkan seiyaku," 1849, in Fukui-ken Ishikai, *Fukui-ken igakushi*, 545–52.
25.　Kasahara, *Hakushinki*, 200–201, 239.
26.　Ibid., 239.

At the time there was no way to preserve fresh lymph outside the human body, and doctors required steady access to unvaccinated children to prevent the vaccine from going extinct. Parents, however, were initially so wary of the new treatment that even doctors in larger cities such as Osaka had trouble procuring volunteers.[27] There were many reasons to be skeptical. Unlike previous inoculation techniques of Chinese origin, the administration of the cowpox vaccine required cutting the body and transmitting bodily fluids directly from child to child. To make matters worse, the lymph had been derived from beasts in a foreign land by barbarians adhering to the evil creed of Christianity—a concern that was widespread, not just among uneducated people and practitioners of Chinese medicine but even among advocates of vaccination.[28] Some physicians opposed the new technique on grounds of Chinese medical theory or because they doubted its benefits. After all, the vaccine could be deadly if it triggered an actual outbreak of smallpox or resulted in the transmission of other illnesses. Furthermore, not all vaccinations were effective, leaving some patients vulnerable to disease.[29]

To implement the program and override the doubts of the "ignorant people,"[30] Ōno's government soon felt compelled to blend benevolence with coercion. After the first delivery of lymph had died out in 1850 due to a lack of volunteers, the lord had the physicians carry out a survey of unvaccinated children and began to offer free vaccinations to the poor.[31] A domain edict of 1851 advertised the example of Motodo, the doctors' first test village in the Southern Mountains, where peasants had initially opposed the treatment but changed their minds when they witnessed a small group of vaccinated children be unharmed during an outbreak of smallpox.[32] But the number of volunteers remained low, and in 1852, after a

27. Kōzai, "Yobō sesshu to iu 'eisei,'" 222–23.

28. Soekawa, "Gyūtō shutōhō shōrei no hanga ni tsuite," 62–63; Soekawa, *Nihon tōbyōshi josetsu*, 76–78; Trambaiolo, "Writing, Authority and Practice," 221–31, 251–52.

29. Kōzai, "Yobō sesshu to iu 'eisei,'" 223–24; Trambaiolo, "Writing, Authority and Practice," 231–47.

30. "Shutō shōrei ni tsuki furegaki," 1851, in *Fukui kenshi*, Shiryō-hen 7, 458–59.

31. Ibid. On compensation, see also MT goyōdome 1857.8.19, YH 1109, 798–99.

32. "Shutō shōrei ni tsuki furegaki," 1851, in *Fukui kenshi*, Shiryō-hen 7, 458–59; letter from Nakamura Taisuke and Hayashi Unkei to Kasahara Hakuō, 1851.2.25, in Kasahara, *Hakushinki*, 144–45; Ōno-han yōdome bassui eisei shokusan kōgyō, 1850.6.6, 1851.1.11, 1852.7.26, Echizen Ōno Doi-ke monjo.

consultation with his doctors, Toshitada decided to make vaccinations compulsory for castle town residents. Doctors were to vaccinate all eligible children from every block association in the town, and *chō* officials were asked to facilitate the process by applying pressure on reluctant parents.[33] By 1855, parents of unvaccinated children were being punished with house arrest if their offspring was found out to have contracted the disease, and *chō* officials faced punishment if parents within their block neglected to report for the vaccinations. The domain also disciplined town children who vandalized the sign in front of the vaccination clinic.[34]

In late 1857, the lord moved beyond smallpox and announced the establishment of a hospital—referred to as *byōin* (the emerging term for "hospital") or Saiseikan (House of Saving Life)—in Upper Ichibanmachi, one of the central town neighborhoods, in place of an earlier "vaccination house" (Shutōkan) the domain had run with financial help from wealthy townspeople (see fig. 18).[35] The new facility offered medical treatment to domain subjects of all backgrounds, including the poor, whom it treated free of charge. One purpose of the hospital was to serve as a training site to improve the skills of local doctors. Physicians and peddlers of medicine were no longer allowed to operate on domain territory without the hospital's approval.[36] During an undated cholera outbreak in one of those years, the domain ordered all villages to report cases to the hospital so sufferers could receive proper instruction on treatments rather than rely on rumors or the advice of unlicensed drug peddlers.[37] The hospital thus became the centerpiece of the domain's emerging public health care system.

The domain tirelessly advertised the benevolent intentions behind the vaccinations, and by 1860 the method had indeed become more widely accepted; even subjects of other domains appear to have taken advantage

33. MT goyōdome 1852.4.28; Shoyōdome (Nojiri) 1852, fourth month, YH 1001 and 1002, 734–35.
34. MT goyōdome 1855.4.11, 8.8, YH 1067 and 1070, 782–83; 1856.9.16, 10.21, YH 1091 and 1095, 792–93; Iwaji, *Ōno-han no yōgaku*, 69.
35. Edict of 1857, twelfth month, Yasukawa Yozaemon-ke monjo; Iwaji, *Ōno-han no yōgaku*, 70; MT goyōdome 1860.4.16, YH 1146, 820–21.
36. Edict of 1857, twelfth month, Yasukawa Yozaemon-ke monjo; Yoshida Setsuzō, "Ryūin kiji," 394–95; MT goyōdome 1860.12.6, NGM.
37. See the edict dated 9.16, Yasukawa Yozaemon-ke monjo.

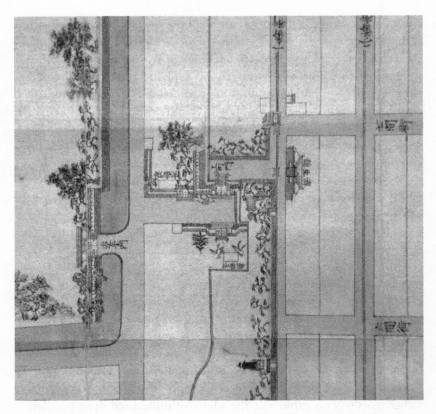

FIGURE 18 The Saiseikan Hospital on a town map of 1858 or later. Note the bell tower of the town elders' office in the southern part of Ichibanmachi and the two domain academies Meirinkan and Yōgakkan inside the castle compound. Courtesy of Ōno-shi Rekishi Hakubutsukan.

of Ōno's facilities. The domain now ordered the Koshirō and leatherworkers to have their children vaccinated.[38] But vaccinations were a favor the subjects had not asked for, and the lord's proclamations expressed increasing frustration at the inability of the domain population to comprehend the benefits of this and other new forms of medical welfare. In an edict of 1859, which followed up on an earlier announcement of changes at the hospital, the government deplored widespread misunderstandings regard-

38.   MT goyōdome 1860.7.11, YH 1173, 839; 1860.10.6, YH 1204, 862.

ing the lord's intentions among ordinary villagers and even village officials. The edict urged village headmen to consider the following:

> In such a situation, the lord can bestow as much kind benevolence as he
> wants—it is entirely pointless. So far, in the past few years, the lord has
> majestically bestowed kind benevolence on the poor on a number of oc-
> casions, and he has done so not merely to relieve a temporary want, but
> with the deeply felt conviction that eventually, as even ignorant people
> feel thankful, they would automatically develop a sense of gratitude and
> repay their ruler's favor [*on-kokuon*] and reform their hearts. From there
> on, they would each work hard in their respective professions, abandon
> selfish desires, preserve a simple and frugal lifestyle, and strive to benefit
> not only the lord but also the people. And in the course of practicing this
> diligently and continuously, each of their livelihoods would naturally be-
> come comfortable; making this happen is the lord's deepest wish.[39]

The edict shows that the government tried to use the clinic and the vaccinations to strike a moral bargain with the domain population. The lord
was not content to simply save the lives of his subjects through the application of new medical knowledge. He expected the gratitude due to a
good Confucian ruler and hoped to initiate a virtuous circle by which
subjects repaid the initial favor through frugality and hard work,
eventually benefiting themselves and everyone else in the domain.
Toshitada's vision of welfare emphasized the well-being of the domain
population in the long term and for the state's sake. Rather than granting only temporary aid, he sought to increase his subjects' health and
wealth so that they could help themselves and contribute to the common good through thrifty and diligent behavior.

The idea that medical relief could be instrumentalized to cultivate
popular loyalty was not limited to Ōno domain. As mentioned, the shogunate's vaccination program on the island of Ezo was part of a larger
effort to assimilate the Ainu, boost their population, and inspire gratitude for benevolent treatment to prevent them from submitting to the
Russian czar.[40] Yoshida Shōin, a loyalist thinker, saw poor relief and
health care as battlegrounds for a future competition between the Japanese

39. Rokuban kiroku (Suzuki) 1859, seventh month, YH 1125, 808–9.
40. Walker, "The Early Modern Japanese State and Ainu Vaccinations."

government and Western powers. In a memorandum of 1858, he warned his lord, the daimyo of Chōshū:[41]

> There are many beggars in our country, so [the Americans] will certainly set up poorhouses for them; there are also many abandoned children, so they will establish children's homes; and again, there are in our country many who are old and decrepit, crippled or unable to get medical care; they will probably build apothecaries and hospitals. If [the Americans] turn their hands in earnest to these projects, it will be easy enough to win the hearts of the ignorant people by such means.

Although Ōno's domain government was more concerned with the success of its domestic reforms than with foreign invasion, its officials were no less aware than Shōin of the potential impact of medical benevolence on the hearts and minds of the common people. Whether Ōno's reformers ever corresponded with Shōin is uncertain, but they were exchanging views with some of the most progressive intellectuals of their time. Several of Ōno's vassals were closely acquainted with Ogata Kōan, a physician, vaccinator, and teacher of Western learning who educated many future Meiji leaders in his Osaka academy and in 1856 sent one of his students to Ōno to head the domain's new Academy of Western Learning (Yōgakkan). One of Ōno's boldest reformers, Uchiyama Ryūsuke, was a student of prominent military scholar Sakuma Shōzan.[42] In the 1850s, Ōno's powerful neighbor domain Fukui came under the influence of Yokoi Shōnan, a Confucian political thinker who emphasized the importance of mercantilism and foreign trade. Despite their remote home base, Ōno's leaders thus had access to some of the most innovative minds of the Bakumatsu era.

The Grain Price Crisis of 1860

Ōno's above-discussed edict of 1859 emphasized not only medical welfare but also hard work, thrift, and self-reliance. This was not an unusual statement to make by the standards of Tokugawa Confucian thought. In the

41. Yoshida Shōin, "Testimony of a Madman," 126.
42. Iwaji, *Ōno-han no yōgaku*, 18–20, 32–56.

seventeenth century, Yamaga Sokō argued that too generous and indiscriminate relief would encourage depravity and idleness among the poor and advocated strict limitations.[43] At the same time, however, the idea of benevolent government allowed for an inversion of Sokō's welfare logic. Because benevolence was extraordinary by definition and believed to inspire gratitude, it could be put to work as a moral incentive. To fight the economic crisis in his domain, Ōno's Lord Toshitada (see fig. 19) greatly expanded his involvement in welfare matters and invested heavily in public health, granaries, and relief handouts, hoping that generous welfare would result in more, not less, frugality and self-reliance and persuade subjects to support his mercantilist reforms.

In 1860, Ōno domain experienced a sudden spike in the price of grain, due in part to countrywide inflation. Although the government provided subjects with generous food aid during that crisis, the townspeople, far from showing gratitude, reacted with criticism, rumors, and threats of unrest. Officials initially responded with punitive sanctions against the townspeople, but then resolved the standoff by establishing new relief granaries for the domain poor. The events of 1860 can be read as a temporary breakdown of communication between ruler and town subjects, followed by a reaffirmation of the relationship.[44] The town elders meticulously recorded the exchanges between the townspeople and the domain. Their journals show how strongly the domain leadership insisted on the proper performance of the dialogue between high and low and the lengths it could go to if the expected gratitude did not materialize.

The crisis of 1860 also reveals the challenges the lord faced with his new vision of benevolent rule. For Toshitada, poor relief was both an economic policy and a means of committing his subjects to the project of building a prosperous domain state. Subjects, however, had already been asked to make major sacrifices on behalf of the domain budget since

43. Yamaga Sokō, "Yamaga gorui," 40–44; Yoshida Kyūichi, *Nihon shakai fukushi shisōshi*, 218–24.

44. In Ōno as elsewhere, the dialogue between high and low had a theatrical and ritualistic quality while conveying concrete political messages that could be decoded by all participants and affected their legitimacy. Compare with Esherick and Wasserstrom's analysis of the Tiananmen protests as political theater, "Acting Out Democracy."

FIGURE 19 Photograph of Doi Toshitada. Courtesy of Ōno-shi Rekishi Hakubutsukan.

before the start of the reforms in 1842.[45] They had seen the domain found a trade company in 1855 and were most likely looking for a sign that despite his profit-seeking inclinations, their lord would still act as a loving father who had their best interests in mind. The volatile economic climate of the Bakumatsu years did not make such understanding any easier to achieve. In 1860, Japan's economy was reeling from the impact of the unequal treaties with foreign powers and major harvest shortfalls, and Ōno's lord was not in a position to protect his people from the consequences of these events. Changes in local society added to the potential for unrest. Vagrancy was rampant, and since the 1830s firefighting com-

45. These included import controls, sumptuary regulations, forced loans, and forced donations; see *Fukui kenshi*, Tsūshi-hen 4, 813–17, 823–26.

panies were proliferating among the younger townspeople and instigated at least one grain riot in 1850.[46]

The weather in the spring and summer of 1860 was rainier than usual, and domain officials, still haunted by the memory of the Tenpō famine, wasted no time putting countermeasures such as export controls into place.[47] In the fifth month, when the high price of rice had already begun to cause unemployment in the castle town, the government sold its grain reserves to the poor (*konkyūmono*) at a cheaper rate and distributed free rice to the "extremely, extremely poor" (*gokugoku-konkyūmono*)—a category that probably included old, sick, and unemployed people with no prospects of repaying the more common relief loans.[48] Officials then restocked the reserves by buying up grain inside and outside the domain, using commoners as intermediaries to keep a low profile and dispel suspicions of hoarding.[49] In the beginning of the seventh month, the lord again offered grants, loans, and cheap sales of grain to the town poor and indigent people in the countryside.[50]

Although the government seems to have acted in the townspeople's best interest, many poorer townspeople reacted to the price hike by accusing their government and merchants of hoarding. Some of them threatened to riot. In the fifth month, a sticker found on a stone wall in the town directly blamed the domain for the high cost of rice and the starvation it caused among the poor: "The deeds of Doi Noto-no-kami [Toshitada]'s vassal minions may be highly acclaimed across the provinces, but we will take down this pack of governor [*bugyō*] officials with fire hooks, plows, and hoes."[51] The anonymous scribbler did not know that in this case, the government had merely been guilty of bad timing.

46. Shogandome and MT goyōdome 1834, eighth and tenth month, YH 688–90, 500–501; Shoyōdome (Nojiri) 1850, ninth month, YH 983, 724; MT goyōdome 1857. i5.16, YH 1107, 797.

47. The domain also forced all vassals to sell their rice stipends back to the domain beyond their own subsistence needs. For a more detailed discussion of the crisis of 1860, see Ehlers, "Mibun shakai to jinsei."

48. MT goyōdome 1860.5.17, 5.20, 5.25, SSM. For excerpts from these entries, see YH 1152 and 1153, 823–25.

49. For example MT goyōdome 1860.5.20, 5.21, 5.26, 5.29, 6.1, 6.2, SSM and NGM.

50. MT goyōdome 1860.7.2–8, SSM (for excerpts, see YH, 836–39).

51. MT goyōdome 1860.5.27, YH 1157, 830–31. On threats of unrest, see also MT goyōdome 1860.8.1, 8.4, 8.6, YH 1182, 842–46.

Officials were trying to stock grain for relief at the same moment the whole country was entering a period of high inflation. In 1859, the shogunate had dramatically debased the nationwide gold currency to counteract the effects of the trade treaty with the United States of 1858. This treaty had forced Japan to accept an exchange rate between Japanese and foreign silver currency that gave foreigners extraordinarily cheap access to Japanese gold currency in the country's trimetallic monetary system and led to a massive leakage of gold coins from Japan.[52] In Ōno, the result of this debasement was an unexpected spike in the price of rice, from 38 to 54.6 *monme* silver per bale in the course of just one year.[53] At first, the townspeople were not aware of these connections, nor did they trust that their government was "hoarding" rice with the ultimate goal of providing them with relief. As the town elders later reported:

> For a while, when the price of rice rose higher and higher, [the people in the block associations] believed that this was because the authorities were buying up rice, but soon, the authorities started giving it out in form of relief rice and cheap sales. So the people have now realized that their previous belief was hugely mistaken, and there are even some *chō* that express major embarrassment about this.[54]

> Some people were grumbling because they did not comprehend that the high price of rice was an issue that concerned all provinces alike, and believed that it was happening just here.[55]

As expected, the harvest of 1860 was a disappointment, but by that time the domain government had already decided to address the scarcity in a more systematic manner: by establishing permanent relief granaries on its territory. For the townspeople, the government set up the so-called Relief Bureau (*gokyūjo yakusho* or *gokyūjokata*) and placed its management in the hands of six wealthy townspeople.[56] In the villages, it established "Seigneurial Relief Granaries," also called "General Granaries"

52. Frost, *The Bakumatsu Currency Crisis.*
53. Kaidō, "Ōno-machi yōdome ni miru beika no hensen," 35.
54. MT goyōdome 1860.8.22, YH 1188, 850.
55. MT goyōdome 1860.8.16, YH 1185, 849.
56. MT goyōdome 1860.9.6, YH 1197, 855–56.

(*gokyūjogura* or *sōgura*), to be run by prominent peasants.[57] As in the case of the smallpox vaccinations, domain officials insisted that the new granaries were an unmitigated blessing. But instead of allowing subjects to come to this conclusion on their own, they expected open displays of gratitude, both in writing and through obedient behavior. The government used the granaries not only to protect its subjects from scarcity but to reassert control over them, especially over the townspeople, who had been defiant throughout the summer.

Even on strictly economic terms, the construction of granaries made sense for a mercantilist domain. From the late seventeenth century onward, Japanese domains had been experimenting with grain storage systems, often inspired by the "community granaries" (*shasō*, Chinese: *shecang*) proposed by Chinese neo-Confucian thinker Zhu Xi in the twelfth century. While Zhu Xi had insisted that local elites operate the community granaries autonomously from the state, the Tokugawa versions were usually semi-governmental and run jointly by warrior authorities and commoner leaders. Moreover, eighteenth-century intellectuals and officials in Japan envisioned storehouses not only as safeguards against crop failures but also as financial institutions that would stimulate local markets, stem the flow of interest to extraterritorial lenders, generate profits to fund public works, and provide cheap credit to taxpayers in need. Zhu Xi's Japanese followers did not heed the wise man's advice that loans from these granaries should not bear interest beyond the recovery of operational costs. As Mark Ravina has argued, the importance of the community granary model for Tokugawa administrators was not so much in its actual mode of operation but in the legitimacy it seemed to confer on governmental moneylending.[58] Whatever Zhu Xi's original intentions, the combination of neo-Confucian orthodoxy, sustainability, and profitability turned the granaries into a perfect fit for Toshitada's reform agenda. Although the domain had already taken steps toward famine prevention in 1842 by requiring all commoner households to put away annual savings, it waited until 1860 to establish a public system of grain storage.[59]

---

57. Gokyūjogura chokoku ukeharaichō, 1860, Uchikura Jin'emon-ke monjo.
58. Ravina, "Confucian Banking."
59. Goyō narabi ni henji (Miyazawa) 1842.4.12, YH 824, 595–96. In the Bakumatsu era, prompted by the Tenpō famine, territories all across Japan improved their

In the summer of 1860, the domain administration became increasingly annoyed by the persistent rumors and criticisms of its policies that circulated among the townspeople. It repeatedly reminded them of the lord's various relief measures and insisted that benevolent government was not a one-way street. In the seventh month, the domain elder summoned all town officials to the castle and confronted them as follows:

> The lord, thinking that his subjects must be suffering poverty due to the recent high price of rice, has repeatedly provided relief, and yet the subjects fail to comprehend his lordship's benevolent intentions. We even hear that there are people among them who slander domain policy, which is outrageous. Still, [the lord] believes that this surely is because his intentions have not been transmitted to his subjects. Therefore, let us make sure that we, not only us domain officials but also you [the town officials], take extra care and pass on the lord's intentions to subjects to the best of our ability, so that hard workers are created and idlers disappear.[60]

But the popular mood in the castle town did not improve; on the contrary, even vassals began to slander the administration. In the eighth month, the situation had become so serious that the lord, who was in Edo at the time on alternate attendance, decided to make a personal intervention. He sent a "direct letter" (*jikisho*) to Ōno in which he assured townspeople and vassals that the inflation was not a result of domain policy and backed the main target of the rumors, reformer Uchiyama Shichirōemon (fig. 20), by promoting him to the top position of house elder.[61] Apparently, Uchiyama lost no time reasserting control over vassals and subjects. Only two days after his appointment, the domain leadership summoned the town officials for another important announcement: "The lord has repeatedly provided relief rice and cheap rice sales; he has bought expensive rice with the right hand and distributed or sold it cheaply with the left hand, and yet there are people who return favors with ingratitude, spread all kinds of anonymous letters and rumors, and criticize both domain policy and the officials." The domain leadership accused the

---

mechanisms of grain storage; see, for example, Yoshida Nobuyuki, "Bakumatsu-ki, Edo no shūen to minshū sekai."

60. MT goyōdome 1860.7.5, YH 1171, 838.
61. Yoshida Setsuzō, "Ryūin kiji," 399.

FIGURE 20 Photograph of Uchiyama Shichirōemon. Courtesy of Ōno-shi Rekishi Hakubutsukan.

town officials of protecting ungrateful troublemakers and blamed some of the vassals for facilitating the unrest: "If you fail to transmit the lord's deep considerations to the subjects, and do not report the feelings of subjects upwards to the lord, this will affect the safety of the state [*kokka no go-anki*], and will eliminate any possibility of achieving unity between high and low."[62] This time, the three governors reinforced their

62. MT goyōdome 1860.8.16, YH 1185, 847–48.

exhortations with a sterner warning: they announced they would reward individuals who turned in themselves or others and punish those who neglected to report critics within their block or five-people's associations. They also declared that if this kind of attitude persisted, the lord would refuse to relieve the townspeople in the future, "no matter how bad the year or how much you starve." Like an offended parent, the lord threatened to withhold his benevolence from his defiant subjects.[63]

The town elders scrambled to soothe their ruler's paternal wrath. They made each *chō* submit a written apology, in which they expressed gratitude for "the great favor of benevolent government" and stated their determination to report offenders. But the authorities were not so easily moved. They rejected the letters as incomplete,[64] and in the subsequent days subjected the townspeople to a series of disciplinary sanctions. On the sixteenth and twentieth of the eighth month, they imposed a round of duty money on the town's purveyor merchants but exempted the villages, arguing that the villagers at least had not spread any rumors or alarm.[65] On the twenty-sixth day, the domain took the extraordinary step of putting the entire town population under arrest. All townspeople, even traders who traveled out of town for a living, were barred from going to the countryside while the government gathered more evidence on rumormongers.[66] The headmen of the block associations desperately submitted another set of apologies, arguing that day laborers who went to work outside town could not last another day without income.[67]

Moved by this ultimate show of contrition, the government eventually lifted the curfew on the sixth day of the ninth month, and then restored harmony between lord and subjects with a grand gesture of forgiveness. The lord would top up the previously collected duty money from

63. Ibid.

64. MT goyōdome 1860.8.20, NGM. Two of these notes of apology have survived; Seiji-muki hihyō ni tsuki renpan ukesho, Kaseya monjo.

65. MT goyōdome 1860.8.16, 8.20, NGM; Temae yōki, 1860.8.16, NGM; Ōjōya goyōdome 1860.8.21, YH 1187, 850. At least one purveyor merchant was among those found guilty of spreading rumors about impending unrest; MT goyōdome 1860.8.24, 10.3, 12.18, NGM.

66. MT goyōdome 1860.8.24, 8.26, YH 1191 and 1192, 852–53. On the investigations, see MT goyōdome 1860.8.5–11, 8.20, 8.22–24, 8.27, 8.29, NGM; 1860.9.1, SSM.

67. MT goyōdome 1860.9.6, YH 1196, 855.

the purveyors (approximately 2,100 *ryō*) with 500 *ryō* of gold from his own treasury and return all of it to the townspeople by establishing a new type of relief fund—the Relief Bureau described already. The government also announced the creation of granaries in the villages. Again, it intended these granaries not only to protect subjects from distress but also to inspire fresh gratitude that would translate into virtuous behavior and eventually a prosperous domain. In the first granary registers submitted in the tenth month of 1860, peasant leaders had to insert a prewritten preface that laid out the proper understanding of the virtuous circle (see fig. 21). In it, the peasants declared that they had made donations to the granary to thank the lord for his most recent benevolent policies: the smallpox vaccinations, the hospital, rice and silver money for the poor, and monetary gifts (*sakeryō*) for old people. These four constituted actual relief measures the domain had already implemented. The fifth "favor," however, was nothing but an inversion of the punishment the domain had imposed earlier on the townspeople: the duty money in the eighth month, from which the villagers had been exempted.[68] The lord also responded to the villagers' donations by topping them up from his own budget as he had done for the townspeople.[69] The signing village leaders stated that they were at a loss for words at such warm-hearted generosity.

The domain's carrot-and-stick approach proved successful at pacifying the town; in subsequent months, the townspeople were given more opportunities to thank the lord for his benevolence. The wealthier ones reciprocated by making further donations. During the final months of 1860, many rich townspeople offered money to the domain for the new granary, and Ōno's purveyor merchants all returned the IOUs they had received for their duty money in the eighth month, turning these loans into outright gifts. At the end of the year, the lord honored these semivoluntary donors with privileges and words of praise.[70]

68. Gokyūjogura chokoku ukeharaichō, 1860, Uchikura Jin'emon-ke monjo, Nojiri Kiheiji-ke monjo, et al. See also Goyō osukui sō-dozō shoyōdome, Uchikura Jin'emon-ke monjo.

69. The villages received a total of 500 *ryō* of gold and 2,000 bales of millet. For more details on the village granaries, see Ehlers, "Mibun shakai to jinsei," 360–61.

70. See MT goyōdome 1860, ninth to twelfth month, SSM and NGM. On the rewards, see 1860.12.18, NGM.

FIGURE 21 Preface of Gokyūjogura chokoku ukeharaichō, 1860. *Source:* Uchikura Jin'emon-ke monjo.

Poorer subjects did not have the means to reciprocate benevolence with donations, but they could perform gratitude in other ways. At the very least, recipients of aid were expected to be frugal. In the early summer of 1860, for instance, the domain accused some lower-class towns-people of squandering their relief money on nighttime drinking at the Sannō Shrine.[71] Recipients also had to demonstrate a willingness to work. The regulations for the new village granaries stipulated that the granary managers appointed for each village should examine the work ethic of farmers and reject applications for poor relief from idlers.[72] In the town, the situation was more complex because in 1860 many were suffering from unemployment. Although the government harbored the unrealistic hope of sending all excess laborers to the countryside to practice farming,[73] it eventually conducted a series of public works projects—so-called sei-gneurial relief construction (*osukui fushin*)—for "extremely poor" people as winter work to allow them to earn a daily wage. The shogunate had been offering such workfare since the eighteenth century at times of sudden mass unemployment in the cities,[74] but in Ōno, the first project of

71. MT goyōdome 1860.6.6, NGM.

72. Gokyūjogura chokoku ukeharaichō, 1860, Uchikura Jin'emon-ke monjo.

73. The government offered townspeople monetary incentives to become farmers, apparently without much success; MT goyōdome 1860.7.4, YH 1170, 837; 1860.11.6, SSM.

74. Examples include Edo during the Tenpō famine in 1837 (Yoshida Nobuyuki, *Kinsei kyodai toshi no shakai kōzō*, 22), and Osaka during the Kyōhō famine in 1733 (Kitahara, *Toshi to hinkon no shakaishi*, 22, 25).

this kind was the construction of the granary for the town's new Relief Bureau.[75] The domain government went on to open many more sites in 1860 for the repair of roads, moats, and bridges until the snow became too deep for further construction.[76]

There was a huge demand for these jobs among the townspeople. Every day, several hundred people signed up for seigneurial relief construction,[77] in part because the government used these projects as an excuse to limit poor relief to those who were physically unable to work. "Extremely poor" women and children were also forced to work in construction for a lower wage than men, and some were given textile piecework by the domain.[78] The first few people who were granted permission to buy cheap grain from the new granary were those too old or sick to engage in manual labor.[79] In addition, the domain also put heavy pressure on the *chō* to provide their starving residents with mutual relief—an intervention that had probably become necessary because the government had forced all block associations to reshuffle their five-people's groups after the rumor drama, improving mutual supervision but disrupting old constellations of neighborly aid.[80] The domain officials did such a thorough job of portraying seigneurial relief as exceptional that some recipients who had been granted aid felt reluctant to accept it. In 1860 the lord rewarded nine townspeople who had rejected the domain's offer of cheap rice sales because they empathized with the lord's fiscal difficulties.[81] In a similar case of 1865, the households in question

75. MT goyōdome 1860.10.16, NGM.

76. See, for example, MT goyōdome 1860.10.18–19, 10.21–26, 10.29, 12.1–3, 12.6–7, 12.16, 12.21, NGM; 1860.11.1–2, 11.6, 11.10–11, 11.15–16, 11.19, SSM; MT goyōdome 1861.2.1, 2.3, 2.6, 2.17, 2.21, 4.1, 4.4, 6.6, 6.26, SSM.

77. Some town laborers came up with their own proposals for new construction projects; see the testimony of a laborer arrested for rumors in MT goyōdome 1860.8.23, YH 1189, 851.

78. The making of so-called *kase*, which probably involved spinning or winding thread; see MT goyōdome 1860.10.17, NGM, and 1860.11.29, SSM. For women and children carrying sand and soil at seigneurial relief construction sites, see, for example, MT goyōdome 1860.10.18, 10.25, 12.16, NGM; MT goyōdome 1861.2.3, SSM.

79. MT goyōdome 1860.11.6, SSM.

80. MT goyōdome 1860.11.19, 11.22, 11.26, 11.28, 12.1, 12.3, 12.11, 12.16, 12.21, 12.26, NGM.

81. MT goyōdome 1860.6.16, NGM.

promised to take good care of themselves and do whatever was necessary to avoid starvation.[82] Although the motives of these households are not entirely clear, they did use the domain's relief offers as an opportunity to show off their virtue and reenact the paternalist relationship.

Merchant Charity and the State

The granaries of 1860 broadcast a reassuring message to Ōno's domain subjects: behind their white walls of clay they held stocks of actual grain, safely removed from the greedy fingers of government officials and other speculators. This trust-building potential was probably the reason the domain insisted on constructing brand-new buildings on town or village land rather than storing the grain in the existing granaries of wealthy peasants.[83] But the granaries' gleaming facades masked a more complicated reality. Since the late eighteenth century, seigneurial relief and commoner charity had become increasingly intertwined, and wealthy commoners had come to collaborate extensively with the domain in the funding and management of poor relief. The granaries of 1860 represented the culmination of this trend. Moreover, the government had itself begun to behave like a merchant house. In 1855, it established Ōnoya, a trade enterprise for domain products with branches in Osaka and Hakodate that continued to operate well into the Meiji period. In Tokugawa society, the "charity" of both types of "merchants" supported warrior rule and followed the conventions of the status order. After the abolition of the status order, Ōnoya turned into a merchant house of a more straightforward kind and became one of many local leaders who donated money to philanthropic causes.

The relief granary for the townspeople was a joint operation of domain and town elite. In autumn 1860, the domain appointed six wealthy

82. Ōno-han jisha machikata goyōki, 1865.1.16, Echizen shiryō. Ōno's domain subjects had been taught to empathize with their lord's fiscal situation and refrain from petitioning when his finances were bad; see, for example, Kōshi yōdome (Nojiri) 1849.2.11, YH 956, 701–2.

83. Rokuban kiroku (Suzuki) 1860, tenth month, YH 1212, 867; MT goyōdome 1860.12.1, NGM.

townspeople, all members of the purveyor guild, to the post of "commissioner for the relief of the town poor" (*machikata konkyūmono kyūjokata goyōgakari*). The leader of this group was Nunokawa Genbei, a rising sake brewer and moneylender, who was also appointed town elder in 1860.[84] In the villages, too, the managers of the granaries were leading members of their respective communities. Although the domain government established the ground rules for the granaries and had to sign off on every disbursal, these managers decided exactly how the stocks for the granaries were going to be collected and used. They established modes of operation that reflected the economic circumstances of their particular villages.[85]

Whereas the village granaries were intended to make peasant communities self-reliant and independent from governmental aid, the Relief Bureau had a different purpose: it managed the entire town economy. Unlike the village granaries, the Relief Bureau did not collect fixed contributions from all house owners but drew on domain funds and donations from wealthier townspeople.[86] As soon as the bureau was established, the six commissioners received permission to lend out about two-thirds of the endowment to address a credit crunch in the town that had resulted from the inflation in 1860.[87] On at least one occasion it disbursed "seigneurial relief" rice to the Koshirō, who were not part of the community of townspeople.[88] For a while, rice dealers were required to sell all of their rice stocks above a certain limit to the Relief Bureau, and until 1865, the Relief Bureau remained responsible for setting the price of rice. Sake brewers were required to buy their rice supply from the bureau until at least 1863.[89] In 1860 and possibly later, the Relief Bureau was also the only institution allowed to ship rice to the mountain villages and the Omodani

84. *Ōno chōshi*, vol. 4, 548–50; MT goyōdome 1860.9.6, YH 1197, 855–56.

85. Ehlers, "Mibun shakai to jinsei," 360–64.

86. The domain sometimes transferred part of its own reserves to the bureau to have them sold to poor townspeople. It assisted with the purchase of rice outside the domain and sold rice to the bureau on a number of occasions; see MT goyōdome 1861.2.11, 2.21, SSM; Ōno-han jisha machikata goyōki, 1865.7.6, 7.17, 9.16, Echizen shiryō.

87. Temae yōki, 1860.9.6, 9.11, NGM.

88. MT goyōdome 1860.11.26, SSM. Officials cited a precedent from 1836 to justify this handout, which seems to have excluded the wealthy Iemon/Isuke household discussed in chapter 2.

89. On rice sales, see MT goyōdome 1860.9.17, 9.21, YH 1200, 861–62; 1860.12.16, YH 1226, 874; Ōno-han jisha machikata goyōki, 1865.6.11, Echizen shiryō. On restrictions

copper mine, a function that had hitherto been fulfilled by town merchants.[90] The bureau continued to operate until the abolition of domain rule in 1871. Nunokawa and some of the other "former relief commissioners" remained in charge until 1874, collecting payments on loans taken out by wealthy townspeople and disentangling and liquidating the bureau's various assets.[91]

Cheap rice sales by the Relief Bureau were probably one of the reasons Ōno's castle town did not experience any open unrest during the politically and economically unstable years surrounding the Meiji Restoration.[92] Domain leaders were acutely aware of the possibility of riots. In a letter of 1870, house elder Uchiyama Shichirōemon warned his lord that he had a "reputation for being wealthy," and that as the Ōnoya branches in Osaka and Hakodate prospered, they would inspire jealousy among a town population suffering from hunger and high prices.[93] The town merchants must have shared this fear of violence, though their enthusiasm about the Relief Bureau was probably limited. After all, the bureau was an extremely invasive institution that balanced the demands of the town poor with the interests of the domain while cutting into the businesses of town merchants. Although no townsperson seems to have directly commented on this problem, Nojiri Gen'emon, the outspoken wealthy peasant cited in previous chapters, expressed frustration with the domain's attitude toward the poor. In 1869, he complained in his journal that the domain was soft on poor tenant farmers but indifferent about the burdens it placed on rich commoners such as himself. "Last winter, finally, it became apparent that poor and rich alike were suffering from poverty. In Ōno domain, this tendency is particularly strong."[94] If this perception was shared by other elites in the Ōno area, it might have led

---

on sake brewers, see MT goyōdome 1861.10.12, 10.16, 12.16, SSM; Ōno-machi yōdome bassui, 1863.10.11, *Ōno shishi*, Hansei shiryō-hen 2, 454–55.

90. MT goyōdome 1860.9.21, YH 1200, 861–62; MT goyōdome 1861.4.17, SSM; MT goyōdome 1869.4.1, 4.21, 6.6, NGM.

91. See, for example, Nunokawa Genbei yori mairu go-kyūjo no gi, Echizen Ōno Doi-ke monjo; Kōin ukeharai Nunokawa Genbei go-kyūjo ukeharai kanjō, Uchiyama Ryōji-ke monjo; Kanjōbo, 1874, Echizen Ōno Doi-ke monjo.

92. See, for example, MT goyōdome 1869, NGM.

93. Uchiyama Shichirōemon to Doi Toshitsune, 1870, fifth month, Uchiyama Ryōji-ke monjo; *Ōno shishi*, Tsūshi-hen (ge), 96.

94. Shoyōdome (Nojiri) 1869, second month, YH 1368, 969–70.

them to welcome the restrictive welfare policies of the new Meiji state. The Relief Regulations issued by the central government in 1874 strictly limited public assistance to a small number of infirm poor without kin who lacked community support. Many early Meiji leaders and intellectuals, such as Iwakura Tomomi and Fukuzawa Yukichi, sharply opposed public poor relief on the grounds that it would stifle individual initiative. In addition, the early Meiji government was more than eager to rid itself of the financial obligations inherited from its Tokugawa predecessors.[95]

For Ōno's wealthy commoners, the abolition of domain rule brought a release from the pressure to fulfill the government's unpredictable demands for duty money and fund its expensive relief programs.[96] It released them more generally from the business constraints imposed by the Relief Bureau. The political transition also had a liberating effect on Ōnoya, the lord's own commercial enterprise. One year after the Meiji Restoration of 1868, Ōno domain embarked on a project of village reform that illustrates in exemplary form how Ōnoya's evolution from mercantilist state enterprise to private company reshaped its involvement in public assistance for the poor.

The year 1868 had been one of crop failure, and the village reform of 1869 was thus partly intended as an emergency intervention. Yet domain officials were clearly thinking in the long term—only two years before the abolition of domain rule. The government primarily hoped to prevent impoverished peasants from giving up their land and moving into the town, where they would engage in wage labor and become vulnerable to grain price fluctuations.[97] Ironically, the domain had contributed to this problem because it encouraged textile production in the castle town to increase export revenue.[98]

<hr />

95.   Kinzley, "Japan's Discovery of Poverty," 5–9; Garon, *Molding Japanese Minds,* 32–40.

96.   Ōno's case confirms Matsuzawa Yūsaku's argument that the status order had reached an impasse with regard to poor relief by the end of the Tokugawa period. Many village elites chafed under the obligation of providing aid within their village communities, and perceived the abolition of the status order as an opportunity to invest their money more profitably in enterprises that generated local employment; see Matsuzawa, *Meiji chihō jichitaisei no kigen,* 133–208, 333–78.

97.   MT goyōdome 1860.7.4, YH 1170, 837.

98.   *Ōno chōshi,* vol. 5, 311–30.

In the summer of 1869, the Council of Vassals (*retsuza*) appointed vassal Yokota Hagusa to the position of "official of the Bureau of Civil Affairs and official for special tasks."[99] Yokota's job was to implement a reform for the "extremely poor" of Koyato village on the edge of the Ōno plain (see map 5). In the 1820s, the village had 312 residents living in fifty-seven households, twenty-five of them landless.[100] The root causes of the village's poverty are not entirely clear, but in a receipt of 1860 addressed to the domain, village officials explained that their community, poor to begin with, had incurred high expenses due to a legal dispute and only stayed afloat thanks to loans from the domain.[101] The immediate reason for the reform is better documented: sixteen of the village households had recently gone bankrupt. In the nineteenth century, rural revitalization programs were popular among domain and shogunate administrators, especially in eastern Japan, where traveling agricultural reformers offered their services to governments and advised village communities on matters of agriculture and saving.[102]

Yokota also disbursed some aid to the "extremely, extremely poor," but his main concern was refinancing the villagers' debts. He forced bankrupt farmers to sell some of their belongings, persuaded creditors to forgive some of the debt, paid creditors off from the coffers of the *goyōjō* (literally: "purveyor place"; one of the Ōnoya company's alternate names), and made debtors conclude new agreements with the *goyōjō*. For the duration of the reform, Koyato was placed under an unusual administrative arrangement. According to Yokota's journal, the lord transferred the village from the rural intendants' jurisdiction to that of the *goyōjō*, which became the villagers' new lender.[103] The office of the village headman was temporarily closed. At the same time, the reform remained under the direct oversight of the domain. Yokota regularly discussed his

99.   Koyato kaikaku shoyōdome, 1869, Yokota-ke monjo.

100.   *Nihon chimei daijiten*, vol. 18, 507. In the Tokugawa period, Koyato was a shared-revenue village between Ōno domain and the shogunate. Although the shogunate's tax claim was insignificant, it might have been a factor in the lawsuit that contributed to the village's financial troubles.

101.   Sashiagemōsu issatsu no koto, 1860, Uchiyama Ryōji-ke monjo.

102.   Havens, "Religion and Agriculture in Nineteenth-Century Japan"; Yasumaru, *Nihon no kindaika to minshū shisō*, 35–51.

103.   Goyōdome (journal of the censor=*metsuke*), 1863, Echizen Ōno Doi-ke monjo; Koyato kaikaku shoyōdome, 1869, Yokota-ke monjo.

plans with the Council of Vassals and made decisions on many aspects of village life. As usual, the domain hoped to achieve economic self-reliance for the village by combining relief with exhortations to be frugal and work hard. Yokota and his subordinates occasionally roamed through the village to observe the work ethic of farmers laboring in the fields and drafted a set of sumptuary regulations. It is unclear whether the domain also used Ōnoya to provide loans to villages other than Koyato,[104] but the company's entanglement with seigneurial relief policies can be traced back to at least 1860, when Ōnoya accepted payments from poor townspeople for cheap rice they bought from the domain government.[105]

Yokota's journal ends in the autumn of 1870. In 1877, a lawsuit occurred that sheds some light on the aftermath of the Koyato village reform. The plaintiff was Ōsakaya Shichitarō, merchant of Ōno town, who was represented by his "guardian," a former domain vassal named Takemura Junsaburō. The defendant was a farmer from Koyato village, Ishimoto Kichisaburō, who was sued over an outstanding payment of over 30 yen, the annual installment due in 1876 on a very large loan of 453.64 yen. The IOU in question was the renegotiation of an earlier loan given to Ishimoto in the context of the Koyato village reform. The high amount might be explained by the fact that Ishimoto once served as one of several peasant representatives (*komae sōdai*) of the village and had probably borrowed money for the whole community in that capacity.[106] The conditions of the loan were very favorable for the borrower. Not only could repayment be delayed in years of bad harvest, the loan was interest-free and repayable over a period of thirty years. In the IOU, Ishimoto called the loan an "extraordinary favor," and as a "sign of my gratitude" (*myōga no tame*) promised to continue paying a voluntary amount every year, even after the principal had been paid back. Long repayment schedules were a typical feature of charitable loans in this region. For example, in Tokugawa times there had been a form of IOU on the Ōno plain that required pawning land but delayed repayment until the borrower had economically recovered.[107]

---

104. For other villages under reform, see, for example, Shichiban yōdome (Suzuki) 1869, twelfth month, and Shoyōdome (Nojiri) 1870.1.23, YH 1384 and 1386, 976–77.

105. Goyōdome (*kōribugyō*) 1865.3.1, 3.6, SSM; MT goyōdome 1860.5.20, 7.4, SSM.

106. Sashiagemōsu issatsu no koto, 1860, Uchiyama Ryōji-ke monjo.

107. The so-called *chikarazuki shōmon*; see, for example, Chikarazuki ni aiwatashi-mōsu asabatake shōmon no koto, 1836, Matsuda Gorōbei-ke monjo. I am grateful to Motokawa Mikio for this reference.

Ishimoto defended his failure to pay by arguing (through a man from Fukui—perhaps legal counsel) that, first, he had concluded an agreement with the plaintiff that allowed a deferral of payment in case of an "extraordinarily bad" harvest or another "unforeseen disaster."[108] Second, he contested Ōsakaya Shichitarō's right to sue him at all, claiming that he had borrowed the money not from him but from "the former prefectural governor," that is, Ōno's former lord, who had briefly served in that capacity between 1869 and 1871. Ōsakaya Shichitarō, he argued, had originally been no more than a manager (*shihainin*) of the domain's trade company, the *goyōjō*.

As shown, the domain government had entrusted the refinancing of the villagers' debt to the *goyōjō*, and Ishimoto was not mistaken to assume a close connection between the *goyōjō* and Ōsakaya Shichitarō. The *goyōjō* (Ōnoya) had been established in the 1850s by Uchiyama Shichirōemon, a business-savvy vassal and close adviser to the domain lord. In 1869, the year of the village reform, Shichirōemon occupied the position of house elder and was the dominant figure on the Council of Vassals. From the outset, Shichirōemon deliberately obscured the identity of the *goyōjō* as a domain-run enterprise. In 1855, he opened a store outlet for domain products in a town neighborhood in Osaka by posing as a townsman under the name of Ōnoya Shichibei.[109] The goal of this unconventional step was to reduce the domain's dependency on outside merchants. Initially, the shop in Osaka primarily sold specialty goods from Ōno, such as copper, tobacco, lacquer, mosquito nets, textiles, and medicinal herbs, but soon Shichirōemon and his colleagues expanded the operation and linked it up with other interregional trade routes, especially Ezochi (Hokkaido) and with foreign merchants in Yokohama. They also turned toward moneylending, which became one of the company's most profitable activities.[110] In the 1860s, Shichirōemon and his peers opened further branches in Hakodate, Ota village (Echizen Province), Yokohama, and in Ōno itself.

The Ōno branch, like the earlier shop in Osaka, took on a fictitious merchant identity. It was located in Upper Ichibanmachi on land origi-

108. Koyato-mura ikken-chō, 1877, Echizen Ōno Doi-ke monjo.

109. On the history of Ōnoya, see Sakata, "Hanten 'Ōnoya' no kenkyū"; *Fukui kenshi*, Tsūshi-hen 4, 833–41; *Ōno shishi*, Tsūshi-hen (ge), 94–112.

110. Reels 2704 and 2705 of Uchiyama Ryōji-ke monjo contain many examples of IOUs from the 1860s addressed to the domain's "product bureau" (*sanbutsukata*) or to Ōsakaya Shichitarō.

nally reserved for townspeople, and was required to pay taxes on its land like any other merchant house in town.[111] It went by a variety of names, such as *goyōjō*, *sanbutsu kaisho* (product bureau), and Ōsakaya Shichitarō, which did not refer to a proper person but was the merchant name of the Ōno shop. The branch in Ōno town became the headquarters of the domain's growing Ōnoya network.

After 1871, its ambiguous identity between domain bureau and merchant house served the enterprise well in making the transition from a domain-run to a private company. The Doi family remained the proprietor, and Uchiyama Shichirōemon continued as the main manager of the enterprise, although he preferred to stay behind the scenes and had the branches registered in the name of others, often minors, who required guardians such as Takemura who served as the actual managers.[112] In the first years of the Meiji period, the Ōnoya network was highly profitable and expanded to additional towns like Gifu, Kobe, Nagoya, and Mikuni. Ōsaka(ya) Shichitarō became Ōno town's greatest taxpayer and a major employer and benefactor of impoverished former vassals, who suffered from the loss of their hereditary stipends.[113]

Its fabricated town origins also helped the firm win a qualified victory in the Koyato village lawsuit. The court rejected Ishimoto's claim that Ōno's lord had been the original provider of the contested loan.[114] After all, the judge ruled, Ōsakaya Shichitarō had been paying taxes on town land before 1871 and therefore counted as a townsperson, independent from the domain. The court accepted the plaintiff's argument that domain officials such as Yokota had not issued loans to Koyato's villagers on behalf of the domain but merely "introduced" them to "private" lenders like Ōsaka. With regard to the actual payment, the court ultimately supported the debtor's side. It ruled that Ishimoto was allowed to withhold the annual payment for 1876 because the agreement had failed to define the severity of an "extraordinarily bad" harvest.

The Relief Bureau and the Koyato village reform reveal both breaks and continuities in merchant involvement in welfare policies across the Meiji Restoration. The Ōnoya business was a remnant of the domain

---

111. Yōroku, 1852, SSM.
112. Sakata, "Hanten 'Ōnoya' no kenkyū," 1–4.
113. *Ōno shishi*, Tsūshi-hen (ge), 94–97.
114. Koyato-mura kinsu deiri go-saikyo no utsushi, 1877.7.31, Yokota-ke monjo.

government and as such inherited the financial legacies of the domain's village reforms. Although it rejected its governmental roots after 1871, it subsequently became an important contributor to local philanthropic initiatives, as the following section shows. The abolition of domain rule removed the "benevolent" authority of the lord, who had imposed duties on his subjects and marshaled his own and wealthy commoners' resources for his ambitious quest to raise domain prosperity. Whereas the domain leadership of the Bakumatsu era had paid scant regard to the distinction between seigneurial and commoner money and even obscured it intentionally, the new social order required drawing a clear line between the governmental and the private sphere. The lawsuit against Ishimoto indicates that these new boundaries remained ambiguous and contested for some time. The withdrawal of domain authority and dismantling of the Relief Bureau allowed Ōnoya and merchants of commoner background to invest their money more freely into causes of their own choice, which ranged from poverty relief to other philanthropic initiatives that promoted economic growth.[115] As we shall see, their activism retained a public quality because it compensated for the Meiji state's weakness on the ground and meshed well with the national goal of self-strengthening.

Local Philanthropy after the Meiji Restoration

In 1871, Ōno domain was formally abolished and its territory integrated into a number of successive prefectures.[116] Two years later, inner Echizen erupted in a large uprising that was particularly violent on the Ōno plain. The trigger was the Meiji government's policy toward religion, especially

---

115. This overlap of interest between former vassals and former commoner elites recalls E. H. Norman's view of the Meiji Restoration as a "thorough house-cleaning," driven by a "feudal-merchant coalition" between lower-ranking samurai and capitalist commoner elites intent on removing the institutional strictures of the status order without upsetting the class hierarchy; see Norman, "Japan's Emergence as a Modern State," 177–87. See also Matsuzawa, *Meiji chihō jichitaisei no kigen*, 133–208, 333–78.

116. Ōno Prefecture (1871), Fukui Prefecture (1871), Asuwa Prefecture (1871–73), Tsuruga Prefecture (1873–76), Ishikawa Prefecture (1876–81), Fukui Prefecture (1881–today).

its restrictions on Buddhist sermons and its strict separation of Buddhist and Shinto worship. Believers of the True Pure Land school mistook these policies as an attempt to eradicate Buddhism and replace it with Christianity, which they had come to associate with Western-style reform. A total of 30,000 peasants, townspeople, and priests in the counties of Ōno, Imadate, and Sakai rallied in defense of Buddha's law and demanded a ban on Christianity and Western learning.[117] Ōno's lord had already moved to Tokyo and some of the protesters in fact demanded a return of Tokugawa rule, but the uprising in Ōno also released some of the discontent pent up during Toshitada's reforms. For example, protesters destroyed the houses of Ōsakaya Shichitarō (Uchiyama Shichirōemon) and his son Gonjirō, the headquarters of the Ōnoya business, the houses of the three new district leaders including former town elder Nunokawa Genbei, and the house of a wealthy landowner known for his love of Western culture. The crowd of protesters and sympathizers included a handful of former vassals who had been demoted under Toshitada or resented the appropriation of domain property by Ōnoya and its affiliates. The uprising illustrated just how little the composition of the local elites had changed after 1871, and how much resentment these leaders continued to generate among lower-class subjects, who saw their millenarian hopes of "world renewal" dashed after the rise of the imperial regime.[118]

The emerging Meiji government harshly punished the leaders of this uprising and rejected all their demands, sending out a strong message that it would no longer tolerate popular protest as an appeal to the ruler's benevolence and as means of collective bargaining.[119] But in 1878, it granted the wealthiest taxpayers across the nation the right to vote in elections for the new prefectural assemblies, where representatives opposed any attempt of the central government and prefecture administrations to raise

---

117. For detailed analyses of this uprising, see Mikami, *Meiji shonen Shinshū monto dai-kekki no kenkyū*; Sakata, *Echizen Ōno ikki*; *Ōno shishi*, Tsūshi-hen (ge), 50–58.

118. E. H. Norman cites the Echizen uprising to support his point that peasant unrest around the Meiji Restoration constituted "a strange mixture of reaction and revolution, of superstition and shrewd estimate of class interest." Ōno's protesters were indeed influenced by millenarian and xenophobic ideas current at the time, while also attacking those whom they saw as the main beneficiaries of the domain reforms. See Norman, "Japan's Emergence as a Modern State," 168–69.

119. See also Makihara, *Kyakubun to kokumin no aida*, 70–74.

the land tax and allocate more money for welfare-related expenses. The members of Fukui's prefectural assembly in the 1880s frequently criticized tax appropriations for poor relief and public health, concerned that the money would spoil the poor, fail to benefit their localities, and open the door to exploitation by the state.[120] Although the Meiji government provided some relief for poor people and disaster victims on the basis of the Relief Regulations of 1874, the number of recipients of governmental relief seems to have been much smaller than before the Restoration. In the three years between 1881 and 1883, only twenty-six residents of Ōno County, an area larger than the former domain, received aid from the national treasury. A higher number—eighty-five—was supported from prefectural reserves, thanks to the Law on Disaster Relief Funds (*Bikō Chochikuhō*) the central government had passed in 1880.[121]

Despite their skepticism about state-managed relief, many of these same taxpayers did not hesitate to donate large sums to causes of their own choice. Rather than regulating commodity prices or giving money directly to the poor, they preferred to donate to institutions of public health and education[122] and invested in local infrastructure and enterprises that promoted self-help in the form of work and saving. In doing so, they rejected Toshitada's relatively generous approach toward poor relief while perpetuating his belief that hard work, frugality, and health were necessary to generate local prosperity. For some of Ōno's Meiji-era leaders, the former lord's welfare agenda had been identical with their own. Many of Ōno's doctors, teachers, district administrators, and some of the merchants were former domain vassals who had formulated and carried out the domain reforms' various components. Even the former lord continued to address welfare matters in his old domain, partly to help

---

120. McClain, "Local Politics and National Integration."

121. Tsuruga-ken rekishi seiji-bu 7—kyūjutsu, and Fukui-ken rekishi seiji-bu 7—kyūjutsu, Naikaku bunko; Fueki, "Meiji shoki kyūhin rippō no kōzō"; Garon, *Molding Japanese Minds*, 33–34.

122. On education, see Yanagisawa, "Gakku torishimari Yoshida Setsuzō no 'Seisai nisshi,'" 485–87. As Brian Platt has shown, commoner elites in Shinano Province played a leading role in funding and organizing schools before and after the Meiji Restoration. Although the case of poor relief differs from education in that Tokugawa governments were more deeply involved in the former, the two were closely related in the minds of local elites; see Platt, *Burning and Building*.

his impoverished former vassals and partly to preserve the proud memory of Toshitada's "enlightened" rule.

From the outset, Meiji government officials expressed a strong interest in public health but lacked the funds and administrative framework to implement policies without the support of local leaders. In 1874, the Meiji government issued regulations for smallpox vaccinations and made the vaccinations mandatory in 1876. In 1876, the Home Ministry ordered medical overseers (*imu torishimari*), who had recently been appointed for each of the new administrative districts (*daiku*), to cooperate with local village and neighborhood headmen to ensure that all newborns were vaccinated within the first year of their lives.[123]

Ōno's vaccination program had been discontinued when the domain was abolished, but in 1875, an exalted personality (presumably the former lord) extended a loan of 1,000 yen to a number of physicians, among them Tsuchida Suzu, successor of Ryūwan, who had been one of the initiators of the lord's vaccination program in 1850.[124] The donor cited his desire to carry on the vision of "Kenshōin-sama," that is, Toshitada, who had retired in 1862 and died in 1869. He wanted the interest accruing on the fund to be used for treating poor patients and gradual repayment of the principal over an undefined period of time. The money was borrowed by Tsuchida himself and a number of well-heeled townspeople and villagers on the Ōno plain, at least some of whom appear to have been personally related to Tsuchida. Through his medical work, Tsuchida seems to have been acquainted with many local villagers outside his former domain and included some of them in the new scheme. The donation was probably connected to the implementation of the new vaccination guidelines: in 1876, Tsuchida Suzu was serving as the medical overseer of Ōno's two administrative districts.[125] In 1875, villages in the Ōno area started to produce registers that listed the name, age, and vaccination status of all local children.[126] The scheme suggests that building vaccination infrastructure in the early Meiji period in this region

123. Fukui-ken Ishikai, *Fukui-ken igakushi*, 262–79.
124. Shoyōdome, 1873.3.28, Uchiyama Ryōji-ke monjo; Shutō saikō kashitsuke, 1875.7.1, Echizen Ono Doi-ke monjo. On Tsuchida Ryūwan, see Fukuda Gen'ichirō, *Echizen jinbutsushi* (chū), 385.
125. Fukui-ken Ishikai, *Fukui-ken igakushi*, 273–79.
126. Shutō kisai misai torishirabechō, 1875, Yamada Saburōbei-ke monjo.

continued to draw on the former lord and on physicians' border-crossing networks.

After the abolition of Ōno domain, Toshitada's hospital, too, was forced to close its doors. In the late 1870s, the central government ordered the election of hygiene commissioners (*eisei iin*) in every community as a response to cholera epidemics, but public funding for hospitals and health care remained extremely limited. In 1878, the assembly of Ishikawa Prefecture (to which Ōno belonged between 1876 and 1881) approved some funds for public hospitals in Ōno and other smaller centers.[127] In 1882, Ōno was finally able to open a new hospital, which was administered by the Ōno Public Hospital Federation (Kōritsu Ōno Byōin Rengōkai)—a body composed of local village and neighborhood headmen[128]—and funded by the neighborhoods of Ōno town and 120 villages in five different sections of Ōno County.[129] The construction of the building was financed by a large number of voluntary donors—most prominently the Ōsakaya Shichitarō firm and affiliates, town merchants Ozaki Yaemon and Nunokawa Genbei, and the Rōkyūsha, an endowment created by Uchiyama Shichirōemon to promote the welfare of former domain vassals.[130] The hospital initially attracted high numbers of patients and became the designated site of the public smallpox vaccination program, which inoculated the children of "extremely poor people" free of charge.[131] Local leaders such as physician Tsuchida Suzu and ex-domain reformers Yoshida Setsuzō and Yokota Hagusa—now a school official—described the new clinic as a continuation of Toshitada's legacy, which had made Ōno a forerunner of modern medicine in the region.[132] But the hospital operation turned out to be financially unsustainable in its public form.

127. Yuki no yogatari, 1882.5.19, in *Ōno shishi*, Shinbun shiryō-hen, 4; Fukui-ken Gikaishi Hensan Iinkai, *Fukui-ken gikaishi*, vol. 1, 271–72, 293.

128. Kaitatsu, year unknown, 5.18, Nojiri Kiheiji-ke monjo.

129. The burden differed by section, and less than a quarter of all households were required to pay; Meiji jūshichi nendo Kōritsu Ōno Byōin hiyō shishutsu yosan gian, 1884, Nojiri Kiheiji-ke monjo.

130. "Kōritsu Ōno Byōin kenchikuhi dō kifukin suitōroku," 1882, in *Ōno shishi*, Shoke monjo-hen 2, 668.

131. Meiji jūshichi nendo Kōritsu Ōno Byōin hiyō shishutsu yosan gian, 1884, Nojiri Kiheiji-ke monjo. In early 1882, the hospital treated an average of 120 people a day; *Fukui Shinbun*, 1882.1.7, 1.21.

132. Yoshida Setsuzō to Yokota Hagusa et al., year unknown, 4.19, NGM.

After losing its prefectural subsidies during the economic crisis of the mid-1880s, the hospital had to close in 1889,[133] and Ōno's leaders now pinned their hopes on a private institution—the Saisei Hospital, set up by some of Ōno's physicians with much support from local notables.[134] Despite its ultimate failure, the case of Ōno's public hospital shows how crucial the initiative and collaboration of local elites and physicians was for promoting public health and Western medicine in the early Meiji period, especially in rural areas.

Ozaki Yaemon, one of the main donors of the hospital building, is today remembered as Ōno's greatest philanthropist.[135] A close relative of Nunokawa Genbei—and of Kameya Moemon, the wealthy merchant featured in chapter 5—Ozaki was a former purveyor merchant who served several terms as representative in Fukui's prefectural assembly.[136] He earned his benevolent reputation despite—or because of?—the fact that he had been one of the people targeted during the uprising of 1873. Although the archives of Ozaki and most of Ōno's other Meiji-era town elites are no longer accessible to researchers today, Saitō's biography of Ozaki suggests that Ōno's wealthy continued to act collectively when organizing food aid for starving townspeople. After a bad harvest in 1880, for example, Ozaki encouraged Ōno's sake brewers and other leaders to donate rice and money for the poor and purchased rice in the port town of Mikuni.[137] When economic depression hit the town around 1885–86, wealthy townspeople, among them many members of the former purveyor guild, donated on behalf of the "extremely poor."[138] In 1882, Nunokawa and Ozaki, together with a few other townsmen, founded Ōno's Chamber of Commerce. From the make-up of this body, it would not be far-fetched

133. *Fukui Shinpō*, 1889.4.6, in *Ōno shishi*, Shinbun shiryō-hen, 126–27. Closing public hospitals and replacing them with private practices was a nationwide trend in the 1880s and 1890s. Prefectural taxpayers were often hesitant to fund institutions that only benefited specific regions and questioned whether hospitals were still needed for the training of local physicians; see Ikai, *Byōin no seiki no riron*, 80–85.

134. *Fukui Shinpō*, 1888.2.11, 2.28, 3.4, 4.8, in *Ōno shishi*, Shinbun shiryō-hen, 75.

135. Ōno-shi Kyōiku Iinkai (ed.), *Do ni ikita Ozaki Kindō*.

136. Saitō Shūsuke, *Ozaki Yaemon (Kindō)-den*; *Ōno chōshi*, vol. 4, 538–40, 554–56.

137. Saitō Shūsuke, *Ozaki Yaemon (Kindō)-den*, 190.

138. Sekihinsha kyūjo yūshi meiretsu, 1885, NGM. On the depression, see *Fukui Shinbun*, 1886.3.9, in *Ōno shishi*, Shinbun shiryō-hen, 61–62.

to call it the modern incarnation of the purveyor guild, with former samurai enterprises such as Ōsakaya Shichitarō now joining the ranks.[139]

Although Ozaki and his colleagues still offered charity in very bad years, their priority was creating economic growth, and they expected the poor to contribute to that goal through labor and savings. In the first decades of Meiji, Ōno's elites founded a variety of associations under names such as Kōseisha (Welfare Society), Bikōsha (Society for Emergency Provision), Shinsōsha (Society for Household Vitalization; established by Ozaki to coordinate the elite response to the food crisis of 1880), and Kinkensha (Society for Diligence and Thrift) that provided credit and grants to the poor and encouraged saving.[140] Although the details of these schemes are obscure, many of them seem to have gathered funds from members, invested them, and used the return to benefit their members, charitable causes, or both. In the case of the vaccination loan, Ōnoya or (probably) the former lord provided the loan, wealthy locals served as borrowers and administrators, and needy people were the beneficiaries. The distinction between for-profit and charitable enterprises was blurred in this style of philanthropy because these schemes needed to make a profit to be beneficial and economic investment could itself be construed as a form of support for the poor. Ozaki Yaemon, for example, invested money into infrastructure, education, copper smelting, forestry, agricultural improvement, and land reclamation and also collaborated with the Chamber of Commerce to promote silk and papermaking, which he liked to refer to as "poor relief" (*saimin kyūsai*).[141] Contemporaries took such claims quite seriously. After Ozaki's death, grateful farmers enshrined him as a protector deity on fields he had helped develop south of Ōno town.[142]

What stands out in these developmentalist approaches to poverty relief is a preference for self-perpetuating endowments—a format clearly informed by Tokugawa precedents. One example is the Relief Bureau of 1860, but many of the new schemes also resembled the so-called loan

---

139. *Ōno shishi*, Tsūshi-hen (ge), 123–26. On trade and industry associations as successors of Tokugawa guilds in rural areas, see Pratt, *Japan's Protoindustrial Elite*, 74.

140. These schemes are briefly mentioned in Saitō Shūsuke, *Ozaki Yaemon (Kindō)-den*, 187–91, and some appear in Meiji jūninen yori maitoshi kanjō shirabe, NGM.

141. Saitō Shūsuke, *Ozaki Yaemon (Kindō)-den*, 84–115, 149–59; *Ōno shishi*, Tsūshi-hen (ge), 126.

142. Saitō Shūsuke, *Ozaki Yaemon (Kindō)-den*, 58–61.

societies (*kō*) of the late Tokugawa period, which were present in the Ōno area from at least the late 1700s and became common among local peasants and townspeople. There were many different types of loan societies, some operating like mutual insurance schemes and others like credit unions or even gambling rings. As Tetsuo Najita has shown, *kō* constituted an important continuity in nineteenth-century economic history because they paved the way for modern banks and insurance companies.[143] Ōno's domain government also co-opted the loan society format and used it to raise funds while promoting community welfare in the nineteenth century. For example, in the 1850s and 1860s the domain established the so-called Reform *Kō*,[144] and in 1864 the *Kō* to Accumulate Good (Sekizenkō), which functioned like a mutual disaster insurance but was created to gather relief money for villagers whose houses had been intentionally destroyed to deter a rebel band from entering the domain. All households of the domain were forced to join it at the behest of the government.[145]

For the Meiji period, Ōno's best-documented example of a semi-public relief fund is the so-called Ifukukai, which was similar to the Relief Bureau and the *Kō* to Accumulate Good. It was established in 1888 to rebuild the town after a devastating fire had destroyed the homes of more than 1,040 households (out of a total of approximately 1,600).[146] Ozaki Yaemon, one of the initiators, explained the goal of the association as follows:

> Property worth several hundreds of thousands of yen has been destroyed, and a good part of the town has lost hope regarding their future livelihoods and is about to move away. If we do not take action, there is no doubt that this town will soon take on the appearance of an empty and isolated village.

143. Najita, *Ordinary Economies in Japan.*
144. The Reform *Kō* collected contributions from village communities and extended loans for economic improvement whenever the lot fell on them, provided they worked hard and lived frugally. See, for example, Kaikakukō ochikuji shōmon no koto, 1857, Tsunewaki San'emon-ke monjo.
145. See, for example, MT goyōdome 1865.1.10, YH 1297, 929.
146. *Fukui Shinpō*, 1888.4.14.

Fortunately, our former lord has once again approached us privately with kind exhortations and consulted me and a few others regarding the prospect of recovery. With this favor as our foundation, each of us has transferred some agricultural land from our own property to a certain gentleman merchant and borrowed 20,000 yen. We will spread this money widely across the town, hoping that henceforth, this will make the people exert themselves even more, and make them shed the detrimental habits of extravagance and idleness and devote themselves to the promotion of production and industry (*shokusan kōgyō*).

If the people thus honor and appreciate our intentions, we can expect our town to regain its prosperity after some time—and surely, we will see this calamity turn into the happiness of another day! This is the reason we have named this society "Ifukukai"—Association for Turning Bad Into Good Fortune.[147]

The former domain lord took on a coordinating role, and Ozaki's language was strikingly reminiscent of the lord's proclamations prior to 1871. The Ifukukai's funds were intended both to rebuild the town in a physical sense and create prosperity by inspiring gratitude and industry among the local people. Ozaki was an accomplished amateur poet, and he penned some verses such as the following to extol his former ruler's benevolence: "The grass of the people—today, dew of mercy falls on them from Kameyama hill, telling them to grow."[148] (Kameyama hill was the location of the former lord's castle keep.) Clearly, the belief in the transformative power of benevolence had not disappeared from the minds of local leaders. Although the lord was now a retiree in Tokyo and in no position to enforce gratitude, the local elites pretended he had never left, invoking ties of benevolence and gratitude between him, the local leaders, and lowly subjects at this moment of great crisis.[149]

The "gentleman merchant" mentioned in the quote above was of course none other than Ōsakaya Shichitarō. This company had not only

---

147. Ifukukai shogen, 1888, Ozaki Yaemon-ke monjo.
148. Saitō Shūsuke, *Ozaki Yaemon (Kindō)-den*, 146.
149. To transmit his intentions to Ōno's merchants, Toshitsune dispatched his former vassal Ono Rissei—the same man who had carried the lord's direct letter from Edo days before the founding of the Relief Bureau in 1860; Ifukukai kiroku, Miyazawa Yoshizaemon-ke monjo; *Ōno gunshi*, 622–23.

been the main benefactor of the hospital but also made large donations to public schools[150] and was heavily involved in the relief of impoverished former samurai. In 1881, for example, Doi and Uchiyama decided to divert 15,000 yen from the company's profits to establish the Shigensha, a fund that invested in commercial ventures and distributed earnings among its members, former domain vassals.[151] The Ifukukai had seven members, all of them prominent members of Ōno's Chamber of Commerce, including some former town elder families, who put up their agricultural land as collateral and themselves received some aid from the fund. The society provided reconstruction loans and emergency aid to fire victims on two occasions (in 1888 and 1899) before it was dissolved in 1911.[152] Like many of Ōno's philanthropic schemes in the nineteenth century, it was semi-public and combined welfare and disaster relief with a broader interest in boosting the local economy.

When did this structure of social welfare funding come to an end? Around the turn of the century, the vestiges of domain wealth in the area gradually disappeared. In 1899, the Ōnoya business was disbanded after a period of decline that had commenced with branch closures in the 1880s.[153] In 1897, the Shigensha dissolved as well; established in 1881 as an endowment to help impoverished former vassals, it unraveled rather quickly as poor members requested the withdrawal of their share of the principal. In 1896, the Rōkyūsha, another of Uchiyama's aid funds for ex-samurai, was abolished, and its remaining capital was used to set up the Daishichi Bank, Ōno's first modern bank.[154] With Ōnoya, Ōno lost its biggest donor, one that had supported former vassals and given major impulses to many charitable ventures. At the same time, the central government finally became more involved in social welfare in rural areas.[155] The Home Ministry began to encourage communities to set up local as-

150. *Ōno shishi*, Tsūshi-hen (ge), 294.

151. Ibid.

152. Yōsho tsuzuri and Ryōshūsho tsuzuri, 1888, Miyazawa Yoshizaemon-ke monjo; Ifukukai seisan hōkokusho, 1898, Miyazawa Yoshizaemon-ke monjo; "Kanshajō," 1911, cited in Saitō Shūsuke, *Ozaki Yaemon (Kindō)-den*, 147–48. See also *Fukui Shinpō*, 1888.6.22.

153. *Ōno shishi*, Tsūshi-hen (ge), 107–12.

154. Ibid., 112–20, 220–26.

155. Kinzley, "Japan's Discovery of Poverty."

sociations of self-help and promoted agricultural cooperatives as well as so-called *hōtokusha* (repaying virtue societies)—associations for mutual assistance and self-help inspired by the village reforms of the Bakumatsu era.[156] Bureaucrats encouraged charitable groups of all kinds to establish and join nation-wide federations, such as the Japanese Red Cross Society, which had been expanding since the 1890s.[157] In the Ōno area, repaying virtue societies and Red Cross chapters began to appear around the late 1890s.[158] These national associations ushered in a new era of collaboration between state bureaucracy and citizen's groups in social welfare that intensified after World War I.

The nineteenth century was a time of continuity in the history of social welfare in the Ōno area, despite the break of the Meiji Restoration. The main factor behind this continuity was the domain reform from the 1840s to the early 1870s, which influenced responses to poverty through the first three decades of the Meiji era. Toshitada's mercantilism anticipated the theme of state strengthening that became dominant in Japan after 1868. Moreover, during the first half of the Meiji period, local social structures and initiatives still mattered more than central government directives in determining what kinds of aid the poor could expect from their wealthier neighbors. In Ōno, such continuity was perhaps more conspicuous than in other regions because the domain's mercantilist reforms had peaked right before the Meiji Restoration, and its public health measures and economic interventions translated almost seamlessly into reform measures by the Meiji regime under the leadership of essentially the same local elites as in the final decades of domain rule.

In the Bakumatsu era, Ōno's domain government was still working with occupation-based groups and the idea of reciprocity between ruler

---

156. Garon, *Molding Japanese Minds*, 40–49; Miyachi, *Nichiro sengo seijishi no kenkyū*; *Ono shishi*, Tsūshi-hen (ge), 158–64; Pyle, "The Technology of Japanese Nationalism."

157. On the Tokugawa roots of the Japanese Red Cross, see Konishi, "The Emergence of an International Humanitarian Organization in Japan."

158. On the Red Cross and *hōtokusha* activity in the Ōno area, see Kasamatsu Sōemon-ke monjo, NGM, and Ashikaga Shūtoku-ke monjo. In 1919, the Home Ministry prompted the founding of the Fukui Prefectural Relief Improvement Society (Fukui-ken Kyūsai Kairyō Kyōkai) with a branch office in Ōno County; see *Ono shishi*, Tsūshi-hen (ge), 185–86; Fukui-ken Naimu-bu Chihōka (ed.), *Fukui-ken shakai jigyō ippan*.

and subjects. Toshitada and his advisers tried whatever they could to accomplish state strengthening under these conditions. They gave new responsibilities to purveyor merchants, physicians, villages, and block associations, persuading them that such collaboration was in their mutual best interest. In the absence of a strong unifying ideology such as nationalism, the domain government modified the idea of benevolent rule to discipline subjects and put them to work in the service of the domain state. Although this strategy seems to have worked reasonably well for a while, there were limitations to this kind of self-strengthening because wealthy and poor commoners alike were being asked to make sacrifices on behalf of a warrior house that was involved in profit-making and unable to balance the interests of different social groups at a time of economic instability. The abolition of the domain enabled village and town elites to join hands with members of the former retainer band to continue Toshitada's agenda without the restraint of feudal obligations.

Despite the massive social changes that accompanied the removal of domain authority, the field of social welfare was marked by continuity in terms of ideology and concrete social structures. The Ōnoya trading company—a product of the domain reforms—contributed to the building of health and education infrastructure in the area and promoted the welfare of impoverished former samurai. Town merchants reenacted older forms of collaboration, such as the purveyor guild, to collect money and food for townspeople at times of hunger and disaster. They collaborated with physicians and former vassals to resurrect Toshitada's public health initiatives that had vanished with the domain. Endowments and mutual insurance schemes remained important after 1871 as vehicles for collecting and investing welfare money, even as community leaders were dismantling the domain's semi-public funds such as the Relief Bureau and the village granaries.[159] Certainly, much more remains to be known about the communal bodies, business ties, and family networks of Ōno's town and village elites during the Meiji era, not to speak of their relationships with their poorer neighbors, who rarely appear in

---

159. On the dismantling of one of the village granaries, see Oboe, 1873, Tōhō Haruo-ke monjo.

contemporary documents. But there can be no doubt that these kinds of structures deeply affected the organization of social welfare in the region.

Toshitada's instrumentalization of benevolence had a long afterlife under the Meiji regime. Although Ōno's town leaders did not long for a return of feudal rule, the strategy of mobilizing subjects through paternalist appeals retained some currency among them, and the Meiji oligarchs also remained interested in the idea. Even though the Meiji government rigorously suppressed uprisings that followed the moral mold of Tokugawa protests, it did not discard the idea of benevolent rule but modified it by reinventing the emperor as a benevolent parent and patron of charity, whose rare displays of benevolence had to be repaid with personal sacrifices on behalf of the nation. In the early years of the twentieth century, the government intensified its rhetoric of imperial benevolence to combat the spread of socialism and discourage the poor from feeling entitled to public assistance.[160] One example is the Imperial Gift Foundation Saiseikai, an endowment for health care for the poor established in 1911. To set up the Saiseikai, the government used an imperial donation as seed money to collect capital from private donors all over the country and then granted medical aid in the name of the emperor, even though the majority of funds had actually been contributed by subjects.[161] The idea of reciprocity between high and low thus took on a new life in a national context.

160.　Ikeda, *Nihon shakai fukushishi*, 179–99; Endō, *Tennōsei jikei shugi no seiritsu*, 35–67; Makihara, *Kyakubun to kokumin no aida*, 204–25.

161.　Ikeda, "Onshi Zaidan Saiseikai no seiritsu"; Endō, "Onshi Zaidan Saiseikai no seiritsu to tenkai," two parts.

CONCLUSION

Ōno's last preserved town elders' journal ends before the final lunar month of 1869. Shortly thereafter, the world in which these journals belonged came to an end. In 1870, the domain government gave the town elders new titles to place them within the new imperial order, but one year later their position was abolished, together with the concept of the domain. In a radical departure from previous practice, former townspeople and vassals were brought together in so-called large districts (*daiku*), which were subdivided into several small districts (*shōku*) of about 300 households. Ōno town comprised two large districts in 1872, and one in 1873. Within each small district, so-called town groups (*machigumi*) replaced the old block associations and samurai neighborhoods, which in many cases had to merge or split to meet the target size of about 100 households each. The next major reform step in 1878 did away with the districts and divided the town groups (now called *chō*) up between three elected head officials (*kochō*). In 1884, all nineteen *chō* were placed under the control of one government-appointed headman. In 1888, Ōno finally settled into the status it retained until the founding of Ōno City in 1954: that of a town (*chō*) with an elected mayor and town council. The Meiji state confiscated the castle grounds and auctioned most of them off to private bidders but reserved some land for the new county office, where a former vassal of Ōno domain began to serve as the head of Ōno County on behalf of the central government.[1]

---

1. *Ōno shishi*, Tsūshi-hen (ge), 35–37, 68–81, 87–93, 139–43.

Perhaps as a result of these frequent reorganizations, relatively few documents have survived from the entities that governed Ōno town after the abolition of the domain. But the absence of documentation is particularly striking with regard to the poorer residents of the area. After 1869, and especially after the Great Uprising of 1873, the surviving sources cease to convey the presence and struggles of poor widows, day laborers, peddlers, tenant farmers, cormorant fishermen, itinerant entertainers, and beggars. The main exceptions were the emerging newspapers of the region, which occasionally reported on incidents involving lower-class people and often denounced them as backward and benighted.[2] This is not to say that Tokugawa sources ever provided a direct window onto the lives of the poor; they, too, need to be read against the grain and in context to yield meaningful insights. Nor is it entirely impossible to reconstruct the lives of lower-class people in Meiji Japan from materials such as court notes, petitions, surveys, and miscellaneous private and administrative records. But the state of documentation in Ōno and many other localities certainly makes it much more difficult to see beyond the condescending paternalism of well-meaning elites that featured so prominently in the last chapter of this book.

The case of Meiji Japan illustrates that increasing literacy and a more invasive state do not always result in better documentation. Administrative changes are only one possible reason poor people in the Meiji period were less likely to leave a paper trail than were their Tokugawa predecessors. Another major factor was the abolition of the Tokugawa mode of governance. When the status order was dismantled, for example, mendicant groups such as the Koshirō and blind professionals disappeared as self-governing entities and became invisible in documentary terms. The former villages and block associations often continued to practice a limited form of communal recordkeeping after the Restoration (as seen in chapter 1, some chō in Ōno started to keep journals in the middle of the nineteenth century and continued them over many decades), but their political influence declined because they had been absorbed and reorganized within the new administrative districts and lost the ability to write their own laws, acquire privileges in return for duties and tax payments, and include and exclude people as residents and members. Officials of

2.   Imanishi, "Bunmei kaika to sabetsu"; *Satsuyō Shinbun*; etc.

the new state no longer needed to keep extensive records of their interactions with such associations because the precedents established in these interactions no longer mattered for the day-to-day conduct of local government.

The Tokugawa archive stands out in its detailed portrayal of lower-class subjects, not merely as objects of observation and control but as assertive political actors. The representatives of self-governing groups were able to speak in an official capacity irrespective of wealth or reputation and were in turn held accountable by the full and often hereditary members of their associations. Because these groups wielded real power over subjects, even over those who did not enjoy the benefits of membership, samurai and commoner officials were compelled to record their interactions with group leaders and preserve such information over time. By the same token, the leaders of status groups were eager to keep track of agreements and incidents that affected their privileges and duties and increasingly wrote them down to prevent them from being forgotten. Officials such as Ōno's town elders, who played a pivotal role in governing the complex society of a castle town, produced particularly rich records that touch on a great variety of social relationships and groups, but there were many other levels of authority in Tokugawa society whose officials kept journals and precedent manuals comparable to those in Ōno. If we add the many other forms of administrative and private documentation that existed, we arrive at an archive of enormous proportions.

The preceding chapters explored one of the most active areas of Tokugawa politics: the give and take between rulers and subjects. Tokugawa politics was reciprocal in more than one sense. Authorities maintained relationships of mutual obligation with self-governing status groups by granting them privileges in exchange for duties and deploying a rhetoric of gratitude and protection that reinforced the power asymmetry between high and low. Status groups also cultivated relationships of give and take with one another, forming lasting agreements that benefited both sides and were occasionally managed by samurai officials. This book has focused primarily on interactions in the context of dealing with poverty, but the status order with its web of relationships also manifested itself in many other areas of public life. It allowed the Tokugawa state to adapt to social change and gave ordinary subjects some room to influence their fortunes.

I deliberately refrained from proposing a strict definition of the term "status group" because I wanted to draw attention to dynamic processes of group formation and capture the structural diversity between groups. Many occupational groups developed gradually and often received official recognition only after they had already operated in practice for some time, as was the case with six bathhouse owners in Ōno who petitioned in 1834 for recognition as a guild so as to eliminate competition.[3] Although I generally regard status groups as occupation-based, self-governing, privileged, and duty-performing, this definition would exclude some groups that were also a product of rule by status. Ōno's purveyor guild, for example, was self-governing, called itself a "guild" (*nakama*), and performed duties for the authorities but did not have a shared occupation aside from a broad merchant identity and admitted new members primarily on the basis of wealth. Duty rather than occupation was this group's defining rationale. I also blurred the distinction between land-based occupational communities such as villages and *chō* and other associations such as trade and crafts guilds, mendicant confraternities, and monastic groups. Although these differences mattered and might in fact justify a classification into separate categories, all of these groups resulted from the same mode of governance.

Give and take between rulers and subjects was pervasive throughout the realm, but not all sources are equally suitable to studying it because Tokugawa rulers projected an aura of absolute authority and did not advertise how responsive they could be behind their intimidating facade. In his work on the structure of Tokugawa warrior rule, Luke Roberts has emphasized the need to differentiate between two kinds of documents in Tokugawa archives: those recording the superficial performance (*omote*) of rule and those recording actual practice (*naishō*).[4] Roberts shows that the people of Tokugawa Japan were able to tolerate discrepancies between surface and practice as long as the subordinate party agreed to keep up appearances and performed the expected rituals of submission and gratitude. Officials routinely compromised their own rules by negotiating pragmatic solutions between shogunate and domain lords and between samurai administrations and the status groups among subjects. Roberts's

3. MT goyōdome 1834.8.6, YH 687, 498–500.
4. Roberts, *Performing the Great Peace*.

argument helps explain why some administrative sources contain no hint of the negotiations that took place between rulers and subjects. The reason is that many interactions and informal precedents belonged in the *naishō* sphere of government—the realm of tacitly acknowledged practice. Such solutions were neither illegal nor corrupt but constituted "open secrets" that allowed officials to maintain flexibility while adhering to tradition and the fiction of absolute samurai authority.

Ōno's town elders' journals provide some examples of *naishō*-style solutions. One is the overlooking of temporary beggars who were not officially permitted to beg in Ōno town. Another is the precedent the town elders achieved in 1740 with the leaders of the guild of the male blind, who agreed to issue a receipt for alms money from the lord's household, only to return the Koshirō's share of the alms to the town elders rather than passing it on to the Koshirō themselves. For an example of a (failed) *omote* performance, one need look no further than the grain price crisis of 1860, when Ōno's domain government disciplined the townspeople for their refusal to perform gratitude for the lord's relief policies. The domain had to punish the townspeople in this instance because the townspeople had disrupted the surface of benevolent rule. Most *naishō* solutions in the town elders' journals were open secrets of the kind that either helped the domain government keep up appearances with the town population or allowed the town elders to save face with the domain government. They were indeed "open" in the sense that the town elders wrote them down for posterity and potentially exposed them to the eyes of domain officials, who sometimes asked to inspect those journals. At the same time, the journals must have obscured other *naishō* solutions that were more likely to be recorded in the documents of guilds, block associations, households, and other entities.

However, the town elders' journals did far more than just record open secrets. They documented many interactions between the domain government and the town's self-governing associations that fully conformed to the framework of Tokugawa rule. The status groups themselves were no open secrets—not even the mendicant groups that had formed among marginalized people. They enjoyed governmental recognition and tried to perform their duties as openly as possible to assert their value to the government and society at large. It was precisely because these groups had an *omote* presence that they were sometimes able to negotiate *naishō* solutions with the authorities. Although government officials and ideo-logues could play down the complexity of the status order and some-times obscured inconvenient changes that had occurred in the social roles of particular groups, they could not deny the privileges that status groups had acquired over time. The status order was a living entity, and officials on all levels of society produced sources such as "journals of of-ficial business" or precedent manuals to keep track of the changes that regularly occurred in the relationships, privileges, and duties of specific groups.

The theme of poverty and poor relief is well suited to highlighting the adaptability of the status order because poor people lived under un-stable circumstances and were themselves often seen as a source of insta-bility. The authorities dealt with the poor by allowing mendicants to form self-governing groups and mobilizing them and other status groups to support and control indigent people. The status order not only benefited the rulers but gave all subjects, rich and poor, a legitimate language to voice grievances and pursue their aspirations for economic security and social status. The status order was shaped by the collective actions and interac-tions of millions of people who sought to defend livelihoods and stake out autonomous spheres for themselves. Wealthy people such as Ōno's purveyor merchants and sake brewers were just as capable as poor ones of using collective action to their advantage, but the poor were the most creative in exploiting the reciprocities and interdependencies inherent in this system. For this reason, their actions have much to teach us about the mechanics of the status order more generally.

If poverty and poor relief offer insights on status, the reverse is true as well: status helps illuminate the character of poverty and poor relief in Tokugawa Japan. Villages, block associations, and mendicant groups played a central role in supporting the poor and placing them in society, and the authorities were therefore slow to build distinct, permanent in-stitutions for relieving impoverished subjects. Once they did, they again relied heavily on the structures of the status order to maintain them: the cohesion of occupation-based associations; the customary ties between mendicant and other communities; and the duties that wealthy mer-chants, guilds, and confraternities shouldered toward their lord. These features help explain why no clear distinction between public welfare and private charity developed in Japan and why the authorities were able to channel and manage poor relief without much direct taxation or significant involvement of religious institutions. The organizing principles of the status order—occupation, privilege, and duty—were reinforced by the ideology of benevolent rule and even enabled some experimentation with modern social welfare in the context of late Tokugawa mercantilism.

The diversity of the self-governing groups, combined with the country's fragmentation into many feudal territories, resulted in an uneven development of welfare institutions. Had I focused on a town or village community other than Ōno to examine the management of poverty, different occupational groups would have come into view, such as temple clerics, flophouse operators, or fishing cooperatives. Conversely, collaborations between the same kinds of groups could result in the formation of different poor relief institutions. For example, Kubota, the castle town of Akita domain, developed an endowment for orphan care, the so-called Kan'onkō of 1829, which did not have a direct equivalent in Ōno but became the site of similar collaborations between wealthy merchants and domain authorities as seen in chapter 5.[5] In addition to comparisons within Japan, there is plenty of meaning in relating the Tokugawa status order to other societies that were disconnected from it in time and space. Some comparative work is already under way on guilds and other self-governing entities, for example, in late imperial China and pre-industrial Europe, and some of it is beginning to take Japan into consideration.[6] But the status groups of Tokugawa Japan also deserve attention in their own right because for millions of individuals in this part of the world at this time, these groups anchored them in society and defined their possibilities in life.

5. Shōji, "Tenpō no kikin-ka no Akita Kan'onkō."
6. See, for example, Lucassen, de Moor, and van Zanden, "The Return of the Guilds"; de Moor, "The Silent Revolution"; Ruggiu, "Mibun gainen to atarashii shakaishi—Anshian rejīmu-ki no Furansu to Edo jidai no Nihon"; Carré, "Rekishi no hikaku/apurōchi no kōsa/gainen no saikentō"; Pomeranz, "Skills, 'Guilds', and Development." On guilds in Qing China and their involvement in communal life, see also Moll-Murata, "Chinese Guilds from the Seventeenth to the Twentieth Centuries"; Rowe, "Social Stability and Social Change"; Rowe, *Hankow: Commerce and Society in a Chinese City*, 213–340; Rowe, *Hankow: Conflict and Community in a Chinese City*, 91–134. On the social structures underlying charity in late Ming China, see Joanna Smith, *The Art of Doing Good*.

Character List

aikyū 相給
aitai nite, aitai shidai 相対ニ而、
　相対次第
Ajimi 味見
Akanegawa 赤根川
Anama 穴馬
anma 按摩
Ashimi 芦見

ba 場
bannin 番人
bettō 別当
Bikōsha 備荒社
bikuni 比丘尼
bugyō 奉行
bujikigashi 夫食貸し
bun 分
bungen sōō 分限相応
bunsetsu kōzō 分節構造

chasen 茶筅
chō 町
chōchō nite sōō ni kurashi-sōrō mono-domo
　町々ニ而相応ニ暮候者共
chōgaimono 帳外者
Chōshōji 長勝寺
chūgen 中間
chūkansō 中間層
chūrōsen ちうらう銭

daikan 代官
daiku 大区
dannaba 旦那場
deiri 出入
dezukuri 出作り
Doi Toshifusa 土井利房
Doi Toshinori 土井利義
Doi Toshisada 土井利貞
Doi Toshitada 土井利忠
Doi Toshitsune 土井利恒
dōjō 道場
dōshinmono 道心者

ebisu-uta 戎歌
edamura 枝村
eta 穢多

fudōri 不道理
fusaku 不作
fuse 布施
fuyu-kasegi 冬稼ぎ

gachigyōji 月行事
ganshodome 願書留
gesen no shosa 下賤之所作
gizetsu 義絶
gō 合
go-kaisho 御会所
goku-konkyū 極困窮

gokyūjogura 御救助蔵
gokyūjokata 御救助方
gomen 御免
gomenchi 御免地
goningumi 五人組
gōriki 合力
goyō 御用
goyōdome 御用留
goyōjō 御用場
goyōki 御用記
goyōkin 御用金
goyōtashi 御用達
goze 瞽女
Gujō 郡上
gundai 郡代

hachiningei 八人芸
haitō 配当
Hakariishi 計石
Hanaguro (Hanakura, Matsuda) Yosōzaemon
鼻黒 (花倉、松田) 与惣左衛門
Haniu 羽生
harutauchi 春田打ち
Hayashi Unkei 林雲渓
heijin, heimin 平人、平民
Hiden'in 悲田院
hinin 非人、貧人、疲人
hiningoya 非人小屋
hinin tsukasa 貧人司
hinkyūbarai 貧窮払
hira machiya 平町家
hiyō 日用
Honbo 本保
Hondenji 本伝寺
hondō 本道
honke 本家
hōon 報恩
Hōtokusha 報徳社
hyō 俵

ibuchi 居扶持
ie 家
iegara 家柄
Ifukukai 為福会

jibun hodokoshi 自分施
jige makanai 地下賄
jihi 慈悲
jihigoya 慈悲小屋
jikei kyūsai 慈恵救済
jinago 地名子
jingai 人外
jinsei 仁政
jisha bugyō 寺社奉行
jōmen 定免
jōshu 城主
junzai kange, kaizai kange 巡在勧化、
　廻在勧化
jūsō to fukugō 重層と複合

kaban 加番
kabu 株
kagyō 家業
kai 階
kaihōgoya 介抱小屋
kaku, kakuai 格、格合
Kameya Moemon 亀屋茂右衛門
Kami-Kurodani 上黒谷
kan 官
Kanamori Nagachika 金森長近
Kanazuka 金塚
kandō 勘当
kanjin 勧進
kanjōsho goyōtashi 勘定所御用達
kanka kodoku haishitsu 鰥寡孤独廃疾
kankei 関係
kankin 官金
kanmotsu torihakarawase-ryō 官物為取斗料
kannushi 神主
karei no segyō 嘉例之施行
karekore muzukashiku mōsu 彼是六ヶ数
　申す
kariume 仮埋
kasegi 稼ぎ
kashiya 借屋
katsumei negai 渇命願
Katsuyama 勝山
kawaya 皮屋、革屋
kegare 穢
Keiden'in 敬田院

kemi 毛見、検見
kengyō 検校
kijiya 木地屋
kikkai 乞丐
kinin, kijin 飢人
Kinkensha 勤倹社
kizami 刻
kō 講
kojiki, kotsujiki 乞食
kojikibarai 乞食払
kojikigashira 乞食頭
kokka no go-anki 国家之御安危
kokorozashi shidai 志次第
Kōkō tennō 光孝天皇
koku 石
kokueki 国益
kokuon 国恩
komononari 小物成
kōmotsu 公物
komusō 虚無僧
konkyū 困窮
kōri bugyō 郡奉行
Kōseisha 厚生社
koshifuda 腰札
kōshi no rei 更始ノ令
Koshirō(-domo) 古四郎共、古城共
kōtō 勾当
kouta 小哥
Koyama Yōju 小山養寿
Koyato 小矢戸
kubikiri goyō 首切御用
kudoku 功徳
kumi 組
kumigashira 組頭
Kuzuryūgawa 九頭竜川
kyūikusho 救育所

machi bannin 町番人
machi bugyō 町奉行
machibyakushō 町百姓
machidoshiyori 町年寄
machigumi 町組
machigura 町蔵
machi isha 町医者
machi kaisho 町会所

machikata 町方
makanai-dai 賄代
Managawa 真名川
meakashi 目明
meikun 名君
mentsū 面桶
mibun 身分
Mibunteki Shūen Kenkyūkai 身分的周縁
　研究会
Minami Yamanaka 南山中
minogasu 見逃
Mitani 三谷
mōjin, zoku-mōjin 盲人、俗盲人
mon 文
monme 匁
monogoi 物乞い
monomorai 物貰い
mononari 物成
mōsō 盲僧
mossō 物相、盛相
mujū 無住
muninbetsu-mono 無人別者
muratsugi, muraokuri 村継、村送
mushuku 無宿
mutsushi むつし

Nabeya Seizaemon 鍋屋清左衛門
nagaya 長屋
nainai 内々
naishō 内証
nakadōri 中通り
nakama 仲間
Nakamura Taisuke 中村岱佐
Nakano 中野
nangi 難儀、難義
naritachi 成立
nariwai なりわひ、生業
nenban 年番
ninbetsubarai 人別払
ninbetsunegai 人別願
Nishikata 西方、西潟
Nishitani 西谷
Niu 丹生
Noguchi 野口
Nojiri Gen'emon 野尻源右衛門

Nunokawa Genbei 布川源兵衛
nushikata 主方

o-ie go-sonbō no go-kaikaku 御家御存亡之
　御改革
ōjōya 大庄屋
okakoimomi 御囲籾
Ōkubo 大窪
Oku-Echizen 奥越前
omemie 御目見
Ōmiya 大宮
omodachi-sōrō mono 重立候者
Omodani 面谷
omote 表
Ōno 大野
Ono Jizen'in 小野慈善院
Ōnoya 大野屋
osabyakushō 長百姓
Ōsakaya Shichitarō 大坂屋七太郎
osakete 御酒手
osegyō-yado 御施行宿
ōsetsukerare-sōrōte aisukui 被仰付候而相救
oshigoi 押乞い
osukui 御救
osukui fushin 御救普請
osukuigoya 御救小屋
Ota 織田
Otomi 小当見
Ozaki Yaemon 尾崎弥右衛門

retsuza 列座
rien, ribetsu 離縁、離別
riyaku 利益
Rōkyūsha 良休社
ryō 両
Ryōbyōin 療病院
ryōmin 良民

Sabae 鯖江
saimin 細民
Saiseikan 済生館
sakujiki 作食
sanbutsu kaisho 産物会所
sarukai 猿飼
sasara 簓

sazen 作善
segayu 施粥
segyō, osegyō 施行、御施行
segyōgoya 施行小屋
sejō no fujo o motte tachiyuki-sōrō mibun
　世上之扶助を以立行候身分
Sekizenkō 積善講
senmin 賎民
Seyakuin 施薬院
shachū 社中
shaku 勺
shasō 社倉
Shichikenmachi 七間町
shichiya 質屋
Shigensha 思源社
shikiri-gin 仕切銀
shimin 四民
Shindenno 新田野
shinjō yoroshiki mono 身上宜敷者
shinnai shidai 心内次第
Shinokura 篠座
shinshi 賑賜
Shinsōsha 賑竈社
shintai 賑貸
shiokiyaku 仕置役
shion 四恩
Shirai Hirokage 白井寛蔭
shitayaku 下役
shizoku 士族
shō 升
shōbai no myōga 商売の冥加
shōjin 小人
shokanjin 諸勧進
shōku 小区
shokubun 職分
shōya 庄屋
shūbun 衆分
shūdan 集団
shūgi 祝儀
shuku 夙
Shutōkan 種痘館
shutsuyaku 出役
sōchō segyō 惣町施行
sōdai 惣代
sōgura 惣蔵

sono higurashi no tei 其日暮之体
sono hi kasegi 其日稼
sōroku 惣録
sōshaban 奏者番
sōson 惣村
sotsu 卒
suainin, gajin 牙人
sugiwai すぎわひ、生業
Sugiyama Waichi 杉山和一
sukui 救

tachiai 立会
takamochi 高持
tame 溜
tansakugata 探索方
tegata 手形
tenshoku 天職
to 斗
tōdōza 当道座
toiya, ton'ya 問屋
Tokuganji 徳巌寺、徳岸寺
torishimari-ryō 取締料
tosei 渡世
tōzokukata 盗賊方
Tsuchida Ryūwan/Suzu 土田龍湾・錫
tsukiban 月番

uchikake 打掛
Uchinami 打波
Uchiyama Shichirōemon 内山七郎右衛門
uradanagari 裏店借
Ushikubi 牛首
uwadera 上寺

Wakaino 若猪野

yaku 役
yamabushi 山伏
yamaga no mono 山家者
yashikidaka 屋敷高
Yokomakura 横枕
Yokota Hagusa 横田莩
yōmin 養民
yonai 与内
Yoshida Setsuzō 吉田拙蔵
yuisho 由緒
yukichū osukui 雪中御救
yūmin 遊民

zahō 座法
zamoto 座元
zatō 座頭

APPENDIX I

Rice Price in Ōno Town (per bale)

Year	Rice price in silver (*monme*)	Year	Rice price in silver (*monme*)
1740	34.7	1834	22.1–43.6
1741	22.6	1836	28.5–65.3
1781	18.6	1837	32.4–99.4
1782	18.9	1838	30.4–51
1783	24.4	1840	17.3–31.5
1784	23.4–41.8	1841	18.4–21.4
1785	15.3–25.3	1843	17.5–23.7
1786	16.2–32.5	1844	21.8–26.7
1787	22.7–38.8	1847	25.2–30
1789	21.6–27.5	1852	27–33.7
1793	20.2–28.1	1853	26.5–34.8
1797	22.9–30.8	1855	21.8–30.9
1799	19.2–27.8	1856	20.3–25.7
1800	21–26.2	1857	21.5–28.9
1801	18.3–26.5	1859	38.7–39
1804	17.1–18.1	1860	36.5–56.6
1809	23.6–28.1	1861	37.4–57.5
1815	16.1–20	1864	49.5–59.5
1829	22.5–32.5	1867	88.7–211.8
1832	23–26.9	1868	66–176.5

Note: In Ōno, 1 bale (*hyō*) = 4.56 *to*, that is, 82.26 liters (21.71 gallons).

Source: Kaidō, "Ōno-machi yōdome ni miru beika no hensen."

APPENDIX 2

Sample Commodity Prices and Wages in the Ōno Area before 1860

Item	Price in silver (*monme*)	Other currencies
One night at a regular inn in town	1.5 (1784) 2 (1809)	
One night at an inn in the mountains	2 (1787)	
Reimbursement for domain clerks for an overnight stay within the domain		125 *mon* copper 45 *mon* copper for lunch only
One secondhand cotton-wadded kimono (*nunoko*)	15.5 or more (1786)	
One secondhand unlined kimono (*hitoemono*)	9 (1786)	
Food for one jailed vagrant per day	1 (1838)	
One *shō* of sake (once sterilized)	1.25 (1787)	
Annual wage of a samurai servant (service in Edo, excl. room and board)	105 (1787)	
Five-month wage of a samurai servant (service in Osaka, excl. room and board)	43.75 (1802)	
Porter service (mountain road, one post station)	1 (1787)	
Daily wage of a mine worker (*horiko*)	approx. 1	100 *mon* copper (1785)
Domain reward for firefighting	1 or 3 (1786)	

(*continued*)

Item	Price in silver (*monme*)	Other currencies
One long *tobi* (construction tool)	9 (1785)	
Donation to a shrine for prayers for rain	5 (1792)	
Eight construction ropes	4 (1800)	
Thirty bundles of rice straw	3 (1800)	
Five straw mats	0.5 (1800)	
One block of tofu		20 *mon* copper (1800)
Dyeing of textiles, per piece	1–7.8 (1800)	
Annual stipend of a foot soldier (*ashigaru*)		6.9 *koku* of rice

Source: MT goyōdome, SSM, AHM, NGM.

Bibliography

Abbreviations

AHM	Adachi Hiromichi-ke monjo
MT goyōdome	Machi toshiyori goyōdome (town elders' journal)
NGM	Nunokawa Genbei-ke monjo
SSM	Saitō Suzuko-ke monjo
TKM	Tamura Kōsaburō-ke monjo
YH	*Ōno shishi*, vol. 9: Yōdome-hen

Unpublished Documents

Copies of all unpublished documents are accessible at the Office for the Compilation of Ōno City History within the Cultural Preservation Room (Bunkazai Hogoshitsu Shishi Hensanbu) of the Board of Education of Ōno City, if not otherwise indicated.

Adachi Hiromichi-ke monjo (AHM)
    Goyōtashi goyōdome (1799–1819). Doc. 3373:3.
    MT goyōdome=Machi toshiyori goyōdome. Docs. 3373:4 (1853), 3373:5 (1856), and 3374:6 (1857) of Adachi Hiromichi-ke monjo.
    Tenmei hachi tomeki=Tenmei hachi tsuchinoe saru: Takō, sashiyado, shōnin, fushin, konrei tomeki (1783 [*sic*], months 3–7 and petitions from these and other months). Doc. 3373:2.
Ashikaga Shūtoku-ke monjo
    Reel 1336 (sources related to the Red Cross and *hōtokusha*).
Echizen Ōno Doi-ke monjo
    Goyōdome (*metsuke*) (1863). Doc. 887.
    Kanjōbo (1874). Doc. 2603:929.
    Koyato-mura ikken-chō (1877). Doc. 2906:1095.
    Nunokawa Genbei yori mairu go-kyūjo no gi. Doc. 2603:929.

Ōno-chō yakuba no hokan ni kakaru yōdome-chū kyū Ōno-han ni kansuru shorui sono jū-ni: kyūjutsu ni kansuru tsuzuri. Doc. 2516:318.

Ōno-han yōdome bassui eisei shokusan kōgyō kyūjutsu shōbatsu bikō chochiku ni kansuru koto ni oyobu zatsu no bu (1925). Doc. 2511:151.

Sho-hikidaka ni tsuki moto-Ōno-ken todoke. Doc. 2907:1147.

Shutō saikō kashitsuke (1875). Doc. 2559:585.

Echizen shiryō
   Ōno-han jisha machikata goyōki (1865). Doc. 82:45/46.

Fukui Daigaku Toshokan monjo
   Ōjōya goyōdome (1845). Doc. 3527:29.

Hanakura-ke monjo
   Goyōdome (1789–1830). Doc. 2818:126.

   Goyōki (1775–1778). Doc. 2817:119.

   Nikki (1793–1796). Doc. 2804:16.

   Nikki (1798–1800). Doc. 2804:18.

   Nikki (1800–1802). Doc. 2804:19.

Hiyoshi kuyū monjo
   Chōnai yōdome (1860–1977). Doc. 91.

Honda Okuemon monjo
   Goze kudoki jishin no mi no ue (copied in 1839). Doc. 36:1.

Hondenji
   Kakochō (1667–1734). (not publicly accessible)

Honmachi-shimo kuyū monjo
   Chōnai yōdomeki (1831–1948). Doc. 85:1.

Kasamatsu Sōemon-ke monjo
   Reel 4496 (sources related to the Red Cross).

Kaseya monjo
   Seiji-muki hihyō ni tsuki renpan ukesho (1860). Doc. 1177:24 and 1177:25.

Kōbara-ke shūshū monjo
   Goyōnin-yaku yōyō tehikae (1852). Doc. 1037:12.

Komori Seibei-ke monjo
   Murayaku shoyōdome (1809–10). Doc. 2828:40.

Koseki (1878). (not publicly accessible)

Kose Norio-ke monjo
   On-nengu sashihikichō etc. (1714–1871). Reels 2442–2455.

Matsuda Gorōbei-ke monjo
   Chikarazuki ni aiwatashi-mōsu asabatake shōmon no koto (1836). Doc. 2831:82.

Matsumura Toshiaki-ke monjo
   Aikime-mōsu shōmon no koto (1771). Doc. 2761:267.

Miyazawa Yoshizaemon-ke monjo
   Goyōki (1764–1780). Doc. 2784:86.

   Ifukukai kiroku (1900). Doc. 2788:517.

   Ifukukai seisan hōkokusho (1898). Doc. 2788:520.

   Ryōshūsho tsuzuri (1888). Doc. 2788:519.

   Yōsho tsuzuri (1888). Doc. 2788:518.

Mugiya monjo
  Zatō, goze, kojikigashira e shūgi fuse no oboe (1791). Doc. 4553:759.
Naikaku bunko (Fukui Kenritsu Bunshokan)
  Fukui-ken rekishi seiji-bu 7—kyūjutsu. Fukui-ken shiryō 3.
  Tsuruga-ken rekishi seiji-bu 7—kyūjutsu. Fukui-ken shiryō 34.
Nojiri Gen'emon-ke monjo (NGM)
  Jisha machi goyōdome (1781). Doc. 2799:1.
Nojiri Kiheiji-ke monjo
  Gokyūjogura chokoku ukeharaichō (1860). Doc. 2810:8.
  Kaitatsu (Year unknown, 5.18). Doc. I17450051. Fukui Kenritsu Bunshokan.
  Meiji jūshichi nendo Kōritsu Ōno Byōin hiyō shishutsu yosan gian (1884).
  Doc. I17550060. Fukui Kenritsu Bunshokan.
  Mura sashihikichō (1775). Doc. 2811:210.
  Saru mura sashihikichō (1776). Doc. 2813:237.
  Uma no toshi mura sashihikimai chō (1774). Doc. 2812:223.
Nunokawa Genbei-ke monjo
  Horikane goyōdome (1804–1806). Doc. 420:22.
  Kōritsu Ōno Byōin kenchikuhi dō kifukin suitōroku (1882). Doc. 419:3.
  Meiji jūninen yori maitoshi kanjō shirabe (1879-). Doc. 3604:70.
  MT goyōdome=Machi toshiyori goyōdome. Docs. 422:42 (1860, months 1, 3, 4, 6,
  8, 10, 12) and 420:23 (1869).
  Sekihinsha kyūjo yūshi meiretsu (1885). Doc. 3607:131.
  Temae yōki (1859–60). Doc. 421:40.
  Yoshida Setsuzō shojō (year unknown, 4.19). Doc. 421:34-2.
Ōbatake Seiemon-ke monjo
  Manpō kyūkichō (1775). Doc. 2925:197.
Oka Fumio-ke monjo
  Zatō shikiri-gin muramura wappuchō (1856, 1858–65, 1867–69). Docs. G005 007,
  096, 104, 735, 746, 768, 795, 834, 855, 867, 875, 905, 910, 946, and 1030. Fukui
  Kenritsu Bunshokan.
Oka Nioji-ke monjo
  Osukui hiedai kudasare-jō (1807). Doc. 1019:62.
Ōno Kōtō Gakkō Ōkuma-ke monjo
  Kōshi bibō (1870). Doc. 3613:44.
Ozaki Yaemon-ke monjo
  Ifukukai shogen (1888). Doc. 98:3.
  Takuchi jūnanatō tōkyūchō (1877). Uncatalogued.
Saitō Suzuko-ke monjo (SSM)
  Aza fukisho shimo, Sannō ushiro, Shinmei shimo kyōkai sokuryōzu.
  Uncatalogued.
  Goyōdome (county governor) (1865). Doc. 2391:68.
  Goyōdome (county governor) (1866). Doc. 3413:161.
  Goyōtashi goyōdome (1828–39). Doc. 2382:48.
  Mizuchō (1763, 1829, and 1864). Docs. 2394:75, 2394:76, 2394:88, 2394:89, 2394:90,
  2394:91, 2394:93, 2394:94.

MT goyōdome=Machi toshiyori goyōdome. Docs. 2376:26 (1740), 2376:27 (1741), 2376:28 (1765), 2377:29 (1769), 2370:1 (1776), 2377:31 (1777), 2377:32 (1780), 2377:33 (1783, months 9–12), 2378:34 (1784), 2378:35 (1785), 2378:36 (1786), 2379:38 (1787), 2380:39 (1789), 2381:43 (1801), 2382:47 (1815), 2383:51 (1834), 2383:52 (1836), 2384:53 (1837), 2385:54 (1838), 2387:56 (1840), 2387:57 (1841), 2387:58 (1843), 2388:62 (1847), 2388:63 (1852), 2389:64 (1855), 2389:65 (1860, months 2, i3, 5, 7, 9, 11), 2390:66 (1861), 2390:67 (1864), 2391:69 (1867), 2375:17 and 2375:20 (fragments).

Ōno machi ezu (1730). Doc. 2399:145.

Ōno on-ryōbun yonmangoku-chū chōzai ninzū-yose (1726). Doc. 2398:119.

Shogandome (town elder petition book) (1852). Doc. 2372:8.

Shoganshodome (town elder petition book) (1853). Doc. 2373:9.

Sō-ninbetsu yosechō (1855, 1856, 1857, 1861, and 1871). Docs. 2394:80, 2394:81, 2394:82, 2394:83, and 2394:84.

Yōroku (1852). Doc. 3411:153.

Tamura Kōsaburō-ke monjo (TKM)

Oboe (1808). Doc. 1049:675.

Ōno-machi danmen ezu (1743, copied in 1775). Doc. 4448:101.

Osukuikin narabi ni momi hie oboe (1821). Doc. 1056:1530.

Tsutomekata oboegaki Tamura-hikae (1810). Doc. 4450:176.

Untitled. Doc. 1059:1975.

Tōhō Haruo-ke monjo

Oboe (1873). Doc. 106:2.

Tsunewaki San'emon-ke monjo

Issatsu no koto (1793). Doc. 1172:131.

Kaikakukō ochikuji shōmon no koto (1857). Doc. 1173:198.

Uchikura Jin'emon-ke monjo

Gokyūjogura chokoku ukeharaichō (1860). Doc. 2885:38.

Goyō osukui sō-dozō shoyōdome (1860). Doc. 2885:37.

Uchiyama Ryōji-ke monjo

Kōin ukeharai Nunokawa Genbei go-kyūjo ukeharai kanjō Ōsaka nokori-dō no gi, Hakodate-gashi no gi. Doc. 2711:1192.

Sashiagemōsu issatsu no koto (1860). Doc. 2704:706.

Shoyōdome (1873). Doc. 2705:1024.

Uchiyama Shichirōemon to Doi Toshitsune (1870, fifth month). Doc. 2702:476.

Urata Takeshi-ke monjo

On-jōka chōchō kyōyusho (1851). Doc. 86:1.

Yamada Saburōbei-ke monjo

Sairei kamaban narabi ni zatō goze tomariyado oboe-chō (1851). Doc. 2725:31.

Shutō kisai misai torishirabechō (1875). Doc. 10011:00904:I1918 (1). Fukui Kenritsu Bunshokan.

Yasukawa Kaibutsu-ke monjo

Ōno machizukushi. Doc. 4353:4.

Yasukawa Yozaemon-ke monjo

Edict (no year, 9.16). Doc. 3140:29.

Edict (1857, twelfth month). Doc. 3140:22.

Gōchū shoshiki warikata oboe (1725). Doc. 3141:69.

On-ryōbun muramura kyōyusho (1851). Doc. 3140-34.
Yokomachi kuyū monjo
    Yokomachi yashiki tanbetsu shirabechō (1872). Doc. 88:5.
Yokota-ke monjo
    Koyato kaikaku shoyōdome (1869). Doc. 2767:16.
    Koyato-mura kinsu deiri go-saikyo no utsushi (1877). Doc. 2767:18.
    Omodani yashiki narabi ni mura no zu (1843). Doc. 2768:138.

Published Works

Place of publication is Tokyo if not otherwise indicated.

Abercrombie, Nicholas, and Stephen Hill. "Paternalism and Patronage." *British Journal of Sociology* 27:4 (1976): 413–29.
Amino Yoshihiko. *Chūsei no hinin to yūjo.* Akashi Shoten, 1994.
Amos, Timothy. *Embodying Difference: The Making of Burakumin in Modern Japan.* Honolulu: University of Hawai'i Press, 2011.
———. "Portrait of a Tokugawa Outcaste Community." *East Asian History* 32/33 (2006): 83–108.
Aoki Yūichi. "Kinsei toshi ni okeru monjo kanri ni tsuite—'Sunpu machi kaisho monjo' o chūshin ni." *Chiba shigaku* 39 (2001): 8–25.
Araki Kyōko. "'Monogashira-yaku tsutomekata tehikae' kara mita Bakumatsu-ki Ōno-han." In *Monogashira-yaku tsutomekata tehikae kaidoku,* edited by Ōno Komonjokai, 120–30. Ōno: Ōno Komonjokai, 2011.
Asakawa Kan'ichi. "Notes on Village Government in Japan After 1600," part 1. *Journal of the American Oriental Society* 30:3 (1910): 259–300.
Asano Kenshin. *Nihon bukkyō shakai jigyōshi.* Bonjinsha, 1934 (rpt. in *Senzenki shakai jigyō kihon bunkenshū* 37, Nihon Tosho Sentā, 2002).
Asao Naohiro. "Hiden'in to Ōmi no hininban." In *Nihon kokka no shiteki tokushitsu: Kinsei/Kindai,* edited by Asao Naohiro Kyōju Taikan Kinenkai, 3–36. Kyoto: Shibunkaku Shuppan, 1995.
———. "Ikoma-ke to zatō/goze nakama." *Kyoto Tachibana joshi daigaku kenkyū kiyō* 28 (2002): 67–101.
———. "Jūhasseiki no shakai hendō to mibunteki chūkansō." In *Nihon no kinsei,* vol. 10: Kindai e no taidō, edited by Tsuji Tatsuya and Asao Naohiro, 45–94. Chūō Kōronsha, 1993.
———. "Kinsei no mibunsei to senmin." *Buraku mondai kenkyū* 68 (1981): 37–55.
———. "Kinsei no mibun to sono hen'yō." In *Nihon no kinsei,* vol. 7: Mibun to kakushiki, edited by Asao Naohiro, 7–40. Chūō Kōronsha, 1992.
———. "Sōson kara chō e." In *Nihon no shakaishi,* vol. 6: Shakaiteki sho-shūdan, edited by Asao Naohiro et al., 323–62. Iwanami Shoten, 1988.
Azuma Shunsuke. "Bakumatsu-ki Kita Ezochi ni okeru Ōno-han no Ushoro basho keiei." *Hokkaidō kaitaku kinenkan kenkyū kiyō* 35 (2007): 67–86.

Beerens, Anna. *Friends, Acquaintances, Pupils, and Patrons: Japanese Intellectual Life in the Late Eighteenth Century—A Prosopographical Approach.* Leiden: Leiden University Press, 2006.

Botsman, Daniel V. *Punishment and Power in the Making of Modern Japan.* Princeton, NJ: Princeton University Press, 2004.

———. "Recovering Japan's Urban Past: Yoshida Nobuyuki, Tsukada Takashi, and the Cities of the Tokugawa Period." *City, Culture and Society* 3:1 (2012): 9–14.

Brooks, William Lyman. "Outcaste Society in Early Modern Japan." Ph.D. diss., Columbia University, 1976.

Brown, Philip. *Central Authority and Local Autonomy in the Formation of Early Modern Japan: The Case of Kaga Domain.* Stanford, CA: Stanford University Press, 1993.

———. *Cultivating Commons: Joint Ownership of Arable Land in Early Modern Japan.* Honolulu: University of Hawai'i Press, 2011.

Buraku Mondai Kenkyūjo (ed.). *Buraku no rekishi.* Higashi Nihon-hen. Kyoto: Buraku Mondai Kenkyūjo, 1983.

Burakushi yōgo jiten. Edited by Kobayashi Shigeru et al. Kashiwa Shobō, 1985.

Burns, Susan L. "From 'Leper Villages' to Leprosaria: Public Health, Nationalism and the Culture of Exclusion in Japan." In *Isolation: Places and Practices of Exclusion*, edited by Carolyn Strange and Alison Bashford, 104–18. London: Routledge, 2003.

Carré, Guillaume. "Les marges statutaires dans le Japon prémoderne: enjeux et débats." *Annales: Histoire, Sciences Sociales* 66:4 (2011): 955–76.

———. "Rekishi no hikaku/apurōchi no kōsa/gainen no saikentō—Mibunteki shūen/kōsa suru kinsei mibunsei-ron." Translated by Takazawa Norie and Matsumoto Reiko. *Shisō* 1084: Kōsa suru Nihon Kinseishi—Nichifutsu no taiwa kara (2014): 9–28.

Chiba Tokuji and Saigusa Yukihiro. "Chūbu Nihon Hakusanroku jūmin no kisetsuteki hōrō kankō—Ushikubi chiku no jirei o chūshin ni." *Kokuritsu minzokugaku hakubutsukan kenkyū hōkoku* 8:2 (1983): 253–306.

Chiba Yakō. "Edo jidai no ganka shōshi." *Chiba igaku* 78 (2002): 257–62.

Cornell, John B. "'Caste' in Japanese Social Stratification: A Theory and a Case." *Monumenta Nipponica* 25:1/2 (1970): 107–35.

Craig, Albert M. *Chōshū in the Meiji Restoration.* Cambridge, MA: Harvard University Press, 1961.

Crawcour, E. S. "Changes in Japanese Commerce in the Tokugawa Period." In *Studies in the Institutional History of Early Modern Japan*, edited by John W. Hall and Marius B. Jansen, 189–202. Princeton, NJ: Princeton University Press, 1968.

De Moor, Tine. "The Silent Revolution: A New Perspective on the Emergence of Commons, Guilds, and Other Forms of Corporate Collective Action in Western Europe." *International Review of Social History* 53 (2008): 179–212.

De Moor, Tine, Jan Lucassen, and Jan Luiten van Zanden. "The Return of the Guilds: Towards a Global History of the Guilds in Pre-industrial Times." *International Review of Social History* 53 (2008): 5–18.

De Vos, George, and Wagatsuma Hiroshi (eds.). *Japan's Invisible Race: Caste in Culture and Personality.* Berkeley: University of California Press, 1966.

Drixler, Fabian. *Mabiki: Infanticide and Population Growth in Eastern Japan, 1660–1950.* Berkeley: University of California Press, 2013.

Edgerton-Tarpley, Kathryn. "From 'Nourish the People' to 'Sacrifice for the Nation': Changing Responses to Disaster in Late Imperial and Modern China." *Journal of Asian Studies* 73:2 (2014): 447–69.

Ehlers, Maren. "Benevolence, Charity, and Duty: Urban Relief and Domain Society during the Tenmei Famine." *Monumenta Nipponica* 69:1 (2014): 55–101.

———. "Charity Reconstructed: The Transformation of Social Welfare in Rural Japan in the Nineteenth Century." In *Charities in the Non-Western World: The Development and Regulation of Indigenous and Islamic Charities*, edited by Rajeswary Ampalavanar Brown and Justin Pierce, 88–111. New York: Routledge, 2013.

———. "Executing Duty: Ōno Domain and the Employment of *Hinin* in the Bakumatsu Period." *Early Modern Japan* 18 (2010): 76–87.

———. "Mibun shakai no hinmin kyūsai—Tenmei kikin-chū no Echizen Ōno-han o rei ni." In *Mibunteki shūen no hikakushi—Hō to shakai no shiten kara*, edited by Tsukada Takashi, 293–346. Osaka: Seibundō, 2010.

———. "Mibun shakai to jinsei—Bakumatsu Ōno no bikō chochiku." In *Kinsei mibun shakai no hikakushi—Hō to shakai no shiten kara*, edited by Tsukada Takashi, Saga Ashita, and Yagi Shigeru, 345–75. Osaka: Seibundo, 2014.

———. "Ōno-han no Koshirō—Han shakai no naka no hinin shūdan." In *Toshi no shūen ni ikiru* (Mibunteki shūen to kinsei shakai 4), edited by Tsukada Takashi, 87–120. Yoshikawa Kōbunkan, 2006.

Endō Kōichi. "Onshi Zaidan Saiseikai no seiritsu to tenkai katei ni tsuite." Two parts. *Meiji Gakuin Ronsō—Shakaigaku/Shakai Fukushigaku Kenkyū* 131 (2009): 49–99 and 132 (2010): 1–49.

———. *Tennōsei jikei shugi no seiritsu*. Gakubunsha, 2010.

Esherick, Joseph W., and Jeffrey N. Wasserstrom. "Acting Out Democracy: Political Theater in Modern China." In *Popular Protest and Political Culture in Modern China*, edited by Jeffrey N. Wasserstrom and Elizabeth J. Perry, 32–69. Boulder, CO: Westview Press, 1992.

Foucault, Michel. *The Birth of Biopolitics: Lectures at the Collège de France, 1978–1979*. New York: Picador, 2010.

———. *Madness and Civilization: A History of Insanity in the Age of Reason*. Translated by Richard Howard. New York: Vintage Books, 1988.

Fritsch, Ingrid. "Blindheit in Japan: Stigma und Charisma." *Asiatische Studien* 48:1 (1994): 427–38.

———. *Japans blinde Sänger im Schutz der Gottheit Myōon-Benzaiten*. Munich: Iudicium, 1996.

Frost, Peter. *The Bakumatsu Currency Crisis*. Cambridge, MA: Harvard University Press, 1970.

Fueki Shun'ichi. "Meiji shoki kyūhin rippō no kōzō: Bikō chochikuhō kenkyū." Two parts. *Waseda hōgakkai-shi* 23 (1973): 317–47 and 24 (1974): 349–79.

Fujimoto Hiro. "Kinsei iryōshi kenkyū no genzai—Minshū/kō-kenryoku to iryō." *Yōgaku* 21 (2014): 91–125.

Fujimoto Seijirō. *Jōkamachi sekai no seikatsushi—Botsuraku to saisei no shiten kara*. Osaka: Seibundō, 2014.

Fujita Teiichirō. *Kinsei keizai shisō no kenkyū*. Yoshikawa Kōbunkan, 1966.

Fukai Jinzō. *Kinsei no chihō toshi to chōnin.* Yoshikawa Kōbunkan, 1995.

―――. "Kinsei toshi no hattatsu―Toshi kōzō o chūshin ni." In *Genroku/Kyōhōki no seiji to shakai* (Kōza Nihon kinseishi 4), edited by Matsumoto Shirō and Yamada Tadao, 147–94. Yūhikaku, 1980.

Fukaya Katsumi. *Hyakushō naritachi.* Hanawa Shobō, 1993.

Fukuda Chizuru. *Bakuhanseiteki chitsujo to oie sōdō.* Azekura Shobō, 1999.

Fukuda Gen'ichirō. *Echizen jinbutsushi.* Gyokuundō, 1910.

Fukui-ken Gikaishi Hensan Iinkai (ed.). *Fukui-ken gikaishi.* Vol. 1. Fukui: Fukui-ken Gikai Jimukyoku, 1971.

Fukui-ken Ishikai (ed.). *Fukui-ken igakushi.* Fukui: Fukui-ken Ishikai, 1968.

Fukui-ken Keisatsushi Hensan Iinkai (ed.). *Fukui-ken keisatsushi.* Vol. 1. Fukui: Fukui-ken Keisatsu Honbu, 1987.

Fukui-ken Kyōiku Iinkai (ed.). *Mino kaidō/Katsuyama kaidō (Eiheiji-dō/Hakusan zenjōdō)* (Rekishi no michi chōsa hōkokusho 5). Fukui: Fukui-ken Kyōiku Iinkai, 2005.

Fukui-ken Naimu-bu Chihōka (ed.). *Fukui-ken shakai jigyō ippan.* Fukui-ken Naimu-bu Chihōka, 1921.

Fukui-ken (ed.). *Zusetsu Fukui kenshi.* Fukui: Fukui-ken, 1998.

Fukui kenshi. Shiryō-hen 3: Chū-Kinsei 1. Edited by Fukui-ken. Fukui: Fukui-ken, 1982.

―――. Shiryō-hen 6: Chū-Kinsei 4. Edited by Fukui-ken. Fukui: Fukui-ken, 1987.

―――. Shiryō-hen 7: Chū-Kinsei 5. Edited by Fukui-ken. Fukui: Fukui-ken, 1992.

―――. Tsūshi-hen 3: Kinsei 1. Edited by Fukui-ken. Fukui: Fukui-ken, 1994.

―――. Tsūshi-hen 4: Kinsei 2. Edited by Fukui-ken. Fukui: Fukui-ken, 1996.

Fukui shishi. Tsūshi-hen 2: Kinsei. Edited by Fukui-shi. Fukui: Fukui-shi, 2008.

Funazawa Shigeki. "Ōno-han kashindan no shokusei to kyūroku." *Fukui kenshi kenkyū* 9 (1991): 53–74.

Garon, Sheldon. "From Meiji to Heisei: The State and Civil Society in Japan." In *The State of Civil Society in Japan*, edited by Frank J. Schwartz and Susan J. Pharr, 42–62. Cambridge: Cambridge University Press, 2003.

―――. *Molding Japanese Minds: The State in Everyday Life.* Princeton, NJ: Princeton University Press, 1997.

Gay, Suzanne. *The Moneylenders of Late Medieval Kyoto.* Honolulu: University of Hawai'i Press, 2001.

Geremek, Bronisław. *Poverty: A History.* Oxford: Blackwell, 1997.

Goodman, Roger. "The 'Japanese-style Welfare State' and the Delivery of Personal Social Services." In *The East Asian Welfare Model*, edited by Roger Goodman, Gordon White, and Huck-ju Kwon, 139–58. London: Routledge, 1998.

Gotō Masatoshi et al. (eds.). *Mibunteki shūen o kangaeru* (Mibunteki shūen to kinsei shakai 9). Yoshikawa Kōbunkan, 2008.

Gotō Masatoshi and Yoshida Nobuyuki (eds.). *Yamazato no shakaishi.* Yamakawa Shuppansha, 2010.

Gramlich-Oka, Bettina. *Thinking Like a Man: Tadano Makuzu (1763–1825).* Leiden: Brill, 2006.

Groemer, Gerald. "The Creation of the Edo Outcaste Order." *Journal of Japanese Studies* 27:2 (2001): 263–93.

————. *Goze to goze-uta no kenkyū*. 2 vols (Kenkyū-hen, Shiryō-hen). Nagoya: Nagoya Daigaku Shuppankai, 2007.

————. "The Guild of the Blind in Tokugawa Japan." *Monumenta Nipponica* 56:3 (2001): 263–93.

Hall, John Whitney. "Rule by Status in Tokugawa Japan." *Journal of Japanese Studies* 1:1 (1974): 39–49.

Hall, John W., and Marius B. Jansen (eds.). *Studies in the Institutional History of Early Modern Japan*. Princeton, NJ: Princeton University Press, 1968.

Hanley, Susan B. *Everyday Things in Premodern Japan: The Hidden Legacy of Material Culture*. Berkeley: University of California Press, 1997.

Hanley, Susan B., and Kozo Yamamura. *Economic and Demographic Change in Pre-industrial Japan, 1600–1868*. Princeton, NJ: Princeton University Press, 1977.

Hara Naofumi. "Akinai ga musubu hitobito: Jūsō suru nakama to ichiba." In *Akinai ga musubu hitobito* (Mibunteki shūen to kinsei shakai 3), edited by Hara Naofumi, 191–241. Yoshikawa Kōbunkan, 2007.

Hatanaka Toshiyuki. *"Kawata" to heijin—Kinsei mibun shakairon*. Kyoto: Kamogawa Shuppan, 1997.

Hauser, William B. *Economic Institutional Change in Tokugawa Japan: Ōsaka and the Kinai Cotton Trade*. London: Cambridge University Press, 1974.

Havens, Thomas R. H. "Religion and Agriculture in Nineteenth-Century Japan: Ninomiya Sontoku and the Hōtoku Movement." *Japan Christian Quarterly* 38:2 (1972): 98–105.

Heisenji monjo. 2 vols. Edited by Fukui-ken Ōno-gun Heisenji-mura. Heisenji: Heisenji-mura, 1924.

Heisenji shiyō. Edited by Fukui-ken Ōno-gun Heisenji-mura. Heisenji: Heisenji-mura, 1930.

Hermansen, Christian M. "The Hinin Associations in Osaka, 1600–1868." *Copenhagen Journal of Asian Studies* 15 (2001): 47–80.

Hinin Taiheiki. Osaka, 1688. University of Tokyo, Denshiban Katei Bunko. http://kateibunko.dl.itc.u-tokyo.ac.jp.

Hiramatsu Yoshirō. "Kinsei-hō." In *Iwanami kōza: Nihon rekishi* 11, Kinsei 3, edited by Asao Naohiro, 331–78. Iwanami Shoten, 1976.

————. *Kinsei keiji soshōhō no kenkyū*. Sōbunsha, 1960.

————. "Ninsoku yoseba no seiritsu to hensen." In *Ninsoku yoseba shi—Wagakuni jiyūkei/hoan shobun no genryū*, edited by Ninsoku Yoseba Kenshōkai, 83–132. Sōbunsha, 1974.

Hiroe Kiyoshi. "Kinsei goze zatō-kō." *Tosa shidan* 157 (1981): 1–7.

Hosaka Hirooki. "Jūnanaseiki ni okeru komusō no seisei—Boroboro/komozō to no idō to 'kou' kōi no arikata." In *Mibunteki shūen*, edited by Tsukada Takashi, Yoshida Nobuyuki, and Wakita Osamu, 161–216. Kyoto: Buraku Mondai Kenkyūjo, 1994.

Howell, David L. *Capitalism from Within: Economy, Society, and the State in a Japanese Fishery*. Berkeley: University of California Press, 1995.

————. *Geographies of Identity in Nineteenth-Century Japan*. Berkeley: University of California Press, 2005.

————. "Hard Times in the Kantō: Economic Change and Village Life in Late Tokugawa Japan." *Modern Asian Studies* 23:2 (1989): 349–71.

————. "Kinsei shakai ni okeru shiteki bōryoku to kōteki bitoku." In *Shūen bunka to mibunsei*, edited by Wakita Haruko, Martin Collcutt, and Taira Masayuki, 111–35. Kyoto: Shibunkaku Shuppan, 2005.

Hozumi Nobushige (ed.). *Goningumi seidoron.* Third edition. Hozumi Shōgaku Zaidan, 1937.

Hübner, Regina Beate. "State Medicine and the State of Medicine in Japan: *Kōkei Saikyūhō* (1791), an Emergency Handbook Initiated by the Bakufu." Ph.D. diss., Cambridge University, 2014.

Hüchtker, Dietlind. *"Elende Mütter" und "liederliche Weibspersonen": Geschlechterverhältnisse und Armenpolitik in Berlin (1770–1850).* Münster: Westfälisches Dampfboot, 1999.

Hur, Nam-Lin. *Prayer and Play in Tokugawa Japan: Asakusa Sensōji and Edo Society.* Cambridge, MA: Harvard University Asia Center, 2000.

"Iburaku ikkan." In *Nihon shomin seikatsu shiryō shūsei*, vol. 14: Buraku, edited by Tanikawa Ken'ichi, 531–65. San'ichi Shobō, 1971.

Ikai Shūhei. *Byōin no seiki no riron.* Yūhikaku, 2010.

Ikeda Yoshimasa. *Nihon shakai fukushishi.* Kyoto: Hōritsu Bunkasha, 1986.

————. "Nihon zenkindai ni okeru shakai fukushi no kōzō—Nihon shakai fukushishi josetsu." *Shakai fukushigaku* 24:1 (1983): 117–43.

————. "Ono Jizen'in no seiritsu." *Kyoto Furitsu Daigaku gakujutsu hōkoku/jinbun* 41 (1989): 21–54.

————. "Onshi Zaidan Saiseikai no seiritsu." In *Kindai Nihon shakai to shisō*, edited by Gotō Yasushi, 135–82. Yoshikawa Kōbunkan, 1992.

————. "Ryūmin atsumesho kara kyūmin jusansho e." *Buraku mondai kenkyū* 74 (1982): 70–93.

Ikeda Yoshimasa and Ikemoto Miwako. *Nihon fukushishi kōgi.* Osaka: Takasuga Shuppan, 2002.

Ikegami, Eiko. *Bonds of Civility: Aesthetics and the Political Origins of Japanese Culture.* Cambridge: Cambridge University Press, 2005.

Imanishi Hajime. "Bunmei kaika to sabetsu." *Buraku mondai kenkyū* 132 (1995): 129–51.

————. "Bunmeika to 'Ushikubi kojiki.'" In *Bakumatsu/Meiji-ki no kokumin kokka keisei to bunka hen'yō*, edited by Nishikawa Nagao and Matsumiya Hideharu, 345–74. Shin'yōsha, 1995.

Inaba Mitsuhiko. *Kyūmin kyūjo seido no kenkyū: Teikoku gikai kaisetsu izen-shi.* Keiō Tsūshin, 1992.

Inoue Tomoichi. *Kyūsai seido yōgi.* Hakubunkan, 1909.

Inoue Yokushō. *Shintei Echizen no kuni meisekikō.* Edited by Sugihara Takeo. Fukui: Matsumi Bunko, 1980.

Ioka Yasutoki. "Hininban e no kyūmai ni kansuru ichi shiryō o megutte." *Regional* (Journal of the Nara Kenritsu Dōwa Mondai Kankei Shiryō Center) 7 (2007): 10–18.

Ishii Ryōsuke. *Edo no senmin.* 1988; Akashi Shoten, 2012.

Ishikawa Michigorō. "Shinchō kazenroku." In *Ōno shishi*, vol. 6: Shiryō sōkatsu-hen, 334–61. Ōno-shi, 1985.

Iwaji Yūichi. *Ōno-han no yōgaku.* Ōno: printed by author, 1984.

Izumi sonshi. Edited by Izumi-mura. Izumi: Izumi-mura Yakuba, 1977.

Jannetta, Ann. *The Vaccinators: Smallpox, Medical Knowledge, and the "Opening" of Japan.* Stanford, CA: Stanford University Press, 2007.

Jippensha Ikku. *Muda shugyō kane no waraji.* Edited by Imai Kingo. Ōzorasha, 1999.

———. *Shank's Mare.* Translated by Thomas Satchell. Boston: Tuttle, 2001.

Jizen kyūsai shiryō. Edited by Tsuji Zennosuke. Kinkōdō Shoseki, 1932.

Jōetsu shishi. Tsūshi-hen 7: Minzoku. Edited by Jōetsu Shishi Hensan Iinkai. Jōetsu: Jōetsu-shi, 2004.

Jütte, Robert. *Poverty and Deviance in Early Modern Europe.* Cambridge: Cambridge University Press, 1994.

Kaidō Shizuka. "Ōno-machi yōdome ni miru beika no hensen." *Kenshi shiryō* 5 (1995): 25–36.

Kalland, Arne. *Fishing Villages in Tokugawa Japan.* Richmond, UK: Curzon, 1995.

Kalland, Arne, and Jon Pedersen. "Famine and Population in Fukuoka Domain During the Tokugawa Period." *Journal of Japanese Studies* 10:1 (1984): 31–72.

Kanda Yuzuki. "Ameuri shōnin." In *Akinai no ba to shakai* (Shirīzu kinsei no mibunteki shūen 4), edited by Yoshida Nobuyuki, 203–33. Yoshikawa Kōbunkan, 2000.

Kankoku kōgiroku. 3 vols. Annotated by Sugano Noriko. Tōkyōdō Shuppan, 1999.

Karlsson, Anders. "Famine Relief, Social Order, and State Performance in Late Chosŏn Korea." *Journal of Korean Studies* 12:1 (2007): 111–41.

Kasahara Hakuō. *Hakushinki: Hakushin yō ōraidome.* Fukui: Fukui-ken Ishikai, 1997.

Katō Yasuaki. "Kinsei no shōgaisha to mibun seido." In *Nihon no kinsei,* vol. 7: Mibun to kakushiki, edited by Asao Naohiro, 125–78. Chūō Kōronsha, 1992.

———. *Nihon mōjin shakaishi kenkyū.* Miraisha, 1974.

Katsuyama shishi. Shiryō-hen 1: Hanchō/machikata. Edited by Katsuyama-shi. Katsuyama: Katsuyama-shi, 1977.

Katsuyama shishi. Vol. 1: Fūdo to rekishi. Edited by Katsuyama Shishi Hensan Iinkai. Katsuyama: Katsuyama-shi, 1974.

Katsuyama shishi. Vol. 2: Genshi-Kinsei. Edited by Katsuyama Shishi Hensan Iinkai. Katsuyama: Katsuyama-shi, 2006.

Kawamura Kihō. *Kafuku ninpitsu.* Osaka and Kyoto, 1809. British Museum. http://www.britishmuseum.org/research/collection_online/collection_object_details.aspx?objectId=778709&partId=1&searchText=kawamura+kiho&page=1.

Kawato Masato. "Kinsei hisabetsumin no seikatsu to shisō—Tokushima-han o chūshin to shite." *Naruto shigaku* 1 (1987): 133–66.

Kelly, William. *Deference and Defiance in Nineteenth-Century Japan.* Princeton, NJ: Princeton University Press, 1985.

Kenshōbo: Tosa-han hōsei shiryō. Edited by Kōchi Kenritsu Toshokan. Kōchi: Kōchi Kenritsu Toshokan, 1985.

Kikuchi Isao. *Kikin kara yomu kinsei shakai.* Azekura Shobō, 2003.

———. *Kikin no shakaishi.* Azekura Shobō, 1994.

———. *Kinsei no kikin.* Yoshikawa Kōbunkan, 1997.

Kinugasa Yasuyoshi. "Kinsei ni okeru mibunsei shisō to kisen jōe-kan." *Buraku mondai kenkyū* 68 (1981): 18–36.

Kinzley, W. Dean. "Japan's Discovery of Poverty: Changing Views of Poverty and Social Welfare in the Nineteenth Century." *Journal of Asian History* 22:1 (1988): 1–24.

Kishino Toshihiko (ed.). *Owari-han shakai no sōgō kenkyū.* 5 vols. Osaka: Seibundō, 2001–12.

Kishū-han Rōbangashira-ke Monjo Hensankai (ed.). *Jōkamachi keisatsu nikki.* Osaka: Seibundō, 2003.

Kitahara Itoko. *Toshi to hinkon no shakaishi—Edo kara Tokyo e.* Yoshikawa Kōbunkan, 1995.

Kizaki Tekisō. "Shūsui zatsuwa." In *Shūsui zatsuwa/Wakasakō.* Annotated and introduced by Norimoto Yoshihiro. Fukui: Fukui-ken Kyōdoshi Kondankai, 1974.

Kobata Atsushi. "Kinsei no Omodani dōzan ni tsuite." *Fukui kenshi kenkyū* 1 (1984): 2–26.

Kobayashi Takehiro. "Bakumatsu ishinki no toshi shakai—Toshi gyōsei no hen'yō to machi bugyōsho yoriki." In *Toshi no mibun ganbō,* edited by Usami Hideki and Yabuta Tōru, 181–211. Yoshikawa Kōbunkan, 2010.

Koikawa Harumachi. "Kinkin sensei eiga no yume." In *Early Modern Japanese Literature: An Anthology, 1600–1900, Abridged,* edited by Haruo Shirane, 321–35. New York: Columbia University Press, 2008.

Kondō Yoshihiro. *Shikoku henro.* Ōfūsha, 1971.

Konishi, Sho. "The Emergence of an International Humanitarian Organization in Japan: The Tokugawa Origins of the Japanese Red Cross." *American Historical Review* 119:4 (2014): 1129–53.

Koseki Yūichirō. *"Meikun" no kinsei—Gakumon/chishiki to hansei kaikaku.* Yoshikawa Kōbunkan, 2012.

Kouamé, Nathalie. "Le pèlerinage de Shikoku pendant l'époque d'Edo: Mythes et réalités de la pratique du settai." In *Japon Pluriel* 4. Actes du quatrième colloque de la SFEJ, edited by Nadine Lucas and Cécile Sakai, 221–28. Arles: Picquier, 2001.

———. *Pèlerinage et Société dans le Japon des Tokugawa: Le Pèlerinage de Shikoku entre 1598 et 1868.* Paris: École Française d'Extrême-Orient, 2001.

———. "Shikoku's Local Authorities and Henro During the Golden Age of the Pilgrimage." *Japanese Journal of Religious Studies* 24:3–4 (1997): 413–27.

Kōzai Toyoko. "Ainu wa naze 'yama ni nigeta' ka? Bakumatsu Ezochi ni okeru 'wagakuni saisho no kyōsei shutō' no okuyuki." *Shisō* 1017 (2009): 78–101.

———. "Yobō sesshu to iu 'eisei'—Shutō no rekishi no hanshō kara." *Gendai shisō* 38:3 (2010): 216–31.

Kujirai Chisato. "Sendai hanryō no 'raijin-goya' ni tsuite." *Tōhoku Gakuin Daigaku Tōhoku Bunka Kenkyūjo kiyō* 36:11 (2004): 11–38.

Kurihara Ken'ichi. "Kinsei bikō chochiku no keisei to sonraku shakai—Tsuchiura-han 'shūkoku' o chūshin ni." *Kantō kinseishi kenkyū* 63 (2007): 3–33.

Kuriyama Shigehisa. "Fukushin: Some Observations on Economic Development and the Imagination of the Body in Japanese Medicine of the Edo Period." In *Two Faces of the Early Modern World: The Netherlands and Japan in the 17th and 18th Centuries,* edited by Shirahata Yozaburo and W. J. Boot, 47–58. Kyoto: International Research Center for Japanese Studies, 2001.

Kuroda Toshio. *Nihon chūsei no kokka to shūkyō*. Iwanami Shoten, 1975.

Kurushima Hiroshi and Yoshida Nobuyuki (eds.). *Kinsei no shakai shūdan—Yuisho to gensetsu*. Yamakawa Shuppansha, 1995.

Kusayama Iwao. "Sonraku keisatsu-ri hininban ni tsuite—Osaka shikasho to Setsu-Ban ryōgoku murakata no kinchō kankei o jiku to shite." Two parts. *Chiikishi kenkyū* 19:3 (1990): 1–33 and 20:1 (1990): 1–25.

Leupp, Gary P. *Servants, Shophands, and Laborers in the Cities of Tokugawa Japan*. Princeton, NJ: Princeton University Press, 1992.

Li, Lillian. *Fighting Famine in North China: State, Market, and Environmental Decline, 1690s–1990s*. Stanford, CA: Stanford University Press, 2007.

Lu, Hanchao. *Street Criers: A Cultural History of Chinese Beggars*. Stanford, CA: Stanford University Press, 2005.

Lust, Commerce, and Corruption: An Account of What I Have Seen and Heard, by an Edo Samurai, edited and introduced by Mark Teeuwen and Kate Wildman Nakai. New York: Columbia University Press, 2014.

Machida Tetsu. *Kinsei Izumi no chiiki shakai kōzō*. Yamakawa Shuppansha, 2004.

———. "Kinsei kōki Awa ni okeru 'takoku mukitte/uron-mono' tōsei to Shikoku henro—Uchimawari/ban-hinin/osukuigoya." *Buraku mondai kenkyū* 193 (2010): 39–104.

Mae Keiichi. "Yamato ni okeru 'hininban-kyū' shiryō." Two parts. *Buraku mondai kenkyū* 56 (1978): 81–93 and 58 (1978): 88–100.

Maehara Yumiko. "Kyōhō kaikaku-ki Kyoto ni okeru haraimai to beika seisaku." *Hisutoria* 116 (1987): 20–40.

Makihara Norio. *Kyakubun to kokumin no aida—Kindai minshū no seiji ishiki*. Yoshikawa Kōbunkan, 1998.

Matsumoto Eiko. "Kinsei shakai ni okeru zatō/koze [*sic*] no kōsatsu—Tosa/Awa o chūshin ni." *Naruto shigaku* 6 (1992): 53–70.

Matsumoto Sannosuke. "The Idea of Heaven: A Tokugawa Foundation for Natural Rights Theory." In *Japanese Thought in the Tokugawa Period, 1600–1868: Methods and Metaphors*, edited by Tetsuo Najita and Irwin Scheiner, 181–99. Chicago: University of Chicago Press, 1978.

Matsuo Kenji. *Chūsei no toshi to hinin*. Kyoto: Hōzōkan, 1998.

Matsuyama Yōko. "Uchiyama Kaisuke no jinbutsuzō." In *Monogashira-yaku tsutomekata tehikae kaidoku*, edited by Ōno Komonjokai, 119–36. Ōno: Ōno Komonjokai, 2011.

Matsuzaki Noriko. "Kumamoto jōkamachi ni okeru kyūmin no kyūsai to shakai hoshō." *Kumamoto shigaku* 93/94 (2011): 59–83.

Matsuzawa Yūsaku. *Meiji chihō jichitaisei no kigen—Kinsei shakai no kiki to seido hen'yō*. Tokyo Daigaku Shuppankai, 2009.

Maus, Tanya. "Rising Up and Saving the World: Ishii Jūji and the Ethics of Social Relief during the Mid-Meiji Period (1880–1887)." *Japan Review* 25 (2013): 67–87.

McClain, James L. "Edobashi: Power, Space, and Popular Culture in Edo." In *Edo and Paris: Urban Life and the State in the Early Modern Era*, edited by James L. McClain, John M. Merriman, and Ugawa Kaoru, 105–31. Ithaca, NY: Cornell University Press, 1994.

———. "Failed Expectations: Kaga Domain on the Eve of the Meiji Restoration." *Journal of Japanese Studies* 14:2 (1988): 403–47.

———. *Kanazawa: A Seventeenth-Century Japanese Castle Town*. New Haven, CT: Yale University Press, 1982.

———. "Local Politics and National Integration: The Fukui Prefectural Assembly in the 1880s." *Monumenta Nipponica* 31:1 (1976): 51–75.

McClain, James L., John M. Merriman, and Ugawa Kaoru (eds.). *Edo and Paris: Urban Life and the State in the Early Modern Era*. Ithaca, NY: Cornell University Press, 1994.

McClain, James L., and Wakita Osamu (eds.). *Osaka: The Merchant's Capital of Early Modern Japan*. Ithaca, NY: Cornell University Press, 1999.

McCormack, Noah Y. *Japan's Outcaste Abolition*. Abingdon: Routledge, 2013.

Mencius. *The Works of Mencius*. Translated by James Legge. New York: Dover Publications, 1970.

Metzler, Mark. "Policy Space, Polarities, and Regimes." In *Economic Thought in Early Modern Japan*, edited by Bettina Gramlich-Oka and Gregory Smits, 217–50. Leiden: Brill, 2010.

Mibunteki shūen to kinsei shakai. 9 vols. Yoshikawa Kōbunkan, 2006–2008.

Mieda Akiko. "Chūsei inu jinin no sonzai keitai." *Buraku mondai kenkyū* 162 (2002): 2–34.

Mikami Kazuo. "Hyakushō ikki no shitsuteki tenkan ni tsuite—Meiwa no Echizen daiikki no kaimei o chūshin ni." Two parts. *Rekishi kyōiku* 15:11 (1967): 83–93 and 15:12 (1967): 97–101.

———. *Meiji shonen Shinshū monto dai-kekki no kenkyū*. Kyoto: Shibunkaku Shuppan, 1987.

———. "Nihon kindaika to Shinshū chitai no seikaku—Meiji-ki Echizen chihō no jirei yori." *Fukui kenshi kenkyū* 6 (1989): 1–32.

Minami Kazuo. "Bakumatsu Edo chōnin no fukushi shisetsu setsuritsu negai—'Shichū torishimari zoku-ruishū' o chūshin to shite." *Sankō shoshi kenkyū* 51 (1999/10): 1–27.

———. *Edo no shakai kōzō*. Hanawa Shobō, 1969.

Minegishi Kentarō. "Kegare kannen to buraku sabetsu (ge)—Sono fukabunsei to kegare kannen no ichi." *Buraku mondai kenkyū* 162 (2002): 97–119.

———. *Kinsei hisabetsuminshi no kenkyū*. Azekura Shobō, 1996.

———. "Kinsei senminsei no kiso kōzō." *Buraku mondai kenkyū* 89 (1986): 78–111.

Mishima Saiichi. *The History of Ophthalmology in Japan*. Oostende: Wayenborgh, 2004.

Miwa Kiken. "Kyūga taii." In *Nihon keizai sōsho*, vol. 6, edited by Takimoto Seiichi, 449–58. Nihon Keizai Sōsho Kankōkai, 1914.

Miyachi Masato. *Nichiro sengo seijishi no kenkyū—Teikoku shugi keiseiki no toshi to nōson*. Tokyo Daigaku Shuppankai, 1973.

Miyamae Chikako. "'Raijingoya' no kanjin to chiiki shakai." *Buraku kaihō kenkyū* 197 (2013): 16–29.

Miyamoto Tsuneichi. "Shiramine sonki." In *Echizen Itoshiro minzokushi/sono hoka* (Miyamoto Tsuneichi chosakushū 36), 131–67. Miraisha, 1992.

Miyamoto Tsuneichi et al. (eds.). *Nihon zankoku monogatari.* Vol. 1: Mazushiki hito-bito no mure. Heibonsha, 1959.

Miyanaga Takashi. *Bakumatsu ken'ō shisetsudan.* Kōdansha, 2006.

Moll-Murata, Christine. "Chinese Guilds from the Seventeenth to the Twentieth Centuries: An Overview." *International Review of Social History* 53 (2008): 213–47.

Monbushō Futsū Gakumukyoku. *Honchō mōjinden.* 1919; Ōzorasha, 1987.

Mori Osamu. *Nihon mōjinshi-kō—Shiryoku shōgaisha no rekishi to denshō, kinzoku to katamegami.* Tottori: Yonago Imai Shoten, 1993.

Morishita Tōru. *Bushi to iu mibun—Jōkamachi Hagi no daimyō kashindan.* Yoshikawa Kōbunkan, 2012.

———. "Hagi-han no meakashi to autorō sekai." In *Mibunteki shūen to buraku mondai no chiikishiteki kenkyū,* edited by Machida Tetsu and Takenaga Mitsuo, 189–218. Kyoto: Buraku Mondai Kenkyūjo, 2016.

———. "Mibunteki shūen no keifu to hōhō." *Buraku mondai kenkyū* 161 (2002): 2–17.

———. "Tsushima no kakaekudashimono to toshi kasō shakai." *Buraku mondai kenkyū* 168 (2004): 27–61.

Motojima Chishin. *Getsudō kenmonshū.* Vols. 2–4 of *Zoku Nihon zuihitsu taisei bekkan: Kinsei fūzoku kenmonshū.* Yoshikawa Kōbunkan, 1981–82.

Motokawa Mikio. "Jūhasseiki Echizen ni okeru hōkensei no tenkan—Hyakushō ikki no tenkai to Fukui-han no taiō kara." *Fukui-ken chiikishi kenkyū* 3 (1972): 58–88.

Mueller, Doreen. "Documenting Disaster in Japanese Painting: The Case of the Tenpō Era Famine (1833–39) and Its Legacy." Ph.D. diss., University of London, 2016.

Murakami Kazue. "Kinsei ni okeru kyūsai no sōgo fujoteki seikaku no ichi kōsatsu—Komatsu-han Kaisho Nikki yukidaore no kiroku yori." MA thesis, Ehime University, 1995.

Nagai Akiko. "Chikuzen/Chikugo no mōsō shūdan to sono shūhen." In *Mibunteki shūen,* edited by Tsukada Takashi, Yoshida Nobuyuki, and Wakita Osamu, 255–93. Kyoto: Buraku Mondai Kenkyūjo, 1994.

Nagami Shigeo. "Echizen Ōno no kadozuke geinō—Harugoma to Ōno machizukushi to fukubukuro." *Okuetsu shiryō* 29 (2000): 72–82.

Naitō Jirō. "Bakuhanki shomin ryokō to sono hogo shisetsu—Yukidaore to muraokuri ni tsuite." *Nihon rekishi* 175 (1962): 17–25.

Najita Tetsuo. *Ordinary Economies in Japan: A Historical Perspective, 1750–1950.* Berkeley: University of California Press, 2009.

———. *Visions of Virtue in Tokugawa Japan: The Kaitokudō Merchant Academy of Osaka.* Chicago: University of Chicago Press, 1987.

Nakagawa Miyuki. "Bakumatsu/Meiji shoki no junzai zatō ni kansuru nōto." *Nara Kenritsu Dōwa Mondai Kankei Shiryō Sentā kenkyū kiyō* 7 (2000): 127–38.

———. "Chiiki shakai to junzainin—Tenpō-ki Yamato no kuni no junzai zatō torishimari o megutte." *Nara Kenritsu Dōwa Mondai Kankei Shiryō Sentā kenkyū kiyō* 3 (1996): 79–106.

———. "Junzai zatō no katsudō o meguru chiiki shakai no ichi dōkō." *Nara Kenritsu Dōwa Mondai Kankei Shiryō Sentā kenkyū kiyō* 1 (1994): 9–19.

———. "Kinsei ni okeru tōdō soshin denshō no hen'yō—Kamo-sha to Kōkō tennō o megutte." *Nara Kenritsu Dōwa Mondai Kankei Shiryō Sentā kenkyū kiyō* 4 (1997): 94–111.

———. "Kinsei ni okeru tōdō soshin denshō no hen'yō (sono ni)—Kōkō tennō kara Amayo miko e." *Nara Kenritsu Dōwa Mondai Kankei Shiryō Sentā kenkyū kiyō* 5 (1998): 71–96.

———. "Zatō shukusen ni kansuru kenkyū nōto—Zatō to jiin no sōron." *Nara Kenritsu Dōwa Mondai Kankei Shiryō Sentā kenkyū kiyō* 6 (1999): 113–24.

———. "Zatō shukusen o meguru chiiki shakai no dōkō." *Nara Kenritsu Dōwa Mondai Kankei Shiryō Sentā kenkyū kiyō* 2 (1995): 101–12.

Nakagawa Sugane. "Utajamisen no shūhen." In *Mibunteki shūen*, edited by Tsukada Takashi, Yoshida Nobuyuki, and Wakita Osamu, 461–87. Kyoto: Buraku Mondai Kenkyūjo, 1994.

———. *Nikkan mōsō no shakaishi*. Fukuoka: Ashi Shobō, 2002.

Nakaizumi Yukimasa. "Meiji-zen Nihon gankashi." In *Meiji-zen Nihon igakushi*, vol. 4, 211–433. Nihon Gakujutsu Shinkōkai, 1964.

Nakamura, Karen. *Deaf in Japan: Signing and the Politics of Identity*. Ithaca, NY: Cornell University Press, 2006.

Nakamura Tekisai. *Kinmō zui*. Kyoto: Yamagataya, 1666. National Diet Library Digital Collections. http://dl.ndl.go.jp/info:ndljp/pid/2569350?itemId=info%3Andljp%2Fpid%2F2569350&__lang=en.

Nakayama Tarō. *Nihon mōjinshi*. 2 vols. Yagi Shoten, 1965.

Namase Katsumi. "Hoshō: Kin-gendai no 'shikaku shōgaisha' o megutte." In Ōkuma Miyoshi, *Mōjin no seikatsu*, revised and with an afterword by Namase Katsumi, 221–43. Yūzankaku, 1998.

———. *Kinsei Nihon no shōgaisha to minshū*. San'ichi Shobō, 1989.

———. *Nihon no shōgaisha no rekishi*. Kinsei-hen. Akashi Shoten, 1999.

Namikawa Kenji. *Kinsei Hokuō shakai to minshū*. Yoshikawa Kōbunkan, 2005.

Nesaki Mitsuo. *Shōrui awaremi no sekai*. Dōseisha, 2006.

Nihon chimei daijiten. Vol. 18: Fukui-ken. Kadokawa Shoten, 1989.

Nihon jinmei daijiten. Heibonsha, 1979.

Nihon kokugo daijiten. Shōgakkan, 2006.

Nishida Kaoru. "Miko." In *Minkan ni ikiru shūkyōsha* (Shirīzu kinsei no mibunteki shūen 1), edited by Takano Toshihiko, 51–90. Yoshikawa Kōbunkan, 2000.

Nishimura Kazue. "Kinsei Osaka sangō ie ukenin nakama ni tsuite." In *Kinsei Osaka no toshi kūkan to shakai kōzō*, edited by Tsukada Takashi and Yoshida Nobuyuki, 245–88. Yamakawa Shuppansha, 2001.

———. "Kinsei Osaka sangō ie ukenin nakama no tenkai katei—Kashiya-uke no sokumen o chūshin to shite." In *Nenpō toshishi kenkyū*, vol. 10: Dentō toshi to mibunteki shūen, edited by Toshishi Kenkyūkai, 98–113. Yamakawa Shuppansha, 2002.

Nobi Shōji. "Kōiki hininban-sei no tenkai to muramura no teikō." Two parts. *Chiikishi kenkyū* 17:2 (1988): 1–36 and 17:3 (1988): 1–21.

———. "Murakata hininban no seiritsu." *Chiikishi kenkyū* 16:3 (1987): 1–38.

Noda Senkōin. "Nihon kubu shugyō nikki" (excerpt). In *Ōno shishi*, vol. 6: Shiryō sōkatsu-hen, 756–61. Ōno-shi, 1985.

Nojiri Yasuhiro. *Kinsei Nihon no shihai kōzō to han chiiki.* Yoshikawa Kōbunkan, 2014.
Norman, E. H. "Japan's Emergence as a Modern State." In *Origins of the Modern Japanese State: Selected Writings of E.H. Norman*, edited and with an introduction by John W. Dower. New York: Pantheon Books, 1975.

Obinata Sumio. "Bakumatsu/ishinki ni okeru mibunsei no kaitai to kindai keisatsu no seiritsu." *Buraku mondai kenkyū* 132 (1995): 113–28.
O'Brien, Martin, and Sue Penna. *Theorising Welfare: Enlightenment and Modern Society.* London: SAGE Publications, 1998.
Ofuregaki Tenmei shūsei. Third edition. Edited by Takayanagi Shinzō and Ishii Ryōsuke. Iwanami Shoten, 1976.
Ogawa Kazunari. *Bokumin no shisō—Edo no chisha ishiki.* Heibonsha, 2008.
Ogura Osanaga. *Uchinamigawa ryūiki no dezukuri seido to ayumi.* Ōno: printed by author, 2000.
Ogyū Sorai. "Benmei." In *Nihon shisō taikei*, vol. 36, 37–185. Iwanami Shoten, 1973.
Ogyu Sorai's Discourse on Government (Seidan): An Annotated Translation. Translated by Olof G. Lidin. Wiesbaden: Harrassowitz Verlag, 1999.
Ōishi Kyūkei. *Jikata hanreiroku.* 2 vols. Revised and enlarged by Ōishi Shinkei, edited by Ōishi Shinzaburō. Kondō Shuppansha, 1984.
Okamoto Ryōichi. *Ran/ikki/hinin.* Kashiwa Shobō, 1983.
Okayama-han Kenkyūkai (ed.). *Han sekai no ishiki to kankei.* Iwata Shoin, 2000.
Ōno chōshi. 5 vols. Edited by Ōno Chōshi Hensankai. Ōno: Ōno Chōshi Hensankai, 1954–57.
Ōno-gun Kyōikukai. *Ōno gunshi.* 2 vols. 1912; Meicho Shuppan, 1972.
Ōno no ayumi. Kaiteiban. Edited by "Ōno no ayumi" Kaiteiban Henshū Iinkai and Ōno-shi Kyōiku Iinkai. Ōno: Ōno-shi, 2004.
Ōno-shi Kyōiku Iinkai (ed). *Do ni ikita Ozaki Kindō.* Ōno: Ōno Shiyakusho, 1981.
Ōno-shi Rekishi Minzoku Shiryōkan (ed.). *Ezu ga kataru Ōno: Ōno shisei 40-shūnen kinen tokubetsuten kaisetsu zuroku.* Ōno: Ōno-shi Rekishi Minzoku Shiryōkan, 1994.
Ōno shishi. Vol. 1: Shaji monjo-hen. Edited by Ōno Shishi Hensan Iinkai. Ōno: Ōno Shiyakusho, 1978.
———. Vol. 3: Shoke monjo-hen 2. Edited by Ōno Shishi Hensan Iinkai. Ōno: Ōno Shiyakusho, 1981.
———. Vol. 5: Hansei shiryō-hen 2. Edited by Ōno Shishi Hensan Iinkai. Ōno: Ōno Shiyakusho, 1984.
———. Vol. 6: Shiryō sōkatsu-hen. Edited by Ōno Shishi Hensan Iinkai. Ōno: Ōno Shiyakusho, 1985.
———. Vol. 8: Chiku-hen. Edited by Ōno Shishi Hensan Iinkai. Ōno: Ōno Shiyakusho, 1991.
———. Vol. 9: Yōdome-hen (YH). Edited by Ōno Shishi Hensan Iinkai. Ōno: Ōno Shiyakusho, 1995.
———. Vol. 10: Shinbun shiryō-hen. Edited by Ōno Shishi Hensan Iinkai. Ōno: Ōno Shiyakusho, 2000.
———. Vol. 13: Minzoku-hen. Edited by Ōno Shishi Hensan Iinkai. Ōno: Ōno Shiyakusho, 2008.

————. Vol. 14: Tsūshi-hen (ge), Kindai/gendai. Edited by Ōno-shi. Ōno: Ōno Shiyakusho, 2013.

Ono Shō. "Mibunsei shakairon to iu shikaku." *Rekishi hyōron* 564 (1997): 89–102.

Ooms, Herman. *Tokugawa Village Practice: Class, Status, Power, Law.* Berkeley: University of California Press, 1996.

Orikuchi Shinobu. "Kokubungaku no hassei (dai-san-kō)—Marebito no igi." In *Orikuchi Shinobu zenshū*, vol. 1, edited by Orikuchi Shinobu Zenshū Kankōkai, 3–62. Chūō Kōronsha, 1972.

Osaka hennenshi. Vol. 6. Edited by Osaka Shiritsu Chūō Toshokan Shishi Henshūshitsu. Osaka: Osaka Shiritsu Chūō Toshokan, 1969.

Osaka shishi. Vol. 3. Edited by Osaka-shi Sanjikai. Osaka: Osaka-shi Sanjikai, 1911.

Ota chōshi. Shiryō-hen (chū). Edited by Ota Chōshi Hensan Iinkai. Ota: Ota-chō, 1996.

Ōyama Kyōhei. *Nihon chūsei nōsonshi no kenkyū.* Iwanami Shoten, 1978.

Platt, Brian. *Burning and Building: Schooling and State Formation in Japan, 1750–1890.* Cambridge, MA: Harvard University Asia Center, 2004.

Pomeranz, Kenneth. "Skills, 'Guilds', and Development: Asking Epstein's Questions to East Asian Institutions." In *Technology, Skills and the Pre-modern Economy in the East and the West: Essays Dedicated to the Memory of S.R. Epstein*, edited by Maarten Prak and Jan Juiten van Zanden, 93–127. Leiden: Brill, 2013.

Pons, Philippe. *Misère et Crime au Japon: du XVIIe Siècle à Nos Jours.* Paris: Gallimard, 1999.

————. "Ordre marginal dans le Japon moderne (17e–20e siècle): les voyous canalisateurs de l'errance." *Annales: Histoire, Sciences Sociales* 51:5 (1996): 1155–78.

Porter, John. "Meiji shoki Osaka ni okeru hinmin no kyūsai to tōsei." In *Kinsei mibun shakai no hikakushi—Hō to shakai no shiten kara*, edited by Tsukada Takashi, Saga Ashita, and Yagi Shigeru, 323–44. Osaka: Seibundō, 2014.

————. "Meiji shoki Tokyo ni okeru hinmin no kyūsai to tōsei." *Buraku mondai kenkyū* 211 (2015): 89–112.

————. "Tokyo no hinin shūdan no kaitai katei to kaitai-go ni okeru kojiki tōsei." In *Mibunteki shūen to buraku mondai no chiikishiteki kenkyū*, edited by Machida Tetsu and Takenaga Mitsuo, 219–56. Kyoto: Buraku Mondai Kenkyūjo, 2016.

Pratt, Edward. *Japan's Protoindustrial Elite: The Economic Foundations of the Gōnō.* Cambridge, MA: Harvard University Asia Center, 1999.

Pyle, Kenneth. "The Technology of Japanese Nationalism: The Local Improvement Movement, 1900–1918." *Journal of Asian Studies* 33:1 (1973): 51–65.

Ravina, Mark J. "Confucian Banking: The Community Granary (Shasō) in Rhetoric and Practice." In *Economic Thought in Early Modern Japan*, edited by Bettina Gramlich-Oka and Gregory Smits, 179–204. Leiden: Brill, 2010.

————. *Land and Lordship in Early Modern Japan.* Stanford, CA: Stanford University Press, 1999.

Roberts, Luke S. *Mercantilism in a Japanese Domain: The Merchant Origins of Economic Nationalism in 18th-Century Tosa.* Cambridge: Cambridge University Press, 1998.

————. *Performing the Great Peace: Political Space and Open Secrets in Tokugawa Japan.* Honolulu: University of Hawai'i Press, 2012.

Rotermund, Hartmut O. *Pèlerinage au neuf sommets: Carnet de route d'un religieux itinérant dans le Japon du XIXe siècle.* Paris: CNRS, 1983.

Rowe, William T. *Hankow: Commerce and Society in a Chinese City, 1796–1889.* Stanford, CA: Stanford University Press, 1984.

————. *Hankow: Conflict and Community in a Chinese City, 1796–1895.* Stanford, CA: Stanford University Press, 1989.

————. "Social Stability and Social Change." In *The Cambridge History of China,* vol. 9, part one: *The Ch'ing Empire to 1800,* edited by Willard J. Peterson, 473–562. Cambridge: Cambridge University Press, 2002.

Ruggiu, François-Joseph. "Mibun gainen to atarashii shakaishi—Anshian rejīmu-ki no Furansu to Edo jidai no Nihon." Translated by Takeshita Kazuaki. *Shisō* 1084: Kōsa suru Nihon kinseishi—Nichifutsu no taiwa kara (2014): 109–25.

Saitō Hiroko. "Kinsei Izumi no sonraku shakai ni okeru 'konkyūnin' kyūsai—Izumi-gun Ikegami-mura o chūshin ni." In *Kinsei mibun shakai no hikakushi—Hō to shakai no shiten kara,* edited by Tsukada Takashi, Saga Ashita, and Yagi Shigeru, 293–321. Osaka: Seibundō, 2014.

Saitō Shūsuke. *Ozaki Yaemon (Kindō)-den.* Fukui: Privately printed, 1966.

Saitō Shūsuke et al. (eds.). *Okuetsu bunka.* Vol. 7: Yōsui shiryō-hen. Ōno: Ōno-shi Kyōiku Iinkai/Bunkazai Hogo Iinkai, 1967.

Sakaguchi Yuki. "Izumi no kuni zaikata hininban ni tsuite." *Buraku mondai kenkyū* 165 (2003): 2–83.

Sakata Tamako. *Echizen Ōno ikki.* Ōno: Fukui-ken Ōno-shi Kyōiku Iinkai, 1972.

————. "Hanten 'Ōnoya' no kenkyū." *Okuetsu shiryō* 6 (1977): 1–105.

————. "Jōkamachi no seiritsu to yonhyakunen no keika." *Okuetsu shiryō* 12 (1983): 42–60.

————. "Jōkamachi Ōno no dōro to machikado no yagō." *Okuetsu shiryō* 16 (1987): 45–67.

————. "Miryoku aru hanshu Toshiyoshi [*sic*] ni tsuite—Shomin ga zendai mimon no ikki sawagi o okoshita." *Okuetsu shiryō* 13 (1984): 101–27.

————. *Ōno machi ezu.* Ōno-shi: Fumi no Kai, 1975.

Saku Takashi. *Echizen no kuni shūmon ninbetsu on-aratamechō.* Vols. 2 and 3. Yoshikawa Kōbunkan, 1968–69.

Satō Nobuhiro. "Yōzō kaikuron." In *Nihon keizai taiten,* vol. 18, edited by Takimoto Seiichi, 53–109. Keimeisha, 1929.

Satsuyō Shinbun. Fukui: Asuwa-ken Kappankyoku, 1872. Fukui Kenritsu Toshokan.

Sawa Hirokatsu. "Kinsei no chiiki chitsujo keisei to shūkyō." *Rekishi hyōron* 635 (2003): 36–52.

————. "Nihon ni okeru shūkyōteki tairitsu to kyōzon—Kinsei o chūshin ni." *Rekishigaku kenkyū* 808 (2005): 2–13.

Schak, David C. *A Chinese Beggar's Den: Poverty and Mobility in an Underclass Community.* Pittsburgh: University of Pittsburgh Press, 1988.

Scheiner, Irwin. "Benevolent Lords and Honorable Peasants: Rebellion and Peasant Consciousness in Tokugawa Japan." In *Japanese Thought in the Tokugawa Period, 1600–1868: Methods and Metaphors*, edited by Tetsuo Najita and Irwin Scheiner, 39–62. Chicago: University of Chicago Press, 1978.

Scott, James. *Weapons of the Weak: Everyday Forms of Peasant Resistance*. New Haven, CT: Yale University Press, 1985.

Screech, Timon. *The Lens Within the Heart: The Western Scientific Gaze and Popular Imagery in Later Edo Japan*. Richmond, UK: Curzon, 2002.

Selden, Kyoko, and Joshua Young. "Hinin Taiheiki: The Paupers' Chronicle of Peace." *Review of Japanese Culture and Society* 27 (2015): 32–54.

Sen, Amartya. "A Sociological Approach to the Measurement of Poverty: A Reply to Professor Peter Townsend." *Oxford Economic Papers*, New Series, 37:4 (1985): 669–76.

———. *Poverty and Famines: An Essay on Entitlement and Deprivation*. Oxford: Oxford University Press, 1982.

Shinmura Taku. *Nihon iryō shakaishi no kenkyū—Kodai chūsei no minshū seikatsu to iryō*. Hōsei Daigaku Shuppankyoku, 1990.

"Shinpojiumu tōron: Mibun o toinaosu." In *Mibun o toinaosu* (Shirīzu kinsei no mibunteki shūen 6), edited by Kurushima Hiroshi, Takano Toshihiko, Tsukada Takashi, Yokota Fuyuhiko, and Yoshida Nobuyuki, 154–64. Yoshikawa Kōbunkan, 2000.

Shiramine sonshi. Vol. 2. Edited by Shiramine Sonshi Henshū Iinkai. Shiramine: Shiramine-mura Yakuba, 1962.

Shirīzu kinsei no mibunteki shūen. 6 vols. Yoshikawa Kōbunkan, 2000.

Shōji Takuya. "Tenpō no daikikin to Kubota (Akita)-machi ni okeru osukuigoya—Kinsei kōki ni okeru toshi jūmin no sēfutinetto." *Tōhoku shakai fukushishi kenkyū* 21 (2003): 1–10.

———. "Tenpō no kikin-ka no Akita Kan'onkō ni yoru koji kyūsai—Kinsei no saigai to minkan kyūsai katsudō." *Senshū shigaku* 31 (2000): 93–108.

Sippel, Patricia. "Popular Protest in Early Modern Japan: The Bushū Outburst." *Harvard Journal of Asiatic Studies* 37:2 (1977): 273–322.

Smith, Joanna Handlin. *The Art of Doing Good: Charity in Late Ming China*. Berkeley: University of California Press, 2009.

Smith, Thomas C. *The Agrarian Origins of Modern Japan*. Stanford, CA: Stanford University Press, 1984.

Soekawa Masao. "Gyūtō shutōhō shōrei no hanga ni tsuite." *Nihon ishigaku zasshi* 30: 1 (1984): 62–84.

———. *Nihon tōbyōshi josetsu*. Kindai Shuppan, 1987.

"Sorai Sensei tōmonsho (jō)." In *Nihon rinri i-hen*, vol. 6, edited by Inoue Tetsujirō and Kanie Yoshimaru, 147–60. Ikuseikai, 1902.

Stanley, Amy. "Maidservants' Tales: Narrating Domestic and Global History in Eurasia, 1600–1900." *American Historical Review* 121:2 (2016): 437–60.

———. *Selling Women: Prostitution, Markets, and the Household in Early Modern Japan*. Berkeley: University of California Press, 2012.

Sugahara Kenji. "Kinsei Kyoto no chō to sutego." *Rekishi hyōron* 422 (1985): 34–60.

————. "Kinsei Kyoto no hinin—Yojirō o megutte." *Nihonshi kenkyū* 181 (1977): 69–104.

————. "Kinsei zenki Kyoto no hinin—Hiden'in toshiyori shihai o chūshin ni." In *Zen-kindai Kyoto no burakushi*, edited by Buraku Mondai Kenkyūjo, 178–225. Kyoto: Buraku Mondai Kenkyūjo, 1987.

Sugimoto Hisashi. *Nōsanson keizai no kisoteki kenkyū*. Osaka: Yukawa Kōbunsha, 1944.

Sugino Akihiro. "Shōgai no bunka bunseki—Nihon bunka ni okeru 'mōmoku no para-dokusu.'" *Minzokugaku kenkyū* 54 (1990): 439–63.

————. "Shōgaisha undō no soshiki to nettowāku—Nihon ni okeru shōgai tōjisha undō no rekishi to tenbō." In *Soshiki to nettowāku no kenkyū* (Kenkyū sōsho 112), edited by Kansai Daigaku Keizai/Seiji Kenkyūjo, 87–105. Suita: Kansai Daigaku Keizai/Seiji Kenkyūjo, 1999.

Suzuki Bokushi. *Hokuetsu seppu*. Edited by Santō Kyōzan and Okada Takematsu. Iwanami Shoten, 1991.

Suzuki (formerly Yokota) Noriko. "Kinsei raibyōkan no keisei to tenkai." In *Rekishi no naka no "raisha*," edited by Fujino Yutaka, 81–140. Yumiru Shuppan, 1996.

Tachibana Reikichi. "Hakusanroku no yakihata kenkyūshi." *Ishikawa Kenritsu Hakubu-tsukan kiyō* 3 (1990): 16–35.

Tachibana Sōken. "Denrai nenjū nichiroku." In *Fukui shishi*, vol. 9: Shiryō-hen, 498–603. Fukui: Fukui-shi, 1994.

Taira Masayuki. "Sesshō kindan to sesshō zaigōkan." In *Shūen bunka to mibunsei*, edited by Wakita Haruko, Martin Collcutt, and Taira Masayuki, 240–68. Kyoto: Shibunkaku Shuppan, 2005.

Takagi Shōsaku. *Nihon kinsei kokkashi no kenkyū*. Iwanami Shoten, 1990.

Takahashi Bonsen. *Nihon jizen kyūsaishi no kenkyū*. Shakai Jigyō Kenkyūjo, 1940.

Takahashi Kazuo. "Shichiken no asaichi—Sono hassei kara genjō made." *Okuetsu shiryō* 12 (1983): 61–71.

Takahashi Kōsuke. *Kikin to kyūsai no shakaishi*. Aoki Shoten, 2006.

Takebe Aiko. "Jiin ryōshu to chiiki shakai—Ichigyōin fukie ikken o megutte." In *Mibunteki shūen to chiiki shakai*, edited by Tsukada Takashi and Yoshida Nobuyuki, 227–55. Yamakawa Shuppansha, 2013.

Takemura, Eiji. *The Perception of Work in Tokugawa Japan: A Study of Ishida Baigan and Ninomiya Sontoku*. Lanham, MD: University Press of America, 1997.

Takeuchi Makoto. "Kansei kaikaku to 'kanjōsho goyōtashi' no seiritsu." Two parts. *Nihon rekishi* 128 (1959): 23–32 and 129: 49–56.

Tan, WeiYu Wayne. "The Careers of the Blind in Tokugawa Japan, 1603–1868." Ph.D. diss., Harvard University, 2015.

Tanaka Shinji. "Tottori-han hinin seido no seiritsu." *Kaihō kenkyū Tottori* 1 (1999): 12–24.

————. "Tottori-han ni okeru 'zaichū' hiningashira no seikatsu to 'yaku.'" Two parts. *Kaihō kenkyū Tottori* 2 (2000/1): 17–30 and 3 (2000/2): 11–27.

Tanaka Yoshio. "Kaga-han hiningoya-sei seiritsu no jijō ni tsuite." *Nihon rekishi* 183:8 (1963): 45–67.

———. "Kaga-han ni okeru hisabetsu buraku—Tōnai/kawata o chūshin ni shite." In *Kinsei buraku no shiteki kenkyū*, vol. 2, edited by Buraku Kaihō Kenkyūjo, 47–94. Osaka: Kaihō Shuppansha, 1979.

———. "Kaga-han 'tōnai' no kenkyū." In *Tōhoku/Hokuetsu hisabetsu burakushi kenkyū*, edited by Harada Tomohiko and Tanaka Yoshio, 251–300. Meiseki Shoten, 1981.

———. "Kenkyū nōto: Ōno jōkamachi, hiningashira 'Koshirō-domo' to shūen no hitobito (1)—Echizen/Ōno-han." *Buraku/Jinken nōto* 5 (2003/9), edited by Kanazawa B-kenkyūkai, 42–54.

Taniai Susumu. *Mōjin no rekishi*. Akashi Shoten, 1996.

Taniyama Keirin. *Nihon shakai jigyōshi*. Daitō Shuppansha, 1950.

Taniyama Keirin and Yamazaki Seika. *Bukkyō shakai jigyōshi* (jō) (Bukkyō daigaku kōza 5). Bukkyō Nenkansha, 1933.

Tatebe Seian. "Minkan bikōroku." Introduced, transcribed, and translated into modern Japanese by Abiko Rin and Moriya Yoshimi. In *Nihon nōsho zenshū*, vol. 18, 3–196. Nōsangyoson Bunka Kyōkai, 1983.

Teihon: Kaga-han hisabetsu buraku kankei shiryō shūsei. Edited by Tanaka Yoshio. Akashi Shoten, 1995.

Thompson, E. P. "The Moral Economy of the English Crowd in the Eighteenth Century." *Past and Present* 50 (1971): 76–136.

Toby, Ronald P. "Both a Borrower and a Lender Be: From Village Moneylender to Rural Banker in the Tempo Era." *Monumenta Nipponica* 46:4 (1991): 483–512.

"Tōdōyōshū." In *Nihon shomin seikatsu shiryō shūsei*, vol. 17, edited by Tanigawa Ken'ichi et al., 229–41. San'ichi Shobō, 1972.

Tokyo-to (ed.). *Tokyo shishi-kō*. Vol. 52: Shigai-hen. Tokyo-to, 1962.

"Tori nikki." In *Takefu shishi*, Shiryō-hen (Fuchū hansei narabi ni Honbo jin'ya shokiroku), edited by Takefu Shishi Hensan Iinkai, 1–157. Takefu: Takefu-shi, 1968.

Townsend, Peter. "A Sociological Approach to the Measurement of Poverty—A Rejoinder to Professor Amartya Sen." *Oxford Economic Papers*, New Series, 37:4 (1985): 659–68.

Trambaiolo, Daniel. "Writing, Authority and Practice in Tokugawa Medicine, 1650–1850." Ph.D. diss., Princeton University, 2014.

Tsubouchi Susumu. *Hakusan sanroku no Shinshū hatten to dōjō no kenkyū*. Katsuyama: printed by author, 1985.

Tsuji Hidetake. *Ōita-ken no shakai fukushi jigyōshi*. Ōita: Ōita-ken Shakai Fukushi Kyōgikai, 1973.

Tsukada Takashi. "Hinin—Kinsei Osaka no hinin to sono yuisho." In *Shokunin/oyakata/nakama* (Shirīzu kinsei no mibunteki shūen 3), edited by Tsukada Takashi, 229–65. Yoshikawa Kōbunkan, 2000.

———. "Kasōmin no sekai—'Mibunteki shūen' no shiten kara." In *Nihon no kinsei*, vol. 7: Mibun to kakushiki, edited by Asao Naohiro, 225–68. Chūō Kōronsha, 1992.

———. "Kinsei kōki Osaka ni okeru toshi kasō minshū no seikatsu sekai." In *Higashi Ajia kinsei toshi ni okeru shakaiteki ketsugō—Sho-mibun/sho-kaisō no sonzai keitai* (Osaka Shiritsu Daigaku Bungaku Kenkyūka sōsho 3), edited by Inoue Tōru and Tsukada Takashi, 75–127. Osaka: Seibundō Shuppan, 2005.

————. *Kinsei mibunsei to shūen shakai*. Tokyo Daigaku Shuppankai, 1997.

————. *Kinsei Nihon mibunsei no kenkyū*. Kobe: Hyōgo Buraku Mondai Kenkyūjo, 1987.

————. *Kinsei Osaka no hinin to mibunteki shūen*. Kyoto: Buraku Mondai Kenkyūjo, 2007.

————. "Mibunsei no kōzō." In *Iwanami kōza Nihon tsūshi*, vol. 12, edited by Asao Naohiro et al., 107–50. Iwanami Shoten, 1994.

————. *Mibunsei shakai to shimin shakai—Kinsei Nihon no shakai to hō*. Kashiwa Shobō, 1992.

————. "Mibunteki shūenron—Kanjin no heizon o tegakari to shite." In *Nihonshi kōza*, vol. 6: Kinsei shakairon, edited by Rekishigaku Kenkyūkai and Nihonshi Kenkyūkai, 193–230. Tokyo Daigaku Shuppankai, 2005.

————. "Mibunteki shūen to rekishi shakai no kōzō." In *Mibun o toinaosu* (Shirīzu kinsei no mibunteki shūen 6), edited by Kurushima Hiroshi, Takano Toshihiko, Tsukada Takashi, Yokota Fuyuhiko, and Yoshida Nobuyuki, 82–88. Yoshikawa Kōbunkan, 2000.

————. *Osaka no hinin—Kojiki/Shitennōji/Korobi-kirishitan*. Chikuma Shobō, 2013.

————. "Shiryō shōkai: Mitsui Bunko shozō no santo, hinin kankei shiryō." *Mitsui Bunko ronsō* 23 (1989): 141–87.

————. "Toshi ni okeru shakai=bunka kōzōshi no tame ni." *Toshi bunka kenkyū* 1 (2003): 124–41.

————. *Toshi Osaka to hinin*. Yamakawa Shuppansha, 2001 (Nihonshi riburetto).

Tsukada Takashi, Yoshida Nobuyuki, and Wakita Osamu (eds.). *Mibunteki shūen*. Kyoto: Buraku Mondai Kenkyūjo, 1994.

Tsukamoto Akira. *Kinsei Ise jingū-ryō no shokue kannen to hisabetsumin*. Osaka: Seibundō Shuppan, 2014.

Tsukamoto Manabu. *Shōrui o meguru seiji—Genroku no fōkuroa*. 1983; Kōdansha, 2013.

Uchida Kusuo. "Osaka shikasho no soshiki to shūnyū." *Hisutoria* 115 (1987): 73–115.

Uesugi Satoshi. *Meiji ishin to senmin haishirei*. Osaka: Kaihō Shuppansha, 1990.

Umihara Ryō. *Kinsei iryō no shakaishi—Chishiki, gijutsu, jōhō*. Yoshikawa Kōbunkan, 2007.

————. "Toshi Osaka ni okeru shōka hōkōnin no hinkon to kyūsai—Sumitomo-ke no jirei kara." In *Kinsei mibun shakai no hikakushi—Hō to shakai no shiten kara*, edited by Tsukada Takashi, Saga Ashita, and Yagi Shigeru, 267–92. Osaka: Seibundō, 2014.

Van Steenpaal, Niels. "Kankoku kōgiroku—Bakufu jinsei no pafōmansu." In *Dai-32-kai kokusai Nihon bungaku kenkyū shūkai kaigiroku*, 35–52. Kokubungaku Kenkyū Shiryōkan, 2009.

Vlastos, Stephen. *Peasant Protests and Uprisings in Tokugawa Japan*. Berkeley: University of California Press, 1986.

Vollmer, Klaus. "Reinheit und gesellschaftliche Ordnung in Japan: Dimensionen des sogenannten *buraku*-Problems in historischer und zeitgenössischer Perspektive." In *Reinheit—Religiöse, soziale und politische Aspekte*, edited by Peter Burschel and Christoph Marx, 325–46. Vienna: Böhlau, 2011.

Wada Takuma. "'Taiheiki' o matou kanazōshi—*Hinin Taiheiki* o chūshin ni." *Edo bungaku* 41 (2009): 20–32.

Wakabayashi, Bob Tadashi. "In Name Only: Imperial Sovereignty in Early Modern Japan." *Journal of Japanese Studies* 17:1 (1991): 25–57.

Walker, Brett L. "Commercial Growth and Environmental Change in Early Modern Japan: Hachinohe's Wild Boar Famine of 1749." *Journal of Asian Studies* 60:2 (2001): 329–51.

———. "The Early Modern Japanese State and Ainu Vaccinations: Redefining the Body Politic 1799–1868." *Past and Present* 163 (1999): 121–60.

Walthall, Anne. *Social Protest and Popular Culture in Eighteenth-Century Japan.* Tucson: University of Arizona Press, 1986.

———. "Village Networks: Sōdai and the Sale of Edo Nightsoil." *Monumenta Nipponica* 43:3 (1988): 279–303.

Watanabe Takashi (ed.). *Han chiiki no kōzō to hen'yō—Shinano no kuni Matsushiro-han chiiki no kenkyū.* Iwata Shoin, 2005.

———. "Han chiikiron to chiiki shakairon—Matsushiro-han no jirei kara." *Rekishi hyōron* 676 (2006): 53–65.

Wenderoth, Ingrid. *Sekizoro: Geschichte und Wandel einer Strassen- und Bettelkunst marginalisierter Gruppen im vormodernen Japan: Eine Studie zu Übelvertreibung und Segenspende im japanischen Jahresbrauchtum.* Hamburg: Gesellschaft für Natur- und Völkerkunde Ostasiens, 2008.

———. "Von Straßenkünstlern, Scharlatanen und törichtem Volk im 7. Kapitel der edozeitlichen Berufe-Enzyklopädie *Jinrin kinmō zui.*" *Nachrichten der Gesellschaft für Natur- und Völkerkunde Ostasiens* (NOAG) 173–74 (2003): 183–207.

Will, Pierre-Etienne, and R. Bin Wong, with James Lee. *Nourish the People: The State Civilian Granary System in China, 1650–1850.* Ann Arbor: University of Michigan Center for Chinese Studies, 1991.

Woldering, Guido. "*Eta wo osamuru no gi* oder 'Erörterung der Herrschaft über die Schmutzigen': Gedanken eines Schwertadligen der späten Edo-Zeit zum 'Abschaum' seiner Gesellschaft." *Nachrichten der Gesellschaft für Natur- und Völkerkunde Ostasiens* (NOAG) 171–72 (2002): 21–37.

Woodside, Alexander. *Lost Modernities: China, Vietnam, Korea, and the Hazards of World History.* Cambridge, MA: Harvard University Press, 2006.

Yabuta Yutaka. *Kokuso to hyakushō ikki no kenkyū.* Azekura Shobō, 1992.

Yamada Kōta. "Matsushiro hanryō no mōjin—Kōka san umadoshi Higashi Terao-mura Ameya Heisuke joshi ikken." In *Han chiiki no kōzō to hen'yō—Shinano no kuni Matsushiro-han chiiki no kenkyū,* edited by Watanabe Takashi, 179–240. Iwata Shoin, 2005.

Yamaga Sokō. "Yamaga gorui." In *Nihon keizai taiten,* vol. 51, edited by Takimoto Seiichi, 4–194. Keimeisha, 1930.

Yamaguchi Keiji. *Sakoku to kaikoku.* Iwanami Shoten, 2006.

Yamaguchi Takaharu. *Hakusanroku/dezukuri no kenkyū—Ushikubi sonmin no yukue.* Toyama: Katsura Shobō, 1994.

Yamamoto Kaoru. "Senshū no Sakai 'shikasho' chōri to gunchū hininban." *Buraku mondai kenkyū* 159 (2002): 69–95.

Yamaori Tetsuo. *Kojiki no seishinshi.* Kōbundō, 1987.

Yamasaki Yoshihiro. *Kinsei kōki no ryōshu shihai to chiiki shakai—"Hyakushō naritachi" to chūkansō.* Osaka: Seibundō, 2007.

Yamazaki Masukichi. *Yokoi Shōnan no shakai keizai shisō.* Taga Shuppan, 1981.

Yanagisawa Fumiko. "Gakku torishimari Yoshida Setsuzō no 'Seisai nisshi'—Fukui-ken Ōno-gun-ka no gakuseiki shōgakkō no sōsetsu katei." *Fukui-ken Bunshokan kenkyū kiyō* 9 (2012): 51–66.

Yanagita Kunio. "Mino Echizen ōfuku." In *Yanagita Kunio zenshū,* vol. 18, 94–126. Chikuma Shobō, 1999.

———(ed.). *Sanson seikatsu no kenkyū.* Kokusho Kankōkai, 1975.

———. "Tabemono to shinzō." In *Yanagita Kunio zenshū,* vol. 10, 365–511. Chikuma Shobō, 1998.

Yasumaru Yoshio. *Nihon no kindaika to minshū shisō.* 1974; Heibonsha, 1999.

Yasuoka Shigeaki. *Nihon hōken keizai seisaku shiron.* Yūhikaku, 1959.

Yokoi Shōnan. "Kokuze Sanron: The Three Major Problems of State Policy." Translated by D. Y. Miyauchi. *Monumenta Nipponica* 23:1/2 (1968): 156–86.

Yokota Fuyuhiko. "Geinō/bunka to 'mibunteki shūen.'" In *Mibun o toinaosu* (Shirīzu kinsei no mibunteki shūen 6), edited by Kurushima Hiroshi, Takano Toshihiko, Tsukada Takashi, Yokota Fuyuhiko, and Yoshida Nobuyuki, 29–48. Yoshikawa Kōbunkan, 2000.

———. "Imoji—Tsuji-mura imoji to Matsugi-ke." In *Shokunin/oyakata/nakama* (Shirīzu kinsei no mibunteki shūen 3), edited by Tsukada Takashi, 17–46. Yoshikawa Kōbunkan, 2000.

Yokota Noriko. "'Monoyoshi'-kō—Kinsei Kyoto no raisha ni tsuite." *Nihonshi kenkyū* 352 (1991): 1–29.

Yokoyama Yuriko. *Meiji ishin to kinsei mibunsei no kaitai.* Yamakawa Shuppansha, 2005.

———. "Meiji ishin to kinsei mibunsei no kaitai." In *Nihonshi kōza,* vol. 7: Kinsei no kaitai, edited by Rekishigaku Kenkyūkai and Nihonshi Kenkyūkai, 133–62. Tokyo Daigaku Shuppankai, 2005.

———. "Zen-kindai mibunsei kenkyū no dōkō—Seika to kadai." *Buraku mondai kenkyū* 180 (2007): 2–24.

Yoshida Jun'ichi. "Hanseiki ni okeru Ōno jōka/Katsuyama jōka no machiya." In Fukui-ken Kyōiku Iinkai (ed.), *Mino kaidō/Katsuyama kaidō,* 150–62.

Yoshida Kyūichi. "Meiji ishin ni okeru kyūhin seido." In *Nihon no kyūhin seido,* edited by Nihon Shakai Jigyō Daigaku Kyūhin Seido Kenkyūkai, 49–86. Keisō Shobō, 1960.

———. *Nihon hinkonshi.* Kaiteiban. Kawashima Shoten, 1993.

———. *Nihon shakai fukushi shisōshi.* Kawashima Shoten, 1989.

———. *Shin-Nihon shakai jigyō no rekishi.* Keisō Shobō, 1994.

Yoshida Kyūichi and Hasegawa Masatoshi. *Nihon bukkyō fukushi shisōshi.* Kyoto: Hōzōkan, 2001.

Yoshida Mori (ed.). *Nishitani sonshi.* Vol. 1. Nishitani: Nishitani-mura, 1970.

Yoshida Nobuyuki. *21-seiki no "Edo."* Yamakawa Shuppansha, 2004.

———. "Bakumatsu-ki, Edo no shūen to minshū sekai." *Rekishi hyōron* 758 (2013): 44–60.

———. "Chōnin to chō." In *Kōza Nihon rekishi* 5, edited by Rekishigaku Kenkyūkai and Nihonshi Kenkyūkai, 151–88. Tokyo Daigaku Shuppankai, 1985.

———. *Dentō toshi/Edo.* Tokyo Daigaku Shuppankai, 2012.

———. "Dentō toshi no shūen." In *Nihonshi kōza*, vol. 7: Kinsei no kaitai, edited by Rekishigaku Kenkyūkai and Nihonshi Kenkyūkai, 33–64. Tokyo Daigaku Shuppankai, 2005.

———. *Kinsei kyodai toshi no shakai kōzō.* Tokyo Daigaku Shuppankai, 1991.

———. *Kinsei toshi shakai no mibun kōzō.* Tokyo Daigaku Shuppankai, 1998.

———. "Kojiki/kanjin to geinōsha no shoyū ni tsuite." *Buraku mondai kenkyū* 159 (2002): 47–49.

———. *Kyodai jōkamachi Edo no bunsetsu kōzō.* Yamakawa Shuppansha, 1999.

———. *Mibunteki shūen to shakai=bunka kōzō.* Kyoto: Buraku Mondai Kenkyūjo, 2003.

———. "Nihon kinsei ni okeru puroretaria-teki yōso ni tsuite." *Rekishigaku kenkyū* 548 (1985): 67–75 (rept. in Yoshida Nobuyuki, *Kinsei toshi shakai no mibun kōzō*).

———. "Nihon kinsei toshi kasō shakai no sonritsu kōzō." *Rekishigaku kenkyū* 534 (1984): 2–12 (rept. in Yoshida Nobuyuki, *Kinsei toshi shakai no mibun kōzō*).

———. *Seijuku suru Edo* (Nihon no rekishi 17). Kōdansha, 2002.

———. "Shoyū to mibunteki shūen." In *Mibun o toinaosu* (Shirīzu kinsei no mibunteki shūen 6), edited by Kurushima Hiroshi, Takano Toshihiko, Tsukada Takashi, Yokota Fuyuhiko, and Yoshida Nobuyuki, 94–117. Yoshikawa Kōbunkan, 2000.

Yoshida Setsuzō. "Ryūin kiji." In *Ōno shishi*, vol. 6: Shiryō sōkatsu-hen, 361–404.

Yoshida Shōin. *Testimony of a Madman* (1858). Translated by Peter Duus. In *The Japanese Discovery of America: A Brief History with Documents*, edited by Peter Duus, 125–28. Boston: Bedford/St. Martin's, 1997.

Yoshida Yuriko. "Chiiki shakai to mibunteki shūen—Shinano no kuni Shimo-Ina gun o chūshin to shite." *Buraku mondai kenkyū* 174 (2005): 2–32.

———. "Manzai to haruta-uchi—Kinsei Shimo-Ina no mibunteki shūen." *Iida-shi Rekishi Kenkyūjo nenpō* 1 (2003): 50–80.

———. "Shinshū Shimo-Ina chiiki ni okeru mibunteki shūen—Iida-han rōmori/saruhiki to sho-shūdan to no kankei." In *Mibunteki shūen no hikakushi—Hō to shakai no shiten kara*, edited by Tsukada Takashi, 245–91. Osaka: Seibundō, 2010.

Yunoki Manabu. *Nihonshu no rekishi.* Yūzankaku, 1975.

Index

Page numbers for figures and tables are in italics.

seigneurial relief (*continued*)
officials role in, 246; starvation petitions
for, 206, 219, *220*, 221–22, 237, 241–42,
242n127; during Tenmei famine, 202,
236–39, 241–42
self-governance: of beggar households/
guilds, 29–30, 113; of blind profession-
als/guilds, 30–31, 163, 192; of block
associations, 6–7, 45, 87; collaboration
with, 249; defining, 296; in famine/
hunger relief, 26, 202, 203, 240; in
mendicancy management, 116, 158,
298; of occupation-based groups, 9–10,
13, 45; in Ōno, 2, 40–41, 55, 66; pooled
donations impact on, 239–40; reciprocity
in, 16, 249, 295; state control and,
paradox, 12–13; in status order dismantling, 294–95; structure of, 295; town
elders coordination of, 14; warrior/
shogun relationship with, 1–2, 12–13,
27–28, 32, 100, 202–3, 203n6, 240, 249
Sen, Amartya, 21, 21n43
Sendai domain, 241n126
shamisen, 169, 177, 182–83
shared-revenue villages, 39n8, 276n100
shimin. See four estates
Shinokura Shrine, 45, 63
Shinran, 61
shintai. See relief loans
Shinto worship, 62, 63, 84, 281
shion. See four favors
shogun, 36, 245. *See also* warrior class/rule
shokubun, 5, 74–75, 80. *See also* occupa-
tion/occupation-based groups; status
order and groups
smallpox vaccinations, 252–54, 253n16,
256–57
social welfare: contrast to poor relief, 26;
funding shift for, 289–90; Meiji-era,
282–86; mercantilism in development
of, 250–51, 299; state control with,
22n44, 251; taxes for, 282. *See also* poor
relief; public health
Southern Mountains (Minami Yamanaka),
38, 41, 92n66, 256

starvation petitions (*katsumei onegai*),
206, 219, *220*, 221–22, 237, 241–42,
242n127
status (*mibun*), 3; almsgiving as measure
of, 90n59; markers for Koshirō, 75,
75n17, 141; tax-exempt, 48–49, 50, 52,
156n137, 228
Status Marginality Research Group
(Mibunteki Shūen Kenkyūkai), 5, 6,
6n6
status order and groups: abolition of, 252,
275n96, 280n115; adoption for
movement within, 21, 36–37, 54,
109–10; autonomy and state control
paradox in, 12–13; beggar bosses/
guilds/households in, 3, 72, 108–13;
benevolent rule relationship with,
2–3, 24–25; of blind professionals, 49,
85, 179n66, 179–80; of block associations, 5–6; defining, 296; doctors/
physicians in, 49; domain administration through, 114; elements and
categories of, 5–6, 20–21, 299;
exclusion from, 3–4, 21, 22–23, 49,
68–69, 72, 84–85, 104, 109–10, 111–12,
111n126, 162–63; guild expansion in,
8–9; hereditary categories in, 20–21;
hierarchies within and between, 13,
17n32; itinerant entertainers/artists in,
71, 81–82, 85n46; Koshirō transgressing, 108–13; land owners in, 5–6;
leatherworkers in, 71–72; marriage
and, 4, 21, 36–37, 54, 72, 85, 107, 110; in
mendicancy management, 158;
merchants in, 3, 4, 48, 48n37; *naishō*
solutions within, 296–98; occupation/
occupation-based groups in, 2, 4, 5,
12–13, 70, 74, 80, 85, 162, 299; in Ōno,
17–18, 48–54, 85, 113–14; outcastes
organization within, 49–50, 70,
71–72; overview, governance, and
geographies of, 1–13; poor relief
highlighted through study of, 26, 241,
298–99; poverty treatment and, 19–21,
23–24, 32; punitive measures for

Harvard East Asian Monographs
(most recent titles)